PRENTICE HALL

Social Studies

The quality choice for today's classrooms

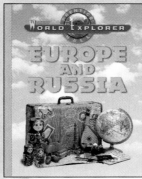
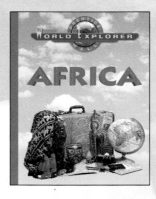

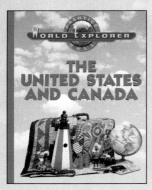

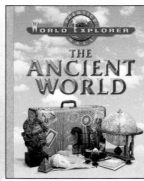

WORLD EXPLORER

The world studies program that lets you choose.

PRENTICE HALL
Simon & Schuster Education Group
A VIACOM COMPANY

Upper Saddle River, New Jersey
Needham, Massachusetts

ISBN 0-13-433688-7

2 3 4 5 6 7 8 9 10   01 00 99 98 97

The only middle grades world that can truly provide the right materials to fit your

Prentice Hall World Explorer lets you choose the right balance of history, geography, and cultures for the regions of the world that you cover in your middle grades curriculum. No more being confined to the contents of a single text. No more having to spend valuable time locating additional resources. All this with hands-on activities and skills; interdisciplinary connections; integrated technology; and manageable resources to support your teaching style.

YOU CHOOSE what's right

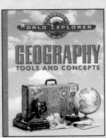  

A few of
the most popular
**COURSE
CONFIGURATIONS:**

Configuration	GEOGRAPHY TOOLS AND CONCEPTS	EUROPE AND RUSSIA	AFRICA
Eastern Hemisphere*	GEOGRAPHY TOOLS AND CONCEPTS	EUROPE AND RUSSIA	AFRICA
Western Hemisphere*	GEOGRAPHY TOOLS AND CONCEPTS		
World History			
Western Civilization		EUROPE AND RUSSIA	
Pacific Rim	GEOGRAPHY TOOLS AND CONCEPTS		
World Cultures		EUROPE AND RUSSIA	AFRICA

studies program curriculum.

for your course of study.

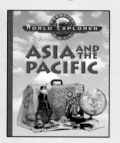 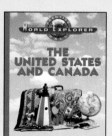  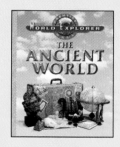 

ASIA AND THE PACIFIC	THE UNITED STATES AND CANADA	LATIN AMERICA	THE ANCIENT WORLD	MEDIEVAL TIMES TO TODAY
ASIA AND THE PACIFIC				
	THE UNITED STATES AND CANADA	LATIN AMERICA		
			THE ANCIENT WORLD	MEDIEVAL TIMES TO TODAY
	THE UNITED STATES AND CANADA		THE ANCIENT WORLD	
ASIA AND THE PACIFIC	THE UNITED STATES AND CANADA	LATIN AMERICA		
ASIA AND THE PACIFIC	THE UNITED STATES AND CANADA	LATIN AMERICA		

* Available in single, hard-bound volume

Only World Explorer provides this many management resources— built right into the program.

Designed from the start to have more time-saving resources for middle grades teachers, the World Explorer program has brand-new ways to help you coordinate your program, scheduling, assessment, team teaching, interdisciplinary connections, and other valuable resources.

- • Managing Time and Instruction
- • Block Scheduling
- • Assessment Opportunities
- • Activities and Projects
- • Resource Pro CD-ROM
- • FYI
- • Technology Options
- • Flexible Planning Guide

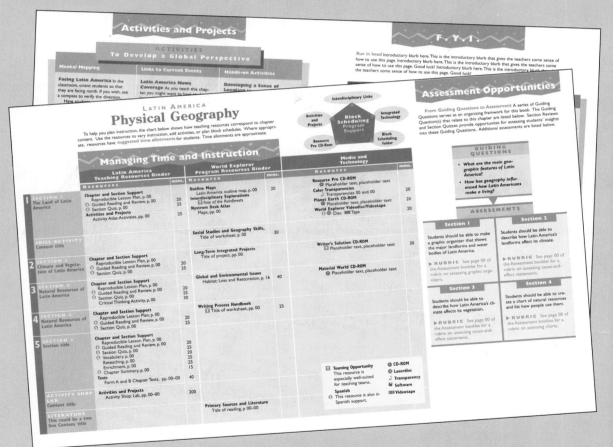

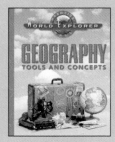

- **Teacher's Edition wraparound with barcodes**
- **Point-of-use technology references**
- **Integrated video presentations**

Guided Reading Audiotapes *
Computer Test Bank
  (MAC/Windows)
 World Video Explorer
    Videodiscs *
    Videotapes
Resource Pro™ CD-ROM
Material World CD-ROM
Planet Earth CD-ROM
Writer's Solution CD-ROM
*available in Spanish

FLEXIBLE PLANNING GUIDE

This key supplement makes it easy to plan, schedule, and coordinate World Explorer's multi-book program.
- **Course configurations**
- **Pacing charts**
- **Scope and sequence of skills**
- **Correlations to national standards**

RESOURCE PRO CD-ROM

- **Teaching Resources**
- **Planning Express™**
- **Computer Test Bank**

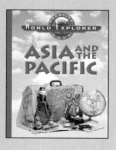
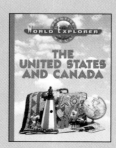

Coverage of all World Explorer program skills is provided in the Student Edition and Teacher's Edition.

Skills Activity
Students learn, practice, and apply core social studies skills through the use of hands-on activities.

Skills Mini-lessons
These lessons supplement and reinforce core social studies skills that are not formally presented in the student book.

THE ANCIENT WORLD SKILLS SCOPE AND SEQUENCE

MAP AND GLOBE SKILLS

SKILL	BOOK	PAGE
Using Parts of a Map	STUDENT	234
Comparing Maps of Different Scale	STUDENT	235
Understanding Distortions in Map Projections	STUDENT	232–233
Using Political and Physical Maps	STUDENT	236–237
Using Regional Maps	TEACHER	61
Using Distribution Maps	TEACHER	157
Using Route Maps	STUDENT	90–91

CRITICAL THINKING SKILLS

Expressing Problems Clearly	TEACHER	215
Identifying Central Issues	STUDENT	56–57
Distinguishing Facts From Opinons	TEACHER	109
Recognizing Bias	TEACHER	175
Recognizing Cause and Effect	TEACHER	23
Drawing Conclusions	STUDENT	180–181

CHART, GRAPH, AND ILLUSTRATION SKILLS

Interpreting Graphs	TEACHER	21
Interpreting Diagrams and Illustrations	TEACHER	137
Using a Time Line	STUDENT	24–25
Reading Tables and Analyzing Statistics	STUDENT	116–117

READING AND WRITING SKILLS

Previewing	TEACHER	31
Reading Actively	STUDENT	218–219
Assessing Your Understanding	TEACHER	133
Using the Writing Process	TEACHER	105
Writing for a Purpose	TEACHER	155

STUDY AND RESEARCH SKILLS

Locating Information	TEACHER	75
Organizing Information	STUDENT	146–147
Organizing Your Time	TEACHER	199

Map and Globe Handbook
Students practice and review basic geography skills that focus on understanding maps and charts.

Use this daily pacing chart to help plan a twelve-week course or an eighteen-week course for The Ancient World.

Block Scheduling
Suggested times are for daily class periods between 40 and 50 minutes long. For planning extended blocks or for teachers who wish to vary the pace of instruction, see the "Managing Time and Instruction" charts before each chapter or the Resource Pro™ CD-ROM

	12-WEEK COURSE	18-WEEK COURSE
ACTIVITY ATLAS	2 DAYS	3 DAYS

CHAPTER 1
THE BEGINNINGS OF HUMAN SOCIETY

	12-WEEK COURSE	18-WEEK COURSE
Section 1 Geography and History	1	2
Section 2 Prehistory	1	2
Section 3 The Beginnings of Civilization	1.5	2
SKILLS ACTIVITY Using a Time Line	1	1.5
CHAPTER 1 REVIEW, ACTIVITIES, AND ASSESSMENT	1.5	1.5

CHAPTER 2
THE FERTILE CRESCENT

	12-WEEK COURSE	18-WEEK COURSE
Section 1 Land Between Two Rivers	1.5	2
Section 2 Babylonia and Assyria	1	2
Section 3 The Legacy of Mesopotamia	1	2
Section 4 Mediterranean Civilizations	1.5	2.5
Section 5 Judaism	1	2
SKILLS ACTIVITY Identifying Central Issues	1	1.5
CHAPTER 2 REVIEW, ACTIVITIES, AND ASSESSMENT	1.5	1.5

CHAPTER 3
ANCIENT EGYPT AND NUBIA

	12-WEEK COURSE	18-WEEK COURSE
Section 1 The Geography of the Nile	1	2
Section 2 Egypt's Powerful Kings and Queens	1	2
Section 3 Egyptian Religion	1	2.5
Section 4 The Culture of the Ancient Egyptians	2	2
Section 5 The Resource-Rich Cultures of Nubia	1.5	2
SKILLS ACTIVITY Reading Route Maps	1	1.5
CHAPTER 3 REVIEW, ACTIVITIES, AND ASSESSMENT	1.5	1.5

CHAPTER 4
ANCIENT INDIA

	12-WEEK COURSE	18-WEEK COURSE
Section 1 The Indus and Ganges River Valleys	1	2
Section 2 The Beginnings of Hinduism	1	1.5
Section 3 The Beginnings of Buddhism	1	1.5
Section 4 The Golden Age of Maurya India	2	2.5
SKILLS ACTIVITY Reading Tables	1	1.5
CHAPTER 4 REVIEW, ACTIVITIES AND ASSESSMENT	1.5	1.5
LITERATURE	1	1

CHAPTER 5
ANCIENT CHINA

	12-WEEK COURSE	18-WEEK COURSE
Section 1 The Geography of China's River Valleys	1	2
Section 2 Confucius and His Teachings	1	1.5
Section 3 Strong Rulers Unite Warring Kingdoms	1	2
Section 4 Achievements of Ancient China	1.5	2
SKILLS ACTIVITY Organizing Information	1	1.5
CHAPTER 5 REVIEW, ACTIVITIES AND ASSESSMENT	1.5	1.5
ACTIVITY SHOP LAB	1	2

CHAPTER 6
ANCIENT GREECE

	12-WEEK COURSE	18-WEEK COURSE
Section 1 The Rise of Greek Civilization	1	2
Section 2 Greek Religion, Philosophy, and Literature	1	2
Section 3 Daily Life of the Ancient Greeks	1.5	2
Section 4 Athens and Sparta: Two Cities in Conflict	1.5	2
Section 5 The Spread of Greek Culture	2	2.5
SKILLS ACTIVITY Drawing Conclusions	1	1.5
CHAPTER 6 REVIEW, ACTIVITIES, AND ASSESSMENT	1.5	1.5
ACTIVITY SHOP INTERDISCIPLINARY	1.5	2
LITERATURE	1	1

CHAPTER 7
ANCIENT ROME

	12-WEEK COURSE	18-WEEK COURSE
Section 1 The Roman Republic	1	2
Section 2 The Roman Empire	1.5	2.5
Section 3 Daily Life Among the Romans	1	2
Section 4 A New Religion: Christianity	1	2
Section 5 The Fall of Rome	1	2
SKILLS ACTIVITY Reading Actively	1	1.5
CHAPTER 7 REVIEW, ACTIVITIES, AND ASSESSMENT	1.5	1.5
TOTAL NUMBER OF DAYS	60	90

WORLD EXPLORER

THE ANCIENT WORLD

PRENTICE HALL
Needham, Massachusetts
Upper Saddle River, New Jersey

Program Authors

Heidi Hayes Jacobs

Heidi Hayes Jacobs has served as an educational consultant to more than 500 schools across the nation. Dr. Jacobs is an adjunct professor in the Department of Curriculum on Teaching at Teachers College, Columbia University. She completed her undergraduate studies at the University of Utah in her hometown of Salt Lake City. She received an M.A. from the University of Massachusetts, Amherst, and completed her doctoral work at Columbia University's Teachers College in 1981.

The backbone of Dr. Jacobs's experience comes from her years as a teacher of high school, middle school, and elementary school students. As an educational consultant, she works with K–12 schools and districts on curriculum reform and strategic planning.

Brenda Randolph

Brenda Randolph is the former Director of the Outreach Resource Center at the African Studies Program at Howard University, Washington, D.C. She is the Founder and Director of Africa Access, a bibliographic service on Africa for schools. She received her B.A. in history with high honors from North Carolina Central University, Durham, and her M.A. in African studies with honors from Howard University. She completed further graduate studies at the University of Maryland, College Park, where she was awarded a Graduate Fellowship.

Brenda Randolph has published numerous articles in professional journals and bulletins. She currently serves as library media specialist in Montgomery County Public Schools, Maryland.

Michal L. LeVasseur

Michal LeVasseur is an educational consultant in the field of geography. She is an adjunct professor of geography at the University of Alabama, Birmingham, and serves with the Alabama Geographic Alliance. Her undergraduate and graduate work is in the fields of anthropology (B.A.), geography (M.A.), and science education (Ph.D.).

Dr. LeVasseur's specialization has moved increasingly into the area of geography education. In 1996, she served as Director of the National Geographic Society's Summer Geography Workshop. As an educational consultant, she has worked with the National Geographic Society as well as with schools to develop programs and curricula for geography.

Special Program Consultant

Yvonne S. Gentzler, Ph.D.
School of Education
University of Idaho, Moscow, Idaho

Content Consultant on The Ancient World

Maud Gleason
Department of Classics
Stanford University
Stanford, California

PRENTICE HALL
Simon & Schuster Education Group
A VIACOM COMPANY

Upper Saddle River, New Jersey
Needham, Massachusetts

ISBN 0-13-433687-9

2 3 4 5 6 7 8 9 10   01 00 99 98 97

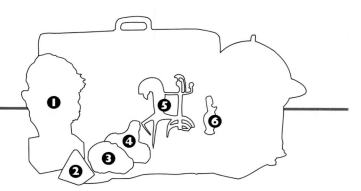

On the Cover

❶ Head of Poseidon, Greek god of the sea

❷ Capstone of an Egyptian pyramid

❸ Fragment of a Roman statue

❹ Model of Egyptian sphinx

❺ Reproduction of an iron sculpture of the goddess Athena in her chariot

❻ Reproduction of an ancient Greek vase

Content Consultants for the World Explorer Program

Africa
Barbara Brown
Africa Studies Center
Boston University
Boston, Massachusetts

East Asia
Leslie Swartz
Harvard University East
    Asian Outreach Program
    at the Children's Museum
    of Boston
Boston, Massachusetts

Latin America
Daniel Mugan
Center for Latin American Studies
University of Florida
Gainesville, Florida

Middle East
Elizabeth Barlow
Center for Middle Eastern and
    North African Studies
University of Michigan
Ann Arbor, Michigan

North Africa
Laurence Michalak
Center for Middle East Studies
University of California
Berkeley, California

Religion
Michael Sells
Department of Religion
Haverford College
Haverford, Pennsylvania

Russia, Eastern Europe, Central Asia
Janet Valliant
Center for Russian, Eastern
    European, and Central Asian
    Studies
Harvard University
Cambridge, Massachusetts

South Asia
Robert Young
South Asia Regional Studies
University of Pennsylvania
Philadelphia, Pennsylvania

Western Europe
Ruth Mitchell-Pitts
Center for West European Studies
University of North Carolina
Chapel Hill, North Carolina

Teacher Advisory Board

Jerome Balin
Lincoln Junior High
    School
Naperville, Illinois

Linda Boaen
Baird School
Fresno, California

Nikki L. Born
Harllee Middle School
Bradenton, Florida

Carla Bridges
Concord Middle School
Concord, North Carolina

Bruce L. Campbell
Walled Lake Middle
    School
Walled Lake, Michigan

Barbara Coats Grabowski
Russell Middle School
Omaha, Nebraska

David Herman
North Carroll Middle
    School
Hampstead, Maryland

Fred Hitz
Wilson Middle School
Muncie, Indiana

William B. Johnson
La Mesa Junior High
    School
Canyon Country,
    California

Kristi Karis
West Ottawa Middle
    School
Holland, Michigan

Kristen Koch
Discovery Middle School
Orlando, Florida

Peggy McCarthy
Beulah School
Beulah, Colorado

Deborah J. Miller
Whitney Young Middle
    School
Detroit, Michigan

Lawrence Peglow
Greenway Middle School
Pittsburgh, Pennsylvania

Lyn Shiver
Northwestern Middle
    School
Alpharetta, Georgia

The World Explorer Team

The editors, designers, marketer, market researcher, manager, production buyer, and manufacturing buyer who made up the World Explorer team are listed below.

Jackie Bedoya, Bruce Bond, Ellen Brown, David Lippman, Catherine Martin-Hetmansky,
Nancy Rogier, Olena Serbyn, Carol Signorino, John Springer, Susan Swan

TABLE OF CONTENTS

THE ANCIENT WORLD 1

Readable, accessible content to motivate your students (see pp. 8-9)

OF SPECIAL INTEREST

A hands-on, active approach to practicing and applying key social studies skills

Engaging, step-by-step activities for exploring important topics in ancient history

High-interest selections from the mythology of ancient civilizations

Active learning approaches to involve and engage students (see pp. 2-7)

READ ACTIVELY

Activating Prior Knowledge

Three sets of reading strategies are introduced on pages viii and ix. Before students read the strategies, use questions like these to prompt a discussion about reading:

- Before you read, what do you do to help you read better?

- How do you figure out the meaning of what you read?

- Do you take a different approach to different kinds of reading, such as a paperback novel or your math textbook?

Discussion of their answers will help students become aware of their own reading processes.

Introducing the Strategies

Point out to students that reading is a process. If students are conscious of their process, they can improve their reading. Point out that there are three sets of reading strategies: **Before You Read, While You Read,** and **After You Read.** Explain that these are the behaviors that good readers exhibit. As students practice these strategies, they too will increase their reading fluency and comprehension.

Be sure to reinforce the idea that students might use several of these strategies at the same time, or they might go back and forth among them. There is no set order for applying them.

How can I get the most out of my social studies book?

How does my reading relate to my world? Answering questions like these means that you are an active reader, an involved reader. As an active reader, you are in charge of the reading situation!

The following strategies tell how to think and read as an active reader. You don't need to use all of these strategies all the time. Feel free to choose the ones that work best in each reading situation. You might use several at a time, or you might go back and forth among them. They can be used in any order.

Give yourself a purpose

The sections in this book begin with a list called "Questions to Explore." These questions focus on key ideas presented in the section. They give you a purpose for reading. You can create your own purpose by asking questions like these: How does the topic relate to your life? How might you use what you learn at school or at home?

Preview

To preview a reading selection, first read its title. Then look at the pictures and read the captions. Also read any headings in the selection. Then ask yourself: What is the reading selection about? What do the pictures and headings tell about the selection?

Reach into your background

What do you already know about the topic of the selection? How can you use what you know to help you understand what you are going to read?

Ask questions

Suppose you are reading about the continent of South America. Some questions you might ask are: Where is South America? What countries are found there? Why are some of the countries large and others small? Asking questions like these can help you gather evidence and gain knowledge.

Predict

As you read, make a prediction about what will happen and why. Or predict how one fact might affect another fact. Suppose you are reading about South America's climate. You might make a prediction about how the climate affects where people live. You can change your mind as you gain new information.

Connect

Connect your reading to your own life. Are the people discussed in the selection like you or someone you know? What would you do in similar situations? Connect your reading to something you have already read. Suppose you have already read about the ancient Greeks. Now you are reading about the ancient Romans. How are they alike? How are they different?

Visualize

What would places, people, and events look like in a movie or a picture? As you read about India, you could visualize the country's heavy rains. What do they look like? How do they sound? As you read about geography, you could visualize a volcanic eruption.

Respond

Talk about what you have read. What did you think? Share your ideas with your classmates.

Assess yourself

What did you find out? Were your predictions on target? Did you find answers to your questions?

Follow up

Show what you know. Use what you have learned to do a project. When you do projects, you continue to learn.

READ ACTIVELY   ix

Introducing the Guiding Questions

This book was developed around five Guiding Questions about the Ancient World. They appear on the reduced Student Edition page to the right. The Guiding Questions are intended as an organizational focus for the book. All of the chapter content, activities, questions, and assessments relate to the Guiding Questions, which act as a kind of umbrella under which all of the material falls. You may wish to add your own Guiding Questions to the list in order to tailor them to your particular course. Or, as a group activity, you may want to ask your class to develop its own Guiding Question.

Ask a volunteer to read the Guiding Questions out loud to the class. These questions will guide students as they learn about the geography, history, and culture of ancient civilizations.

Introducing the Project Preview

The projects for this book are designed to provide students with hands-on involvement in the content area. On the reduced Student Edition page to the right, students are introduced to the projects. Complete information about them appears on pages 222–223. You may assign projects as cooperative activities, whole class projects, or individual projects. Each project relates to one of the Guiding Questions.

THE ANCIENT WORLD

The cities of ancient times bustled with traffic. People shopped at the market, worked, and lived in families, as people do today. Builders, teachers, rulers, and scientists invented objects and systems that we still know and use. The ancient peoples developed great civilizations. They traveled, traded, conquered, and settled. Who could have known how their beliefs and customs would affect the modern world?

Guiding Questions

The readings and activities in this book will help you discover answers to these Guiding Questions.

- What methods do people use today to try to understand cultures of the past?
- How did physical geography affect the growth of ancient civilizations?
- How did the beliefs and values of ancient civilizations affect the lives of their members?
- How did civilizations develop a government and an economic system?
- What accomplishments is each civilization known for?

Project Preview

You can also discover answers to the Guiding Questions by working on projects. Preview the following projects and choose one that you might like to do. For more details, see page 222.

Ancient World Travel Guide Write a travel guide to the world of ancient times, pointing out places of historical interest.

The Hall of Ancient Heritage Create a poster comparing ancient customs to similar customs in today's world.

Ancient Debate Stage a debate to argue which ancient civilization contributed the most to the modern world.

Life in the Ancient World Organize an Ancient World Fair, featuring foods, activities, artwork, and costumes of six ancient civilizations.

Resource Directory

Teaching Resources

📁 **Book Projects,** in the Activities and Projects booklet, provides students with directions on how to complete one of the projects described on these two pages. You may wish to assign or have students choose a project at the beginning of the course.

Program Resources

📁 **Long-Term Integrated Projects** booklet, in the Program Resources Binder, provides opportunities for students to make comparisons across regions through a variety of long-term projects. You may wish to assign or have students choose a project at the beginning of the course.

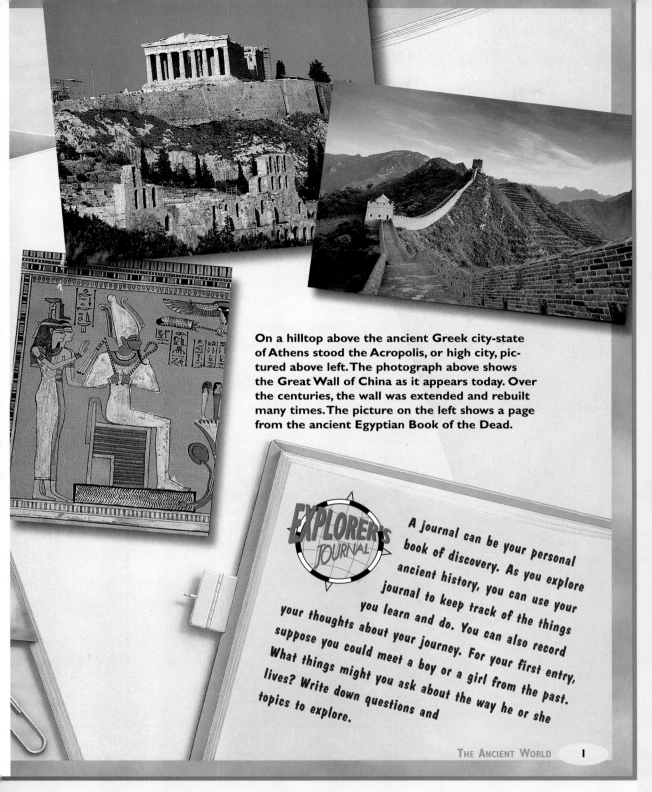

On a hilltop above the ancient Greek city-state of Athens stood the Acropolis, or high city, pictured above left. The photograph above shows the Great Wall of China as it appears today. Over the centuries, the wall was extended and rebuilt many times. The picture on the left shows a page from the ancient Egyptian Book of the Dead.

Explorer's Journal

A journal can be your personal book of discovery. As you explore ancient history, you can use your journal to keep track of the things you learn and do. You can also record your thoughts about your journey. For your first entry, suppose you could meet a boy or a girl from the past. What things might you ask about the way he or she lives? Write down questions and topics to explore.

Using the Pictures

Invite students to discuss the three photographs. Use them as a prompt for discussion of what students know about ancient history. You may want to begin a K-W-L chart on the board with the headings What We Know About the Ancient World, What We Want to Know About the Ancient World, and What We Learned About the Ancient World. Have students fill in the first column with several things they agree they already know. Then ask them to brainstorm what they would like to know about ancient history to add to the second column. Students can fill in the third column as they work through the text.

Using the Explorer's Journal

Have students begin their Explorer's Journal as the paragraph on the student book page suggests. If at all possible, encourage students to use a separate small notebook for their Explorer's Journal entries. They can add to this Journal as they learn more about the Ancient World.

Teacher's Flexible Planning Guide includes a guide to the Prentice Hall World Explorer program, a skills correlation, and a variety of pacing charts for different course configurations. You may wish to refer to the guide as you plan your instruction.

Resource Pro™ CD-ROM allows you to create customized lesson plans and print all Teaching Resources and Program Resources, plus the Computer Test Bank, directly from the CD-ROM.

Lesson Objectives

1 Describe the relative locations of major ancient world civilizations.

2 Identify the time spans in which ancient cultures flourished.

3 List the major geographic features of the ancient world and explain how they affected ancient culture.

Lesson Plan

1 Engage

Ask students to define the word *history*. Encourage them to explain how they think history affects the present.

Activating Prior Knowledge

Ask students how they think the great civilizations of the ancient world might have affected today's world. Have volunteers share knowledge about inventions, languages, architecture, works of art, and so forth. If necessary, prompt students' thinking with examples such as paper and the pyramids.

Answers to...

LOCATION

1. Ancient Rome was the largest; ancient Greece was the smallest. Students should locate ancient civilizations on continents as follows: Africa: ancient Egypt and Nubia; Asia: ancient civilizations of the Fertile Crescent, ancient China, ancient empires of India; Europe: ancient Greece, ancient Rome.

DISCOVERY ACTIVITIES ABOUT
The Ancient World

Learning about the ancient world means being an explorer and a geographer. No explorer would start out without first checking some facts. Begin by exploring the maps of the ancient world on the following pages.

LOCATION

1. Explore the Ancient World's Location To begin your exploration, locate the ancient worlds on the political map. Which was the largest? Which was the smallest? On which continent was each one located?

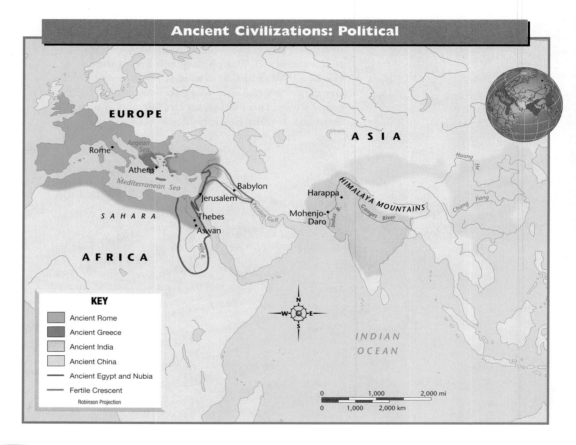

Ancient Civilizations: Political

KEY
- Ancient Rome
- Ancient Greece
- Ancient India
- Ancient China
- Ancient Egypt and Nubia
- Fertile Crescent

Robinson Projection

0   1,000   2,000 mi
0   1,000   2,000 km

Resource Directory

Teaching Resources

Activity Atlas in the Activities and Projects booklet, pp. 3–5, provides a structure that helps students complete the activities in the Ancient World Activity Atlas and encourages discovery learning.

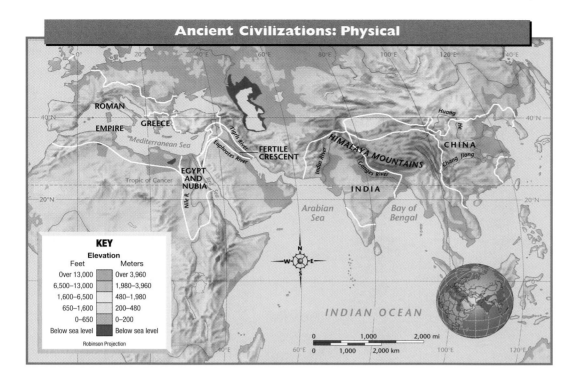

Ancient Civilizations: Physical

ROMAN EMPIRE
GREECE
Mediterranean Sea
Tigris River
Euphrates River
FERTILE CRESCENT
EGYPT AND NUBIA
Tropic of Cancer
Nile R.
Red Sea
India River
HIMALAYA MOUNTAINS
Ganges River
INDIA
Arabian Sea
Bay of Bengal
Huang
He
CHINA
Chang Jiang
INDIAN OCEAN

KEY

Elevation

Feet		Meters
Over 13,000		Over 3,960
6,500–13,000		1,980–3,960
1,600–6,500		480–1,980
650–1,600		200–480
0–650		0–200
Below sea level		Below sea level

Robinson Projection

INTERACTION

2. Consider How Geography Affects Settlement Describe the geographic features of each of the six ancient areas of civilization. How are they different from one another? People often settle in an area because of its physical features. Which features do the six regions have in common?

REGIONS

3. Find the Dates of Ancient Civilizations Look at the table. Which civilization lasted for the longest time? Which ones existed at the same time? Name the civilization that began first. Which was the last to end?

Ancient Civilizations

Location	Time Span
Fertile Crescent	about 3500 B.C.–500 B.C.
Egypt and Nubia	about 3100 B.C.–A.D. 350
India	about 2500 B.C.–185 B.C.
China	about 2000 B.C.–A.D. 1911
Greece	about 2000 B.C.–146 B.C.
Rome	about 900 B.C.–A.D. 476

2 Explore

Point out and explain the five themes of the geography headings in the Activity Atlas. Have students label five pieces of paper with these heads. As students read the Atlas text and study its maps and illustrations, urge them to note interesting facts or questions they have. Let students exchange and combine their theme pages.

3 Teach

Ask students to create a five-column chart about the ancient world with these headings: *Name of Civilization; Time Span; Continent; Key Geographic Features; Effect of Geography on People.* Have students fill in information for each of the headings.

4 Assess

Charts should correctly name, locate, and date each of the civilizations. They should note major rivers and geographic features. Charts should also note that cultures arose in similar locations because of access to waterways and fertile soil.

Answers to . . .

INTERACTION

2. Answers may include mountains, rivers, plains, valleys. All the regions are near water.

REGIONS

3. Egypt and Nubia lasted the longest. All the civilizations co-existed between the years 900 B.C. and 185 B.C. The Fertile Crescent was the site of the first civilization and Rome was the last civilization to end.

ACTIVITY ATLAS
continued

Practice in the Themes of Geography

Ask students to use the Six Ancient Civilizations political and physical maps to find answers to the following questions concerning the five themes of geography.

Location Have students find the civilization that was farthest from the others. (ancient China)

Interaction Ask: *What kind of transportation might the ancient Greeks have used?* (boats) *What kinds of work might have been important to the culture?* (fishing, trading)

Place Have students find the Indus River. Which ancient civilization arose nearby? (ancient India)

Regions Ask students to decide which ancient civilization is in the same region as the possible birthplace of humanity. (ancient Egypt and Nubia)

Movement Ask students to identify two bodies of water that the Egyptians could have used to get to Greece. (the Nile River and the Mediterranean Sea.)

REGIONS

4. Find Geo Cleo Geo Cleo is excited about traveling to the sites of ancient civilizations. Read each of the postcards Geo Cleo sent home to her friends. Unfortunately, part of each message was washed away. Use the maps on the first two pages of this Activity Atlas to fill in the missing information.

The people who lived here in ancient times were cut off from the rest of the world for centuries by a mountain range. The world's highest mountains, the Himalaya Mountains, form a natural barrier to the north. I enjoyed traveling in this Asian country of _____.

This city, called _____, has some of the oldest ruins in the world. Located between two rivers, it was the home of a famous civilization of the Fertile Crescent.

I am on the banks of the world's longest river. It runs for 4,132 miles (6,648 km), about the distance between the American cities of Chicago and Honolulu. This river, called the _____, empties into the Mediterranean Sea. In the distance, I can see pyramids and this huge lionlike sculpture called the Sphinx.

I am standing on an ancient wall in northern China, not far from a muddy, yellow river. In ancient times, this river often flooded and wiped out whole villages. It lies to the north of another major Chinese river, the Chang Jiang. This river is named _____.

GEO CLEO

4   THE ANCIENT WORLD

MOVEMENT

5. Trace Greek Settlements Powerful civilizations often expanded to include more land than they originally had. From time to time throughout their history, the city-states of ancient Greece found that they needed more land. The mountainous countryside made it difficult to farm, and the populations were growing quickly. Many of the city-states sent groups of citizens to look for new homes elsewhere. The Greeks established settlements all across the Mediterranean and Black seas, spreading the Greek civilization. Look at the area of Greek settlements on the map. Compare it to the area of the Greek mainland. Which is greater? Near what physical feature are all of the settlements located? How do you think the settlers traveled to their new homes?

LOCATION

6. Locate the Greek Settlements These new settlements became independent cities. Which new city was the farthest from the Greek mainland? Why do you think the new cities might have become so independent? Explain how you think Greek settlements might have affected Mediterranean cultures in general.

▼ The Ancient Greeks traveled across the sea to find new homes in boats like the one painted on this cup.

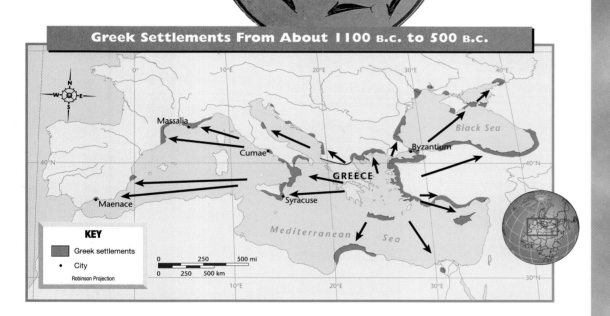

Greek Settlements From About 1100 B.C. to 500 B.C.

KEY
- Greek settlements
- • City

0   250   500 mi
0   250   500 km
Robinson Projection

Massalia
Cumae
Maenace
Syracuse
GREECE
Byzantium
Black Sea
Mediterranean   Sea

Answers to...

MOVEMENT

5. The area of settlements is greater than the Greek mainland. Because all settlements are near the Mediterranean Sea, settlers probably traveled by boat.

PLACE

6. Maenace was farthest from Greece. City-states probably had to act independently since they were so far from the mainland. Greek ideas and culture probably spread throughout the Mediterranean.

Activity

Journal Writing

Making Choices Talk with students about the advantages and disadvantages of living in a culturally isolated or a culturally diverse place. Then have students write in their journals about the type of place they would rather live in. Encourage students to give reasons for their choices.

Background

Links Across Time

The Fertile Crescent Today The Fertile Crescent remains a multicultural region. With the lands around it, this region is now known as the Middle East. People of many different cultural, ethnic, and religious backgrounds live there. As with the ancient civilizations, conflict continues to affect the region. One major cause of strife has been the differences among the three major world religions of the region—Judaism, Christianity, and Islam.

Answers to...

INTERACTION

7. Students should note that the Fertile Crescent could be reached by land or by water and that an exchange of ideas resulted from interaction with other cultures. The Hindu Kush and Himalaya Mountains isolated ancient India, so it probably developed a unique culture.

INTERACTION

7. Think About How Isolation Affects Civilizations You already know that some civilizations existed at the same time but in different places. Look at maps of two of these civilizations below and right.

The Fertile Crescent had few natural barriers to stop invaders. Over time, different peoples conquered and ruled this region. Look at the landforms on the map below. How do you think conquering peoples reached the area? How do you think the culture of this area was affected by these changes?

Look at the map of ancient India. What major landforms do you see? For many years, the people there were left alone. Why do you think this is so? How do you think this affected the culture of ancient Indian empires?

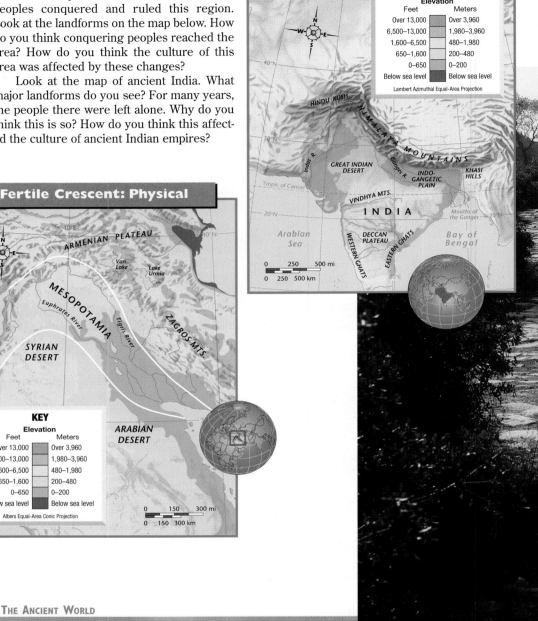

Ancient India: Physical

KEY

Elevation	
Feet	Meters
Over 13,000	Over 3,960
6,500–13,000	1,980–3,960
1,600–6,500	480–1,980
650–1,600	200–480
0–650	0–200
Below sea level	Below sea level

Lambert Azimuthal Equal-Area Projection

Fertile Crescent: Physical

KEY

Elevation	
Feet	Meters
Over 13,000	Over 3,960
6,500–13,000	1,980–3,960
1,600–6,500	480–1,980
650–1,600	200–480
0–650	0–200
Below sea level	Below sea level

Albers Equal-Area Conic Projection

MOVEMENT

8. Consider How Roads Help a Civilization Grow Romans built the largest road system in the ancient world. Look at the roads shown on this map. On how many continents do the roads run? Estimate the greatest distance from one end of the road system to the other. Which city has the most roads leading to it? Why do you think that is? Explain why you think the Romans built so many roads over such a large area.

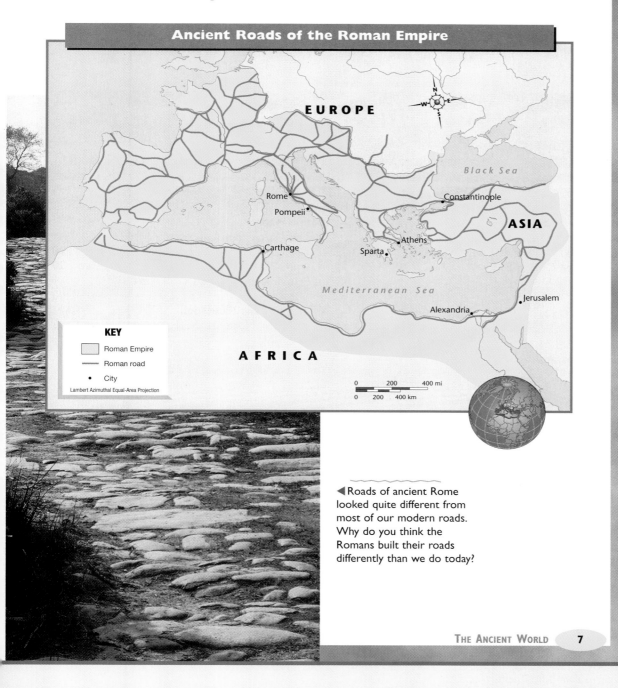

Ancient Roads of the Roman Empire

EUROPE

Black Sea

Rome

Pompeii

Constantinople

ASIA

Carthage

Athens

Sparta

Mediterranean Sea

Jerusalem

Alexandria

KEY

Roman Empire

Roman road

• City

Lambert Azimuthal Equal-Area Projection

AFRICA

0   200   400 mi

0   200   400 km

◄ Roads of ancient Rome looked quite different from most of our modern roads. Why do you think the Romans built their roads differently than we do today?

THE ANCIENT WORLD

The Beginnings of
Human Society

To help you plan instruction, the chart below shows how teaching resources correspond to chapter content. Use the resources to vary instruction, add activities, or plan block schedules. Where appropriate, resources have **suggested time allotments** for students. Time allotments are approximate.

Managing Time and Instruction

	The Ancient World Teaching Resources Binder		World Explorer Program Resources Binder	
	Resource	mins.	Resource	mins.
1 SECTION I **Geography and History**	**Chapter and Section Support** Reproducible Lesson Plan, p. 3 ⓢ Guided Reading and Review, p. 4 ⓢ Section Quiz, p. 5	20 25	**Outline Maps** The Middle East and North Africa: Physical, p. 28 **Nystrom Desk Atlas** Ⓣ **Primary Sources and Literature** Readings **Writing Process Handbook** Preparing Note Cards, pp. 21–22	20 20 40 25
SKILLS ACTIVITY **Using a Time Line**	**Social Studies and Geography Skills,** Reading a Time Line, p. 61	30		
2 SECTION 2 **Prehistory**	**Chapter and Section Support** Reproducible Lesson Plan, p. 6 ⓢ Guided Reading and Review, p. 7 ⓢ Section Quiz, p. 8 Critical Thinking Activity, p. 16 **Social Studies and Geography Skills,** Reading a Natural Vegetation Map, p. 25	20 25 30 30	**Outline Maps** The World: Physical, p. 2	20
3 SECTION 3 **The Beginnings of Civilization**	**Chapter and Section Support** Reproducible Lesson Plan, p. 9 ⓢ Guided Reading and Review, p. 10 ⓢ Section Quiz, p. 11 ⓢ Vocabulary, p. 13 Reteaching, p. 14 Enrichment, p. 15 ⓢ Chapter Summary, p. 12 **Tests** Forms A and B Chapter Tests, pp. 2–7	20 25 20 25 25 15 40		

Block Scheduling Folder
PROGRAM TEACHING RESOURCES

Activities and Projects

Block Scheduling
Program Support

Interdisciplinary Links

Resource Pro™ CD-ROM

Media and Technology

From Guiding Questions to Assessment A series of Guiding Questions serves as an organizing framework for this book. The Guiding Questions that relate to this chapter are listed below. Section Reviews and Section Quizzes provide opportunities for assessing students' insights into these Guiding Questions. Additional assessments are listed below.

Media and Technology

Resource	mins.
◖▶ ◉ ⓢ World Video Explorer	20
◉ Planet Earth CD-ROM	20
▭ Color Transparency 92	20
▭ Color Transparency 121	20
◉ Planet Earth CD-ROM	20
▭ Color Transparency 39	20
♫ ⓢ Guided Reading Audiotapes	20
▭ Color Transparency 171	
(Graphic organizer web template)	20
◉ The Writer's Solution CD-ROM	30
⊟ Computer Test Bank	30

T Teaming Opportunity
This resource is especially well-suited for teaching teams.

ⓢ Spanish
This resource is also in Spanish support.

◉ **CD-ROM**

◉ **Laserdisc**

▭ **Transparency**

⊟ **Software**

◖▶ **Videotape**

♫ **Audiotape**

GUIDING QUESTIONS

- *What methods do people use today to try to understand cultures of the past?*
- *How did physical geography affect the growth of ancient civilizations?*

ASSESSMENTS

Section 1

Students should be able to make a web of the tools used to help understand the past.

▶ **RUBRIC** See the Assessment booklet for a rubric on assessing graphic organizers.

Section 2

Students should be able to write an explanation of the effect geography and climate had on farming during the Stone Age.

▶ **RUBRIC** See the Assessment booklet for a rubric on assessing cause-and-effect statements.

Section 3

Students should be able to create a chart detailing the development of the earliest cities and civilizations.

▶ **RUBRIC** See the Assessment booklet for a rubric on assessing charts.

Activities and Projects

Mental Mapping

The First Human Home Tell students that most of the earliest human fossils and the remains of their living areas have been found in Africa. Early human fossils have been found throughout the African continent, especially in East Africa. Have students draw outline maps of the eastern hemisphere including Africa, Asia, and Europe. You may distribute outline maps if you prefer.

Tell students that important human fossils have been found near Java, Indonesia; Beijing, China; and Heidelberg, Germany, as well as Africa. Invite students to locate these three places on their maps. Have them check the locations. Then have them trace routes that early humans might have traveled to migrate from East Africa to each of those three spots.

Links to Current Events

Uncovering the Past Today, many scientists are working to learn more about early humans. If possible, invite a scientist from a local university, college, or museum to talk to students about the questions scientists are trying to answer with their research. Ask the scientist to explain why so much of human prehistory is a mystery to researchers.

If no scientist is available to visit your classroom, arrange a field trip to a museum of archaeology or natural history. Ask someone at the museum to talk to your class about the ways that museum curators try to bring prehistory alive for the public. If practical, you might arrange "before" and "after" visits to the museum. Discuss how students find the museum displays more interesting after they gain background information by reading the chapter.

Hands-On Activities

Living on the Land Divide students into small groups. Ask each group to imagine that they are a band of Stone Age gathering and hunting people who have moved to your area. Ask them to imagine that they can speak to one another but not write. They have fire and the ability to make tools out of natural materials. Since it is the Stone Age, none of the buildings, roads, and other human-made structures in your area would exist. Have them imagine that the climate and vegetation are as they exist. (In reality, of course, the vegetation would not include many species that exist today.)

Invite each group to spend 15 to 30 minutes walking around outside. Ask them to look for things they might use to create clothing, shelter, tools, and other necessary objects. Ask them what they might eat. Would their band be likely to settle here for a while or move on to another area? Why?

Creating a Civilization Have students think of themselves as people who are to be part of one of the first human colonies on another planet. Ask them to list the things they would take. Have them list the first things they would build or create. Urge them to think about social institutions as well as physical structures. Give students a chance to discuss their ideas in a small group or with the class as a whole. *Basic*

Comic Relief Invite students to discuss the stereotypes they see or have about prehistoric peoples. Have them create cartoon strips portraying those stereotypes. Then ask them to create a second cartoon strip that presents more realistic information about people who lived in prehistoric times. *English Language Learners*

More Than Footsteps Tell students that the theme of human-environment interaction can be used to study even prehistoric peoples who had very simple culture and technology. Invite students to suggest ways that prehistoric people might have changed the land on which they lived. How would they have been affected by the land? Have students work in groups or as a whole class to make a two-column chart listing ways that early humans would have affected and been affected by the land. *Average*

Research a Site Have students research an archaeological site that has provided information about early humans and how they lived. Have them report to the class on what archaeologists or other scientists actually found at the site. What methods did they use to analyze or understand what they found? What conclusions did they draw from the objects they found? *Challenging*

F.Y.I.

This page can help you extend your own and students' understanding of the concepts in this chapter. You may want to browse through some of the suggestions in the **Bibliography. Interdisciplinary Links** can connect social studies understandings to areas elsewhere in the curriculum through the use of other Prentice Hall products. **National Geography Standards** reflected specifically in this chapter are listed for your convenience. Some hints about appropriate **Internet Access** are also provided. **School to Careers** provides insights into the practical uses of some of the concepts in this chapter as they might pertain to various careers.

BIBLIOGRAPHY

FOR THE TEACHER

Ancient Cities: A Geographic Perspective. National Geographic, 1991. Sound filmstrip.

Martell, Hazel Mary. *The Kingfisher Book of the Ancient World: From the Ice Age to the Fall of Rome.* Kingfisher, 1995.

Place, Robin. *Bodies from the Past.* Thomson, 1995.

Wood, Michael. *Legacy: The Search for Ancient Cultures.* Sterling, 1994.

FOR THE STUDENT

Easy

Lessem, Don. *The Iceman.* Crown, 1994.

Caselli, Giovanni. *An Ice Age Hunter.* Bedrick, 1992.

Average

Charley, Catherine. *Tombs and Treasures.* Viking, 1995.

Hill, Emily, ed. *The Visual Dictionary of Ancient Civilizations.* Dorling Kindersley, 1994.

Challenging

Scarre, Chris. *Smithsonian Timelines of the Ancient World.* Dorling Kindersley, 1993.

LITERATURE CONNECTION

Brennan, J. H. *Shiva: An Adventure of the Ice Age.* Harper, 1992.

Cowley, Marjorie. *Dar and the Spear Thrower.* Clarion Books, 1994.

Turnbull, Ann. *Maroo of the Winter Caves.* Clarion Books, 1984.

INTERDISCIPLINARY LINKS

Subject	Theme: Origins
MATH	Middle Grades Math: Tools for Success *Course 1*, Lesson 1-6, **Constructing Bar and Line Graphs** *Course 2*, Lesson 1-2, **Using a Computer to Graph Data**
SCIENCE	Prentice Hall Science *Evolution: Change Over Time*, Lesson 3-1, **The Search for Human Ancestors,** Lesson 3-2, **Human Ancestors and Relatives** *Exploring Earth's Weather*, Lesson 2-3, **Changes in Climate, Connections: The Birth of Agriculture**

NATIONAL GEOGRAPHY STANDARDS

Students explore the 18 National Geography Standards throughout *The Ancient World.* Chapter 1, however, concentrates on investigating the following standards: 1, 2, 3, 4, 5, 6, 9, 10, 11, 12, 14, 15, 17. For a complete list of the standards, see the *Teacher's Flexible Planning Guide.*

SCHOOL TO CAREERS

In Chapter 1, The Beginnings of Human Society, students learn about the beginning of civilization and prehistory. Additionally, they address the skill of using a time line. Understanding early human history can help students prepare for careers in many fields such as history, archaeology, urban planning, and so on. Understanding time relationships is a skill particularly useful for administrators, office managers, historians, politicians, and others. The curriculum presented in this book, as in all eight titles of Prentice Hall's *World Explorer* program, is designed to prepare students not only for careers but also for good citizenship—of the world as well as of this country.

INTERNET ACCESS

Many social studies teachers and students use Internet browsers, or search engines, to investigate particular topics. For the best results, use narrow rather than broad topics. Try these for Chapter 1: irrigation, Nile River, Iceman, prehistoric civilizations. Finding age-appropriate sites is an important consideration when using the Internet. For links to age-appropriate sites in world studies and geography, visit the Prentice Hall Home Page at: **http://www.phschool.com**

Connecting to the Guiding Questions

As students complete this chapter, they will focus on how archaeologists learn about prehistoric peoples, how historians search for clues in written records, and how human society developed. Students will also investigate how the geography of a land contributed to the development of cities. The content of this chapter corresponds to the following Guiding Questions:

● What methods do people use today to try to understand cultures of the past?

● How did physical geography affect the growth of ancient civilizations?

Using the Picture Activities

Point out that these pictures tell us that the people who painted them hunted animals for food. Encourage class discussion of the questions.

● Possible responses may include: The paintings may have some spiritual meaning. Paintings inside caves would last longer.

● Before asking students to draw their pictures, have the class generate a list of items that indicate something about American culture.

CHAPTER 1

The Beginnings of Human Society

SECTION 1
Geography and History

SECTION 2
Prehistory

SECTION 3
The Beginnings of Civilization

PICTURE ACTIVITIES

This bull is one of hundreds of animals painted on the walls and ceilings of Lascaux (las COH) Cave in France. The people who painted these pictures lived about 15,000 years ago. To create their paintings, the artists traveled hundreds of yards into the dark cave. Often, they had to crawl through narrow, dangerous passages. To paint on the ceilings, they built rickety wooden platforms.

Understand the mind of the artist
Why do you suppose these people faced such dangers just to paint pictures on the walls? Why do you think they painted in caves rather than on rocks outside the caves?

Create a picture for the future
While the people who painted these cave pictures had no written language, they left pictures that tell us something about their lives. Draw a picture that will tell people a thousand years in the future about your life.

Resource Directory

Media and Technology

Journey Over the Ancient World, from the World Video Explorer, introduces students to the regions where the world's first civilizations developed.

A Trip To: The Cave Paintings at Lascaux, from the World Video Explorer, enhances students' understanding of prehistoric culture through an exploration of the cave paintings at Lascaux, France.

Chapter 2

Chapter 3

Geography and History

BEFORE YOU READ

Reach Into Your Background

Have you ever read a detective story or watched a mystery movie? Then you know what it's like to solve a mystery by using clues. The mystery you are about to read even begins with a dead body! Was he the victim of foul play? How can people figure out how he died? Read on . . .

Questions to Explore

1. What tools do we use to understand the past?

2. What is the connection between the geography of a place and its history?

Key Terms

history
prehistory
archaeologist
oral tradition

Key People

The Iceman of the Alps

His frozen body was found in a high mountain pass in the Alps, in the European country of Italy, so he is called the Iceman.

The Iceman was used to traveling the mountains. Usually, he was well able to survive alone. This day, however, he probably was caught by surprise by a fierce mountain storm. He stretched out near some rocks and covered himself with a cape made of woven grass. Soon, he fell asleep. As he slept, it grew colder. The Iceman froze to death without ever waking.

For thousands of years, the Iceman lay covered with snow and ice. In 1991, two hikers discovered him by chance. His body and possessions were taken to a laboratory, where scientists learned more about him. The Iceman lived before people kept written records. However, his clothing, tools, and his body were well preserved. They provided clues about the Iceman's life.

Scientists determined that the Iceman lived about 5,000 years ago, in about 3000 B.C. His clothes were made of finely stitched animal skins. That showed that the Iceman probably came from a community with people skilled in sewing.

▼ The Iceman was a skilled outdoorsman. Among his belongings were a wood frame pack, a bow, a flint dagger, and other gear suited to wilderness survival.

Teaching Resources

📁 **Reproducible Lesson Plan** in the Chapter and Section Resources booklet, p. 3, provides a summary of the section lesson.

📁 **Guided Reading and Review** in the Chapter and Section Resources booklet, p. 4, provides a structure for mastering key concepts and reviewing key terms in the section. Available in Spanish in the Spanish Chapter and Section Resources booklet, p. 3.

Program Resources

Material in the **Primary Sources and Literature Readings** booklet extends content with a selection related to the concepts in this chapter.

Outline Maps The Middle East and North Africa: Physical, p. 28

Heterogeneous Groups

The following Teacher's Edition strategies are suitable for heterogeneous groups.

Interdisciplinary Connections

Critical Thinking

Cooperative Learning

Lesson Objectives

① Describe how archaeologists use clues to learn about prehistoric people.

② Differentiate between prehistory and history.

③ Explain how geography affects civilizations.

Lesson Plan

1 Engage

Warm-Up Activity

Ask a volunteer to place the contents of his or her pockets or backpack on a table. Have the class imagine that they live thousands of years in the future. Have students discuss how the objects serve as clues to the way people live today.

Activating Prior Knowledge

Have students read Reach Into Your Background in the Before You Read box. Encourage students to discuss the methods used in solving mysteries in detective stories.

2 Explore

Have students read the section and explore the following questions: Why do archaeologists sift through the remains of ancient campsites? How do stories that have been passed down by word of mouth help people understand the past? How do rivers affect the development of civilizations?

3 Teach

Have students work in small groups to develop a dictionary of terms for this section. Each group should locate unfamiliar terms in the section and write their definitions based on contextual clues. Encourage groups to begin with the key terms listed at the beginning of the section. Direct students to use each term in a sentence as well. Students may check their definitions against those in a classroom dictionary if necessary. Invite groups to share their completed dictionary of terms with the class. This activity should take about 25 minutes.

4 Assess

See the answers to the Section Review. You may also use students' completed dictionaries as an assessment.

Acceptable dictionaries include all key terms with correct definitions as well as appropriate sentences.

Commendable dictionaries include all key terms plus two additional terms with correct definitions and appropriate sentences.

Outstanding dictionaries show a thorough understanding of all key terms as well as several other terms.

Putting a Face on Prehistory

Experts analyzed many clues to learn about the Iceman. An artist studied the Iceman's skull to make this model of his head (below left). The Iceman's copper ax (below right) and unfinished arrows and a bow without a string suggest that he had been looking for materials needed to finish his weapons, when he met his death.

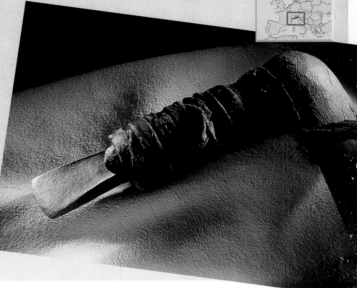

The Iceman's Face Using measurements, X-rays, and computer views of the Iceman's head, a sculptor made a model of the skull. Then, with the help of other information, the sculptor added clay to the skull to show flesh. Finally, he used soft plastic and real hair to make a finished sculpture. It is an accurate model of the way the Iceman probably looked in life.

The most important clue about the Iceman's life was his copper ax. Copper was the first metal used by Europeans, beginning about 4000 B.C. There was no doubt that the Iceman lived after people had learned to use copper. Although the Iceman's people left no written record, scientists put together the clues he left to build a story of his life.

Understanding History

The scientists' curiosity about the Iceman's life was natural. We all are curious about our past. We want to know how our parents and grandparents and great-grandparents lived. We want to know where people in our community came from.

As human beings, we are curious about our origins. What was life like many thousands of years ago? About 5,000 years ago, people in Southwest Asia and in Africa developed systems of writing. With this, they began to keep written records of their experiences. That was the beginning of **history,** since history means the recorded events of people.

If you add the prefix *pre-* to the word *history,* you get the word *prehistory.* The prefix *pre-* means *before.* Therefore, **prehistory** means *before history.* Prehistory is the period of time in the past before writing was invented. How can we learn about the people who lived before written history?

Resource Directory

Program Resources

Nystrom Desk Atlas

Media and Technology

 Planet Earth CD-ROM includes physical maps of Africa and Asia that allow students to view the areas that gave birth to human prehistory.

Color Transparency 92

Prehistory: Digging Up the Past   To learn about life in prehistoric times, scientists must rely on clues other than written records. Scientists known as **archaeologists** examine objects to learn about past people and cultures. They sift through the dirt of prehistoric camps to find bones, tools, and other objects. These objects may tell them something about the people who lived there. For example, the size of spear points made from a stone called flint shows what kinds of game the people hunted. To kill big game, such as bears, hunters had to use large, heavy spear points. Such points, however, would not work very well with birds and small animals.

History: A Record in Writing   Historians do not have to rely on the objects discovered by archaeologists to learn about the past. They study the written record of human life and accomplishments to understand a society—its wars, its religion, and its rulers, among other things. Historians also look at what other groups living at the same time wrote about that society.

The Tools of Survival

Prehistoric peoples made tools and weapons from stone. These handaxes (1 and 3) and the sharp spear point (2) were fashioned from quartz some 50,000 years ago. **Critical Thinking** Which tool do you think would have been best for hunting? Why?

Radiocarbon Dating All plants and animals have tiny amounts of a substance called radiocarbon in their bodies. After they die, the radiocarbon changes into another substance. Scientists know how long this change takes. They have tests that measure how much radiocarbon is left in ancient wood, grass, cloth, and flesh. Scientists can then calculate the age of the material.

Oral Traditions: A Record in the Spoken Word The written records studied by historians often began as oral traditions, which are stories passed down by word of mouth. Oral history can tell family history, such as stories of parents, grandparents, and great-grandparents. It can also tell stories about heroes or events in the past.

Oral traditions are still an important part of many societies today. Not all oral stories are historically accurate. Like myths and legends, they often mix facts with beliefs and exaggerations about heroes. Still, oral traditions tell about how a society lived and what the people considered important.

Linking Geography and History

Knowing when something happened is only the beginning for historians. Understanding why historic events took place is also important. Knowing the connection between geography and history is often the

Carrying On a Tradition

This man is a griot from the African country of Mali. Griots memorize important events from a village's past such as births, deaths, hunts, and wars. Griots may spend hours or even days retelling important events. Griots pass their knowledge on to young men who have been selected to become griots themselves. **Critical Thinking** How are oral traditions different from written history?

Rice Fields in the Hills

Wherever people farm, they must discover the most efficient way to grow crops and the best way to use available land. Rice grows best in fields covered with shallow water. On these hillsides along the Chang Jiang in China, rice farmers have built terraces into the hillsides. Terraces catch and hold rainwater and make it possible to grow crops on hilly land.

key to understanding why events happened. For example, to explain why the ancient Egyptians developed a successful civilization, you must look at the geography of Egypt.

Egyptian civilization was built on the banks of the great Nile River. Each year, the Nile flooded, depositing rich black soil on its banks. Because the soil was so rich, Egyptian farmers could grow enough crops to feed the large numbers of people in the cities. That meant everyone did not have to farm, so some people could do other things that helped develop the civilization. Without the Nile and its regular flooding, Egyptian civilization would not have become so successful. This is one way that geography affects history.

SECTION 1 REVIEW

1. **Define** (a) history, (b) prehistory, (c) archaeologist, (d) oral tradition.

2. **Identify** The Iceman of the Alps.

3. How do we learn what happened throughout history and prehistory?

4. Describe how geography can affect the history of a group of people.

Critical Thinking

5. **Understanding Cause and Effect** What effect has the geography of your community had on the way people live there?

Activity

6. **Writing to Learn** You may know stories that have been passed on by oral tradi-

tion. Ask a family member, teacher, or friend to share a story with you. The story should be about an important event in the person's life. Moving to a new country or home, the birth of a baby, or a move to a new school are all events that people share stories about. Write the words down. Try to write so the story sounds as if someone is speaking.

Resource Directory

Teaching Resources

Section Quiz in the Chapter and Section Resources booklet, p. 5, covers the main ideas and key terms in the section. Available in Spanish in the Spanish Chapter and Section Resources booklet, p. 4.

Activity

Critical Thinking

Drawing Conclusions Tell students that they can combine new knowledge with what they already know to draw conclusions about a place or a culture. Point out to students that they need to think carefully in order to draw sound conclusions, then pose the following question: *Several of the world's great civilizations and large cities are located along the banks of rivers. Why do you think this is so?* (Rivers supplied water for drinking and farming, as well as serving as a means of transportation for trading.)

Section 1 Review

1. (a) the recorded events of people (b) the period of time before writing was invented (c) a scientist who studies ancient objects to learn about the people who used the objects (d) stories passed down by word of mouth

2. a prehistoric man whose body and possessions provided clues about how people lived 5,000 years ago

3. Students may say that archaeologists use clues from objects left by prehistoric people and that historians use written records to learn about ancient societies.

4. Students may mention that ancient Egyptian farmers relied on the flooding of the Nile.

5. Students should show an understanding of the connection between landforms and certain human activities.

6. Stories should reflect an attempt to capture the natural voice of the storyteller.

Prehistory

Lesson Objectives

1 Describe how humans lived during the Old Stone Age and the developments that led to the New Stone Age.

2 Summarize how the development of farming changed the way people lived.

Lesson Plan

1 Engage

Warm-Up Activity

Discuss with students the skills people need to survive in the wilderness. Have students discuss how to get food, make clothing and shelter, and so on.

Background

Biography

Mary Douglas Leakey (1913–1996) The leader of the team of scientists who discovered the footprints in eastern Africa was Mary Leakey, a woman responsible for some of the most noteworthy archaeological and anthropological finds of the twentieth century. For 30 years, she and her husband, Louis S.B. Leakey, made many important discoveries at prehistoric sites in Africa. They discovered the earliest known stone tools. The Leakeys called these tools "choppers." Choppers are sharply pointed stone tools that could be used for cutting, sawing, smashing, or crushing.

BEFORE YOU READ

Reach Into Your Background
For tens of thousands of years, our human ancestors lived and prospered using mainly stone tools. They used no metal of any kind. Look around the room in which you are reading this. What items are made of metal? How would your life be different if everything metal did not exist?

Questions to Explore
1. How did people live in the Old and New Stone Ages?

2. What is the effect of geography and climate on farming?

Key Terms
nomad
fertile
domesticate

Key Places
East Africa

▲ Prehistoric peoples had to make tools and other items out of materials they could find. This carving was made from a bone or tusk of a mammoth, or prehistoric elephant.

Long before humans used metal, about three-and-a-half million years ago, a huge explosion shook a part of what is now the country of Tanzania in East Africa. A volcano spit out clouds of fine ash that fell on the surrounding land. Then rain came. It turned the blanket of ash into thick mud. Before the mud dried, two individuals walked across the landscape. As they walked, they left their footprints in the mud.

In 1976, a group of scientists looking for evidence of early humans discovered the footprints, preserved in stone. They were amazed at their find. The footprints are almost identical to those made by modern humans walking in wet sand.

The Stone Age: From Hunting and Gathering to Farming

A million years after these footprints were made, human ancestors used tools. They used stones as hammers. With these hammers, they chipped sharp flakes from soft volcanic rock. They used the points they made to cut plants or meat.

This first use of stone to create tools began what we now call the Stone Age. The Stone Age gets its name from the fact that people made tools and weapons mainly from stone. These tools were very simple. Gradually, people began to make more complex tools from stone. Scientists think that the Stone Age continued for hundreds of thousands of years, until people learned to use metal for tools and weapons.

Resource Directory

Media and Technology

 Color Transparency 121

Teaching Resources

📁 **Reproducible Lesson Plan** in the Chapter and Section Resources booklet, p. 6, provides a summary of the section lesson.

📁 **Guided Reading and Review** in the Chapter and Section Resources booklet, p. 7, provides a structure for mastering key concepts and reviewing key terms in the section. Available in Spanish in the Spanish Chapter and Section Resources booklet, p. 5.

Prehistoric Shelter

Some 18,000 years ago, people in central Russia depended on mammoths not only for food but also for shelter. People built huts like this one by fitting mammoth bones together. **Critical Thinking** Name some shelters other people have made from natural materials they gathered.

Archaeologists divide the Stone Age into two periods, the Old Stone Age and the New Stone Age. During the Old Stone Age, people did not yet know how to farm. They lived by hunting animals and gathering roots, berries, leaves, and seeds. They used stone to make hunting weapons and tools to cut meat, scrape animal hides, cut skins to make clothing, and many other things. They also used other materials—bone and animal horns and tusks.

Gradually, Old Stone Age people learned to hunt in groups. Soon, they had developed the skill of cooperating in the hunt. Almost all of human prehistory took place during the Old Stone Age.

Fire! About 500,000 years ago, there was another important development in human prehistory—the discovery of fire. No one knows for sure how it happened. Perhaps one day a small band of hunters saw a grass fire caused by lightning on the open plain. Terrified by the fire, they probably ran from it.

A great advance came when humans discovered how to make fire when they wanted it. They probably did this by rubbing two sticks together or by striking stones together to produce a spark. With the ability to make fire as they needed it, people could move to areas that had cold climates.

READ ACTIVELY

Predict Why would fire be useful to early people?

Program Resources

Outline Maps The World: Physical, p. 2

Activating Prior Knowledge

Have students read Reach Into Your Background in the Before You Read box. As students look around, be sure to remind them that many of the plastic items they see once would have been fashioned from metal or wood. Have students also consider these items as they discuss how their lives would be different without metal.

2 Explore

Ask students to read the section and explore the following questions: *What important steps did our ancient ancestors take that led to modern civilization? Why did Old Stone Age people move from place to place? What allowed New Stone Age people to settle down? How did they get food?*

3 Teach

Ask students to create a sequencing map, showing some important developments in human prehistory with an explanation of why each step was important. For example, stone tools allowed the ancestors of modern humans to become efficient hunters. This activity should take about 20 minutes.

Answers to . . .

PREHISTORIC SHELTER

Possible answers: tepees, hogans, earth lodges, stone buildings, log cabins

4 Assess

See the answers to the Section Review. You may also use students' completed sequencing maps as an assessment.

Acceptable maps include at least three developments in proper sequence with an explanation of the importance of each.

Commendable maps include more than three developments in proper sequence with an explanation of their importance.

Outstanding maps include an explanation of all developments, and show an understanding of the interrelatedness of the developments.

Background

Links Across Time

Nomads Today The word *nomad* comes from a Greek word that means "one who wanders for pasture." Nomads exist today. For example, in the deserts of Southwest Asia, Bedouins move their camels, goats, and sheep from place to place to ensure that the herds have suitable pastures for grazing.

Answers to . . .
MAP STUDY

They probably abandoned the area and searched for a more fertile place to settle.

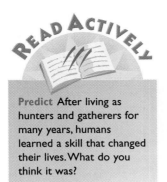

Predict After living as hunters and gatherers for many years, humans learned a skill that changed their lives. What do you think it was?

Settling New Areas As people developed the use of tools, they left their original homes in Africa. This may have begun as early as 1 million years ago. Many Stone Age people became **nomads,** or people who had no single, settled home. They moved around to places where they were sure they would find food. These nomads stayed at a campsite for several days. When they had gathered all the food around, they moved on.

Humans eventually spread out over much of the Earth. There is evidence that people were living in Asia and Europe at least 500,000 years ago. Perhaps 30,000 years ago, humans crossed from Asia into North America. By 10,000 B.C., humans had reached Peru in South America. Though few in number, people lived in regions as different as the steamy rain forests in Asia, the cold lands near the Arctic Circle, and the very high altitudes of the Andes Mountains in South America.

The Beginning of Farming

For tens of thousands of years, humans continued to live as hunters and gatherers. Then, about 11,000 years ago, people in Southwest Asia made an amazing discovery. They learned that if they planted the seeds of wild grasses, new crops of grass would come up. Thus began the

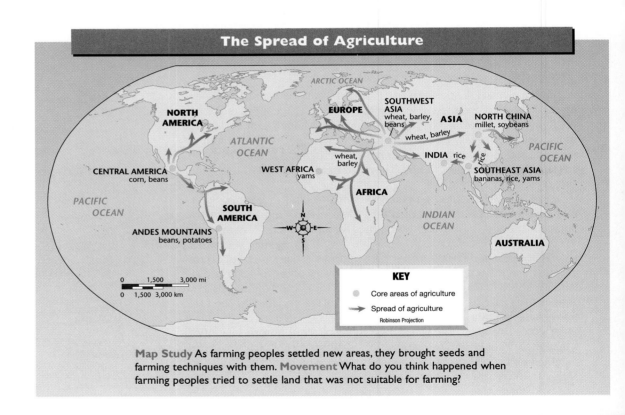

The Spread of Agriculture

Map Study As farming peoples settled new areas, they brought seeds and farming techniques with them. **Movement** What do you think happened when farming peoples tried to settle land that was not suitable for farming?

Resource Directory

Teaching Resources

Reading a Natural Vegetation Map in the Social Studies and Geography Skills booklet, p. 25, provides additional skill practice.

► Seven thousand years ago, an ear of corn did not make much of a meal (top). It took thousands of years of careful breeding for ears of corn to reach their present size.

New Stone Age in Southwest Asia. It was called the New Stone Age because people began to grow their own food. They were no longer nomads, although they still depended on stone tools. However, in many other parts of the world, the Old Stone Age continued for many thousands of years. In some areas, Old Stone Age societies existed into the 1900s.

Since in most societies women were responsible for gathering plants and seeds, they may have first gotten the idea of planting seeds. Men usually were the hunters. Women began planting and harvesting their crops in the same place year after year.

Farming in Other Places

Some places were better for farming than others. Soil in some areas was very **fertile,** which means that the soil contained substances that plants need to grow. Plants also need light and warmth, so areas that had long springs and summers were good places to farm. Gentle rains were important sources of water for plants. In several places around the world, many miles apart, people discovered that the soil, the water, and the length of the summers were good for plants. These people took up the farming way of life. About 7,000 years ago, Chinese farmers began planting rice and other crops. A little later in Central America, people began to grow corn, beans, and squash.

While the kinds of plants grown by those first farmers are still important today, they looked very different. When people first began to plant seeds, they carefully chose the biggest, best-tasting plants. They selected those seeds to plant. Gradually, this careful selection of the biggest and best seeds and roots from each crop led to the kind of food that we eat today. For example, the earliest corn came from cobs only two or three inches long. Today, the corn-on-the-cob we eat may be four times that size.

Taming Animals

Humans learned another important skill during the New Stone Age. They learned to **domesticate,** or tame, animals. The first domesticated animals may have been dogs, because

ACROSS TIME

Not Just Thousands of Years Ago Not all human groups took up farming. Even today, a few groups still live the way we believe Old Stone Age people did. Such groups include some living in the rain forests of the Amazon River Valley in South America, in the Kalahari Desert of Africa, and in parts of New Guinea, a Pacific Ocean island.

Beast of Burden

Camels are native to north Africa, southwest Asia, India, and the highlands of central Asia. They were domesticated long ago and have been used for their meat, milk, wool, and hides. Mostly, however, they have been used to carry loads. People in these regions still use camels to help them in their work. **Interaction** How did humans benefit from domesticating animals?

they were valuable in hunting. By taming sheep, cows, and pigs, people developed a ready source of meat, milk, wool, and skins. Through careful breeding, the herders developed animals that were gentler than their wild ancestors and gave more milk or wool. By about 3000 B.C., cattle, camels, horses, and donkeys were trained to carry heavy loads.

SECTION 2 REVIEW

1. Define (a) nomad, (b) fertile, (c) domesticate.

2. Identify East Africa.

3. How did people of the Old Stone Age get their food?

4. How was life in the New Stone Age different from life in the Old Stone Age?

Critical Thinking

5. Identifying Central Issues Over the past two million years, human beings have made important discoveries and developed new ways of doing things. Name two of the most important developments and explain how they affect us today.

Activity

6. Writing to Learn Pretend you are a member of a hunting and gathering society. You get the idea to try growing plants for food. Write a journal entry describing what gave you the idea. Tell the differences your idea might make to your people.

The Beginnings of Civilization

Section 3

BEFORE YOU READ

Reach Into Your Background

Look at the shoes you are wearing and the shirt or sweater you have on today.

Who made the fabric for your clothes? Who prepared the leather or canvas for your shoes? Who grew the grain for the cereal you ate for breakfast? All of these jobs were done by people who have special skills—weavers, shoemakers, farmers. Think what life would be like if families had to do all these things for themselves.

Questions to Explore

1. How did early cities develop?
2. What is civilization?

Key Terms

irrigation
surplus
artisan
civilization
social class

U nder a fierce desert sun, long lines of people are digging a long trench, soon to become a deep canal. Other people lift heavy baskets of dirt dug from the canal onto their shoulders. They dump the dirt near the river where another crew of men is building a huge earthen dam.

These are some of the world's first construction workers. They are building an **irrigation** system, a network of canals to supply land with water from another place. One person directs the work at each site. Like the big construction projects of today, this job takes teamwork.

Soon, the dam will hold the spring flood waters of the river. A group of people are building wooden gates in the dam. Officials will open the gates in the dry summer. Water will flow through the canals, irrigating the growing crops.

▼ These people use traditional methods—an animal-powered pump—to irrigate their crops in the Nile Valley of Egypt.

Advantages of a Settled Life

Farming and raising animals was much harder work than hunting and gathering. However, it had far greater rewards. Producing food allowed people

---

Lesson Objectives

1. Explain how early farming villages grew into cities.
2. Describe how some societies grew into civilizations.
3. Summarize the role of trade in the development of civilizations.

Lesson Plan

1 Engage

Warm-Up Activity

Tell students that early hunter-gatherers moved from place to place, carrying all their possessions. Ask students to imagine that they have to carry all their belongings with them to a new home. What things would they carry? What kinds of things would they *not* be able to own and carry with them?

Activating Prior Knowledge

Have students read Reach Into Your Background in the Before You Read box. Ask student volunteers to describe a camping or backpacking trip they have taken. Have them explain how being away from some of the things they take for granted (television, telephones, automobiles) affected them. How did they manage without these things? What was most enjoyable? What item was the most difficult to do without?

---

2 Explore

Have students read the section and explore the following questions: *Why did populations grow after people settled in farming villages? How were farming villages different from cities? What are the features of a civilization? What effects did trade have on civilizations?*

3 Teach

Have students develop their own quiz for the section. Suggest that they include five multiple-choice questions and one short essay question. This activity should take about 25 minutes.

Background

Daily Life

A Farmer's Work Hunter-gatherers who lived in an area with plenty of game and vegetation had to work only about 20 hours a week to get enough food for their families. Early farmers, on the other hand, had to work many more hours planting, tending, and harvesting their crops. Children worked alongside adults, and mothers carried babies on their backs while they worked the fields.

Answers to ...

GRAPH STUDY

Population grew slowly before the year A.D. 1.

---

to have a steady supply of food year around. This meant they could stay in one place. People often had a food **surplus**—more than they needed. Surplus food could be stored for use at another time.

The Population Grows Having surplus food also affected the size of families. The hunting-gathering life did not allow parents to have many children. How could they feed them all? Now, food surpluses would feed many more people.

Larger families brought rapid population growth. Scientists estimate that about 10,000 years ago the population of the world was about 10 million people, which is about the number of people living in Los Angeles today. By 7,000 years ago, many people had settled into the farming life. The population had grown to about 66 million.

Early Villages and Towns People lived in New Stone Age farming settlements for many centuries before towns developed. Gradually, as the population increased, the settlements grew larger.

With food surpluses, people did not have to spend all their days producing food. Some people were able to switch from farming to other kinds of work. For example, some people became **artisans,** or workers who are especially skilled in making items such as baskets, leather goods, tools, pottery, or cloth.

The Growth of Cities

Not all early farming settlements grew into cities. Cities could develop where rich soil created large surpluses of food. People also needed a dependable source of drinking water and materials to build shelters.

READ ACTIVELY

Ask Questions Think of several questions you would like to have answered about the world's first cities.

World Population, 2000 B.C. to A.D. 2000

Graph Study By A.D. 1000, world population had reached 275 million. By 2000, the world's population is expected to be more than 6 billion. **Critical Thinking** How would you describe the rate of world population growth before the year A.D. 1?

Millions of People

7,000
6,000
5,000
4,000
3,000
2,000
1,000
0

2000 B.C.   1000 B.C.   A.D. 1   A.D. 1000   A.D. 2000*

Year

*Projected

Resource Directory

Teaching Resources

Section Quiz in the Chapter and Section Resources booklet, p. 11, covers the main ideas and key terms in the section. Available in Spanish in the Spanish Chapter and Section Resources booklet, p. 8.

Vocabulary in the Chapter and Section Resources booklet, p. 13, provides a review of key terms in the chapter.

Available in Spanish in the Spanish Chapter and Section Resources booklet, p. 10.

Reteaching in the Chapter and Section Resources booklet, p. 14, provides a structure for students who may need additional help in mastering chapter content.

Enrichment in the Chapter and Section Resources booklet, p. 15, extends chapter content and enriches students' understanding.

Skara Brae: Village of the Hilly Dunes

These ruins of the village of Skara Brae are on one of the Orkney Islands, north of Scotland. Archaeologists think that farmers and herders settled here around 3500 B.C. People used stone to build shelters for themselves and their cattle, sheep, and pigs. Villagers spent their days tending their animals, collecting shellfish, hunting, making pottery, and repairing buildings. Experts think that a violent storm struck the area around 2400 B.C., causing the villagers to abandon Skara Brae. **Critical Thinking** Why do you think the villagers built their homes out of stone?

Some of the earliest cities grew up along big rivers, such as the Nile in Egypt, the Tigris and Euphrates (yoo FRAYT eez) rivers in Iraq, the Huang He (hwahng hay) in China, and the Indus River in Pakistan. Cities grew up there because the soil for farming is rich near riverbeds.

The Earliest Cities   The chart on the next page shows when the first cities developed in Asia, Africa, and the Americas.

Early cities were different from farming villages in some important ways. Cities were larger, of course. Cities also had large public buildings. There were buildings to store surplus grain, buildings for the worship of gods, and buildings where people could buy and sell goods. In villages, most people were farmers. In cities, workers had a wide variety of occupations. Most worked at a craft. As new skills developed, so did new occupations.

Governments Form   As the population of cities grew, so did the need for effective rules. Someone needed to be responsible for keeping order. Others had to settle disputes or manage such things as irrigation projects. People developed government to keep order in their society and to provide services.

The First Civilizations

Over time, some New Stone Age societies grew into civilizations. A **civilization** is a society that has cities, a central government run by official leaders, and workers who specialize in various jobs. This job

Early Jewelry Prehistoric people strung pebbles, shells, bones, and feathers to make necklaces. When people learned to work with copper, they made jewelry from it. By about 3000 B.C., they had learned to use gold. Archaeologists have found gold jewelry in a prehistoric cemetery in Eastern Europe and in ancient tombs in Southwest Asia and Egypt.

specialization leads to another feature of civilizations, social classes. Writing, art, and architecture also characterize a civilization.

By 6600 B.C., artisans in Europe and Asia had learned a key skill. They discovered that melting a certain rock at high temperatures would separate the metal copper from the rock. By 3000 B.C., artisans had learned to mix copper with another metal, tin, to make a mixture called bronze. Because bronze was much harder than copper, it had more uses—weapons, tools, helmets, and shields. This began the Bronze Age.

Trade Helps Civilizations Spread Traders took valuable items such as pottery, tools and weapons, baskets, cloth, and spices to faraway cities. They traded these items for food and goods that people at home wanted. By around 3500 B.C., some civilizations had developed a simple but amazing invention: the wheel and axle. With the wheel and axle, trade goods could be loaded into carts and pushed through the city to market. More goods could be transported farther and more easily.

Trade over water also developed. Merchant ships now carried goods across seas and rivers. With all this travel, people of many different cultures came into contact with one another. New tools and ideas from one society soon spread to others as people from different places traded information along with goods.

Cities and Civilization

Chart Study Cities arose at different times in different places. The city of Harappa (right) was one of the first cities built in what is now Pakistan. **Critical Thinking** About when was Harappa built?

Locations of the First Cities

Area	Date City Was Founded
Southwestern Asia	about 3500 B.C.
Egypt	about 3100 B.C.
Pakistan	about 2500 B.C.
China	about 1700 B.C.
Central America	about 200 B.C.

Ancient Jewelry

The artisan class arose because there was a demand for handicrafts. A European artisan made this bronze bracelet (left) in about 1000 B.C. The gold jewelry (right) was made in Southwest Asia as early as 2900 B.C.

Social Classes Develop Growing trade links brought new prosperity to the cities. This led to another major change in society—the development of **social classes.** Each person was part of a group, or class, made up of others with similar backgrounds, wealth, and ways of living. In the large cities, the king was by far the most powerful person. Next in importance were two classes of people. One was the priests of the city's religion. The other was the nobles, who were government officials and military officers. Below them were the artisans, small traders, and merchants. At the very bottom of the social ladder were common workers and farmers.

SECTION 3 REVIEW

1. **Define** (a) irrigation, (b) surplus, (c) artisan, (d) civilization, (e) social class.

2. Describe the important developments that led from the hunting-and-gathering way of life to villages and cities.

3. How were the large cities of early civilizations different from the early farming villages?

Critical Thinking

4. **Recognizing Cause and Effect** Name some reasons for the development of early civilizations.

Activity

5. **Writing to Learn** You are an early trader bringing tools and weapons made of bronze to people who have never seen this metal. Write a speech to persuade these people to trade for your bronze goods.

SKILLS MINI LESSON

Recognizing Cause and Effect

To **introduce** the skill, explain that cause and effect means that one event happens because of a different event. Remind students that just because one event follows another in time does not mean that there is a cause-and-effect relationship. To **practice** the skill, have students discuss the events leading up to the development of civilizations. Ask them to point out one thing that directly led to another. (For example, surplus food allowed some people to specialize in other work.) Discuss the cause-and-effect relationship, and then ask them to **apply** the skill by listing and explaining other causes that led to the development of civilizations.

Lesson Objectives

❶ Define the elements and function of a time line.

❷ Use a time line to relate historical events to each other.

1 Engage

Warm-Up Activity

Invite two volunteers to role-play the introductory dialogue. Write the term *time line* on the chalkboard. Ask students to suggest how a time line might help Maria explain *prehistory*.

Activating Prior Knowledge

Ask students to think of time lines they have encountered. Have they seen time lines in other textbooks? In magazines or on television? Discuss with students why time lines are useful in a variety of contexts.

2 Explore

To **introduce** the skill, read the Get Ready text with students, noting the definition of a time line in the first paragraph. Allow students time to study the From Prehistory to Today time line. Ask students whether events studied in this chapter would be on the left end or the right end of the time line (left). Then ask students where events that occurred in our present century would be placed (right).

Using a Time Line

"Okay. If something happened in 1000 B.C., it happened 1,000 years ago. Right?" Derek looked at Maria.

"No." Maria smiled. " 'B.C.' stands for 'Before Christ.' That means it happened 1,000 years before Jesus was born. Christians believe he was born about 2,000 years ago. If something happened in 1000 B.C., it really happened about 3,000 years ago."

Derek was still puzzled. "Okay," he said slowly. "Then what does A.D. stand for? Does it mean After the Death of Christ?"

"No," said Maria. "It stands for *Anno Domini,* which is Latin for 'in the year of the Lord.' That is what the Christians called the time after Jesus was born. We still call it that—the years we count now are A.D."

Get Ready

A time line is an easy way to make sense of the dates and events of the past. A time line is a simple diagram that shows how dates and events relate to one another. It has a title, reads from left to right, has years that are evenly spaced, and labels major events.

The best way to understand how to use a time line is to make one yourself. Try making one of your own life! All you need is a pencil, a sheet of paper, and a ruler.

Resource Directory

Teaching Resources

📁 **Reading a Time Line** in the Social Studies and Geography Skills booklet, p. 61, provides additional skill practice.

From Prehistory to Today

c. 3500 B.C.
Written history begins when writing is invented in the Tigris-Euphrates Valley.

A.D. 1776
The United States Declaration of Independence is signed.

4000 B.C.	3000 B.C.	2000 B.C.	1000 B.C.	A.D. 1	A.D. 1000	A.D. 2000

c. 3000 B.C.
Bronze tools are invented.

c. A.D. 1
Jesus is born.

A.D. 476
Roman Empire ends.

■ **BEFORE CHRIST (B.C.)**

■ **ANNO DOMINI ("in the year of the Lord") (A.D.)**

Try It Out

A. Turn the sheet of paper sideways. Use the ruler to draw a straight line 7 inches long across the middle of the paper. Draw a big dot on the left end of the line.

B. Mark the years. Under the dot on the left, write the year you were born. Measure 1/2 inch along the line to the right, mark the spot with another dot, and write the next year under the dot. Continue until you reach the current year. Then write "Present" under the last dot. Your time line goes left to right, just as you read from left to right. Each space between two dots, or interval, represents twelve months.

C. Add the events. Above the first dot, write "Born in (write the name of the town where you were born)." Now write several other important events in your life above other dates on the time line. Connect each label to the right place on the time line with a vertical, or up-and-down, line. Remember, the space between the dots is the year; the dots themselves represent the first day of each year.

D. Give your time line an appropriate title. Now look at your time line, and ask yourself, "Does this make it easy for someone to learn about my life?" If you answer "yes," then you did a good job.

Apply the Skill

Complete the following steps by using the time line on these two pages.

1 Familiarize yourself with the time line. Look it over to get a sense of what the time line shows. What is the title? When does it begin and end? What types of events are shown? You used one-year intervals in your time line. What time intervals does this time line use?

2 Read the time line. Do you understand all of the labels and the dates on the time line? The Latin abbreviation *c.* stands for the word *circa*. *Circa* means "about." Why do you think some dates are marked "*c.*"? Why is 1776 not marked "*c.*"?

3 Learn from the time line. When did written history begin? Were bronze tools invented before or after writing? Can you tell if some events happened closer together than others? Which event happened closer to the birth of Jesus—the signing of the Declaration of Independence or the invention of writing?

4 Use the time line as a reference. A time line can help you remember dates and the order of important events. You may want to look back at the time line here as you read through this book.

3 Teach

Have students **practice** by creating the personal time line outlined in Try It Out. Check students' progress as they identify and sequence events they plan to include. Clarify any confusion and assist students with scale.

For additional reinforcement, ask students to list three important events in sequence for a classroom time line.

4 Assess

Have students **apply** their time line skills by completing the final part of the activity. To **assess,** work through the questions in the text with students. Invite all students to help answer each question. Highlight and review time line conventions such as B.C., A.D., and *c.*

Answers to ...

APPLY THE SKILL

1. The title of the time line is From Prehistory to Today. It begins in 4000 B.C. and ends in A.D. 2000. Events listed include the invention of bronze tools and the birth of Jesus. Intervals of 1,000 years are shown.

2. *Circa* indicates that historians cannot precisely date these events. Historians know exactly when the Declaration of Independence was signed.

3. Written history began *c.* 3500 B.C. Bronze tools were invented after writing. The scale of time lines shows which events happened close to other events. The signing of the Declaration of Independence happened closer to the birth of Jesus.

Review and Activities

Reviewing Main Ideas

1. by examining objects for clues about the ways of life of early peoples

2. Answers will vary. Students may suggest that a river or a lake provides fish to eat as well as water to drink and use for irrigation.

3. They ate plant foods and hunted animals.

4. They grew crops and raised domesticated animals for meat and milk.

5. Farming led to surplus crops, which led to population growth and also allowed some people to become specialized workers and artisans.

6. Cities grew prosperous through trade. People began to identify themselves as part of a group according to their background, wealth, and way of living.

Reviewing Key Terms

Sentences will vary, but should show correct meaning through context.

Critical Thinking

1. Answers may vary, but students may suggest that rich soil and plenty of water would be attractive, while dry, arid conditions would be unattractive.

2. New Stone Age farmers lived in villages where almost everyone farmed. They grew all their own food. Many city people were specialized workers and artisans of different sorts. In cities, people could buy, sell, and trade goods.

Reviewing Main Ideas

1. How do people today learn about people who lived tens of thousands of years ago?
2. Choose a landform or water body such as a river, mountain range, or lake and describe how it can affect the people who live around it.
3. Describe how Old Stone Age people in East Africa millions of years ago got food.
4. How did New Stone Age people get food?
5. Explain the connection between farming and the growth of early cities.
6. What caused social classes to develop?

Reviewing Key Terms

Use each key term below in a sentence that shows the meaning of the term.

1. prehistory
2. archaeologist
3. history
4. oral tradition
5. nomad
6. fertile
7. domesticate
8. irrigation
9. civilization
10. surplus
11. artisan
12. social class

Critical Thinking

1. **Drawing Conclusions** How does the geography of a place make it attractive or unattractive to settlers?
2. **Making Comparisons** Compare how New Stone Age farmers lived with how city people in early civilizations lived.

Graphic Organizer

Copy the web onto a sheet of paper. Then fill in the empty spaces with features of civilization to complete the web.

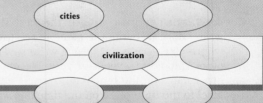

Graphic Organizer

Students' webs may vary.

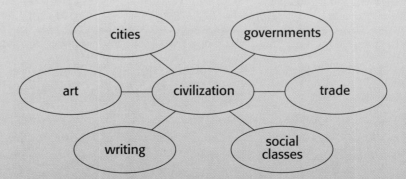

Map Activity

Place Location

Agriculture
For each place listed below, write the letter from the map that shows its location.

1. Central America
2. Southwest Asia
3. North China
4. Southeast Asia
5. West Africa
6. India

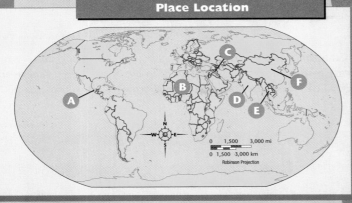

0 1,500 3,000 mi
0 1,500 3,000 km
Robinson Projection

Writing Activity

Writing Archaeology Notes

When archaeologists uncover prehistoric sites, they keep careful notes of each item they find. They use the items to help figure out things about the people who lived there. Choose a place you know well. Pick two or three items from the place and make detailed notes. From the items, tell what you can about the people who used them.

Internet Activity

Use a search engine to find **Flints and Stones: Real Life in Prehistory.** Click on Meet the Shaman to explore the world of the hunter-gatherer. Then click on Archaeologist Consult. Choose Do the Food Quiz. Take the quiz to see if you could survive today as a hunter-gatherer. Then write a journal entry recounting a typical day.

Skills Review

Turn to the Skills Activity. Review the steps for using a time line. Then complete the following: (a) Write a short definition of a time line. (b) How can you tell what the spaces between the years on a time line stand for?

How Am I Doing?

Answer these questions to help you check your progress.

1. Can I identify the methods that archaeologists and historians use to learn about the past?
2. Can I identify ways in which geography and history are connected?
3. Can I describe how Old Stone Age and New Stone Age people lived?
4. Do I understand how civilizations developed?

Internet Activity

If students are having difficulty finding this site, you may wish to have them use the following URL, which was accurate at the time this textbook was published:

http://www.ncl.ac.uk/ ~nantiq/menu.html

You might also guide students to a search engine. Four of the most useful are Infoseek, AltaVista, Lycos, and Yahoo. For additional suggestions on using the Internet, refer to the Prentice Hall Social Studies' Educator's Handbook "Using the Internet," in the Prentice Hall World Explorer Program Resources.

For additional links to world history and culture topics, visit the Prentice Hall Home Page at:
http://www.phschool.com

How Am I Doing?

Point out to students that this checklist is a quick reminder for them of what they learned in the chapter. If their answer to any of the questions is *no* or if they are unsure, they may need to review the topic.

Map Activity

1. A
2. C
3. F
4. E
5. B
6. D

Writing Activity

Students should describe the items objectively, without simply naming them. For example: "9″ × 12″ paper booklet with color pictures and numbered grid" rather than "calendar." Students should show evidence that they have put themselves in the place of an archaeologist thousands of years in the future and that they are using the items as clues to human activity.

Skills Review

Answers may vary. Sample answer: (a) A time line is a way to show the time order of history. (b) by looking at the labels on the time line

Resource Directory

Teaching Resources

Chapter Tests Forms A and B are in the Tests booklet, pp. 2–7.

Program Resources

Writing Process Handbook includes Preparing Note Cards, pp. 21–22, to help students with the Writing Activity.

Media and Technology

Color Transparencies
Color Transparency 171
(Graphic organizer web template)
Prentice Hall Writer's Solution
Writing Lab CD-ROM
Computer Test Bank
Resource Pro™ CD-ROM

The Fertile Crescent

To help you plan instruction, the chart below shows how teaching resources correspond to chapter content. Use the resources to vary instruction, add activities, or plan block schedules. Where appropriate, resources have **suggested time allotments** for students. Time allotments are approximate.

Managing Time and Instruction

	The Ancient World Teaching Resources Binder		World Explorer Program Resources Binder	
	Resource	**mins.**	**Resource**	**mins.**
SECTION 1 Land Between Two Rivers	**Chapter and Section Support** Reproducible Lesson Plan, p. 18 ⓢ Guided Reading and Review, p. 19 ⓢ Section Quiz, p. 20 Critical Thinking Activity, p. 37	20 25 30	**Outline Maps** The Middle East and North Africa: Physical, p. 28 **Nystrom Desk Atlas** Ⓣ **Primary Sources and Literature Readings** **Writing Process Handbook** Writing Effective Paragraphs, pp. 27–28	20 20 40 25
SKILLS ACTIVITY Identifying Central Issues	**Social Studies and Geography Skills,** Identifying Central Issues, p. 42	30		
2 SECTION 2 Babylonia and Assyria	**Chapter and Section Support** Reproducible Lesson Plan, p. 21 ⓢ Guided Reading and Review, p. 22 ⓢ Section Quiz, p. 23 **Social Studies and Geography Skills,** Reading a Diagram, p. 56	20 25 30	**Outline Maps** The Middle East and North Africa: Political, p. 29	20
3 SECTION 3 The Legacy of Mesopotamia	**Chapter and Section Support** Reproducible Lesson Plan, p. 24 ⓢ Guided Reading and Review, p. 25 ⓢ Section Quiz, p. 26	20 25		
4 SECTION 4 Mediterranean Civilizations	**Chapter and Section Support** Reproducible Lesson Plan, p. 27 ⓢ Guided Reading and Review, p. 28 ⓢ Section Quiz, p. 29	20 25	**Outline Maps** Western Europe: Political, p. 18	20
5 SECTION 5 Judaism	**Chapter and Section Support** Reproducible Lesson Plan, p. 30 ⓢ Guided Reading and Review, p. 31 ⓢ Section Quiz, p. 32 ⓢ Vocabulary, p. 34 Reteaching, p. 35 Enrichment, p. 36 ⓢ Chapter Summary, p. 33 **Tests** Forms A and B Chapter Tests, pp. 8–13	20 25 20 25 25 15 40	**Outline Maps** The Middle East and North Africa: Political, p. 29	20

Block Scheduling Folder
PROGRAM TEACHING RESOURCES

Activities and Projects

Interdisciplinary Links

Block Scheduling
Program Support

Resource Pro™ CD-ROM

Media and Technology

Media and Technology

Resource	mins.
◖◗ ⊘ ⑤ World Video Explorer	20
⊘ Planet Earth CD-ROM	20
⊔ Color Transparency 92	20
⊔ Color Transparency 70	20
⊔ Color Transparencies 67, 92	20
⌒ ⑤ Guided Reading Audiotapes	20
⊔ Color Transparency 174 (Graphic organizer table template)	20
⊘ The Writer's Solution CD-ROM	30
⊟ Computer Test Bank	30

T	**Teaming Opportunity** This resource is especially well-suited for teaching teams.	⊘	**CD-ROM**
		⊘	**Laserdisc**
		⊔	**Transparency**
⑤	**Spanish** This resource is also in Spanish support.	⊟	**Software**
		◖◗	**Videotape**
		⌒	**Audiotape**

Assessment Opportunities

From Guiding Questions to Assessment   A series of Guiding Questions serves as an organizing framework for this book. The Guiding Questions that relate to this chapter are listed below. Section Reviews and Section Quizzes provide opportunities for assessing students' insights into these Guiding Questions. Additional assessments are listed below.

GUIDING QUESTIONS

- *How did physical geography affect the growth of ancient civilizations?*
- *What accomplishments is each civilization known for?*

ASSESSMENTS

Section 1

Students should be able to write a poem about what it was like to live in a Sumerian city.

▶ **RUBRIC**   See the Assessment booklet for a rubric on assessing a student poem.

Section 2

Students should be able to create a map of the Babylonian and Assyrian empires.

▶ **RUBRIC**   See the Assessment booklet for a rubric on assessing a map produced by a student.

Section 3

Students should be able to write a brief report on the development of writing in Mesopotamia.

▶ **RUBRIC**   See the Assessment booklet for a rubric on assessing a report.

Section 4

Students should be able to create a time line of the major events in the history of the Israelites.

▶ **RUBRIC**   See the Assessment booklet for a rubric on assessing a time line.

Section 5

Students should be able to give an oral presentation on an Israelite value of their choice.

▶ **RUBRIC**   See the Assessment booklet for a rubric on assessing an oral presentation.

Activities and Projects

Mental Mapping	Links to Current Events	Hands-On Activities

Ancient Geography Ask students what kind of a map they would use to locate Babylonia and Assyria. If necessary, explain that these civilizations do not exist any longer. They would need a historic map to locate them. Tell them that Babylonia and Assyria were located on land held today by the countries of Iraq, Syria, and Turkey.

Have students identify the other countries of this region. Have them identify the bodies of water found in this region as well. After discussing the features of this area, give students a few minutes to sketch a map from memory.

Give students a chance to compare their sketched maps with a published map. Ask them to talk about what features were easy to remember and which were difficult to remember or place correctly.

In the News The region of Mesopotamia, known today as Southwest Asia, is often in the news. Invite students to describe what kinds of issues they associate with this region. Students may offer topics such as Israeli-Palestinian conflict; conflict over oil; or conflicts over land. List the topics students offer.

Ask students to find one news story from the past several months that deals with one of these topics. Have them identify the parties involved in the conflict or issue described in the news story they find. Can they locate these parties on a map?

Bulletin Board of Civilizations Before beginning this chapter, have students skim the material to collect the names of all the civilizations they will be studying. Direct them to create a bulletin board with space for each of the civilizations in the chapter. As they work through the chapter, tell them to fill in the bulletin board space for each civilization. Each space should include information about the time when the civilization existed, its location, and other interesting facts about the technology, government, social system, and trade of the civilization. Encourage students to create an appropriate illustration for each civilization's bulletin board space.

Living in the Past Invite students to form small teams of three or four. Have each team choose one of the ancient civilizations discussed in this chapter. Have the team members find out what they can about daily life in that civilization. Encourage them to share the results with the rest of the class by presenting a skit, making a diorama, painting a poster, or giving a report. *Challenging*

Location, Location Review with students the role of the Mesopotamian climate and geography in creating the conditions for the growth of early civilizations. Then ask students to write a real estate ad explaining the advantages of the

Mesopotamian geography and climate to early civilizations. *Basic*

Color-Coded Time Line Have students create a color-coded time line for the civilizations of this chapter. Since some of the civilizations overlap in time, some of the colors used will overlap. *English Language Learners*

Graphic Organizer Have students create a graphic organizer that links civilizations, major cities, and their rulers. Make a box containing the name of each civilization. Under each box include a column with the names of cities of the civilization. Under a second column, have students list the names of notable rulers or leaders of

the civilization along with significant achievements of those individuals. *Average*

F.Y.I.

This page can help you extend your own and students' understanding of the concepts in this chapter. You may want to browse through some of the suggestions in the **Bibliography. Interdisciplinary Links** can connect social studies understandings to areas elsewhere in the curriculum through the use of other Prentice Hall products. **National Geography Standards** reflected specifically in this chapter are listed for your convenience. Some hints about appropriate **Internet Access** are also provided. **School to Careers** provides insights into the practical uses of some of the concepts in this chapter as they might pertain to various careers.

BIBLIOGRAPHY

FOR THE TEACHER
Brookfield, Karen. *Book.* Dorling Kindersley, 1993.

Odijk, Pamela. *The Phoenicians.* Silver Burdett, 1989.

Sumer: Cities of Eden. Time-Life Books, 1993.

Tubb, Jonathan N. *Bible Lands.* Knopf, 1991.

FOR THE STUDENT
Easy
Cribb, Joe. *Eyewitness Books: Money.* Knopf, 1990.

Average
Bender, Lionel. *Invention.* Dorling Kindersley, 1991.

Moss, Carol. *Science in Ancient Mesopotamia.* Watts, 1988.

Challenging
Wilkinson, Philip. *The Lands of the Bible.* Chelsea House Publishers, 1994.

LITERATURE CONNECTION
Gardner, John and John Maier. *Gilgamesh.* Knopf, 1984.

INTERDISCIPLINARY LINKS

Subject	Theme: Civilization
MATH	Middle Grades Math: Tools for Success *Course 1*, Lesson 2-7, **Problem Solving: Use Logical Reasoning** *Course 2*, Lesson 4-7, **Problem Solving: Make a Table**
SCIENCE	Prentice Hall Science *Dynamic Earth*, Lesson 6-4, **Running Water** *Heredity: The Code of Life*, Lesson 4-1, **Plant and Animal Breeding**
LANGUAGE ARTS	Prentice Hall Literature *Copper*, **The Scribe**

NATIONAL GEOGRAPHY STANDARDS

Students explore the 18 National Geography Standards throughout *The Ancient World.* Chapter 2, however, concentrates on investigating the following standards: 2, 4, 5, 6, 9, 10, 11, 12, 13, 15, 16, 17. For a complete list of the standards, see the *Teacher's Flexible Planning Guide.*

SCHOOL TO CAREERS

In Chapter 2, The Fertile Crescent, students learn about the ancient civilizations that developed near the Mediterranean. Additionally, they address the skill of identifying central issues. Understanding how civilizations developed can help students prepare for careers in many fields such as history, archaeology, psychology, and so on.

Identifying central issues is a skill particularly useful for journalists, historians, educators, and others. The curriculum presented in this book, as in all eight titles of Prentice Hall's *World Explorer* program, is designed to prepare students not only for careers but also for good citizenship—of the world as well as of this country.

INTERNET ACCESS

Many social studies teachers and students use Internet browsers, or search engines, to investigate particular topics. For the best results, use narrow rather than broad topics. Try these for Chapter 2: Tigris River, Babylonian Empire, Hammurabi's Code, Torah. Finding age-appropriate sites is an important consideration when using the Internet. For links to age-appropriate sites in world studies and geography, visit the Prentice Hall Home Page at: **http://www.phschool.com**

In this chapter, students will focus on the rise of civilization in the Fertile Crescent. They will explore how ideas, values, religious beliefs, and inventions developed and will learn how certain concepts and beliefs have shaped our world. Content in this chapter focuses on the following Guiding Questions:

● How did physical geography affect the growth of ancient civilizations?

● What accomplishments is each civilization known for?

Using the Map Activities

Be sure students understand that for ancient peoples, survival depended almost entirely upon the geography of their region. Have students look at the map. Ask: *What difficulties would a desert region present? What difficulties might a mountainous region present?*

• Students might place cities in areas that are fertile, near rivers or the Mediterranean Sea, indicating that these locations would provide sources of food and transportation.

• Students may answer that invaders might attack regions with no natural barriers (mountains). Attackers might choose open plains or areas near large bodies of water. For protection, people might arm themselves or build walls.

CHAPTER 2

The Fertile Crescent

KEY

Fertile Crescent

Albers Equal-Area Conic Projection

MAP ACTIVITIES

The land that stretched in an arc from the Mediterranean Sea to the Persian Gulf had many attractions to the people of the ancient world. Get to know this land by completing the following activities.

Build a city
If you were to build three cities in the region shown on the map, where would you locate them? What makes these locations good places to build a city?

Protect yourself against invaders
Which areas might attract invaders? Why? How could people living in these areas protect their cities from invaders?

Resource Directory

Media and Technology

Geography: River Civilizations, from the World Video Explorer, enhances students' understanding of the geographic location for the civilizations of the Fertile Crescent.

Chapter 4

Land Between Two Rivers

BEFORE YOU READ

Reach Into Your Background

What is the land like where you live? Is the area flat, hilly, or mountainous? Does it have any deserts, lakes, rivers, or cities nearby? What in the geography of the area do you think attracted people to first settle in your community?

Questions to Explore

1. How did the geography of Mesopotamia make this a likely area for the rise of civilization?
2. What was it like to live in a Sumerian city?

Key Terms

scribe
city-state
polytheism
myth

Key Places

Sumer
Mesopotamia
Fertile Crescent
Tigris River
Euphrates River

> "**M**y headmaster read my tablet and said: 'There is something missing,' and hit me with a cane . . . The fellow in charge of silence said: 'Why did you talk without permission?' and caned me."

These words from the past come from a student at one of the world's first schools. He told what happened to him when his homework was sloppy or when he spoke without permission. Punishment was severe.

The first known schools were set up in the land of Sumer (SOO mur) over 4,000 years ago. Sumerian schools taught boys—and a few girls—the new invention of writing. Graduates of the schools became professional writers called **scribes**. Scribes were important people in Sumer because they were the only people in the land who could keep records for the kings and priests.

Learning to be a scribe was hard work. Boys normally began school at the age of 8 and didn't finish until they were 20.

The Geographic Setting of the Fertile Crescent

As you can see on the map on the next page, Sumer was located in a region called Mesopotamia (meh suh pah TAY mee uh). Like the place where you live, ancient

▼ The language on this clay tablet—Sumerian—is the oldest known written language.

Teaching Resources

📁 **Reproducible Lesson Plan** in the Chapter and Section Resources booklet, p. 18, provides a summary of the section lesson.

📁 **Guided Reading and Review** in the Chapter and Section Resources booklet, p. 19, provides a structure for mastering key concepts and reviewing key terms in the section. Available in Spanish in the Spanish Chapter and Section Resources booklet, p. 12.

Program Resources

Material in the **Primary Sources and Literature Readings** booklet extends content with a selection related to the concepts in this chapter.

Outline Maps The Middle East and North Africa: Physical, p. 28

Heterogeneous Groups

The following Teacher's Edition strategies are suitable for heterogeneous groups.

Cooperative Learning

Lesson Objectives

1. Describe the geography of the Fertile Crescent.

2. Explain the role of geographic features in the growth of cities.

Lesson Plan

1 Engage

Warm-Up Activity

Ask volunteers to locate some large cities on a United States map. Point out that almost all of the largest cities are near bodies of water. Explain that throughout history, people have settled near water.

Activating Prior Knowledge

Have students read Reach Into Your Background in the Before You Read box. Ask students to list the uses humans have for water.

2 Explore

Ask students to read the section. Then discuss the following questions: Why did the civilizations of the Fertile Crescent settle near rivers? What were some features of the first Mesopotamian cities? What do the Sumerians' religious beliefs tell us?

3 Teach

Ask students to make a chart that shows the link between geography and the rise of cities. In the left column, have students list resources and geographic features. In the right column, have them list how these resources led to the growth of cities. This activity should take about 20 minutes.

Background

Links Across Time

Uncovering the Past For a long time, the ruins of the once-great cities of the Fertile Crescent lay buried beneath the bleak deserts of Syria and Iraq. Archaeologists who excavate these sites have to be very dedicated to their jobs. The climate presents many challenges to diggers. These can include vipers, sandstorms, scorpions, and the unrelenting heat of the sun.

Answers to ...

MAP STUDY

The Syrian Desert and the Arabian Desert to the northwest and southwest of Sumer would not be attractive because there is no nearby water.

Predict What might be some advantages and disadvantages to living between two rivers?

Mesopotamia had special attractions that drew people to settle there. Most important to the people, it had rich soil and life-giving rivers. These attractions drew people who became farmers and city builders. Sumer's central location within the ancient world drew many traders. Sumer became one of the most prosperous areas of the ancient world.

The Location of Mesopotamia Mesopotamia's name describes its location. The word *Mesopotamia* comes from Greek words that mean *between the rivers*. The map below shows that Mesopotamia lies between two rivers, the Tigris and the Euphrates.

Mesopotamia is part of a larger area that is called the Fertile Crescent. The Fertile Crescent is shown on the map at the beginning of this chapter. To see how this region got its name, place your finger at the eastern edge of the Mediterranean (med uh tuh RAY nee un) Sea on the map. Move eastward from the Mediterranean coast to Mesopotamia. Then move south to the Persian Gulf. Notice that the region you've traced is shaped like a crescent moon. The rivers of this crescent-shaped region made it one of the best places in Southwest Asia for growing crops.

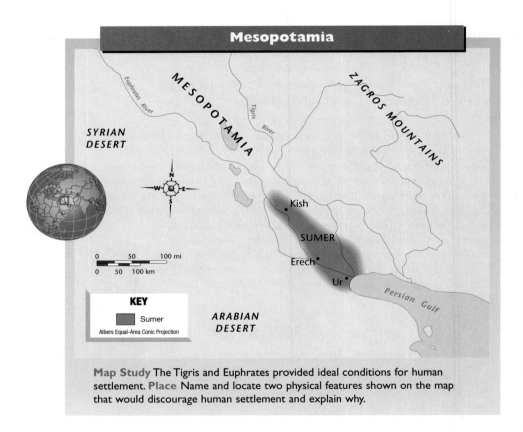

Map Study The Tigris and Euphrates provided ideal conditions for human settlement. **Place** Name and locate two physical features shown on the map that would discourage human settlement and explain why.

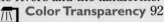

Resource Directory

Program Resources

Nystrom Desk Atlas

Media and Technology

Planet Earth CD-ROM includes satellite images of Africa and Asia that provide students with a visual aid for understanding the spatial relationships between the rivers and the landforms.

Color Transparency 92

Where Two Rivers Meet

The Tigris and Euphrates meet in the southern part of modern Iraq. The land between the rivers continues to be good farmland. Iraqi farmers grow dates, barley, grapes, rice, and tomatoes in the Tigris-Euphrates valley.

Rivers of Life and Death   The Tigris and Euphrates rivers were the source of life for the peoples of Mesopotamia. In the spring, melting snow picked up tons of topsoil as it rushed down from the mountains and flooded the land. The floods left this topsoil on the plain below. Farmers grew crops in this soil. The rivers also supplied fish; tall, strong reeds used to make boats; and clay for building.

The flood waters sometimes brought sorrows as well as gifts. The floods did not always happen at the same time each year. Racing down without warning, they sometimes swept away people, animals, and houses. Then, the survivors would slowly rebuild and pray that the next flood would not be so destructive.

The First Cities

As farming succeeded in Mesopotamia, communities began to have surpluses of food. In time, food surpluses encouraged the building of cities. By 3500 B.C., Mesopotamia had a number of growing cities in the region of Sumer. People coming to these cities were probably amazed. They saw high walls, built to keep out invaders. They stared at the large temples, the houses, the busy shops, and the splendid royal palace. They may have envied the large farms of the nobles outside the walls.

Independent Cities Form   As the map on the previous page shows, cities grew up at different points along the Tigris and Euphrates rivers. These cities were separated by long distances, usually including

SKILLS MINI LESSON

Previewing
To **introduce** the skill, tell students that chapter and section titles, boldfaced heads, maps, graphs, diagrams, and photographs all serve as guideposts to the main ideas. Before reading, it is always a good idea to preview material by taking a quick look at these guideposts. Have students **practice** the skill by asking them to look for the above-mentioned guideposts as they flip through Section 1. Allow students one minute to do this and then tell them to close their books. Ask students to identify topics or information that will be covered in the section. Point out to students that previewing is not a substitute for careful reading but can, in fact, help them read more carefully. Invite students to **apply** the skill of previewing whenever they prepare to read.

Copper: The Multipurpose Metal of Mesopotamia
Copper was one of the first metals people used to fashion useful and decorative objects. Craftspeople worked the soft metal by hammering and soldering it. At a grave site in Ur, archaeologists found a strange-looking ornament—an animal that looked like an eagle with a lion's head. The beast held two stags by their tails. The object was probably made around 2500 B.C. and shows a high level of skill and artistic ability. Copper was also useful for everyday objects. Archeologists have uncovered a wide variety of copper drinking and cooking vessels that date back to the 3000s B.C.

Peacetime in Sumer

Around 2500 B.C., artists from the Sumerian city-state of Ur created this record of peacetime activities. The reverse side documents a battle. **Critical Thinking** How do the activities shown in the three rows provide clues about jobs and social classes in Ur?

a desert. This made it difficult for Sumerians in different cities to unite under one ruler. Each city acted as a state with its own special god or goddess, its own government, and, eventually, its own king. That is why they are called **city-states.**

A Brief Tour of a Sumerian City Some of the earliest cities arose in the region of Sumer. If you visited a Sumerian city, you'd spend much time in traffic jams. The streets were so narrow that carts could not get through them. People had to press themselves against the buildings to let donkeys squeeze by.

Sumerian houses faced away from the crowded streets, onto inner courtyards where families ate and children played. On hot nights, people slept outdoors on their homes' flat roofs. Oil lamps supplied light for Sumerian homes. Clay pipes, buried deep in the ground, carried liquid wastes away. Inventions like plumbing would not come to most other parts of the world for thousands of years.

The public squares buzzed with activity. Merchants displayed goods in outdoor stalls, shouting out to passersby to admire their goods. The streets filled with musicians, acrobats, beggars, and water sellers. Scribes wrote letters for those who could not read or write—for a price.

Visualize What kinds of sights would you see and sounds would you hear on market day in a Sumerian city?

Sumerian Religion

A stranger coming to a Sumerian city would first notice a giant stone building at the center of the city. This was the ziggurat (ZIHG uh raht), the main temple to the gods of the city. Ziggurats were made of terraces, one on top of the other, linked by ramps and stairs. Some were more than seven stories high. At the top of the ziggurat was a temple. The Sumerians believed that gods descended to the Earth using the ziggurat as a ladder.

The people of Sumer worshipped not one, but many, gods and goddesses. This belief in many gods is called **polytheism.** To understand this word, break it up into its parts. *Poly,* a Greek word, means "many." *Theism* refers to gods.

Sumerian **myths,** or stories about gods that explain people's beliefs, warned that the gods would punish people who angered them. The myths also promised rewards to people who served the gods well. Sumerians made sure that their gods were properly cared for. Temple priests washed the statues of gods before and after each meal. Music sounded and incense burned as huge plates of food were laid before them. The god Anu was offered the following meal daily:

21 rams	7 ducks	3 cranes
60 birds	2 bulls	1 bullock
8 lambs	4 wild boars	3 duck eggs
3 ostrich eggs	29 bushels of	243 loaves of bread
2 vessels of milk	dates	

Ur—Then and Now The Sumerian city-state of Ur was destroyed by war in 2006 B.C. In 1991, war came again to Ur. During the Persian Gulf War, the armies of the United States and Iraq fought not far from the ruins of this ancient city. Fortunately, what's left of Ur has survived the latest battles.

▼ This restored brick ziggurat once towered over the city of Ur.

Activity

Cooperative Learning

Scenes From Mesopotamia Invite students to work in groups to perform plays showing how farming communities grew into cities. Remind students that, unlike hunter-gatherers, farmers settled in one place, cooperating to drain and irrigate lands and tend crops. Farming provided a surplus of food. Craftspeople did ironwork, carpentry, pottery, and weaving. Encourage students to research daily life in Mesopotamia and to create costumes and props for their plays. *English Language Learner, Visual, Kinesthetic*

Resource Directory

Teaching Resources

Critical Thinking Activity in the Chapter and Section Resources booklet, p. 37, helps students apply the skill of identifying central issues.

The religious beliefs of the Sumerians give us an idea of what was really important to them. Notice the love of the city expressed in this Sumerian poem.

▼ In this statue grouping of Sumerian gods and worshipers from about 2500 B.C., height indicates importance. The tallest figure represents Abu, the god of vegetation. The smallest figures are worshipers.

> "Behold the bond of Heaven and Earth, the city.
> Behold the kindly wall, the city,
> its pure river,
> its dock where the boats stand.
> Behold . . . its well of good water.
> Behold . . . its pure canal."

Unfortunately for Sumer, the wealth of the city-states became their downfall. Sumerian city-states fought each other over land and, especially, the use of river water. Constant warfare weakened Sumer's rulers and exhausted its armies. Sumer was no longer a major power after 2000 B.C. It fell to a northern rival—Babylonia—in 1759 B.C.

SECTION 1 REVIEW

1. Define (a) scribe, (b) city-state, (c) polytheism, (d) myth.

2. Identify (a) Sumer, (b) Mesopotamia, (c) Fertile Crescent, (d) Tigris River, (e) Euphrates River.

3. What geographic features helped civilizations develop in Mesopotamia?

4. How did Mesopotamia become a center of trade?

Critical Thinking

5. Distinguishing Fact From Opinion Write one fact about Sumerian religion. Write one opinion.

Activity

6. Writing to Learn Pretend you are a student scribe in Sumer. Write a journal entry describing what you see on your walk to school.

Babylonia and Assyria

Reach Into Your Background

Why do you think one country might decide to invade another country? List two or three reasons.

Questions to Explore

1. Why did civilizations rise and fall in Mesopotamia?
2. What characteristics describe the Babylonian and Assyrian empires?

Key Terms

empire
caravan
bazaar

Key People and Places

Nebuchadnezzar II
Babylonia
Assyria
New Babylonian empire

Section 2

Lesson Objectives

1. Explore how empires formed in Mesopotamia.
2. Compare and contrast the Assyrian and Babylonian cultures.
3. Describe the effects of trade and conquest on ancient cultures.

Lesson Plan

1 Engage

Warm-Up Activity

Ask students to consider how the daily routines of people living in peacetime might be different than the daily routines of people living through a war. Guide the discussion to focus on how much time people might spend defending themselves and obtaining food and other basic necessities. Have them also consider how the absence or lessening of these activities during peacetime might leave time for culture and learning.

Activating Prior Knowledge

Have students read Reach Into Your Background in the Before You Read box. Ask several volunteers to share their ideas about why some countries invade others. Record ideas on the chalkboard. When students have finished reading, discuss whether students' ideas applied.

King Sargon II of Assyria (uh SEER ee uh) must have scowled when he heard the news. The nearby kingdoms of Urartu and Zikirtu had joined forces against him. How dare they challenge the most powerful monarch in the world? In the summer of 714 B.C., Sargon set out to "muzzle the mouths" of his enemies.

The rebels were no match for the powerful Sargon. His armies quickly overcame the forces of Urartu and killed all who resisted. The Assyrians howled with laughter when they saw the king of Urartu fleeing on an old horse. Sargon let him go. He knew that the survivors would serve as a grim warning to others who might later be tempted to oppose the mighty Assyrians.

The Two Empires of Mesopotamia

Sargon II was one of many kings who ruled Mesopotamia after the fall of Sumer. The history of Mesopotamia is filled with stories of conquest by one powerful warrior after another. This was a land worth taking. It brought great wealth to the army that could conquer it. But after winning it, each ruler became a target for another conqueror.

▼ This carving shows the powerful Assyrian warrior-king, Sargon II (left), and one of his officials.

2 Explore

When students have read the section, discuss the following questions: What was important about Babylon's location? Why did the Assyrians find that the best method of defense was to attack? Why did conquered people revolt, even while fearing the might of the Assyrians?

3 Teach

Have students draw a time line for recording events from 1760 B.C. to 540 B.C. Suggest that they mark the time line every $\frac{1}{2}$ inch to represent time intervals of 100 years. Encourage students to create simple, captioned illustrations showing conquests and cultural achievements. This activity should take about 25 minutes.

4 Assess

See the answers to the Section Review. You may also use students' completed time lines for assessment.

Acceptable time lines include dates in the correct sequence for at least three events mentioned in the section.

Commendable time lines include each event and date in sequence and several captioned illustrations.

Outstanding time lines show each event and date in sequence and include a complete set of captioned illustrations.

Answers to ...

MAP STUDY

the Mediterranean Sea and the Red Sea

Babylonian and Assyrian Empires

Map Study During different periods of history, the Babylonians and Assyrians controlled vast empires. **Place** Rulers of empires wanted to gain control of the sea, so they could increase their trade and wealth. What bodies of water did the Assyrians reach that the Babylonians did not?

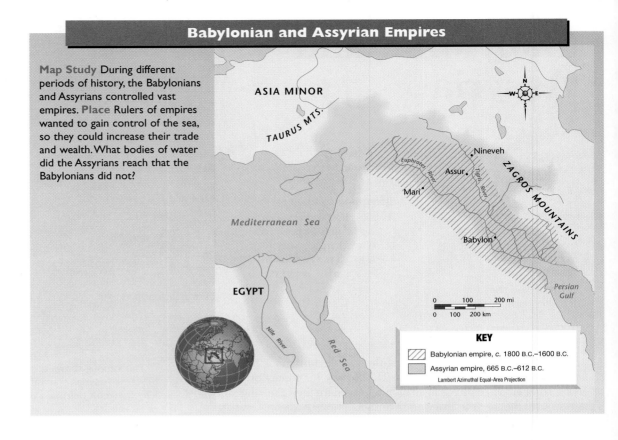

KEY

Babylonian empire, *c.* 1800 B.C.–1600 B.C.

Assyrian empire, 665 B.C.–612 B.C.

Lambert Azimuthal Equal-Area Projection

Ask Questions What questions would you like to ask about the Babylonian empire?

The biggest and most important Mesopotamian civilizations were the empires of Babylonia (bab uh LOH nee uh) and Assyria. An **empire** is an area of many territories and people that are controlled by one government. The beautiful city of Babylon was the center of the Babylonian empire. This empire reached its height around 1750 B.C. The Assyrians, who got their name from the northern city of Assur, began expanding their lands in the 1300s B.C. By the 600s B.C., they controlled a huge empire. It stretched from the Persian Gulf across the Fertile Crescent and through Egypt.

The Babylonians and the Assyrians had two things in common. In their quest for riches, they were vicious warriors. And in the enjoyment of their riches, they built grand cities where culture and learning were highly valued.

The Babylonian Empire

A Babylonian king named Hammurabi (hahm uh RAH bee) created the Babylonian empire by uniting the cities of Sumer. Then, he conquered lands all the way to Asia Minor, the present-day country of Turkey, as you can see on the map above.

Resource Directory

Media and Technology

 Color Transparency 70

A Crossroads of Trade Babylon's location made it a crossroads of trade. Caravans, or groups of travelers, coming and going from the cities of Sumer to the south and Akkad to the north, stopped in Babylon. In the city's bazaars, or markets, you could buy cotton cloth from India and spices from Egypt. Trade made Babylon rich. So did conquest.

Wealth Through Conquest A conqueror—if successful—reaped great rewards. In about 1760 B.C., Hammurabi conquered the city of Mari. He seized Mari's war chariots, weapons, and tools, which were the best in the world. But all the wealth that Babylon gathered could not save it from conquest. By about 1600 B.C., the empire first conquered by Hammurabi had shrunk and was finally destroyed.

Royal Palace Complex at Mari

Plan of the Palace at Mari

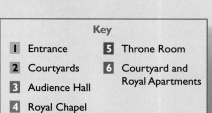

Hammurabi (below) completely destroyed Mari's 300-room royal palace. The design of the palace (left) included several courtyards. In the courtyard near the audience hall, the palace held public gatherings. The richly decorated throne room had a private courtyard. **Critical Thinking** Why do you think the Royal Chapel was smaller than the throne room?

Key

1 Entrance
2 Courtyards
3 Audience Hall
4 Royal Chapel
5 Throne Room
6 Courtyard and Royal Apartments

Teaching Resources

Reading a Diagram in the Social Studies and Geography Skills booklet, p. 56, provides additional skill practice.

Hidden Treasure The Assyrians created numerous sculptures and carvings that depicted images of warfare. In 1993, a carving of an Assyrian armed with a mace and a bow and arrows was rediscovered in a very unlikely place—a boys' school in England! A reconstruction of the carving's travels through history reveals the following: In the mid-1800s, a British archaeologist gave the carving to his benefactor. In the 1950s, the benefactor's home was converted into a school and his "Assyrian Building," which had housed the carving, became the school's candy shop. At some point, the flat carving was whitewashed and a dartboard was placed next to it. For years the carving went unrecognized—even when it became the unfortunate target of stray darts. Shortly after experts had identified the carving as genuine Assyrian art from the 800s B.C., it sold at an auction for the record price of $11.9 million.

The Epic of Gilgamesh Several clay tablets discovered in the great library of Nineveh contained a long narrative poem, or epic. This epic told of the Sumerian hero-king Gilgamesh. It described his adventures and his search for eternal life. It is the oldest epic ever discovered.

The Empire of the Assyrians

North of Babylon was a small kingdom of a few walled cities known as Assyria. Its capital, Nineveh (NIHN uh vuh), was a sleepy village on the Tigris River. Assyria, as you can see on the map in this section, lay in an open land, which other peoples could easily invade.

Because they were constantly defending themselves, the Assyrians became skilled warriors. About 1365 B.C., they decided the best method of defense was to attack. By 650 B.C., Assyria had conquered a large empire. It stretched across the Fertile Crescent, from the Nile River to the Persian Gulf.

Assyria's Contributions The Assyrians were more than warriors. As Assyrian power grew, Nineveh became a city of great learning. Nineveh had a fabulous library that held thousands of clay tablets with writings from Sumer and Babylon. Because the Assyrians kept these records, we now know a great deal about life in early Mesopotamia.

Most of all, however, the Assyrians were geniuses at waging war. They invented the battering ram, a powerful weapon on wheels that pounded city walls to rubble. Slingers hurled stones at the enemy. Expert archers were protected with helmets and armor. But the most feared part of the army were the armed charioteers who slashed their way through the enemy.

The Assyrian War Machine

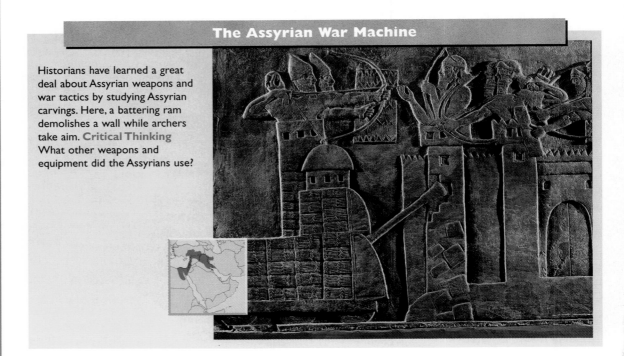

Historians have learned a great deal about Assyrian weapons and war tactics by studying Assyrian carvings. Here, a battering ram demolishes a wall while archers take aim. **Critical Thinking** What other weapons and equipment did the Assyrians use?

Assyria Overthrown The Assyrians had few friends in the lands that they ruled. Conquered peoples attempted a number of rebellions against Assyrian rule. Two groups, the Medes and Chaldeans (kal DEE uhns), joined together to smash the Assyrian empire in 612 B.C.

Babylonia Rises Again

Under the Chaldeans, Babylon rose again. It became the center of an even more splendid kingdom, known as the New Babylonian empire. Its greatest king was Nebuchadnezzar (nehb uh kuhd NEHZ uhr) II. Nebuchadnezzar rebuilt the city of Babylon, which the Assyrians had destroyed. He put up massive walls around the city for protection. He also built a gigantic palace, decorated with colored tiles. Carved on the tiles were plants, animals, birds, designs—and a boastful sentence by the king. "I am Nebuchadnezzar, King of Babylon," it said.

Nebuchadnezzar's royal palace was built on several terraces that rose to the height of some 350 feet (110 m). It had a dazzling landscape of trees and gardens. According to legend, he built the gardens for his wife, who came from the high plateau and hated the dry plains of Mesopotamia.

Under the Chaldeans, the New Babylonian empire became a center of learning and science. Chaldean astronomers charted the paths of the stars and measured the length of a year that was only a few minutes different from the length modern scientists have calculated. And Chaldean farmers raised "the flies which collect honey"—wild bees.

Like other Mesopotamian empires, the Chaldeans were open to attack by powerful neighbors. In 539 B.C., the New Babylonian empire fell. But the city of Babylon was spared.

▲ This clay tablet contains a map of the known world, which shows that the Babylonians were well aware of lands beyond their empire.

SECTION 2 REVIEW

1. Define (a) empire, (b) caravan, (c) bazaar.

2. Identify
(a) Nebuchadnezzar II,
(b) Babylonia, (c) Assyria,
(d) New Babylonian empire.

3. Why did civilizations rise and fall in Mesopotamia?

4. How did Babylon become rich?

5. What accomplishments is Assyria known for?

Critical Thinking
6. Cause and Effect How did Babylon's location affect what happened to it?

Activity
7. Writing to Learn Write an epitaph, a statement carved on a tombstone, for Nebuchadnezzar.

Teaching Resources

📁 **Section Quiz** in the Chapter and Section Resources booklet, p. 23, covers the main ideas and key terms in the section. Available in Spanish in the Spanish Chapter and Section Resources booklet, p. 15.

SECTION 3

The Legacy of Mesopotamia

1. Identify key points of Hammurabi's Code.

2. Explain the importance of the development of writing in Mesopotamia.

3. Describe the way Mesopotamians kept records.

1 Engage

Warm-Up Activity

Ask students to think about how different our lives would be if we did not have a form of writing. Have them consider how little we would know about the achievements and mistakes of people in history. How would we communicate over long distances, keep records, or understand the laws of our country?

Activating Prior Knowledge

Have students read Reach Into Your Background in the Before You Read box. Discuss with students what they could do to preserve a permanent record of their accomplishments for people of the future.

BEFORE YOU READ

Reach Into Your Background

What is your most prized accomplishment? Was it a sport or musical instrument you mastered? A friend you made? A job you did? Why does this accomplishment mean so much to you?

Questions to Explore

1. Why was Hammurabi's Code a major step forward for humankind?

2. How did writing develop in Mesopotamia?

Key Terms
code
cuneiform

Key People
Hammurabi

▼ King Hammurabi stands before Shamash, the god of justice. According to Babylonian legend, Shamash presented the code of laws to Hammurabi.

"If a man has destroyed the eye of a man of the class of gentlemen, they shall destroy his eye. If he has broken a gentleman's bone, they shall break his bone. If he has destroyed the eye of a commoner or broken a bone of a commoner, he shall pay one mina of silver. If he has destroyed the eye of a gentleman's slave, or broken a bone of a gentleman's slave, he shall pay half [the slave's] price. If a gentleman's slave strikes the cheek of a gentleman, they shall cut off [the slave's] ear."
—*from Hammurabi's Code*

Hammurabi's Code

What kind of justice system do you think we would have if our laws were not written down? What if a judge was free to make any law he or she wanted? What if the judge could give any punishment? Would people think that laws were fair? A written **code,** or organized list, of laws helps make sure laws are applied fairly to all.

We owe the idea that all laws should be written down and applied fairly to the Babylonians. It was King Hammurabi who set down rules for everyone in his empire to follow. These rules are known as

Teaching Resources

📁 **Reproducible Lesson Plan** in the Chapter and Section Resources booklet, p. 24, provides a summary of the section lesson.

📁 **Guided Reading and Review** in the Chapter and Section Resources booklet, p. 25, provides a structure for mastering key concepts and reviewing key terms in the section. Available in Spanish in the Spanish Chapter and Section Resources booklet, p. 16.

Hammurabi's Code. The code told the people of Babylon how to settle conflicts in all areas of life.

Hammurabi's Code contained 282 laws organized in different categories. These included trade, labor, property, and family. The code had laws for adopting children, practicing medicine, hiring wagons or boats, and controlling dangerous animals.

An Eye for an Eye   Hammurabi's Code was based on the idea of "an eye for an eye." In other words, a man who blinded another person would have his own eye put out. However, the code did not apply equally to all people. As the laws at the beginning of this section show, the code gave different punishments for breaking the same rules. The harshness of the punishment depended on how important the victim was. The higher the class of the victim, the stiffer the penalty. Thus, an ox owner would pay half a mina of silver if the ox gored a noble. If the victim was a slave, the owner would pay only one third of a mina.

◀ This statue of a fierce lion dates from Hammurabi's time and probably served as a temple "guardian."

2 Explore

After students have read the section, begin a discussion by asking students to explain the advantages of a written code of laws over a set of spoken laws. Ask: *What can you learn about life in Babylon from the punishments listed?* Continue the discussion by asking students why scribes were so highly respected in Mesopotamia. Discuss why it was important to simplify writing.

3 Teach

Ask students to create problem-solution charts for the issues discussed in this section. Ask them to find problems encountered by the Sumerians and describe how their inventions or ideas solved these problems. Use the completed charts when discussing the importance of laws, writing, and record-keeping.

4 Assess

See the answers to the Section Review. You may also use students' charts for assessment.

Acceptable charts identify three problems and describe solutions.

Commendable charts list four problems and describe solutions in detail.

Outstanding charts list four problems and describe solutions in detail. Charts demonstrate an understanding of the cause-and-effect relationship between the problems and the solutions.

Activity

Cooperative Learning

The People v. Hammurabi
The laws of Hammurabi's Code may seem exceedingly harsh to people today. However, applying today's values to events of the past is not fair or instructive. Have students debate the harshness of Hammurabi's Code. Ask one group of students to argue on behalf of Hammurabi and his supporters. This group might propose that the harshness of the code had beneficial preventive effects and helped maintain order. Ask another group to argue on behalf of poor people and slaves. This group might point out unfair aspects of the code.

Background

Daily Life

Laws for Women A significant part of Hammurabi's Code was devoted to the category identified as "Women, marriage, family property, and inheritance." Although the code sought to protect widows and allowed a woman to own property that would be passed on to her children, the laws reflected the idea that women were expected to be strictly obedient to their husbands or fathers. A man could even sell his wife or children into slavery to pay off a debt.

Connect What other kinds of rules or codes of behavior do you know about? How do they compare in fairness to Hammurabi's Code?

A person who accidentally broke a rule was just as guilty as a criminal. Results were what mattered. People such as doctors, who could not control the outcome of their work, had to be very careful, as the following law shows:

> "If a surgeon performed a major operation on a citizen with a bronze lancet [knife] and has caused the death of this citizen . . . his hand shall be cut off."

Laws for Everyone You probably know a lot of rules. There are rules for taking tests, playing ball, and just living in your home. People follow—or break—rules all the time. What, then, was the importance of Hammurabi's Code?

The laws are important to us because they were written down. With written laws, everyone could know the rules—and the punishments. These punishments may seem harsh to us. But they were the first attempt by a society to set up a code of laws that would apply to everyone.

The Art of Writing

Think how difficult it would be to carry on life if no one knew how to read and write. But writing did not just naturally develop. For most of human life, people did not have the art of writing.

Laws Set in Stone

This shows a detail of a stone pillar that has Hammurabi's Code written on it. Many of the laws in Hammurabi's Code were based upon the laws of earlier Mesopotamian civilizations. Hammurabi's great achievement was organizing the laws and preserving them in written form.

▼ Scribes sometimes enclosed a message (left) in an envelope (right) made from wet clay. As the envelope dried, it formed a seal around the tablet.

Writing developed in Mesopotamia in about 3500 B.C. Long before Hammurabi issued his code, the people of Sumer developed a system of writing. Writing met the need of Sumerians to keep records. Record keepers were very important—and busy—people in Sumer. Since only a few people could write, it was one of the most valuable skills in the ancient world. Scribes held positions of great respect in Mesopotamia.

The scribes of Sumer recorded sales and trades, tax payments, gifts for the gods, and marriages and deaths. Some scribes had special tasks. Military scribes calculated the amount of food and supplies that an army would need. Government scribes figured out the number of diggers needed to build a canal. Written records then went out to local officials who had to provide these supplies or workers.

"Pages" of Hard Clay What did the scribes of Mesopotamia write on? The Tigris and Euphrates rivers provided a perfect material —clay. Each spring, the rivers brought down clay from the mountains. Scribes shaped the soft, wet clay into smooth, flat surfaces called tablets. They marked their letters in it with sharp tools. When the clay dried, it left an almost permanent record.

The shape and size of a tablet depended on its purpose. Larger tablets were used for reference. They stayed in one place, like the heavy atlases and dictionaries in today's libraries. Smaller tablets, the size of

LINKS TO MATH

Babylonian Mathematics
The Babylonians developed a useful system of mathematics for solving everyday problems. For example, they learned to calculate areas of geometric shapes. Such calculations were important for making building plans. Their number system was based on numbers from 1 to 60. We still divide minutes and hours into units of 60.

Daily Life

Wisdom Literature
Scholars think that the pithy sayings known as Mesopotamian "wisdom literature" were intended to document pieces of sound advice such as the following:

Utter no evil statement; grief will not drag at your heart.

Some examples betray a sly sense of humor:

Flatter a young man, he'll give you anything you want.

The Development of Writing

Meaning	Outline Character, About 3000 B.C.	Sumerian, About 2000 B.C.	Assyrian, About 700 B.C.	Chaldean, About 500 B.C.
Sun				
God or Heaven				
Mountain				

Table Study This table shows how writing based on pictures changed over time. These characters were used by civilizations in Southwest Asia for more than 3,000 years. The last clay tablets using them were written about 2,100 years ago. Then the languages of the tablets were forgotten. Scholars did not figure out how to read the tablets until the A.D. 1800s. **Critical Thinking** How does this form of writing differ from your own?

letters or postcards, were used for personal messages. Even today, these personal tablets can be fun to read. They show that Mesopotamians used writing during the ups and downs of everyday life:

> "This is really a fine way of behaving! The gardeners keep breaking into the date storehouse and taking dates. You yourselves cover it up and do not report it to me! Bring these men to me—after they have paid for the dates."

From Pictures to Writing
Like most inventions, writing developed over time. At first, people drew pictures to represent what they wanted to say. Grain, oxen, water, stars—each important object had its own symbol.

As people learned to record ideas as well as facts, the symbols changed. Eventually, scribes combined symbols to make groups of wedges and lines known as **cuneiform** (kyoo NEE uh form). Cuneiform script could be used to represent different languages. This made it highly useful in a land of many peoples.

SECTION 3 REVIEW

1. Define (a) code, (b) cuneiform.

2. Identify Hammurabi.

3. Why was Hammurabi's Code important?

4. Why was the development of writing a big step in human history?

Critical Thinking

5. Drawing Conclusions What skills would help a student scribe succeed?

Activity

6. Writing to Learn Reread the letter that complains about the gardeners. Write a law that relates to the gardeners who stole the dates. What should their punishment be? What should happen to the people who didn't tell about the theft?

Mediterranean Civilizations

Lesson Objectives

1. Explain the Phoenicians' contributions to ancient societies.

2. Describe the history of the Israelites.

3. Identify historical leaders of the Israelites.

Lesson Plan

1 Engage
Warm-Up Activity

Ask volunteers to explain how the stories of ancient history have reached us. Lead a discussion about how stories have been told and retold from one generation to the next. Explain that as stories are retold, different versions develop. Point out that when writing was invented, stories were written down and became permanent records.

Activating Prior Knowledge

Have students read Reach Into Your Background in the Before You Read box. Discuss with students the sources they drew upon to make their time lines. Did they rely on their own memories of events, stories told to them by other family members, or photographs and home videos? Ask students to give their opinions about which sources are most reliable.

BEFORE YOU READ

Reach Into Your Background

Just as people can chart the history of a civilization on a timeline, you can also chart your own personal history. What are some major events in the history of your family?

In what year did your family move to the home where you live now, for example? Make a time line that shows major events in your family history.

Questions to Explore

1. How did the Phoenicians help spread civilization throughout the Mediterranean area?

2. What were the major events in the history of the Israelites?

Key Terms

alphabet
monotheism
famine
exile

Key People and Places

Moses
Phoenicia
Canaan
Jerusalem
Israel
Judah

While the great empire of Hammurabi was rising and falling, the people of a poor city on the shores of the Mediterranean Sea were getting rich by gathering snails.

The snails that washed up on the shores of the city of Tyre (TY uhr) were not ordinary snails. These snails produced a rich purple dye. This dye was highly valued by wealthy people throughout the Mediterranean region. Ships from Tyre sold the dye at extremely high prices. The profits soon made Tyre a wealthy and active city.

▶ The Phoenicians left few details about the appearance of their ships. An Assyrian artist made this carving.

Teaching Resources

📁 **Reproducible Lesson Plan** in the Chapter and Section Resources booklet, p. 27, provides a summary of the section lesson.

📁 **Guided Reading and Review** in the Chapter and Section Resources booklet, p. 28, provides a structure for mastering key concepts and reviewing key terms in the section. Available in Spanish in the Spanish Chapter and Section Resources booklet, p. 18.

Program Resources

Outline Maps Western Europe: Political, p. 18

2 Explore

After reading, discuss these questions: Why was the sea so important to the Phoenicians? How did the Phoenicians revolutionize writing? How did Abraham serve as a leader of the Israelites? What obstacles did the Israelites face in trying to establish a homeland?

3 Teach

Ask students to make an outline of the important topics covered in the section. Encourage students to include phrases or sentences that describe why each topic included in the outline is important. This activity should take about 20 minutes.

Journal Writing

Letter Home Have students suppose that they are writing as Phoenician sailors. Give students two options for their correspondent—a friend or a potential competitor. Discuss the different purposes of each type of letter. Ask: *What kinds of things would you describe to a friend?* (the ship's cargo, conditions on board, sights seen) *What would you include in a letter intended to discourage a competitor?* (the roughness of the voyage, sea sickness, the sighting of a sea monster)

Answers to ...
MAP STUDY

Cadiz

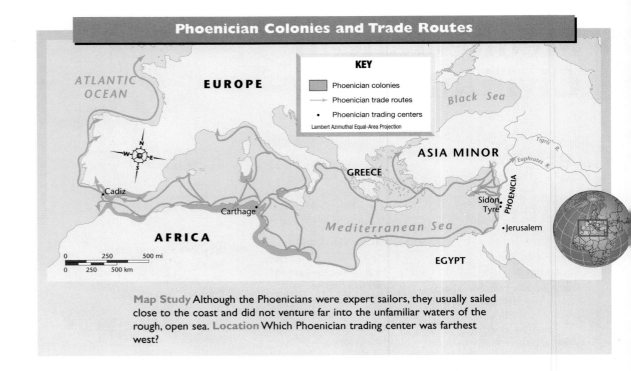

Phoenician Colonies and Trade Routes

KEY

☐ Phoenician colonies
→ Phoenician trade routes
• Phoenician trading centers
Lambert Azimuthal Equal-Area Projection

Map Study Although the Phoenicians were expert sailors, they usually sailed close to the coast and did not venture far into the unfamiliar waters of the rough, open sea. **Location** Which Phoenician trading center was farthest west?

The Phoenicians: Sailors of the Mediterranean

Tyre was the major city in a region called Phoenicia (fuh NEE shuh), shown on the map. The Phoenicians' outlook was not eastward, toward Mesopotamia. Rather, the Phoenicians looked westward, toward the Mediterranean Sea and the cities that were growing up around it.

The Phoenicians had settled in a land that had few, but important, resources. Besides the snails, there were dense forests of cedar trees. Phoenicians sold these resources to neighboring peoples.

As trade grew, the Phoenicians looked to the sea to increase their profits. In time, they became the world's first trading empire. From about 1100 B.C. to 800 B.C., Phoenicia was a great sea power. Phoenician ships sailed all over the Mediterranean Sea. They even sailed out into the stormy Atlantic Ocean. They came back from these trips with stories of horrible monsters who lived in the ocean depths. Did the Phoenicians really believe these stories? Nobody knows for sure. But the stories did help keep other people from trying to compete for trade in the Atlantic.

Trade brought rich goods from lands around the Mediterranean Sea to the Phoenician cities of Tyre and Sidon (SY duhn). Bazaars swelled with foods brought from faraway places. These foods included figs, olives, honey, and spices. In the bazaars, merchants sold strange animals, such as giraffes and warthogs from Africa and bears from Europe.

READ ACTIVELY

Ask Questions What kinds of questions might you ask about the different and unusual lands that Phoenician sailors visited on their trading voyages?

Travelers throughout the Mediterranean area were awed by the grand ships and the overflowing markets of Tyre. This little poem was written by one ancient traveler who visited Tyre's bazaars:

> "When your wares came from the seas,
> you satisfied many peoples.
> With your great wealth and merchandise,
> you enriched the kings of the earth."

Predict What would be some results of an easier, simpler system of writing?

The Phoenician Alphabet: One Sound, One Letter

Because they had so much trade, the Phoenicians needed to simplify writing. Cuneiform, with its hundreds of symbols, was just too complicated.

The Phoenicians found a way to write using just 22 symbols. This was the Phoenician alphabet, a set of symbols that represented the sounds of the language. It forms the basis of the alphabet that people in the United States and many other countries use today. Each of the 22 letters in the Phoenician alphabet stood for one consonant sound.

The simple Phoenician alphabet was far easier to learn than cuneiform. Before the alphabet, highly educated scribes controlled the power of writing. With the alphabet, many more people could learn.

The Phoenician Alphabet

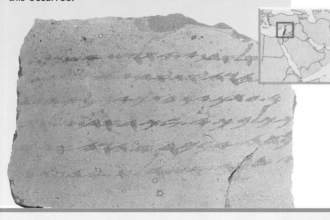

The Phoenician Alphabet

Chart Study The chart (left) shows the Phoenician letters that correspond to our alphabet. The tablet (below) is an example of cursive Phoenician writing. **Critical Thinking** Use of the Phoenician alphabet spread throughout the Mediterranean. How do you think this occurred?

4 Assess

See the answers to the Section Review. You may also assess students' outlines.

Acceptable outlines have headings on the Phoenicians and the Israelites and describe one achievement or event for each group.

Commendable outlines have headings on the Phoenicians and the Israelites and describe two or more achievements or events for each group.

Outstanding outlines have headings and subheadings on the Phoenicians and the Israelites and describe three or more achievements or events for each group.

Background

Global Perspectives

Royal Customers Royalty from around the ancient world prized Phoenician goods. Purple cloth, because of its rarity, was a symbol of royalty. In Rome, only the emperor wore expensive purple robes. The fragrant cedar from Phoenicia's forests was also valued by royalty. According to the Bible, King Solomon of Israel built his temple in Jerusalem with cedar from Phoenicia.

Answers to ...

CHART STUDY

Phoenician traders were partly responsible for helping to spread the alphabet to areas in which they traded.

Critical Thinking

Recognizing Cause and Effect *Suitable as either a whole class or an individual activity.* Ask students to read the material under the heading *The Rise of the Israelites.* Mention that causes are the reasons for an action or a condition. Effects are the actions or conditions that have been brought about. Then write the following pairs of events on the chalkboard and have students identify which pairs have a cause and effect relationship and which do not.

Early Israelites were shepherds—they lived outside of Sumerian cities

Famine—Israelites fled to Egypt

Israelites prospered in Egypt—a jealous Egyptian king enslaved them

LINKS TO LANGUAGE ARTS

The Exodus The name given to the Israelites' escape from Egypt is the Exodus. It comes from an ancient Greek word meaning "going out." Scholars think the Exodus happened in the early 1200s B.C.

The Rise of the Israelites

South of Phoenicia, a small band of people settled along the shores of the Mediterranean. They were called the Israelites. Although the Israelites never built a large empire, they made a deep impact on our civilization.

The Israelites traced their beginnings to Mesopotamia. For hundreds of years, they lived as shepherds and merchants who grazed their flocks outside Sumerian cities.

According to the Bible, a leader named Abraham led his people to a belief in one God. This practice is called **monotheism**. *Mono* is the Greek word for "one." *Theism,* as you know, refers to *gods.* The Bible explains that God promised Abraham that his people would have their own land if they would follow his word:

"Get you out of your country, and from your kindred [relatives], and from your father's house, to the land that I will show you. And I will make of you a great nation."

The Bible goes on to explain how, around 1900 B.C., Abraham led the Israelites from Mesopotamia to a new home in Canaan (KAY nuhn). Find Canaan on the map. Around 1800 B.C., a famine spread across Canaan. A **famine** is a time when there is so little food that many people starve. The famine caused the Israelites to flee south to Egypt.

In Egypt, the Israelites lived well for about 600 years. Many of them reached high positions in the government. Later, they were enslaved when an Egyptian king grew jealous of their wealth and suspicious of their power.

Return to Canaan The Bible tells how an Israelite hero named Moses led his enslaved people out of Egypt. For the next 40 years, the Israelites wandered through the desert of the Sinai (SY ny) Peninsula. Find the Sinai on the map to the left. The Bible says that while in the desert, God gave the Israelites the Ten Commandments, a code of laws. At last, the Israelites returned to Canaan. There, over time, the Israelites moved from herding to farming and built their own cities.

Conquest of Canaan As they moved further north into Canaan, the Israelites faced opposition. Slowly, through

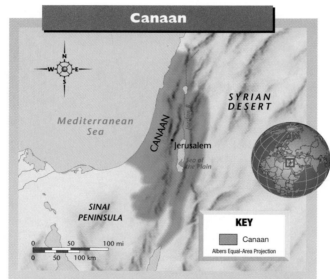

Canaan

Mediterranean Sea

CANAAN

Jerusalem

Sea of the Plain

SYRIAN DESERT

SINAI PENINSULA

0   50   100 mi
0   50   100 km

KEY

Canaan

Albers Equal-Area Projection

Map Study Canaan's location between two deserts made trade over land difficult. Since Canaan bordered the Mediterranean Sea, the Israelites developed a sea trade. **Location** In what direction did the Israelites travel to return to Canaan from the Sinai Peninsula?

fierce wars, the Israelites conquered all of Canaan. Two kings led them to victory. Saul, considered the first king of the Israelites, defended them against many enemies. The next king, David, united the 12 Israelite tribes into a single nation. David established his capital at the city of Jerusalem.

After David died, his son, Solomon, inherited the kingdom. Under Solomon's rule, Israel grew prosperous through trade. The Israelites sold palm and olive oils, honey, fruits, vegetables, and grain to neighboring peoples. King Solomon also developed a sea trade with neighboring lands. On the very first voyage, an Israelite ship brought back more than 13 tons (11.8 metric tons) of gold.

▼ People have lived in Jerusalem since 1800 B.C. Today, centuries-old buildings stand not far from modern hospitals, apartments, and hotels.

Background

Global Perspectives

A Holy City Followers of three of the world's major religions consider Jerusalem to be a holy city and a destination for pilgrimages. Jews regard Jerusalem, the location of two important temples that were both destroyed, as the center of their religion. Jews from around the world visit the Wailing Wall, the only existing remains of the second temple, and slip written prayers into the cracks of the wall. Christians view Jerusalem as holy because important events in Jesus' life took place here. To Muslims, Jerusalem ranks as the third-holiest city after Mecca and Medina in Saudi Arabia. Muslims believe that the prophet Muhammad ascended to heaven from Jerusalem to receive the word of God.

1. (a) a set of symbols that represents the sounds of a language (b) belief in one God (c) a time when people starve because there is little food (d) to force people to live in another country

2. (a) Israelite hero who led his people out of slavery (b) an empire that became a great trading power along the Mediterranean and beyond (c) area of land many Israelites left because of famine; they later returned and reclaimed the land (d) the capital city of the Israelites (e) kingdom composed of 12 united Israelite tribes (f) the southern portion of the kingdom of Israel

3. They were excellent sailors and exchanged goods throughout the Mediterranean. They also developed the Phoenician alphabet.

4. The Phoenician alphabet was easier to use than cuneiform. More people were able to learn to use it.

5. Abraham led the Israelites through Egypt to Canaan. During a famine, many Israelites fled to Egypt, where they prospered and then were enslaved. Moses led them out of Egypt. Eventually, they returned to Canaan. Kings Saul and David reclaimed Canaan and unified the Israelite nation. Israel prospered under King Solomon.

6. The Israelites moved to Egypt to escape a famine. When they left Egypt, they wandered in the desert for 40 years. They won a war to regain Canaan and live as a united nation.

7. Students' poems may refer to the fine wares or strange animals in the marketplace.

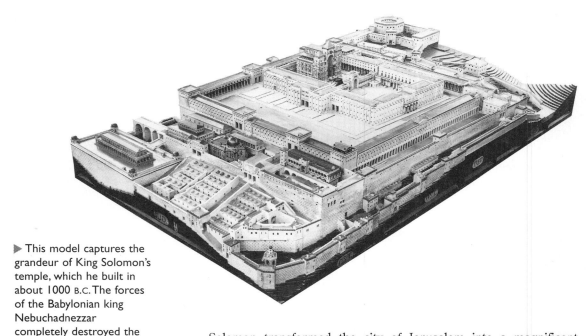

▶ This model captures the grandeur of King Solomon's temple, which he built in about 1000 B.C. The forces of the Babylonian king Nebuchadnezzar completely destroyed the temple in 586 B.C.

Solomon transformed the city of Jerusalem into a magnificent capital. His most prized monument was a beautiful temple in the center of Jerusalem. It became the central place of worship for the Israelites.

Solomon's building projects were very expensive, however. The country faced hard times, and after his death, it split into two kingdoms. The northern kingdom was called Israel. The southern kingdom took the name Judah. The divided kingdom was ripe for invasion, and its dangerous neighbor, Assyria, was gaining power.

In 722 B.C., the Assyrians seized the kingdom of Israel. They punished the Israelites by exiling thousands to distant parts of their empire. To **exile** people means to force them to live in another country. About 135 years later, the kingdom of Judah fell to the Chaldeans. The Judeans were exiled as well.

SECTION 4 REVIEW

1. Define (a) alphabet, (b) monotheism, (c) famine, (d) exile.

2. Identify (a) Moses, (b) Phoenicia, (c) Canaan, (d) Jerusalem, (e) Israel, (f) Judah.

3. What impact did the Phoenicians have on the Mediterranean world?

4. Explain the importance of Phoenician writing.

5. Briefly trace the history of the Israelites from the leadership of Abraham to King Solomon.

Critical Thinking

6. Identifying Central Issues What important events in the history of the Israelites were shaped by movement and by war?

Activity

7. Writing to Learn Look at the poem about Tyre. Write one humorous verse about Tyre's markets.

Resource Directory

Teaching Resources

📁 **Section Quiz** in the Chapter and Section Resources booklet, p. 29, covers the main ideas and key terms in the section. Available in Spanish in the Spanish Chapter and Section Resources booklet, p. 19.

Judaism

BEFORE YOU READ

Reach Into Your Background

Have you ever spent time away from home? If so, what did you do to stay in contact with family and friends?

Questions to Explore

1. How were Israelite religious beliefs unique in the ancient world?
2. What values did the Israelites have?

Key Terms

covenant
prophet
diaspora

Key People

Abraham
Deborah

The Bible records a promise made by God to the Israelite leader Abraham:

> "I will give you many descendants, and some of them will be kings. You will have so many descendants that they will become nations. . . . I will keep my promise to you and your descendants in future generations as an everlasting covenant. I will be your God and the God of your descendants."

This was the promise of a special relationship with God. It helped shape the history of the people of Israel from ancient times to the present.

The Israelites were among many peoples who lived in the Fertile Crescent. They came into contact with many other people and ideas. Over time, the Israelites developed their own ideas. These ideas reflected a blend of many traditions.

The early Israelites came to believe that God was taking part in their history. They recorded events and laws in their most sacred text, the Torah. The Torah is made up of five books. They are called Genesis, Exodus, Leviticus, Numbers, and Deuteronomy. The promise that you just read is from the Book of Genesis. Later, Christians adopted these books as the first five books of the Old Testament.

▲ All Jewish synagogues have a copy of the Torah, like the one above. The Torah's sacred text is handwritten on a parchment scroll.

Teaching Resources

📁 **Reproducible Lesson Plan** in the Chapter and Section Resources booklet, p. 30, provides a summary of the section lesson.

📁 **Guided Reading and Review** in the Chapter and Section Resources booklet, p. 31, provides a structure for mastering key concepts and reviewing key terms in the section. Available in Spanish in the Spanish Chapter and Section Resources booklet, p. 20.

Program Resources

Outline Maps The Middle East and North Africa: Political, p. 29

Lesson Objectives

1. Summarize how the religious beliefs of the Israelites shaped their history.
2. Explain the rules and laws that guided the Israelites.
3. Describe how Jews living in different parts of the world preserved their heritage.

Lesson Plan

1 Engage

Warm-Up Activity

Talk about how shared values help shape people's lives and help people develop a sense of community. Ask students to suggest values shared by people in your community. Have students explain what happens when these values are ignored. What are the consequences for the individuals who ignore them? What are the consequences for the community?

Activating Prior Knowledge

Have students read Reach Into Your Background in the Before You Read box. Ask students how they feel when they get a piece of e-mail or a letter from someone far away. Is it exciting? Do they learn new things? Do they feel a connection to the person who sent the message?

2 Explore

As students read the section, encourage them to find answers to these questions: Why did the Israelites believe that they were God's chosen people? Why were special religious laws and traditions important to the Jews? What were some reasons for the Israelites' having to leave their homeland?

3 Teach

After students have read the section, ask them to make a list of the ideas and beliefs held by the Israelites. This activity should take about 20 minutes.

4 Assess

See the answers to the Section Review. You may also use students' completed lists for assessment.

Acceptable lists correctly identify two important beliefs as presented in the section.

Commendable lists correctly identify at least three important beliefs as presented in the section.

Outstanding lists correctly identify at least three important beliefs as presented in the section. They also include other beliefs implied by the content of the section.

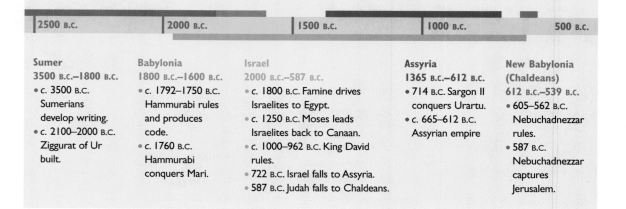

Major Ancient Civilizations of the Fertile Crescent

2500 B.C.	2000 B.C.	1500 B.C.	1000 B.C.	500 B.C.
Sumer 3500 B.C.–1800 B.C.	**Babylonia** 1800 B.C.–1600 B.C.	**Israel** 2000 B.C.–587 B.C.	**Assyria** 1365 B.C.–612 B.C.	**New Babylonia (Chaldeans)** 612 B.C.–539 B.C.
• c. 3500 B.C. Sumerians develop writing.	• c. 1792–1750 B.C. Hammurabi rules and produces code.	• c. 1800 B.C. Famine drives Israelites to Egypt.	• 714 B.C. Sargon II conquers Urartu.	• 605–562 B.C. Nebuchadnezzar rules.
• c. 2100–2000 B.C. Ziggurat of Ur built.	• c. 1760 B.C. Hammurabi conquers Mari.	• c. 1250 B.C. Moses leads Israelites back to Canaan.	• c. 665–612 B.C. Assyrian empire	• 587 B.C. Nebuchadnezzar captures Jerusalem.
		• c. 1000–962 B.C. King David rules.		
		• 722 B.C. Israel falls to Assyria.		
		• 587 B.C. Judah falls to Chaldeans.		

A Covenant With God

To the Israelites, history and religion were closely joined. Each event showed God's plan for the Israelite people. In time, Israelite beliefs changed into the religion we know today as Judaism. You already know that Judaism was monotheistic from its beginning. It also differed in other ways from the beliefs of nearby peoples.

Most ancient people thought of their gods as being connected to certain places or people. The Israelites, however, believed that God was present everywhere. They believed that God knew everything and had complete power.

As you read, Israelites believed that God had made a **covenant,** or binding agreement, with Abraham. For this reason, Israelites considered themselves to be God's "chosen people." Moses renewed this covenant. He told the Israelites that God would lead them to Canaan, "the promised land." In return for God doing this, the Israelites had to obey Him faithfully.

The Ten Commandments At the heart of Judaism are the Ten Commandments. These are laws that Israelites believed God gave them through Moses. Some set out religious duties toward God. Others are rules for moral behavior toward other people. Here are four.

Ask Questions What would you like to know about the Israelites' covenant with God?

> " I the Lord am your God who brought you out of the land of Egypt. . . . You shall have no other gods beside Me. . . .
> Honor your father and your mother, as the Lord your God has commanded. . . .
> You shall not murder.
> You shall not steal. " .

Resource Directory

Media and Technology

 Color Transparency 70

In addition to the Ten Commandments, the Torah set out many other laws. Some had to do with everyday matters, such as how food should be prepared. Others had to do with crimes. Like Hammurabi's Code, many of the Israelites' laws demanded an eye for an eye. At the same time, preachers called on leaders to carry out the laws with justice and mercy.

Some laws protected women. The Ten Commandments, for example, make respect for mothers a basic law. But, as in many other religions, women were of lower status than men. A man who was head of a family owned his wife and children. A father could sell his daughters into marriage. Only a husband could seek a divorce.

Early in Israelite history, a few women leaders, such as the judge Deborah, won honor and respect. Later on, women were not allowed to take part in many religious ceremonies.

▼▶ Several ancient scrolls, concealed in jars like the one on the right, were found near the Dead Sea in 1947. Named the Dead Sea Scrolls, these manuscripts helped historians reconstruct the early history of the Israelites.

Background

Biography

Deborah According to tradition, the prophet Deborah lived during the 1100s B.C. She held the highly respected position of judge and acted as an adviser to her people. Upon hearing that her people were being mistreated by the Canaanites, Deborah and another Israelite leader developed a plan to defeat the Canaanites. According to the Bible, Deborah predicted that a woman would lead the Israelites to victory. The Israelites engaged the Canaanites in battle. During the battle, a thunderstorm struck. The Canaanites' chariots become mired in the muddy battlefield. Later, a woman killed the Canaanite leader. As prophesied by Deborah, the Israelites emerged victorious over the Canaanites.

Cooperative Learning

Traditions Invite students to research Jewish traditions so that they can create a museum display celebrating Jewish culture. You might suggest that students find out about foods served at the Passover feast and the significance of such items as the menorah, shofar, and dreidel. Suggest that some group members do the research, some draw pictures or construct models, and some prepare explanations of the objects. Invite another class to visit the display. *Visual*

Justice and Morality Often in the history of the Israelites, **prophets,** or religious leaders, appeared. They told the Israelites what God wanted them to do. The prophets warned the people not to disobey God's law. Disobedience would bring disaster.

Prophets preached a strong code of moral behavior. They urged the Israelites to lead moral lives. They also called on the rich and powerful to protect the poor and weak. All people, the prophets said, were equal before God. In many ancient societies, the ruler was seen as a god. To the Israelites, however, their leaders were human. Kings had to obey God's law just the way shepherds and merchants did.

Looking Ahead

In A.D. 135, the Romans added to the **diaspora** (dy AS puhr uh), or scattering of people, begun by the Assyrians and Chaldeans. After a rebellion, the Romans drove the Israelites out of their homeland. As a result, Israelites scattered to different parts of the world.

Wherever they settled, the Jews, as they had come to be called, preserved their heritage. They did so by living together in close communities. They took care to obey their religious laws and follow their traditions. These traditions set Jews apart. Yet, they also helped the Jews survive harsh treatment by others.

ACROSS THE WORLD

The Diaspora Because of the Diaspora, there were Jewish communities as far west as Spain and as far east as India. The first Jewish settlers in the Americas arrived in Brazil in the 1500s.

▶ After defeating the Jews in battle in A.D. 78, Roman soldiers carried off precious and sacred objects from the temple in Jerusalem.

Resource Directory

Teaching Resources

Section Quiz in the Chapter and Section Resources booklet, p. 32, covers the main ideas and key terms in the section. Available in Spanish in the Spanish Chapter and Section Resources booklet, p. 21.

Vocabulary in the Chapter and Section Resources booklet, p. 34, provides a review of key terms in the chapter.

Available in Spanish in the Spanish Chapter and Section Resources booklet, p. 23.

Reteaching in the Chapter and Section Resources booklet, p. 35, provides a structure for students who may need additional help in mastering chapter content.

Enrichment in the Chapter and Section Resources booklet, p. 36, extends chapter content and enriches students' understanding.

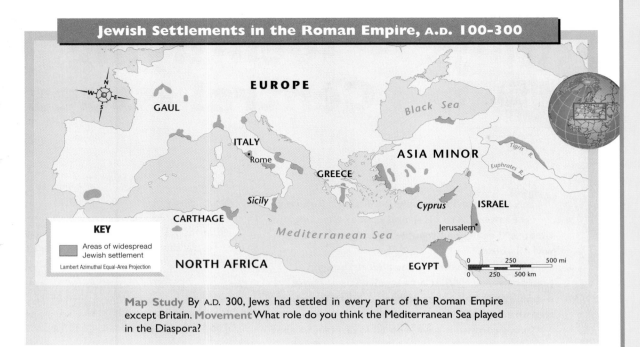

Jewish Settlements in the Roman Empire, A.D. 100–300

EUROPE

GAUL

ITALY
Rome

Black Sea

ASIA MINOR

Tigris R.

GREECE

Euphrates R.

Sicily

Cyprus

ISRAEL

CARTHAGE

Mediterranean Sea

Jerusalem

KEY

Areas of widespread Jewish settlement

Lambert Azimuthal Equal-Area Projection

NORTH AFRICA

EGYPT

0 250 500 mi
0 250 500 km

Map Study By A.D. 300, Jews had settled in every part of the Roman Empire except Britain. **Movement** What role do you think the Mediterranean Sea played in the Diaspora?

Judaism is one of the world's major religions because of its special religious ideas. It also had an important influence on two later religions, Christianity and Islam. Both of those faiths came from the same geographical area. Both were monotheistic. Jews, Christians, and followers of Islam all honor Abraham, Moses, and the prophets. They also share the same moral point of view that the Israelites first developed.

SECTION 5 REVIEW

1. **Define** (a) covenant, (b) prophet, (c) diaspora.

2. **Identify** (a) Abraham, (b) Deborah.

3. How were the Israelites' religious beliefs different from those of other peoples in the ancient world?

4. What values of the Israelites are shown in the Ten Commandments and the covenant?

Critical Thinking

5. **Drawing Conclusions** Why did the Israelites believe that they were God's chosen people?

Activity

6. **Writing to Learn** Suppose you have a friend who wants to learn more about Judaism. Write him or her a letter explaining the special relationship that Israelites felt they had with God.

Spanish Glossary in the Spanish Chapter and Section Resources, pp. 85–89, provides key terms translated from English to Spanish as well as definitions in Spanish.

Chapter Summary in the Chapter and Section Resources booklet, p. 33, provides a summary of chapter content. Available in Spanish in the Spanish Chapter and Section Resources booklet, p. 22.

Cooperative Learning Activity in the Activities and Projects booklet, pp. 24–27, provides two student handouts, one page of teacher's directions, and a scoring rubric for a cooperative learning activity on making an illustrated diagram about the wheel.

Media and Technology

Guided Reading Audiotapes (English and Spanish)

Section 5 Review

1. (a) a binding agreement (b) one of the religious leaders who told the Israelites what God wanted them to do (c) a scattering of people

2. (a) Israelite prophet who made a covenant with God (b) an important female Israelite judge and leader

3. Many ancient peoples believed in many gods, connected with specific places or people. The Israelites believed in one all-powerful God.

4. The Ten Commandments outline the Israelites' religious duties toward God and set rules for moral behavior. The covenant shows how religion and history were closely tied in Israelite beliefs.

5. The Israelites believed that they had a special relationship with God because He had made a solemn covenant with the prophets, Abraham and Moses.

6. Students' letters should explain that the Israelites believed that they were God's chosen people, that he had selected Canaan as their holy land, and that he had given them a set of rules about how they were to behave toward God and the people around them.

Answers to . . .

MAP STUDY

Since some settlements are on islands and others are along the Mediterranean coast, the sea undoubtedly served as a travel route.

1 Describe strategies for identifying central issues.

2 Identify central issues in context.

Lesson Plan

1 Engage

Warm-Up Activity

To **introduce** the skill, read the opening scenario with students. Ask volunteers to recount a similar experience, perhaps relating to a television show or book.

Activating Prior Knowledge

Ask students to define the term *central issue*. Prompt them with the related term *main idea*. Invite volunteers to write some suggested definitions on the chalkboard.

2 Explore

Use students' definitions to clarify and explain central issues. Review the earlier examples that students provided and discard any that no longer apply. Then have students read the rest of the skills activity.

SKILLS ACTIVITY

Identifying Central Issues

"That movie was sure confusing," Bob commented to his friend Juan as they left the theater. "I really had trouble figuring out what it was all about."

"Well, it had some great action, though," Juan answered. "What a neat adventure! Those people really had to go through a lot to find that treasure."

Juan's comment gave Bob an idea. "Maybe that was the point of the movie," he said. "Maybe the whole idea was just to show the great adventures they had while they tried to find the lost treasure."

Get Ready

Juan and Bob got the idea. You can, too. To understand anything you read or see, you need to identify the main idea, or the central issue.

Try It Out

Try identifying central issues by reading the following paragraph. Think about its main idea. Then complete the steps that follow.

◀ A scene from *Raiders of the Lost Ark*. The adventure of finding lost treasure was a central issue of this movie.

Resource Directory

Teaching Resources

📁 **Identifying Central Issues** in the Social Studies and Geography Skills booklet, p. 42, provides additional skill practice.

In 1901, the Code of Hammurabi was discovered when a huge stele (STEE lee), or monument, was found. The stele was almost eight feet tall and more than seven feet around—a huge piece of deep black stone. At its top was a carved scene of a sun-god on a throne handing a scepter to the man in front of him. The scene represented Hammurabi receiving the code of laws from the sun-god. Below the scene, the laws were listed in more than 1,000 lines of writing in cuneiform characters. On the other side of the monument were 2,500 more lines. People soon translated the writing. They realized they had discovered a set of ancient laws.

A. Look for something that identifies the central issue. If you are trying to find the central issue in something you have read, you may find it in the title. Also, look for a sentence that identifies the central issue. Which sentence in the paragraph you just read does this?

B. Look for an idea that all the sentences (or scenes in a movie) have in common. Usually, most of the sentences provide details that support or explain the central issue. The idea they have in common is the central issue. What idea do the sentences in the paragraph have in common?

C. State the central issue in your own words. Write in your own words what you think the central issue is. You might want to write it in the form of a title. Write one or two versions, and then reread the passage to make sure that what you wrote accurately identifies the central issue. What might be a title for the paragraph?

Apply the Skill

The text in the box at right lists some laws from the Code of Hammurabi. Read them, and then follow the steps below.

1 **Follow the three steps for identifying a central issue.** Repeat the three steps you followed before. Does anything in the list of laws state the central issue? What do all the laws have in common? How would you state the central issue of the information in the box?

2 **Consider other peoples' statements of the central issue.** Compare your statement of the central issue with those of some of your classmates. Then, work with your classmates to compare your statements with what some scholars have identified as the central issue in the Code of Hammurabi. Do you agree with the the the following statements? Explain your answers.

- The underlying principle of the Code of Hammurabi is that "the strong shall not injure the weak."
- The basic idea of the Code of Hammurabi is that "the punishment shall fit the crime."
- Every law in Hammurabi's Code follows this central idea: "the punishment for a crime shall be retaliation (revenge)."

Selections From the Code of Hammurabi

If a shepherd is careless and brings about an accident in the flock, the shepherd shall repay in cattle and sheep the loss he caused.

If a physician sets a broken bone, the patient shall give five shekels (Babylonian coins) of silver to the physician.

If a man cuts down a tree in another man's orchard without the consent of the owner of the orchard, he shall pay one-half mina (another Babylonian coin) of silver.

If a man opens his canal for irrigation and neglects it so that the water carries away soil from a nearby field, he shall give the owner of the field enough grain to replace what the field would have grown.

If a builder builds a house for someone and does not make its construction meet the requirements, and a wall falls in, that builder shall strengthen that wall at his own expense.

3 Teach

Group students in threes to **practice** the skill with the Try It Out paragraph. Suggest that students sift out supporting details to help them identify the central issue.

For additional reinforcement, have students identify central issues in paragraphs from recent classroom readings.

4 Assess

Direct students to **apply** the skill to the boxed excerpt from the Code of Hammurabi, and ask them to write down their own statements of the central issue. Then have them compare them with those of the scholars. **Assess** their statements by evaluating their ability to recognize as a central issue the idea that the strong should not injure the weak and that the punishment should fit the crime.

Reviewing Main Ideas

1. They provided water for irrigation, fish for food, and reeds for building. They also deposited fertile soil when they flooded.

2. Mesopotamia lay between the Tigris and Euphrates rivers.

3. Because of its nearness to rivers, Mesopotamia's land was fertile, and people established farming communities. The communities then developed into cities.

4. Students should name two of the following people: Sargon of Assyria, Hammurabi, or Nebuchadnezzar II.

5. Answers will vary. Students may mention that Hammurabi established written laws for his people to obey or that Nebuchadnezzar rebuilt the city of Babylon into a center of learning and science.

6. The Assyrians were warriors. They conquered cities and for centuries ruled a huge empire by force.

7. Because Hammurabi's Code was written, there was less confusion about the laws and the punishments for breaking the laws.

8. People first drew pictures in clay to represent what they wanted to say. These pictures were later simplified into wedge-shaped marks called cuneiform.

9. The Phoenicians developed an alphabet that represented the sounds of the language. The Phoenicians also expanded trade in the Mediterranean, exchanging goods and culture throughout the ancient world.

10. Answers will vary. Students might name God's covenant with Abraham, the Exodus, the conquest and settlement of Canaan, the union of the tribes, or the writing of the Ten Commandments. Students might explain that the covenant with God made the Israelites believe they were the "chosen people" and that they had to obey God faithfully.

11. Answers will vary. A possible answer might explain that the Israelites were unique because they believed in only one God.

Reviewing Key Terms

Sentences should show the correct meanings of terms through context.

Reviewing Main Ideas

1. Explain the importance of the Tigris and Euphrates rivers in the Fertile Crescent.
2. Describe Mesopotamia's location in the ancient world.
3. Explain how Mesopotamia's location shaped its development.
4. Give two examples of strong rulers in the Fertile Crescent.
5. How did rulers in the Fertile Crescent help shape the civilizations they ruled?
6. Explain how Assyria gained and used its power.
7. Name one improvement that Hammurabi's Code made in Babylonian society.
8. List two steps in the development of writing in Mesopotamia.
9. Explain two important cultural contributions of the Phoenicians.
10. List three major events in the history of the Israelites. Then, choose one of them, and describe its importance.
11. Identify one way in which the Israelites' religious beliefs were unique in the ancient world.

Reviewing Key Terms

Use each key term below in a sentence that shows the meaning of the term.

1. scribe
2. city-state
3. polytheism
4. myth
5. empire
6. caravan
7. bazaar
8. code
9. cuneiform
10. alphabet
11. monotheism
12. famine
13. exile
14. covenant
15. prophet
16. diaspora

Critical Thinking

1. **Comparing and Contrasting** Mesopotamian rulers used different methods of uniting their people behind the government. Contrast the ways of Sargon II with those of Hammurabi. How were they similar? How were they different?
2. **Expressing Problems Clearly** How did Assyria's location aid its development as a military power?

Graphic Organizer

Copy the chart onto a sheet of paper. Then fill in the empty boxes to complete the chart.

Civilization	Where They Lived	Their Challenges or Problems	Their Achievements
Sumerians			
Babylonians			
Assyrians			
Chaldeans			
Phoenicians			
Israelites			

Graphic Organizer

Civilization	Where They Lived	Their Challenges or Problems	Their Lasting Achievements
Sumerians	between the Tigris and Euphrates, just north of the Persian Gulf	destructive floods constant warfare	They developed a system of writing.
Babylonians	between the Tigris and Euphrates, north of Sumer	destroyed by Assyrians	Babylon became a center of learning; strides were made in astronomy and mathematics.
Assyrians	north of Babylon on open land	continually open to invasion	They developed sophisticated weapons and conquered many lands.
Chaldeans	king ruled Mesopotamia from Babylon	overthrown by fierce Assyrians	They gained control of the Assyrian empire and rebuilt Babylon.
Phoenicians	small area on eastern shores of Mediterranean Sea	land area small, resources limited	They established trade routes throughout the Mediterranean and developed an alphabet.
Israelites	traveled from Canaan to Egypt and back, settled in Canaan	endured famine and slavery	They built the city of Jerusalem and established a monotheistic religion that survives today.

Map Activity

Place Location

Fertile Crescent
For each place listed below, write the letter from the map that shows its location.

1. Tigris River
2. Euphrates River
3. Mesopotamia
4. Fertile Crescent
5. Canaan
6. Mediterranean Sea

Writing Activity

Writing a Brochure
Choose a civilization that you read about in this chapter. Write a short, imaginary travel brochure telling an ancient visitor about the interesting features of the civilization.

Internet Activity

Use a search engine to search for the site **Cuneiform Connections**. Read the chart to learn some common cuneiform symbols. With a toothpick, scratch symbols from the chart onto self-hardening clay to create a list in cuneiform of items you would sell at a public market. Give your dried tablet to a friend to translate.

Skills Review

Turn to the Skills Activity. Look again at the steps for identifying central issues. Then complete the following: (a) How would you define the term "central issue"? (b) Explain why understanding the central issue is important when you are reading social studies.

How Am I Doing?

Answer these questions to help you check your progress.

1. Do I understand how geography helped shape the civilizations of the Fertile Crescent?
2. Can I explain how civilizations in Mesopotamia and other areas of the Fertile Crescent affected human history?
3. Can I identify some historic events that shaped the culture and beliefs of the Israelites?
4. What information from this chapter can I use in my book project?

Critical Thinking

1. Hammurabi conquered neighboring cities and united them in a great empire, ruling with a recorded code of laws that promised consistent justice. Sargon II also ruled an empire. He used fear and force to rule his subjects. Both kings built centers of learning and trade.

2. Assyria's location on open land made it easy to invade. To defend their land, the Assyrians became skilled warriors. They used their skills to conquer other lands and build an empire.

Map Activity

1. F	**3.** E	**5.** B
2. D	**4.** C	**6.** A

Writing Activity

Students' brochures will vary, but should be based on facts from the section.

Skills Review

Students may say that the central issue is the main idea. Students may suggest that it is important to understand central issues in social studies so that they will understand the ideas that shaped history and continue to be important today.

Resource Directory

Teaching Resources

Chapter Tests Forms A and B are in the Tests booklet, pp. 8–13.

Program Resources

Writing Process Handbook includes Writing Effective Paragraphs, pp. 27–28, to help students with the Writing Activity.

Media and Technology

Color Transparencies
Color Transparency 174
(Graphic organizer table template)
Prentice Hall Writer's Solution
Writing Lab CD-ROM
Computer Test Bank
Resource Pro™ CD-ROM

Internet Activity

If students are having difficulty finding this site, you may wish to have them use the following URLs, which were accurate at the time this textbook was published:

http://www.dia.org/
galleries/ancient/
mesopotamia/
mesopotamia.html

http://www.uiowa.edu/
~english/litcult20/
danielaucutt/
cuneiform.html

You might also guide students to a search engine. Four of the most useful are Infoseek, AltaVista, Lycos, and Yahoo. For additional suggestions on using the Internet, refer to the Prentice Hall Social Studies' Educator's Handbook "Using the Internet," in the *Prentice Hall World Explorer Program Resources.*

For additional links to world history and culture topics, visit the Prentice Hall Home Page at:
http://www.phschool.com

How Am I Doing?

Point out to students that this checklist is a quick reminder of what they learned in the chapter. If their answer to any of the questions is *no* or if they are unsure, they may need to review the topic.

Ancient Egypt and Nubia

To help you plan instruction, the chart below shows how teaching resources correspond to chapter content. Use the resources to vary instruction, add activities, or plan block schedules. Where appropriate, resources have suggested time allotments for students. Time allotments are approximate.

Managing Time and Instruction

	The Ancient World Teaching Resources Binder		World Explorer Program Resources Binder	
	Resource	mins.	Resource	mins.
1 SECTION I The Geography of the Nile	**Chapter and Section Support** Reproducible Lesson Plan, p. 39 Ⓢ Guided Reading and Review, p. 40 Ⓢ Section Quiz, p. 41	 20 25	**Outline Maps** The Middle East and North Africa: Physical, p. 28 **Nystrom Desk Atlas** Ⓣ **Primary Sources and Literature** Readings **Writing Process Handbook** Using Transitions, p. 30	 20 20 40 25
SKILLS ACTIVITY Reading Route Maps	**Social Studies and Geography Skills,** Reading a Trade Map, p. 39	30		
2 SECTION 2 Egypt's Powerful Kings and Queens	**Chapter and Section Support** Reproducible Lesson Plan, p. 42 Ⓢ Guided Reading and Review, p. 43 Ⓢ Section Quiz, p. 44 **Social Studies and Geography Skills,** Reading a Historical Map, p. 28	 20 25 30	Ⓣ **Interdisciplinary Explorations** *Riddles of the Pharaohs: Exploring Ancient Egypt*	
3 SECTION 3 Egyptian Religion	**Chapter and Section Support** Reproducible Lesson Plan, p. 45 Ⓢ Guided Reading and Review, p. 46 Ⓢ Section Quiz, p. 47	 20 25		
4 SECTION 4 The Culture of the Ancient Egyptians	**Chapter and Section Support** Reproducible Lesson Plan, p. 48 Ⓢ Guided Reading and Review, p. 49 Ⓢ Section Quiz, p. 50 Critical Thinking Activity, p. 58	 20 25 30		
5 SECTION 5 The Resource-Rich Cultures of Nubia	**Chapter and Section Support** Reproducible Lesson Plan, p. 51 Ⓢ Guided Reading and Review, p. 52 Ⓢ Section Quiz, p. 53 Ⓢ Vocabulary, p. 55 Reteaching, p. 56 Enrichment, p. 57 Ⓢ Chapter Summary, p. 54 **Tests** Forms A and B Chapter Tests, pp. 14–19	 20 25 20 25 25 15 40		

Block Scheduling Folder
PROGRAM TEACHING RESOURCES

- Activities and Projects
- **Block Scheduling Program Support**
- Interdisciplinary Links
- Resource Pro™ CD-ROM
- Media and Technology

Media and Technology

Resource	mins.
▣ ⊘ Ⓢ **World Video Explorer**	20
⊘ **Planet Earth CD-ROM**	20
⊘ **Material World CD-ROM**	20
▭ **Color Transparencies 92, 93**	20
▭ **Color Transparencies 70, 92**	20
⊘ **Planet Earth CD-ROM**	20
▭ **Color Transparency 92**	20
▭ **Color Transparency 92**	20
⌒ Ⓢ **Guided Reading Audiotapes**	20
▭ **Color Transparency 174** (Graphic organizer table template)	20
⊘ **The Writer's Solution CD-ROM**	30
▯ **Computer Test Bank**	30

- Ⓣ **Teaming Opportunity** This resource is especially well-suited for teaching teams.
- Ⓢ **Spanish** This resource is also in Spanish support.
- ⊘ **CD-ROM**
- ⊘ **Laserdisc**
- ▭ **Transparency**
- ▯ **Software**
- ▣ **Videotape**
- ⌒ **Audiotape**

Assessment Opportunities

From Guiding Questions to Assessment   A series of Guiding Questions serves as an organizing framework for this book. The Guiding Questions that relate to this chapter are listed below. Section Reviews and Section Quizzes provide opportunities for assessing students' insights into these Guiding Questions. Additional assessments are listed below.

GUIDING QUESTIONS

- *How did physical geography affect the growth of ancient civilizations?*
- *What accomplishments is each civilization known for?*

ASSESSMENTS

Section 1

Students should be able to create a map showing the course of the Nile River.

▶ **RUBRIC**   See the Assessment booklet for a rubric on assessing a map produced by a student.

Section 2

Students should be able to write a paragraph revealing how Egyptian rulers unified their country.

▶ **RUBRIC**   See the Assessment booklet for a rubric on assessing a writing assignment.

Section 3

Students should be able to write a glossary of the key terms in the section.

▶ **RUBRIC**   See the Assessment booklet for a rubric on assessing a glossary.

Section 4

Students should be able to role-play a day in the life of the ancient Egyptians.

▶ **RUBRIC**   See the Assessment booklet for a rubric on assessing a role-playing activity.

Section 5

Students should be able to write an explanation of the effect of iron on the wealth of the kingdom of Meroë.

▶ **RUBRIC**   See the Assessment booklet for a rubric on assessing cause-and-effect statements.

Activities and Projects

Mental Mapping

A Mighty Long River Tell students that the Nile River is the longest river in the world (though the Amazon carries a much greater volume of water). The Nile is over 4,100 miles long. The White Nile, the main branch of the river, begins in Burundi and flows through Rwanda, Uganda, Sudan, and Egypt before reaching the Mediterranean. Tributaries that flow through Ethiopia, Kenya, and Tanzania also drain into the Nile.

Give students a few minutes to sketch an outline map of Africa, locating the countries drained by the Nile and sketching the course of the White Nile. When their sketches are finished, allow them to compare their guesses with a published map. Have them make any corrections necessary to their sketches.

Links to Current Events

On Display The climate and customs of ancient Egypt have preserved many artifacts from this civilization. Many objects from ancient Egypt can be seen in museums of art, history, and archaeology.

Have students plan a visit to a museum that has a collection of Egyptian artifacts. They can begin by identifying a museum in your area with such a collection. Have them make a presentation describing the museum and explaining where it is located. Ask each student to identify at least one Egyptian object that they would especially want to see. If possible, arrange a field trip to the museum

Hands-On Activities

Create a Flood Plain Have students work in pairs or in small groups to make salt-and-flour relief maps of the Egyptian Nile. Tell them that the flood plain was long and narrow, with an average width of about 19 miles, but it reached an area as broad as 154 miles in the delta region.

Have students use a relief map for information about the course of the Nile and its flood plain. Encourage them to use color-coding on their models to show the area of Egypt that would have been productive agricultural land. Point out that the area flooded varied from year to year. Students can use gradations of color to distinguish land that was nearly always productive from land that was in use some of the time or only rarely.

Picture Books Ancient Egyptians used a system of hieroglyphs, or highly stylized pictures, to keep records and write stories and histories. A single picture might be used to express the same idea in different stories or accounts. For example, "flood" might always be shown by the same picture, no matter which flood was being discussed. Ask students to develop a system of ten or twenty hieroglyphs, then use it to tell a simple story. The story may be fact or fiction. *English Language Learners*

Time Capsule Egyptian kings and queens were buried with objects they believed they would need in the next life.

By doing this, they provided the archaeologists of our time with a time capsule containing lots of information about their religion, civilization, and technology. Ask students what objects from our civilization they would choose to put into an air-proof, moisture-proof container for archaeologists of the distant future to find. Remind them that these archaeologists may not be able to read English or other present-day languages. Have students make a collage with pictures of the objects they would include in their time capsule. *Basic*

Talk Show Host Present this imaginary scenario to students: Through a fluke in the chemicals used to preserve a

mummy, an Egyptian pharaoh has been found who is not really dead but rather is in a state of hibernation. The pharaoh has been revived. Now students are being sought to interview the mummy on a television talk show. Students must submit a list of questions to the television show's producers, who will evaluate questions on the basis of what the answers might tell viewers about ancient Egyptian social organization, religion, and daily life. Have each student write three questions, and then share them in small groups. You may wish to allow students to act out the "talk show" with a volunteer playing the part of the mummy. *Average*

F.Y.I.

This page can help you extend your own and students' understanding of the concepts in this chapter. You may want to browse through some of the suggestions in the **Bibliography. Interdisciplinary Links** can connect social studies understandings to areas elsewhere in the curriculum through the use of other Prentice Hall products. **National Geography Standards** reflected specifically in this chapter are listed for your convenience. Some hints about appropriate **Internet Access** are also provided. **School to Careers** provides insights into the practical uses of some of the concepts in this chapter as they might pertain to various careers.

BIBLIOGRAPHY

FOR THE TEACHER

Bianchi, Robert Steven. *The Nubians: People of the Ancient Nile.* Millbrook, 1994.

Clarke, Sue. *The Tombs of the Pharaohs: A Three-Dimensional Discovery.* Hyperion, 1994.

Crosher, Judith. *Ancient Egypt.* Viking, 1993.

FOR THE STUDENT

Easy

David, Rosalie. *Growing Up in Ancient Egypt.* Troll, 1993.

Lattimore, Deborah. *The Winged Cat: A Tale of Ancient Egypt.* Harper, 1992.

Average

Jenkins, Earnestine. *A Glorious Past: Ancient Egypt, Ethiopia, and Nubia.* Chelsea House, 1995.

Putnam, James. *Pyramid.* Dorling Kindersley, 1994.

Challenging

Deem, James. *How to Make a Mummy Talk.* Houghton, 1995.

LITERATURE CONNECTION

Bradshaw, Gillian. *The Dragon and the Thief.* Greenwillow, 1991.

Carter, Dorothy Sharp. *His Majesty, Queen Hatshepsut.* Lippincott, 1987.

McGraw, Eloise Jarvis. *Mara, Daughter of the Nile.* Penguin, 1985.

INTERDISCIPLINARY LINKS

Subject	Theme: Culture
MATH	Middle Grades Math: Tools for Success *Course 2*, Lesson 5-11, **Math and Remodeling: Perimeter, Area, and Volume**
SCIENCE	Prentice Hall Science *Dynamic Earth*, Lesson 4-1, **What Is a Mineral?** *Dynamic Earth*, Chapter 6, **Connections: Nature's Gift From the Nile**
LANGUAGE ARTS	Choices in Literature *It's Up to You*, **Egyptian Mystery Tour** *The Adventures of Me*, **The Egyptian Cinderella**

NATIONAL GEOGRAPHY STANDARDS

Students explore the 18 National Geography Standards throughout *The Ancient World.* Chapter 3, however, concentrates on investigating the following standards: 1, 2, 3, 4, 5, 6, 7, 8, 9, 10, 11, 12, 13, 14, 15, 16, 17. For a complete list of the standards, see the *Teacher's Flexible Planning Guide.*

SCHOOL TO CAREERS

In Chapter 3, Ancient Egypt and Nubia, students learn more about the development of ancient civilizations. Additionally, they address the skill of using route maps. Understanding Egypt and Nubia can help students prepare for careers in many fields such as education, art, museum administration, history, and so on. Using route maps is a skill particularly useful for truck drivers and other workers in transportation, such as shipping. The curriculum presented in this book, as in all eight titles of Prentice Hall's *World Explorer* program, is designed to prepare students not only for careers but also for good citizenship—of the world as well as of this country.

INTERNET ACCESS

Many social studies teachers and students use Internet browsers, or search engines, to investigate particular topics. For the best results, use narrow rather than broad topics. Try these for Chapter 3: pyramids, hieroglyphs, Hatshepsut, Meroë. Finding age-appropriate sites is an important consideration when using the Internet. For links to age-appropriate sites in world studies and geography, visit the Prentice Hall Home Page at: **http://www.phschool.com**

Connecting to the Guiding Questions

In this chapter, students study the geographic settings, cultures, and histories of ancient Egyptian and Nubian civilizations. Content in this chapter corresponds to the following Guiding Questions:

● How did physical geography affect the growth of ancient civilizations?

● What accomplishments is each civilization known for?

Using the Map Activities

Ask students to give meanings for *downriver* and *upstream.* Tell them that these terms refer to the direction of a river's flow.

• The compass rose shows that the Nile flows north.

• north; Upper Egypt is up river from Lower Egypt. The land in Upper Egypt is higher because rivers flow downhill.

Heterogeneous Groups

The following Teacher's Edition strategies are suitable for heterogeneous groups.

Critical Thinking
Recognizing Cause
and Effect   p. 65
Drawing Conclusions   p. 69
Interdisciplinary
Connections
Language Arts   p. 82
Language Arts/Music   p. 87
Cooperative Learning
Egypt Exhibit   p. 83
Planning a Lesson   p. 88

CHAPTER 3
Ancient Egypt and Nubia

SECTION 1
The Geography of the Nile

SECTION 2
Egypt's Powerful Kings and Queens

SECTION 3
Egyptian Religion

SECTION 4
The Culture of the Ancient Egyptians

SECTION 5
The Resource-Rich Cultures of Nubia

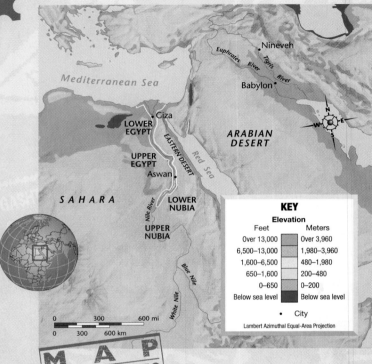

MAP ACTIVITIES

Water, as you know, always flows downhill. Whether the downhill direction is to the east, west, north, or south, water will flow that way. Study the map, and then carry out the following activities to understand the difference between up and down and north and south.

Find the direction of flow
Locate the Nile River and with your finger, trace its route. In what direction does the Nile flow? How do you know this?

Find Upper Egypt and Lower Egypt
Find the two areas labeled Upper Egypt and Lower Egypt. Is Lower Egypt north or south of Upper Egypt? Which area is up river from the other? In which region is the land higher? How do you know this?

Resource Directory

Media and Technology

 Spotlight On: Secrets of the Pyramids, from the World Video Explorer, enhances students' understanding of how and why the pyramids were built.

Chapter 5

The Geography of the Nile

Lesson Objectives

1 Trace the course of the Nile River through ancient Egypt and Nubia.

2 Summarize how the Nile affected trade and the ways of life of ancient Egyptians and Nubians.

Lesson Plan

1 Engage

Warm-Up Activity

Ask students to list the reasons why a river might overflow its banks. Prompt the discussion by asking: *What happens in spring to snow on mountains? How does this affect mountain streams that flow into rivers?* Ask students to explain why water in a river flowing downhill might gather force and move rapidly.

Activating Prior Knowledge

Have students read Reach Into Your Background in the Before You Read box. Ask students to think of several things they would not be able to do if they did not have a body of water nearby. How would the absence of a body of water affect certain livelihoods?

BEFORE YOU READ

Reach Into Your Background

Perhaps you live near a river, lake, or ocean. If so, then you know that bodies of water affect your environment. You enjoy them for recreation. Perhaps your family depends on them for a living. Think of several ways nearby water can affect the way people live.

Questions to Explore

1. How does the geography of the Nile River change as it runs from its sources to the delta?

2. How did the Nile support human life in ancient times?

Key Terms
cataract
delta
silt

Key People and Places
Herodotus
Lower Nubia
Upper Nubia
Upper Egypt
Lower Egypt

"**E**gypt is the gift of the Nile," wrote the Greek historian Herodotus (huh RAHD uh tuhs). He explored Egypt in the 400s B.C. He saw the life-giving waters of its great river. He traveled upriver until he was stopped by churning rapids of white water. Unable to get past the rapids, he turned back. He never found the source of the river.

Herodotus wrote down his observations of Egypt and other lands. They still make interesting reading today. Despite his failure to locate the source of the Nile, Herodotus had learned a basic truth. There would be no Egypt without the Nile.

The Course of the Nile

The Nile is the world's longest river. It flows north from its sources in central Africa to the Mediterranean Sea for more than 4,000 miles (6,400 km). This is more than the distance across the United States.

The Nile has two main sources. The Blue Nile rises in the highlands of the present-day country of Ethiopia and races down to the desert in thundering torrents. The White Nile is calmer. It begins deep in central Africa and flows northward through swamps. The two

▼ Food was one of the gifts of the Nile. This Egyptian hunts waterbirds as he drifts along in a reed boat.

SKILLS MINI LESSON

Using Regional Maps

You might **introduce** the skill by informing students that they can learn a lot about the geography of a place by "reading" regional maps. Show students how to read the key, distance scale, and compass rose on the map on the previous page. Help students **practice** the skill by asking them to identify the lowlands, highlands, and bodies of water of the region. Have them identify land that could be used for farming. Encourage students to **apply** the skill by asking them to write a statement about the geography of the Nile River region based on information from the map. Students may assemble their statements into a class fact sheet.

2 Explore

After students read the section, have them discuss questions such as the following: Why is Egypt called "the gift of the Nile"? How did both the Nile River and the deserts on either side of it help Egypt's civilization to grow? Where was Nubia located? What was Nubia's relationship to Egypt?

3 Teach

Have students work in pairs to make a picture map of the course of the Nile River through Upper and Lower Egypt and Nubia. Students should use the text and photos from the section to create their maps. This activity should take about 20 minutes.

4 Assess

See the answers to the Section Review. You can use students' picture maps for assessment as well.

Acceptable maps include the locations of civilizations relative to the river.

Commendable maps illustrate the farming and trading activities that took place along the river and include the basic geographic facts presented in this section.

Outstanding maps have illustrations that indicate an understanding of the Nile's influence on civilization and the spread of farming from its banks into the surrounding deserts.

READ ACTIVELY

Ask Questions What questions would you like answered about the importance of the Nile River to the ancient Egyptians and Nubians?

▼ Gold was an important Nubian resource. In this wall painting, Nubian princes bring gifts of gold to an Egyptian ruler.

rivers meet at what is today the city of Khartoum (kahr TOOM) in the present-day country of Sudan. There, the Nile begins its journey through desert lands to the Mediterranean Sea.

The Nile Through Ancient Nubia   From Khartoum northward, the Nile makes two huge bends, forming an *S* shape. The northern tip of the *S* is at the city of Aswan in Egypt. Along this 1,000-mile (1,600 km) stretch of the Nile was a land called Nubia.

The Nubian section of the Nile contained six rock-filled rapids called **cataracts.** Between the First and Second Cataracts was Lower Nubia. In this region, the desert and granite mountains lined the riverbanks, leaving very little farmable land. Because it rarely rained in Lower Nubia, people had to live close to the Nile for their water supply.

Farther south, between the Second and Sixth Cataracts, lies the area that was known as Upper Nubia. In this region, rain does fall, so people could farm in the summer and fall. But the farmland was in a very narrow strip, no more than 2 miles (3 km) wide on each side of the river.

The Nile Through Ancient Egypt   The ancient Egyptian section of the Nile ran for about 700 miles (1,100 km) from the First Cataract at Aswan to the Mediterranean Sea. On its way, it passed through a narrow region called Upper Egypt. This fertile strip had an average width of around 6 miles (10 km) on each side of the river. In the north, the Nile spread out to form a fertile, marshy area called Lower Egypt. Dry deserts stretched on each side of the river's green banks.

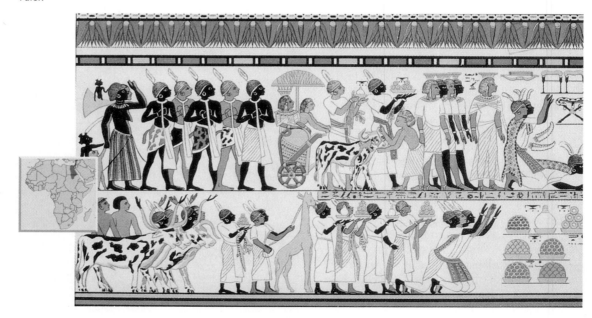

Resource Directory

Teaching Resources

📁 **Reproducible Lesson Plan** in the Chapter and Section Resources booklet, p. 39, provides a summary of the section lesson.

📁 **Guided Reading and Review** in the Chapter and Section Resources booklet, p. 40, provides a structure for mastering key concepts and reviewing key terms in the section. Available in Spanish in the Spanish Chapter and Section Resources booklet, p. 25.

Program Resources

Material in the **Primary Sources and Literature Readings** booklet extends content with a selection related to the concepts in this chapter.
Outline Maps The Middle East and North Africa: Physical, p. 28

The Flooding Nile

The flood waters of the Nile River spread as far as the eye could see. They washed against tree trunks and covered fields. Modern dams like the Aswan High Dam have been built to control flooding, while still providing water for irrigating crops.

Background

Links Across Time

Ancient and Modern Crops
Farming is still an important part of life in Egypt. The Nile is still relied upon to provide water for farming, but today, systems of canals and dams along the Nile supply year-round irrigation. As in ancient Egypt, most farmland is in the Nile Valley, and the wheat and date crops that were grown by the ancient Egyptians are still major crops. Because of irrigation, modern Egypt grows some crops, such as cotton, that were not grown in ancient times. In fact, thanks to irrigation, Egypt is one of the world's most important producers of cotton.

At the end of the Nile in the north, the river split into several streams that flowed to the Mediterranean Sea. These streams formed an area shaped like a triangle and called the **delta.** The delta contained very fertile farmland.

The Gifts of the Nile   Every spring, far away in the highlands of Africa, waters came rushing down from the highlands. As they flowed, they brought rich, fertile soil called **silt.** Each spring the Nile spilled over its banks. It flooded the dry land and deposited a layer of thick silt that was ideal for farming. In gratitude, the Egyptians praised Hapi (HAH pea), the god of the Nile:

> "Hail to you, O Nile, who flows from the Earth and comes to keep Egypt alive."

Black Land and Red Land   The ancient Egyptians called their land *Kemet* (KEH meht), "the black land," because of the dark soil left by the Nile's floods. The timing of the floods and the height of the flood waters might vary from year to year. But unlike the Mesopotamians, the Egyptians usually did not have to worry about flash floods. Dry years were rare, but they could cause famine.

Program Resources

Nystrom Desk Atlas

Media and Technology

Color Transparencies 92, 93

Daily Life

The Technology of Transportation The earliest Egyptian traders constructed boats made from papyrus reeds. They propelled the boats with the help of poles. In later years, traders used oars to move their boats. By about 3200 B.C., the Egyptians had some sailing boats, and by about 3000 B.C., they had started to build sturdy wooden ships to carry the silver, iron, and horses they obtained in Southwest Asia.

Saving Temples Lake Nasser is a lake created by the building of a dam on the Nile in the 1960s. The creation of Lake Nasser threatened to flood ancient temples that the Egyptians had carved in the cliffs above the Nubian Nile. Egypt, with the help of about 50 nations, saved the temples. Workers cut the temples into blocks. They moved the blocks to higher ground and rebuilt the temples.

Beyond the fertile river banks lay the "red land," the vast desert. It spread out on either side of the river. Most of the Sahara lay to the west, and the part of the Sahara called the Eastern Desert lay to the east. These lands were not friendly to human life. They were useless for farming. Only those who knew the deserts well dared travel over this blistering-hot land.

Yet the hostile deserts were a blessing to the Egyptians and Nubians. The hot sands shielded Egypt and Nubia from foreign attacks. This was a protection Mesopotamia did not have. The land between the Tigris and Euphrates rivers was wide-open to the raids of outsiders. The people of Mesopotamia were constantly facing invasions. Over a period of 2,000 years, the people of ancient Egypt and Nubia faced few invasions. Yet they were not isolated. The Nile Valley provided a path for trade with Central Africa. The Mediterranean Sea and the Red Sea provided access to Southwest Asia.

▼ The thriving crops and vegetation of the fertile Nile Valley contrast with the barren cliffs in the distance.

Although a modern tractor waits at the end of the field, this Egyptian farmer uses oxen and a traditional wooden plow to turn the soil in his field.

Civilizations Along the Nile

Communities appeared in the Nile delta of Lower Egypt by around 4000 B.C. The people of the delta built villages around the fertile river beds. Their homes were built of straw or of bricks made from a mix of mud and straw. To the south, in Upper Egypt, people built scattered farming villages along the banks of the Nile.

The first Nubian communities emerged around 3800 B.C. Because farming was difficult, Nubians also fished in the Nile and hunted ducks and other birds along its banks.

The Growth of Trade

The Nile was a highway for trade. Ships could float downriver because the Nile flowed north. But they could also sail upriver because the winds blew toward the south. Another trade link ran east across the desert and the Red Sea to Mesopotamia. Caravans loaded with gold, silver, copper, and fine pottery traveled the overland trade routes. Valuable goods such as cedar from the eastern coast of the Mediterranean Sea and gold from Nubia were sold in the bazaars of Egypt's towns.

READ ACTIVELY

Visualize Picture in your mind the way the Nile River valley looked before and after the yearly floods.

1. (a) rock-filled rapid in a river (b) an area of rich farmland shaped like a triangle and formed by several streams (c) rich fertile soil carried by rivers

2. (a) Greek historian who tried to find the source of the Nile River (b) region between the First and Second Cataracts of the Nile (c) region between the Second and Sixth Cataracts of the Nile (d) the southern part of ancient Egypt (e) the northern part of ancient Egypt that borders on the Mediterranean Sea

3. Students' answers should include the fact that the annual flooding of the Nile River left fertile land for Egyptians and Nubians to farm.

4. Answers may vary, but should indicate that the Nile was a natural highway for Egyptian boats to sail to other African and Southwest Asian countries for trading.

5. Answers may vary, but should indicate that without flooding, the land would be less fertile, and there would be less farming. This, in turn, would affect the growth and development of communities along the Nile.

6. Journal entries should trace the Nile from its sources: the highlands of Ethiopia for the Blue Nile and Central Africa for the White Nile. The two Niles meet at Khartoum in Sudan and travel through Upper and Lower Egypt as one river.

The Final Voyage

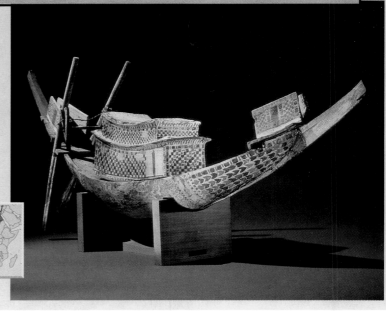

The ancient Egyptians built several kinds of boats for use on the Nile. Boats such as this one have been found in the tombs of Egyptian kings. Royal tombs contained objects that were thought to be needed by the dead—boats would help in making the voyage to the afterlife.

Because of the cataracts, people could not travel through Nubia by river. Instead, the Nubians developed trade routes over land. One of these routes was through the Nile Valley. The Nubians became famous traders of the ancient world as they carried goods from central Africa and Nubia into Egypt and southwestern Asia and back.

One Nubian caravan into Egypt had 300 donkeys. They carried ebony wood, ivory from elephant tusks, ostrich feathers and eggs, and panther skins. Another popular item was a "throw-stick," an African version of a boomerang.

SECTION 1 REVIEW

1. Define (a) cataract, (b) delta, (c) silt.

2. Identify (a) Herodotus, (b) Lower Nubia, (c) Upper Nubia, (d) Upper Egypt, (e) Lower Egypt.

3. How did the Nile River affect the lives of the early Egyptians and Nubians?

4. How did trade develop in various places along the Nile?

Critical Thinking

5. Recognizing Cause and Effect If the Nile River did not flood regularly, how might life along the Nile have been different?

Activity

6. Writing to Learn You are traveling along the Nile from its source to the Nile delta. Write a journal entry about the changes in the river you notice as you travel.

Resource Directory

Teaching Resources

Section Quiz in the Chapter and Section Resources booklet, p. 41, covers the main ideas and key terms in the section. Available in Spanish in the Spanish Chapter and Section Resources booklet, p. 26.

Egypt's Powerful Kings and Queens

BEFORE YOU READ

Reach Into Your Background

What would it be like to have total power over the lives of people? Very few leaders today have such sweeping powers. But at one time, kings and queens had the power of life and death over their people. How would it feel to be responsible for the well-being of thousands of subjects who looked upon you as a god?

Questions to Explore

1. How did Egyptian rulers unify their country?

2. What were some of the accomplishments of Egypt's greatest pharaohs?

Key Terms

pharaoh   regent
dynasty

Key People

Hatshepsut
Menes
Thutmose III

Lesson Objectives

1. Summarize how Egyptian pharaohs unified their country.
2. Explain the power the pharaohs held as political and religious leaders.
3. Describe the achievements of the pharaohs.

Lesson Plan

1 Engage

Warm-Up Activity

Ask students to imagine that one class in their school has no teacher. Even so, this class is still required to pass all the tests given to classes with teachers. Ask students what they think would happen. How might the class work together to pass the tests? How would order be maintained? Do they think students could learn in such a class? Why or why not? Indicate to students that this situation is rather like a country without a president or other strong leader.

Activating Prior Knowledge

Have students read Reach Into Your Background in the Before You Read box. Direct students' discussion so that they consider the problem from the point of view of the all-powerful ruler.

The statue you see here looks like the face of a powerful king of ancient Egypt. And indeed it is. But there's something wrong with this face. You see, there's a woman behind that beard.

The woman is Hatshepsut (haht SHEHP soot), who ruled Egypt during the New Kingdom. Hatshepsut was a bold leader who led her army into battle when enemies threatened Egypt's borders. But she is most known for creating a time of great peace and economic success. She encouraged trade with faraway places, sending a famous expedition to the land of Punt (puhnt) on the east coast of Africa. Egyptian traders returned with shiploads of ivory, gold, and spices.

Hatshepsut was not the only woman to rule Egypt. But the respected title of **pharaoh** (FAIR oh), or king, traditionally referred to a man. For this reason, Hatshepsut appears here with the clothing and symbols of a pharaoh—beard and all.

◀ Hatshepsut declared herself pharaoh of Egypt in 1503 B.C. She ruled with shrewdness and skill until her death.

Teaching Resources

 Reproducible Lesson Plan in the Chapter and Section Resources booklet, p. 42, provides a summary of the section lesson.

Guided Reading and Review in the Chapter and Section Resources booklet, p. 43, provides a structure for mastering key concepts and reviewing key terms in the section. Available in Spanish in the Spanish Chapter and Section Resources booklet, p. 27.

Program Resources

Interdisciplinary Explorations *Riddles of the Pharaohs: Exploring Ancient Egypt*

Media and Technology

Color Transparencies 70, 92

2 Explore

Have students read the section with the following questions in mind: Why were the pharaohs of Egypt so powerful? How did the pharaohs make Egypt strong and prosperous? What happened when a pharaoh was weak? Discuss the accomplishments of the Old, Middle, and New kingdoms.

3 Teach

Organize students into groups of four. Direct them to create an illustrated chart of the dynasties of ancient Egypt and the accomplishments of the pharaohs. This activity should take about 25 minutes.

4 Assess

See the answers to the Section Review. You may also use students' completed charts as an assessment.

Acceptable charts have accurate dates and names and at least one accomplishment of each key pharaoh.

Commendable charts contain additional accomplishments.

Outstanding charts are well-organized, complete, and include cause-and-effect relationships between appropriate events.

CITIZEN HEROES

Overcoming Obstacles A man named Nekhebu worked his way up from the bottom of society to become an architect during the Old Kingdom. At first, he carried other builders' tools for them. Eventually, his hard work paid off. The pharaoh made him Royal Architect. Nekhebu believed in always doing satisfactory work, and in never "going to bed angry against anybody."

▼ This plaque from about 3000 B.C. glorifies events of Menes' reign. At the left of the plaque, Menes looks victoriously on his dead enemies.

Egypt's God-Kings

Hatshepsut was one of many famous Egyptian pharaohs to rule Egypt. Some, like her, were wise. Others were careless or cruel. Egypt's fortunes rested on the strength of its pharaohs.

From Dynasty to Dynasty   The history of ancient Egypt is the history of each of its dynasties. A **dynasty** is a family of rulers. Egypt had 31 dynasties until it was conquered by the Greek ruler Alexander the Great in 332 B.C. Historians group Egypt's dynasties into three main time periods, called kingdoms. The earliest time period is called the Old Kingdom. Next came the Middle Kingdom. The latest time period is called the New Kingdom. The time line on the next page shows the dates of each kingdom. Remember, these kingdoms are not places. They are time periods.

The gaps between the kingdoms were times of troubles—wars, invasions, weak rulers. These in-between periods were rare, however. For most of ancient Egyptian history, there was stable rule.

According to legend, Egypt's first dynasty began when a king named Menes (MEE neez) united Upper and Lower Egypt. Menes built a city named Memphis near the present-day city of Cairo (KY roh). From there, he ruled over the Two Lands, which is what the ancient Egyptians

3000 B.C.	2700 B.C.	2400 B.C.	2100 B.C.	1800 B.C.	1500 B.C.	1200 B.C.

c. 2700 B.C.–2200 B.C.
Old Kingdom

2050 B.C.–1800 B.C.
Middle Kingdom

1550 B.C.–1100 B.C.
New Kingdom

OLD KINGDOM

c. 2600 B.C. Builders begin Great Pyramid.

c. 2550 B.C. Statue of Sphinx built at Giza.

MIDDLE KINGDOM

c. 1991 B.C.–1800 B.C. Egypt expands into Lower Nubia.

c. 1991 B.C.–1800 B.C. Literature and art flourish.

c. 1878 B.C.–1840 B.C. Senusret III strengthens government.

NEW KINGDOM

c. 1503 B.C.–1482 B.C. Queen Hatshepsut rules.

1361 B.C.–1351 B.C. King Tut rules.

1290 B.C.–1224 B.C. Ramses II expands Egyptian territory.

c. 750 B.C.–660 B.C. Nubian pharaohs rule Egypt.

▲ **Time Line Study** This time line shows the dates for each kingdom and lists important events and accomplishments of the kingdoms.

called Upper and Lower Egypt. Carvings from Menes's time show the pharaoh wearing two crowns—the white crown of Upper Egypt and the red crown of Lower Egypt. The uniting of Egypt began one of the most stable civilizations in history. It lasted for more than 2,500 years.

All-Powerful Pharaohs   The pharaohs had absolute power over their people. Whatever the pharaoh decided became law. He decided when the fields would be planted. He received crops from the workers on his estates.

The pharaoh was also a religious leader. It was the pharaoh, Egyptians believed, who provided his people with the Nile's yearly floods and the harvests that followed. As one official wrote:

> "He is the god Re whose beams enable us to see. He gives more light to the Two Lands than the sun's disc. He makes the Earth more green than the Nile in flood. He has filled the Two Lands with strength and life."

Two Thousand Years of Power

Egypt grew and prospered during its first six dynasties, which included the Old Kingdom. It was blessed with able rulers and a well-run system of government. The pharaohs kept the peace and trade with Nubia, with only occasional conflicts. They sent merchants to the eastern coast of the Mediterranean to find timber. This timber was used in the building of houses, boats, and furniture. Egyptian merchants may have even traveled north across the Mediterranean in search of trade items.

About 2250 B.C., near the end of the Old Kingdom, governors in the provinces began to challenge the power of the pharaohs' government. Egypt's unity crumbled, and the dynasties grew weak.

READ ACTIVELY

Connect Compare the role of the Egyptian pharaoh with the role of the President of the United States.

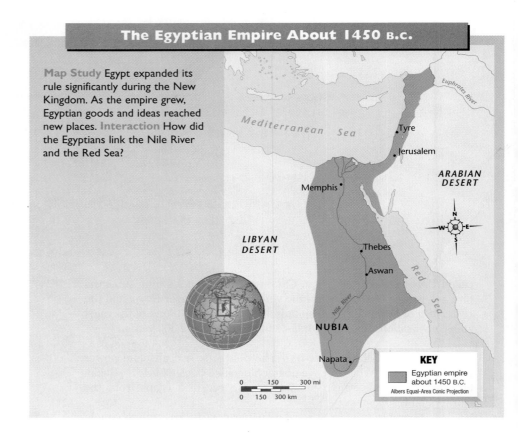

The Egyptian Empire About 1450 B.C.

Map Study Egypt expanded its rule significantly during the New Kingdom. As the empire grew, Egyptian goods and ideas reached new places. **Interaction** How did the Egyptians link the Nile River and the Red Sea?

KEY
Egyptian empire about 1450 B.C.

Albers Equal-Area Conic Projection

The early dynasties of the Middle Kingdom restored order and reunited the country. With calmer times, the pharaohs spent the nation's wealth on works such as irrigation projects instead of on wars. They also built a canal between the Nile and the Red Sea. Egypt grew even richer. However, less able rulers followed. In time, they lost control of the country to foreign invaders.

Egyptian princes became strong enough to drive out the foreign invaders around 1550 B.C. This event marks the start of the New Kingdom.

The first pharaohs of the New Kingdom were not content just to drive foreigners out of their country. They wanted to build an empire. The pharaohs created huge armies of foot soldiers, mounted warriors, and war chariots. Bronze swords and body armor made the Egyptians nearly unbeatable.

A Powerful Queen, a Great Pharaoh

Around 1500 B.C., a child named Thutmose III (thoot MOH suh) became pharaoh. Because of his youth, his stepmother was appointed **regent**. A regent is someone who rules for a child until the child is old enough to rule. His stepmother was Hatshepsut, whom you read about at the beginning of this section. Not content to be regent, Hatshepsut had herself proclaimed pharaoh. She ruled Egypt for about 22 years.

Hatshepsut's reign was good for Egypt. She apparently enjoyed her power, too. When Thutmose grew up, she refused to yield the throne to him. He took over when she died and had all her statues destroyed. We don't know if Thutmose had a hand in Hatshepsut's death.

Thutmose III was one of the greatest pharaohs of the New Kingdom. He led his army in wars against Syria and Phoenicia, in Southwest Asia. Egyptian troops advanced as far east as the Euphrates River and south into Nubia. Yet Thutmose was more than a conqueror. He was an educated man who loved to study plants. Unlike most rulers of his time, he treated defeated peoples with mercy.

▼ Queen Hatshepsut's temple at the foot of a dramatic limestone cliff in Dayr al-Bahri, Egypt, is one of the masterpieces of New Kingdom architecture.

Activity

Journal Writing

Assessing the Pharaohs Suggest that students further research one of the pharaohs discussed in this section or do some reading about another important ruler such as Akhenaton, Cleopatra, Khufu, Ramses II, Ptolemy I, or Seti I. In their journals, have students write an assessment of the ruler's strengths and weaknesses and of his or her contributions to Egyptian life and culture.

Background

Biography

Tutankhamen (reigned 1333–1323 B.C.) After Thutmose, another, even more famous child ruled Egypt. Tutankhamen reigned as pharaoh from the age of nine until his death at 18. Tutankhamen was probably the son of Akhenaton. After Akhenaton's death, priests forced the boy-king to declare Amon-Re the chief god of Egypt. The boy-king was then worshipped as the living form of Amon-Re. His presence in the temple was needed twice a day to give thanks for the rising and setting of the sun. Some historians believe Tutankhamen was murdered by those seeking to replace him.

1. (a) ruler of Egypt (b) family of rulers (c) someone who rules for a child until the child is old enough to rule

2. (a) regent for Thutmose III who declared herself pharaoh (b) the first pharaoh; according to legend, he united Upper and Lower Egypt (c) one of the greatest pharaohs of the New Kingdom

3. Because people believed the pharaoh was a god on the Earth, he or she received the respect and fear of the people. This meant that the pharaohs had total power over the government, economy, and military of Egypt.

4. The Old Kingdom was a time of peace, prosperity, and able rulers. Near the end, though, governors challenged the power of the pharaohs, and the kingdom grew weak. The Middle Kingdom restored order, united the country, and completed irrigation projects. The New Kingdom drove foreigners out of the country, created huge armies, and began building an empire.

5. Egypt's pharaohs were considered gods and had complete authority over their people. Most people today would not accept the idea of a "god-king."

6. Explanations should include the idea that strong pharaohs brought peace and prosperity, while weak pharaohs invited corruption, invasion, and social disorder.

Cleopatra: A Woman of Ambition

Cleopatra ruled Egypt from 69 B.C. to 30 B.C. The Egyptian carving (right) shows Cleopatra and Isis, a popular Egyptian goddess. Cleopatra, however, was not content to be queen of just Egypt. She wanted to rule the Roman Empire—and she almost succeeded. Cleopatra gained so much influence in Rome that her likeness appeared on roman coins (below).

The New Kingdom began to decline around 1075 B.C. Civil war left Egypt weak and poorly defended. The mighty kingdom fell to the famous conqueror Alexander the Great in 332 B.C. About 300 years later, Egypt was conquered by another powerful civilization of the ancient world: the Romans. Egypt became part of the Roman Empire. It would not govern itself again for almost 2,000 years.

SECTION 2 REVIEW

1. Define (a) pharaoh, (b) dynasty, (c) regent.

2. Identify (a) Hatshepsut, (b) Menes, (c) Thutmose III.

3. How did Egypt's rulers govern their empire?

4. Describe some of the accomplishments of each of the three Egyptian kingdoms.

Critical Thinking

5. Expressing Problems Clearly Explain why Egypt's rulers had more authority than most rulers have today.

Activity

6. Writing to Learn Write a paragraph explaining this statement: "Ancient Egypt was strongest when its rulers were strong."

Resource Directory

Teaching Resources

Section Quiz in the Chapter and Section Resources booklet, p. 44, covers the main ideas and key terms in the section. Available in Spanish in the Spanish Chapter and Section Resources booklet, p. 28.

Egyptian Religion

SECTION 3

Section 3

BEFORE YOU READ

Reach Into Your Background

Have you ever tried to organize your friends or family to take a trip or to do something around the house?

If so, you've probably realized that getting people to do something together sounds easier than it actually is. People have their own opinions. It takes special skills to get the best work out of people. What do you think those skills are?

Questions to Explore

1. What role did religion play in ancient Egypt?

2. How did the Egyptians manage to build the pyramids without knowledge of the wheel?

Key Terms

afterlife
mummy

pyramid

Key Places

Giza

> "You will live again. You will live forever. Behold, you will be young forever."

The priest chanted the words as the royal family wept over the body of their most important member, the pharaoh. One hundred days had passed since he had died. During this time, the royal officials had worked on his body. After wrapping the body in many strips of fine linen, they placed the king in a gold-covered coffin. It was decorated to resemble the man in all of his royal glory.

The Egyptians believed in an **afterlife**, a life after death. With each step of the funeral, there were prayers to help the pharaoh's soul on the way to the afterlife. Then the nobles and royal family followed the body as it was carried to the royal tomb. Workers closed the tomb and the mourners went home. The pharaoh's journey to the afterlife had begun.

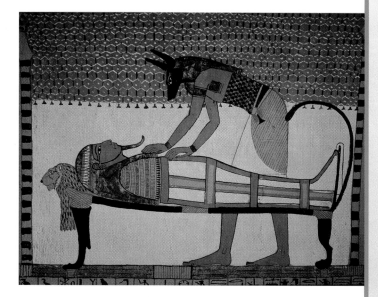

▼ The Egyptian god of the dead, Anubis, tends a dead pharaoh. According to myth, Anubis invented mummification.

Teaching Resources

📁 **Reproducible Lesson Plan** in the Chapter and Section Resources booklet, p. 45, provides a summary of the section lesson.

📁 **Guided Reading and Review** in the Chapter and Section Resources booklet, p. 46, provides a structure for mastering key concepts and reviewing key terms in the section. Available in Spanish in the Spanish Chapter and Section Resources booklet, p. 29.

Media and Technology

🖵 **Color Transparency** 92

Lesson Objectives

1. Describe the importance of religion and the afterlife to ancient Egyptians.

2. Determine the reasons Egyptians made mummies and constructed pyramids.

3. Explain how Egyptians used technology and organization to build the pyramids.

Lesson Plan

1 Engage

Warm-Up Activity

Suggest that students work with a partner to make a chart listing what they know about Egyptian gods and mummies, and why and how the pyramids were built. Then have them write three questions they wish to have answered as they read.

Activating Prior Knowledge

Have students read Reach Into Your Background in the Before You Read box. Ask them to describe how they would organize a group of people to move a huge stone from one place to another. Tell students to suppose that they do not have the assistance of trucks, elevators, cranes, or forklifts. How would they accomplish the task without using machines that have engines?

SECTION 3 73

2 Explore

After students read the section, discuss the Egyptians' beliefs about the afterlife. What were their reasons for mummifying dead people? For building the pyramids? Review the processes of mummification and of building pyramids as described in the text.

3 Teach

Organize students to work in small groups. Each group should prepare a three-minute television news brief. Allow groups to choose from the following topics: Egyptian gods, the afterlife, mummies, tombs, and pyramids. Remind students that their news briefs should include pictures or illustrations. This activity should take about 30 minutes.

4 Assess

See the answers to the Section Review. You may also use students' completed news briefs as an assessment.

Acceptable news briefs cover the information from the text.

Commendable reports include information on the who, what, where, when, and how of the topic.

Outstanding reports include factual information from the text as well as original ideas supported by facts.

READ ACTIVELY

Predict Why do you think the afterlife was so important to the Egyptians? What do you think people did to prepare the dead for the afterlife?

▶Amon-Re's name meant "the hidden one." Some Egyptians believed that Amon-Re watched over and judged all human affairs from an unknown, hidden place.

Religion in Egyptian Life

For the people of ancient Egypt, religion was an important part of daily life. It was the way people explained the workings of nature. Why was there an unexpected long period without rain? What caused sickness and death? The Egyptians believed that only magical spirits could control these events. So they tried to please these spirits, their gods.

Each part of Egypt had its own gods and goddesses who had their own temples. The gods of Upper Egypt were different from those of Lower Egypt. Over the centuries, however, ancient Egyptians came to believe in several groups of gods. These included gods who were often shown as humans with animal heads. Among them was Osiris (oh SY rihs), the god of the living and the dead.

The chief god of the ancient Egyptians was Amon-Re. He protected the rich and the poor. The Egyptians believed that Amon-Re was born each morning in the east and died each evening in the west. That is why the west was believed to be the home of the dead. Egyptians preferred not to be on the west bank of the Nile after nightfall because they believed the spirits of the dead lived there.

According to Egyptian belief, Osiris, the god of the afterlife, had a family. Isis (EYE sihs), one of the most powerful of all Egyptian goddesses, was his wife. The god of the sky, Horus (HOH ruhs), was his son. Egyptians worshipped Isis as the great mother who protected the health of her children. In Egyptian art, Isis and Osiris are often shown together.

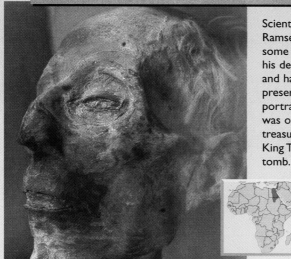

Scientists unwrapped the mummy of Ramses II and found that, although some 3,000 years had passed since his death, his facial structure and hair remained well preserved (left). The gold portrait mask (right) was one of many treasures found in King Tutankhamen's tomb.

Background

Links Across Time

Treasures Unearthed In 1922, an Egyptologist named Howard Carter discovered a buried staircase that led to a sealed tomb. When the tomb was opened, Carter and others in his party found fantastic treasures—items made of gold, alabaster, ebony, and precious stones. Within the burial chamber was the greatest treasure—the mummified body of King Tutankhamen, the 18-year-old boy-king, encased in three nested coffins. The outer two were wooden, but the innermost coffin was made of solid gold.

Life Ever After

The ancient Egyptians believed the spirits of the dead made their way to the afterlife in heavenly boats. Once there, if they lived right in this life, they joined with Osiris and lived a life of ease and pleasure. They spent their days meeting and eating and drinking with their friends and family who had died. The souls of the dead could not survive without food, clothing, and other items from this life, however. The Egyptians took care of this by burying the dead with the possessions they had enjoyed in life. A pharaoh's tomb could contain everything from sandals to furniture to even his favorite horse.

Egyptians believed that if bodies were preserved, or made into **mummies,** the spirit would exist in the afterlife. The bodies of important people, usually royalty, were mummified. The process took two or three months. Workers carefully removed the organs. The body was then filled with a natural salt and stored for at least 42 days. During that time, it completely dried out.

Once dry, the body was cleaned and bathed in spices. Then it was wrapped with long linen bandages. Arms and legs were bandaged tightly to the body. A well-wrapped mummy had up to 20 layers of bandages.

While workers were preparing the mummy, artisans were busy carving the coffin. Actually, there were more than one of these wooden coffins. A pharaoh had three or four coffins. The coffins fit one inside the other like a nest of boxes. The innermost coffin was usually shaped like a human body, with the dead person's face painted on the cover.

LINKS ACROSS THE WORLD

A King With One God Akhenaton (ah kuh NAH tuhn), who became pharaoh in 1353 B.C., gave up the old gods. He had their names chipped off temples. Like the Israelites, Akhenaton worshipped only one god. His god was Aton, the life-giving disk of the sun. The Egyptian people did not accept this monotheism. After the king's death, they went back to worshipping many gods.

SKILLS MINI LESSON

Locating Information
You might **introduce** the skill by indicating to students that there is more to know about making a mummy than is presented in the text. Ask students how they would find more information on making a mummy. Help students **practice** the skill by working with them to make a list of possible subjects and places to search for information. Record their suggestions on the chalkboard. To **apply** the skill, have partners draft one question about mummies that they would like to have answered. Direct students to keep track of where they look for information and to record which locations supply the information they need. Invite students to share their questions, the answers they found, and their search techniques with the class.

Peering Into a Pyramid

Allow students a few minutes to study the diagram of the pyramid. Be sure students understand that the diagram is a cutaway, which permits them to see the interior of the pyramid.

Review with students the tools the Egyptians used to build the pyramids. Then help students use the diagram to consider how such tools were used. Ask students why they think the pyramid, which was used as a tomb, would contain air passages and escape passageways. (People constructing the interior of the pyramid needed to breathe and needed a way to get out.)

Help students visualize the size of the Grand Gallery by telling them that 151 feet (50 m) is about the width of a football field and that 28 feet (9 m) is about the height of a three-story building. Ask students to use information from the diagram to write an assessment of the level of ingenuity and the technological skill of the ancient Egyptians.

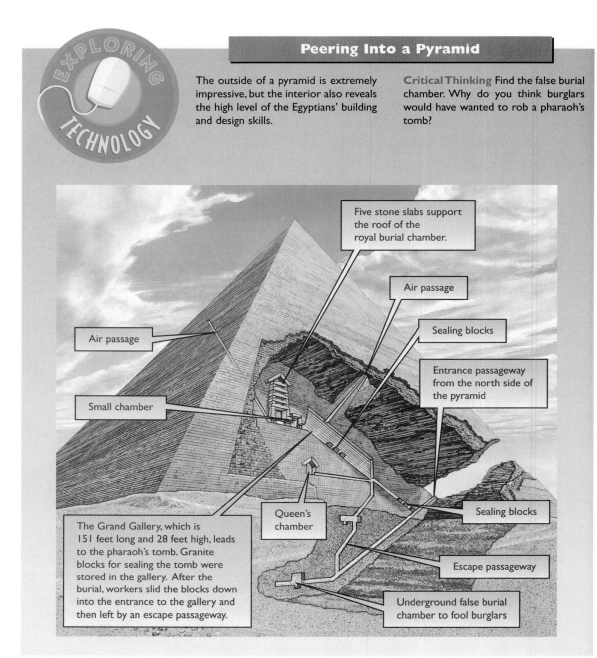

EXPLORING TECHNOLOGY

Peering Into a Pyramid

The outside of a pyramid is extremely impressive, but the interior also reveals the high level of the Egyptians' building and design skills.

Critical Thinking Find the false burial chamber. Why do you think burglars would have wanted to rob a pharaoh's tomb?

Five stone slabs support the roof of the royal burial chamber.

Air passage

Sealing blocks

Entrance passageway from the north side of the pyramid

Air passage

Small chamber

Sealing blocks

The Grand Gallery, which is 151 feet long and 28 feet high, leads to the pharaoh's tomb. Granite blocks for sealing the tomb were stored in the gallery. After the burial, workers slid the blocks down into the entrance to the gallery and then left by an escape passageway.

Queen's chamber

Escape passageway

Underground false burial chamber to fool burglars

Tombs for the Pharaohs

The planning for a pharaoh's tomb began as soon as he was crowned. The earliest royal tombs were made of mud brick. However, as time went on, tomb building became an art. The pharaohs of the

Answers to . . .

PEERING INTO A PYRAMID

Pharaohs were always buried with their possessions, many of which were very valuable.

Fourth Dynasty built the largest and most famous tombs of all. These were the **pyramids,** huge buildings with four sloping outside walls shaped like triangles.

Most of the pyramids were built during the Old Kingdom. The largest is the Great Pyramid. It is one of several enormous monuments at a site called Giza. Find Giza on the map at the beginning of this chapter.

Building the pyramids required a great deal of organization. The Great Pyramid, for example, is made up of more than 2 million stones. The average weight of each stone is 5,000 pounds (2,270 kg). Each stone had to be hauled up the side and put into its right place.

It could take 20 or more years to build a pyramid. The project began with the selection of a site on the west bank of the Nile. Remember that the west bank was the land of the dead. Once the site was chosen, workers cleared the ground. Engineers set the pyramid square so that the sides faced the main points of the compass—north, south, east, and west.

Workers then cut the building blocks. Stone for the inner parts of the pyramids came from nearby quarries. But fine stone for the outside came from farther away. Some came all the way from Nubia. It had to be loaded onto barges and carried along the Nile or canals near the Nile to the building site.

READ ACTIVELY

Visualize What do you think the building site of a half-finished pyramid looked like? How many workers do you think were needed to push the huge blocks of stone up ramps?

Activity

Journal Writing

On the Death of Pharaohs Suggest that students write a journal entry from the point of view of an Egyptian worker who is building the tomb of a pharaoh. Ask students to record what their thoughts and feelings would be as they toiled to prepare the pharaoh's final resting place.

▼ The Great Pyramid (center) is one of 10 located in Giza, Egypt. It stands about 450 feet (140 m) tall.

1. (a) the next life (b) a preserved body (c) a large structure with four triangular faces

2. site of the Great Pyramid

3. The Egyptian religion claimed that the dead would live on forever in a world of ease and pleasure.

4. Students' answers may vary, but should mention that the tombs were furnished with belongings and personal items such as sandals and gloves.

5. Answers may vary. Students may suggest that engineers needed to know how to use levers to lift stones and ramps on which to transport the heavy blocks of stone. The process could take 20 years. Archaeological evidence of work villages near the pyramids indicates that long-term arrangements for workers were made.

6. Answers may vary. Answers may include descriptions of stones being hauled to the site and of workers using sleds, wooden rollers, and levers to pull the blocks up ramps alongside the pyramid. Students should mention that Egyptians believed in an afterlife, and they thought preserving the body through mummification helped ensure that the soul would make it to the next life.

For a Pharaoh's Last Voyage

This large boat was discovered in the Great Pyramid. It was made of wood from cedar trees. Pharaohs were buried with boats so they could make the voyage to the afterlife.

At this time, the ancient Egyptians did not use the wheel. To get the blocks of stone into place, workers had to use sleds, wooden rollers, and levers. They dragged and pushed the huge blocks up ramps of packed rubble to the level they were working on.

Workers toiled all year either in the quarries or at the pyramid site. They had to be fed at least twice a day. Archaeologists have found the remains of their villages. They know that the builders of the pyramids ate huge quantities of wheat bread. Archaeologists actually found the remains of a bakery among grave sites of the workers.

Building pyramids was dangerous work. Each year, men lost their lives, crushed by falling blocks. But the workers believed in the importance of their work. To build a pyramid was an act of faith. It was a way of ensuring the pharaoh's place in the afterlife.

SECTION 3 REVIEW

1. **Define** (a) afterlife, (b) mummy, (c) pyramid.

2. **Identify** Giza.

3. How did the religion of the ancient Egyptians explain what happened to a person after death?

4. How was a pharaoh's tomb furnished?

Critical Thinking

5. **Expressing Problems Clearly** Describe how the ancient Egyptians organized the building of the pyramids.

Activity

6. **Writing to Learn** The pharaoh invites you to go with him to inspect his pyramid as it is being built. Write a journal entry describing what you see on your visit. What does the project tell about Egyptian religious beliefs? What does it tell about their skills in engineering?

Resource Directory

Teaching Resources

Section Quiz in the Chapter and Section Resources booklet, p. 47, covers the main ideas and key terms in the section. Available in Spanish in the Spanish Chapter and Section Resources booklet, p. 30.

The Culture of the Ancient Egyptians

BEFORE YOU READ

Reach Into Your Background

Imagine writing a school report or a letter to a friend using pictures instead of letters. A picture of an eye could stand for the letter *i*. A wavy line (a wave on the *sea*) could stand for the letter *c*. When you put them together you form the word *icy*. This is similar to the idea behind Egyptian picture writing.

Questions to Explore

1. How did the Egyptians live their daily lives?

2. What scientific contributions did the Egyptians make?

Key Terms

hieroglyph
papyrus
astronomer

Key People

Jean François Champollion

His name was Uni, and he was an Egyptian noble of the Old Kingdom. His life story—a success story—is recorded in his tomb.

Uni began his career in a simple way—running a storehouse. Later, he moved up the ladder to groundskeeper of the royal pyramid. In this job, he oversaw the quarrying and delivery of stone for the pyramid. Uni must have worked hard, because later he was made a general. Then, he became Governor of Upper Egypt, in charge of goods and taxes for half the kingdom. By the time of his death, we learn that Uni was royal tutor at the palace and an honored companion of the pharaoh.

Everyday Life of the Ancient Egyptians

Most of what we know of the everyday life of the Egyptians is based on paintings that cover the walls of tombs and temples. These paintings show royalty and ordinary people involved in all aspects of life. Written records also tell us much about their lives. Like Uni, they were busy and hard-working people. They also had a sense of fun and a love of beauty.

▼ Meri, a noble of the fourth dynasty, had his tomb carved with writings and with scenes of his life. Over the centuries, the paint has worn off the carvings.

Linteau et montant de porte provenant du tombeau du fonctionnaire MERI. Sakkara   IVe dynastie

---

Teaching Resources

📁 **Reproducible Lesson Plan** in the Chapter and Section Resources booklet, p. 48, provides a summary of the section lesson.

📁 **Guided Reading and Review** in the Chapter and Section Resources booklet, p. 49, provides a structure for mastering key concepts and reviewing key terms in the section. Available in Spanish in the Spanish Chapter and Section Resources booklet, p. 31.

Lesson Objectives

❶ Explain the everyday lives of Egyptians of all classes.

❷ Appreciate Egypt's achievements in writing, mathematics, astronomy, and medicine.

❸ Describe hieroglyphics and how they were deciphered.

Lesson Plan

1 Engage

Warm-Up Activity

Allow students to preview the section by looking at the photos. If feasible, supplement these views of Egyptian life with other illustrations showing hunting, fishing, farmwork, nobles, scribes, dress, hairstyles, and so on. Invite students to discuss what the pictures show about Egyptian life.

Activating Prior Knowledge

Have students read Reach Into Your Background in the Before You Read box. Demonstrate a rebus that uses letters and pictures to tell a story. You may want to allow students to write their own short messages using pictures rather than words.

2 Explore

Have students read the section. Ask them to identify the different classes of Egyptian society. Then have them create a pyramid showing the class structure as described in the text. Ask about the roles women took. Discuss what students have learned about hieroglyphics. How were these symbols translated? Why was it important to have a written language? What important contributions to astronomy and medicine did the Egyptians make?

3 Teach

Invite groups of students to make up a short play about daily life in ancient Egypt. Encourage students to present all social classes as they act out their play. Students should show how members of different social classes interacted. This activity should take about 30 minutes.

Social Classes Egyptian society itself resembled a pyramid. At the very top stood the pharaoh. Beneath him was a small upper class. This group included priests, members of the pharaoh's court, and nobles who held the largest estates. The next level was the middle class, made up of merchants and skilled workers. At the base of the pyramid was by far the largest class, the peasants. Mostly, the peasants did farm labor. But they also did other kinds of labor, such as building roads and temples. A person could even rise to a higher class. Generally, the way to rise was through service to the pharaoh, as Uni knew.

Prisoners captured in wars were made slaves. Slaves formed a separate class, which was never very large. Egyptian society was flexible, however. Even slaves had rights. They could own personal items and inherit land from their masters. They could also be set free.

Lives of the Peasants Although peasants could own land, most worked the land of wealthier people. During the season of the flood, the peasants worked on roads, temples, and other buildings. As soon as the waters left the land, the fields had to be planted. This had to be done quickly while the soil was still moist. One farmer plowed the black earth with a team of oxen while another followed behind, scattering the seeds.

▼ These wooden figures depict workers in a bakery. The carved scene was found in a tomb. **Critical Thinking** Why do you think such scenes are useful to archaeologists?

Answers to ...

CRITICAL THINKING

because the scenes help archaeologists learn about life in ancient Egypt

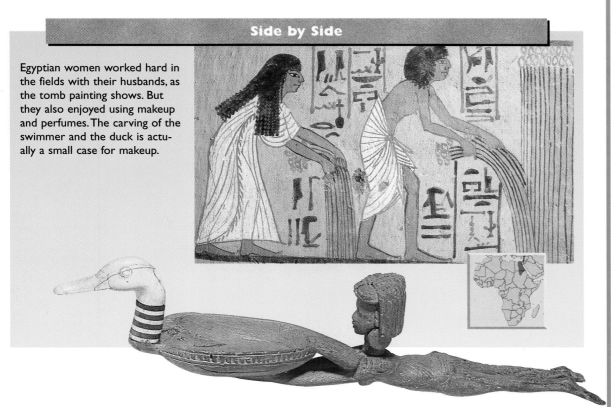

Egyptian women worked hard in the fields with their husbands, as the tomb painting shows. But they also enjoyed using makeup and perfumes. The carving of the swimmer and the duck is actually a small case for makeup.

The harvest was the busiest season for Egypt's peasants. All men, women, and older children went into the fields to gather the crops of wheat or barley. Work went on from sunrise to sunset. Once the crops were gathered, the villagers feasted. Everyone made sure to offer food and drink to the gods in thanks for their help.

Egyptian Women: An Active Role   Egyptian women were looked upon as living models of Isis, the wife of Osiris. They had most of the rights that men had. They could own property, run businesses, and enter into legal contracts. For the most part, women traveled about freely. Egyptian paintings often show them supervising farm work or hunting. And women had many occupations—from priestess to dancer.

Noble women held a special position in Egyptian society. Sometimes they were in charge of temples and religious rites. They could also use their position to influence the pharaoh. Some women acted as regents until the pharaoh was old enough to rule on his own.

Achievements of the Egyptians

From the records of the ancient Egyptians, we know that they possessed an amazing amount of knowledge. They made important advances in such fields as writing, astronomy, and medicine. Among the people of the ancient world, Egypt was known as a land of great learning.

READ ACTIVELY

Connect What American holiday do we celebrate as a day of giving thanks? How is that holiday similar or different from the Egyptians' harvest feast?

4 Assessment

See the answers to the Section Review. You may also use students' plays as an assessment.

Acceptable plays include roles for all members of the social classes.

Commendable plays include roles for all members of the social classes and show through the interaction of the characters an understanding of class relationships.

Outstanding plays include roles for all members of the social classes and women and show through the interaction of the characters an excellent understanding of class relationships.

Background

Daily Life

Fashion Noblewomen of Egypt generally wore fitted linen dresses and linen shawls. Often, they wore adornments such as beaded collars and gold earrings, necklaces, and headpieces set with semiprecious stones. They wore perfumed, braided wigs to protect themselves from the blazing sun. At social events, noblewomen often wore small perfumed cones of fat atop their wigs. As the fat melted, the perfume filled the room. The fat dripped down onto their faces and bodies, softening the skin.

Language Arts Have students use the Egyptian hieroglyphic alphabet shown in the text to write their first names. Students may have to omit some letters of their names, as not all letters can be represented by hieroglyphs. Students might wish to make a personal cartouche. A cartouche is an oblong frame containing a name. Students may spell out their names using markers or paint. Create a bulletin board or wall display of the completed cartouches. *English Language Learner, Visual*

Daily Life

Sacred Cats One ancient cemetery in Egypt contains nearly 300,000 mummies—of cats! Around the year 1500 B.C., Egyptians began to worship cats. Cats were the fond pets of many an Egyptian family. But cats were useful, too. They patrolled grain storehouses and kept the rodent population at bay. Because the cat was sacred, killing a cat was a capital crime. When a pet cat died, its owners shaved off their own eyebrows as a sign of mourning.

Answers to . . .

CHART STUDY

Answers might include man, seem, me, seat, battle, cat, and teeth.

Writing in Egypt

Hieroglyphs

A		P	
AH		F	
AY		M	or
EE		N	
U		L	
B		H	
H		Q	
KH		K	
S		T	
S		DT	
SH		TH	
K		TCH	

To write on papyrus, Egyptian scribes used long, thin, reed brushes. Their ink was a mixture of water and soot, a black powder left from burned wood. **Chart Study** The chart to the left gives some hieroglyphs and the sounds that they stood for. What are some English words you could spell using the hieroglyphs in the chart?

READ ACTIVELY

Ask Questions What would you like to know about the achievements of the Egyptians?

A New System of Writing In ancient Egypt, as in Mesopotamia, ideas were written down in picture-like symbols called **hieroglyphs** (HY ur oh glifs). In this script, some pictures stand for ideas or things. For example, two legs means *go*. Other pictures stand for sounds. For example, a drawing of an owl stands for *m*, as in *mother*.

The Egyptians began to use hieroglyphs because they needed a better way to keep track of the kingdom's growing wealth. As the Egyptian empire grew, it became necessary to create more pictures for more complicated ideas.

At first, the Egyptians wrote on clay and stone, as the Sumerians did. But they needed more convenient writing surfaces. They found it in **papyrus** (puh PY ruhs), an early form of paper made from a reed-like plant found in the marshy areas of the Nile delta. They first cut the stalks of the plant into narrow slivers. Then they soaked the slivers and pounded them flat. Left out in the air to dry, the pieces of papyrus became stiff. Joined side by side, the pieces formed a long roll.

Unlocking a Mystery   The meaning of ancient Egypt's hieroglyphic writing was lost after the A.D. 400s. Scholars could not read the mysterious pictures. It wasn't until about 200 years ago, in 1799, that an important find took place. A soldier digging a fort near the Nile found a large black stone with three different types of writing on it. The upper part showed hieroglyphs, the middle part showed a different form of hieroglyphs, and the lower part showed Greek letters. This stone is called the Rosetta Stone because it was found near Rosetta, a city in the Nile delta near the Mediterranean Sea.

Many scholars tried to use the Greek letters on the Rosetta Stone to figure out the meaning of the hieroglyphs. But it was not an easy task. Then, in the 1820s, a young French scholar named Jean François Champollion (zhahn frahn SWAH shahm poh LYOHN) finally figured it out. When Champollion published his results, a new window onto the world of the ancient Egyptians opened.

Keeping Track of Time   Because they were an agricultural people, the Egyptians needed to be able to predict when the Nile would flood. This was the work of Egyptian **astronomers,** scientists who study the stars and other objects in the sky. They noticed that the Nile appeared to rise rapidly about the same time that they could see Sirius (SIHR ee us), the Dog Star, in the sky shortly before sunrise. They worked out the average time between the appearances of the star. They found that it came to 365 days. This became the length of their year.

LINKS TO MATH

Measurement Some units of measurement used by the Egyptians were based on the human body. The cubit was the distance from an elbow to the tip of the fingers. Of course, this length varied from person to person, so the Egyptians made a standard cubit out of black granite. The Egyptians used their accurate measuring system to build the Great Pyramid.

▼ ▶ The Rosetta Stone honored King Ptolemy V. The hieroglyphs circled by the ring below spell his name. This name and others were the key to finding the meaning of hieroglyphs.

Section 4 Review

1. (a) a symbol or picture that stands for an idea, thing, or sound (b) paper made from a reed with that name (c) a scientist who studies the stars and other objects in the sky

2. French scholar who translated the Egyptian hieroglyphics on the Rosetta Stone

3. The peasants could not plant crops until after the annual summer flooding of the Nile. Then they had to work in the harvest season.

4. Egyptian astronomers predicted the annual flooding of the Nile. Egyptians also knew how to set broken bones and perform surgery. They made medicines from plants.

5. Students' answers may vary, but should include writing (hieroglyphics) and the use of papyrus. These were important because they enabled the Egyptians to keep records.

6. Students' paragraphs should mention that a scribe's work kept track of the pharaoh's wealth or recorded the pharaoh's laws and decrees and important events. Hieroglyphics should show an appropriate word for a scribe to use.

A King's Treasures

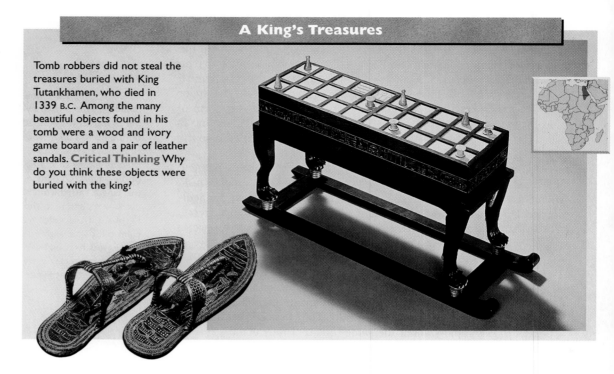

Tomb robbers did not steal the treasures buried with King Tutankhamen, who died in 1339 B.C. Among the many beautiful objects found in his tomb were a wood and ivory game board and a pair of leather sandals. **Critical Thinking** Why do you think these objects were buried with the king?

Medicine   Probably because of their work on mummies, the ancient Egyptians knew a great deal about the body. By studying the body, they learned to perform surgery. They could set broken bones and treat injuries of the spine.

The Egyptians also practiced herbalism, the art of creating medicines from plants. They used these natural remedies to help ease everyday illnesses such as stomachaches and headaches. Mothers prepared their own home remedies to reduce a child's fever. The Egyptians wrote much of their medical knowledge down on papyrus. The ancient Greeks and Romans used these records centuries later.

SECTION 4 REVIEW

1. Define   (a) hieroglyph, (b) papyrus, (c) astronomer.

2. Identify   Jean François Champollion.

3. How were the lives of Egypt's peasants ruled by the seasons?

4. What contributions did the Egyptians make in medicine and astronomy?

Critical Thinking

5. Drawing Conclusions What do you think were the two most important developments of ancient Egyptian culture? Explain your reasoning.

Activity

6. Writing to Learn   You are a scribe at the court of the pharaoh. In a paragraph, describe how you use your skill in his service. Then, use the chart of hieroglyphs in this section to create a word you might have used as a scribe.

Resource Directory

Teaching Resources

Section Quiz in the Chapter and Section Resources booklet, p. 50, covers the main ideas and key terms in the section. Available in Spanish in the Spanish Chapter and Section Resources booklet, p. 32.

Critical Thinking Activity in the Chapter and Section Resources booklet, p. 46, helps students apply the skill of drawing conclusions.

The Resource-Rich Cultures of Nubia

Lesson Objectives

1. Describe the relationship between Nubia and Egypt.

2. Compare and contrast the two civilizations.

3. Trace the developments and achievements of the Nubian kingdoms of Kerma, Napata, and Meroë.

BEFORE YOU READ

Reach Into Your Background

Have you ever been friends with a classmate one week and then rivals the next? How did this affect your relationship with that person?

Questions to Explore

1. What were the achievements of Nubian civilizations?

2. How did the kingdom of Meroë use iron to become rich?

Key Terms

artisan

Key People and Places

Taharka
Kerma
Napata
Meroë

Prince Taharka of Nubia loved a good contest. He once held a 5-hour, 30-mile race across the desert. The athletes, Taharka's soldiers, ran at night to avoid the blazing heat. In the end, he gave prizes to the winners and losers alike.

In 690 B.C., Taharka himself received the ultimate prize: He was to be crowned king of both Nubia and Egypt. Taharka's father, Piye (PEE yeh), had conquered the mighty Egyptians. Now, Taharka was about to inherit this double kingdom. He would become the greatest ruler of his dynasty.

As the kingdom prepared for Taharka's crowning ceremony, what did the powerful warrior do? Like any good son, he invited his mom. And she came, traveling 1,200 miles from Nubia north to Memphis for the big celebration. The king wrote proudly, "She was thrilled to see me upon the throne of Egypt!"

Egypt's Friend and Rival

Taharka's homeland of Nubia was the birthplace of fascinating civilizations. An advanced culture

▼ The pharaoh Taharka of Nubia is shown offering two cups to a god. He is named in the Bible as a warlike and powerful ruler.

Lesson Plan

1 Engage

Warm-Up Activity

With students, locate ancient Nubia on the regional map and follow the course of the Nile River through Nubia. Then locate the region on a modern map and show how it stretches from Khartoum in Sudan to Aswan in Egypt. Discuss how the location of Nubia between Central Africa and Egypt gave it a great advantage in bringing the products of Central Africa to Egypt, Mesopotamia, and the Greek islands of the Aegean Sea.

Activate Prior Knowledge

Have students review the information on Nubia presented in Section 1. Ask them to list facts in a word web with *Nubia* at its center, adding whatever facts they know from other sources. Have students read Reach Into Your Background in the Before You Read box.

Teaching Resources

📁 **Reproducible Lesson Plan** in the Chapter and Section Resources booklet, p. 51, provides a summary of the section lesson.

📁 **Guided Reading and Review** in the Chapter and Section Resources booklet, p. 52, provides a structure for mastering key concepts and reviewing key terms in the section. Available in Spanish in the Spanish Chapter and Section Resources booklet, p. 33.

Media and Technology

🖥 **Color Transparency** 92

2 Explore

Have students read the section. Discuss the following: How did Nubia's location contribute to its wealth and power? Why did the kingdoms of Nubia prosper? What factors led to their downfall? Describe the conflicts between Egypt and Nubia. What were the cultural and technological achievements of the kingdoms of Kerma, Napata, and Meroë?

3 Teach

Ask students to work in pairs to create a Venn diagram of two intersecting circles to illustrate the similarities and differences between life in Nubia and life in Egypt. Instruct students to include both cultural and geographic comparisons. This activity should take about 20 minutes.

LINKS ACROSS THE WORLD

Nubia and Egypt A recent discovery of a Nubian incense burner has some scientists thinking about the early relationship between Egypt and Nubia. Some scientists think the object was made around 3100 B.C. or even earlier. Carved on its side are a seated king and other figures that later became symbols of Egyptian pharaohs. Scientists are debating whether Nubia or Egypt had the first kings.

first appeared in Nubia about 8,000 years ago. This makes it one of the world's oldest cultures. During the long period of Nubian civilization, many kingdoms arose. They would grow and gain power for a time. Then they would become weak and die out. Tracing these events is like taking a slow-motion roller coaster ride through Nubian history.

For most of their long history, Nubia and Egypt both did well as peaceful, friendly neighbors. The Egyptians called Nubia *Ta Sety* (TAH seh tee), "the land of the bow." This probably referred to the Nubians' skill as archers. The Nubian archers were so good that Egypt hired many of them for its armies.

Early in its history, Egypt benefited greatly from goods brought into Egypt by caravans from Lower Nubia. But later, powerful kingdoms arose in Upper Nubia. These kingdoms began to rival Egypt for power and control of land. Three of the more powerful Nubian kingdoms grew up in the cities of Kerma (KUR muh), Napata (NAH pah tah), and Meroë (MER oh ee). Find these three cities on the map below.

The Kingdom of Kerma The Kerma kingdom rose in power at a time when Egypt was weakening. From the city of Kerma at the Third Cataract of the Nile, the kingdom expanded into parts of southern Egypt by 1600 B.C.

The Kingdoms of Nubia and Their Resources

Map Study The natural resources of Nubian kingdoms formed the basis of their wealth. In fact, Nubia was far ahead of most other cultures in the development of metal-working techniques.
Interaction The people of Meroë became skilled at making farm tools and weapons. What do you think these items were made from?

First Cataract

Second Cataract

LOWER NUBIA

Third Cataract

Kerma

Fourth Cataract

Napata

Fifth Cataract

UPPER NUBIA

Sixth Cataract

Meroë

Red Sea

Nile River

Atbara River

Blue Nile

White Nile

0   100   200 mi
0   100   200 km

KEY
• City
⊣ Cataracts
▨ Iron
▨ Copper
▨ Gold

Albers Equal-Area Projection

Answers to ...

MAP STUDY

Students should use the map to identify iron as the metal resource closest to Meroë.

The Art of Kerma

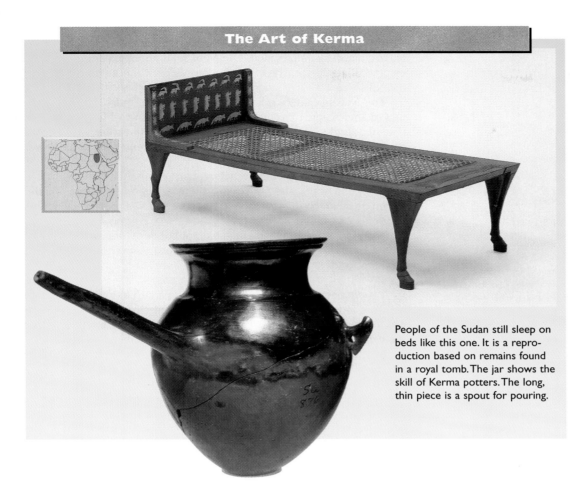

People of the Sudan still sleep on beds like this one. It is a reproduction based on remains found in a royal tomb. The jar shows the skill of Kerma potters. The long, thin piece is a spout for pouring.

Kerma gained not only power but wealth. It was noted for its **artisans,** or skilled workers. They made delicate pottery. Items made by Kerma artisans have been found in the tombs of pharaohs. This means the items were highly prized.

Kerma was a wealthy kingdom. One clue is the way the people buried their kings, in tombs under huge mounds of earth as large as football fields. They placed the kings on gold-covered beds and surrounded them with jewelry, gold, and ivory.

Around the late to mid-1400s B.C., Egypt began to regain its strength. Pharaoh Thutmose III sent his armies into Nubia. After a war that lasted about 50 years, the Egyptians took control of Nubia as far south as the Fourth Cataract. Egypt ruled Nubia for the next 700 years.

During this period, the Nubians adopted many Egyptian ways. They even began to worship Egyptian gods along with their own. Throughout these times of conflict and peace, people and goods continued to pass between Nubia and Egypt. The two cultures became mixed.

4 Assess

See the answers to the Section Review. You may also use students' completed Venn diagrams as an assessment.

Acceptable diagrams indicate at least two similarities and two differences.

Commendable diagrams include at least three similarities and three differences.

Outstanding diagrams indicate three or more similarities and three or more differences.

Activity

Interdisciplinary Connections

Language Arts/Music Tell students that one of the most enduring legends of ancient Egypt tells of the ill-fated love of a Nubian princess for an Egyptian soldier. This legend forms the basis for the popular opera *Aïda*, by Giuseppe Verdi. The story appears in the book *Aïda* as told by Leontyne Price, illustrated by Leo and Diane Dillon. If possible, obtain a copy of the book and/or a recording of the opera. Share parts with students. Discuss how the story focuses on the rivalry and the tensions between Nubia and Egypt. *Auditory*

The Iron Age Iron tools and weapons came into widespread use about 1100 B.C. This began a period known as the Iron Age. The use of iron began near present-day Turkey and spread across Asia, Africa, and Europe. The ancient civilizations of China, India, Babylon, Assyria, and Chaldea all used iron. In addition, the ancient Greeks and Romans used iron long before the peoples of northern Europe did.

Cooperative Learning

Planning a Lesson Have groups choose one of the Nubian kingdoms and ask them to plan a lesson or presentation for another class about the kingdom they chose. Groups may use the material in the text or may find additional information. Encourage students to use illustrations and to act out certain events to make their lesson memorable. Invite small groups of students from other classes to the presentations. *Kinesthetic*

The Kingdom of Napata In the late 700s B.C., Egypt was once again weak and divided. The Nubian kingdom of Napata expanded its power into Egypt. Napata was centered near the Fourth Cataract of the Nile.

The Napatan kings gradually took control of more of Egypt. They moved their capital city first to Thebes and then to Memphis. By the time of Taharka, whose coronation you read about earlier, the Napatans controlled all Egypt. The pharaohs of Egypt's Twenty-fifth Dynasty were Nubians.

The Napatan kings admired Egyptian culture. They brought back old Egyptian ways and preserved them. They even began building pyramids in which to bury their kings. The ruins of these small Nubian pyramids can still be seen today.

The rule of the Napatan kings did not last very long. About 660 B.C., they were forced back into Nubia. The Nubians never again controlled Egyptian land.

The Kingdom of Meroë Moving south of Egypt's reach, the Nubians founded a royal court in the ancient city of Meroë. This city was located on the Nile between the Fifth and Sixth Cataracts. It became the center of an empire that included much of Nubia. It also stretched south into central Africa.

Predict What were some benefits Meroë gained from making and using iron tools and weapons?

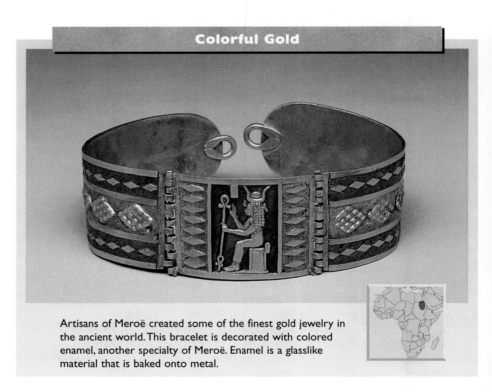

Colorful Gold

Artisans of Meroë created some of the finest gold jewelry in the ancient world. This bracelet is decorated with colored enamel, another specialty of Meroë. Enamel is a glasslike material that is baked onto metal.

Resource Directory

Teaching Resources

📁 **Section Quiz** in the Chapter and Section Resources booklet, p. 53, covers the main ideas and key terms in the section. Available in Spanish in the Spanish Chapter and Section Resources booklet, p. 34.

📁 **Vocabulary** in the Chapter and Section Resources booklet, p. 55, provides a review of key terms in the chapter.

Available in Spanish in the Spanish Chapter and Section Resources booklet, p. 36.

📁 **Reteaching** in the Chapter and Section Resources booklet, p. 56, provides a structure for students who may need additional help in mastering chapter content.

📁 **Enrichment** in the Chapter and Section Resources booklet, p. 57, extends chapter content and enriches students' understanding.

▶ Women like Queen Malakaye, who lived in the early 500s B.C., were important in Nubian culture. Over the centuries, several women held ruling power in Nubia.

The rocky desert east of Meroë held large deposits of iron ore. As a result, the Nubians began making iron weapons and tools. The people of Meroë became the first Africans to specialize in iron-working. Iron plows allowed them to produce good supplies of food. Iron weapons allowed them to control trade routes that ran all the way to the Red Sea. There they traded goods from central Africa for goods from India, the Arabian Peninsula, and Rome. Meroë grew rich on this trade.

Today, Meroë remains largely a mystery. The culture created its own system of hieroglyphic writing. But even today's powerful computers cannot figure out what it means, so scholars must get clues about these people from what they left behind. The kingdom of Meroë began to weaken in the A.D. 200s. However, features of Nubian culture have lasted for 3,500 years. To this day, Nubian styles of pottery, furniture, jewelry, beautiful braided hairstyles, and clothing survive among people of the modern-day country of Sudan.

SECTION 5 REVIEW

1. **Define** artisan.

2. **Identify** (a) Taharka, (b) Kerma, (c) Napata, (d) Meroë.

3. How would you describe the relations between Egypt and Nubia?

4. How did iron help make the kingdom of Meroë rich?

Critical Thinking

5. **Identifying Central Issues** Explain how the Nubians and the Egyptians borrowed from each other's culture. In what ways did each civilization benefit from the other?

Activity

6. **Writing to Learn** List the names of the three major Nubian kingdoms. Then briefly describe each one.

Spanish Glossary in the Spanish Chapter and Section Resources, pp. 85–89, provides key terms translated from English to Spanish as well as definitions in Spanish.

Chapter Summary in the Chapter and Section Resources booklet, p. 54, provides a summary of chapter content. Available in Spanish in the Spanish Chapter and Section Resources booklet, p. 35.

Cooperative Learning Activity in the Activities and Projects booklet, pp. 28–31, provides two student handouts, one page of teacher's directions, and a scoring rubric for a cooperative learning activity on making ancient Egyptian slate palettes.

Media and Technology

Guided Reading Audiotapes (English and Spanish)

1. a skilled worker

2. (a) a Nubian king who also became ruler of Egypt (b) a kingdom centered near the Third Cataract of the Nile (c) a kingdom centered near the Fourth Cataract of the Nile (d) an ancient city near rich deposits of iron; the first African center to specialize in making iron into tools and weapons.

3. For most of their long history, Nubia and Egypt both did well as peaceful, friendly neighbors.

4. Meroë specialized in making iron tools such as plows and weapons. The plows helped Nubia produce ample supplies of food. The weapons allowed Nubia to control trade routes reaching to the Red Sea. Meroë became rich trading ironwork for goods from other parts of the world.

5. The Nubians worshipped Egyptian gods along with their own. The two civilizations benefited from trade and the exchange of ideas and customs.

6. Students' answers will vary but should include Kerma, noted for its artisans; Napata, known for its dominance over Egypt; and Meroë, known for its ironwork.

SKILLS ACTIVITY

Reading Route Maps

Lesson Objectives

1. Describe the purpose and the elements of a route map.

2. Devise a simple route map.

3. Use the elements of a route map to find destinations, distances, and directions.

Lesson Plan

1 Engage

Warm-Up Activity

To **introduce** the skill, begin by having students read the opening scenario. Ask students what they think a route map is and how the caravan leader in the introduction might use one.

Activating Prior Knowledge

Ask students whether they have ever consulted a road atlas, a bus or subway map, or a hiking- or bike-trail map. Have volunteers explain why and how they used such maps. Explain that these maps, though seemingly quite different, are all route maps. Point out that any map that shows established paths is a route map.

2 Explore

When students have read the text under Get Ready, ask them to write a definition of a route map. You might help them by asking what distinguishes a route map from other types of maps.

As the sky began to darken, the cool breeze shifted slightly. The leader of the caravan turned around and saw the storm at the horizon behind them. Then he looked ahead, straining to see some glimpse of Assur. The caravan had been traveling for many days with goods from Giza. Although his men were tired, he signaled for them to move faster. He wanted to reach the city before the storm reached them.

The pharaoh had chosen him to lead this trip because of his experience as a traveler. For years, he had brought goods from Lower Egypt to Syria and Sumer. This particular road, however, was new to him. He hoped they would reach Assur soon.

Get Ready

The caravan leader might have found a route map useful. This is a map that shows the routes, or paths, people follow. Reading a route map is simply a matter of reading a map and then reading the routes that are marked on it. As you do with all maps, you begin by reading the title, the key, the scale, the compass rose, and the labels on the map. Then, you study the map to figure out what it shows. Finally, you read the routes on the map by following the lines that show them.

Try It Out

Perhaps the best way to figure out how to use route maps is to make one of your own. You'll need a blank sheet of paper, colored pencils, and a ruler.

A. **Draw a simple map of the area that includes your school and your home.** Use the ruler as needed to make straight lines. Add a scale and a compass rose.

B. **Mark the location of your school and your home with symbols.** Explain the symbols in a map key.

C. **Draw routes.** Using a colored pencil, draw a line to show the route you take from home to school. Now use a different color to draw a line to show the route you take from your home to a friend's home. In the map key, explain the meaning of the different colored lines.

D. **Add symbols to your map.** For example, you might draw a symbol on the route from home to school to indicate you are carrying your lunch. Identify the symbols you use on the map key.

Resource Directory

Teaching Resources

Reading a Trade Map in the Social Studies and Geography Skills booklet, p. 39, provides additional skill practice.

Apply the Skill

Use the Egyptian trade routes map to complete the steps that follow.

1 Familiarize yourself with the map. The first step in reading any map is to familiarize yourself with it generally. What is the title of the map? What region of the world does it show? What does the map key indicate?

2 Understand what routes are shown. You can learn this by studying the map key. How are Egyptian trade routes shown?

▶ As you might guess, trade routes followed the Nile River as well.

▼ This Egyptian tomb painting shows traders loading grain into a ship.

3 Use the map. According to this map, did Egyptian traders travel more by sea or by land? What city would a trader pass on the way from Giza to Assur? About how far is Assur from Giza?

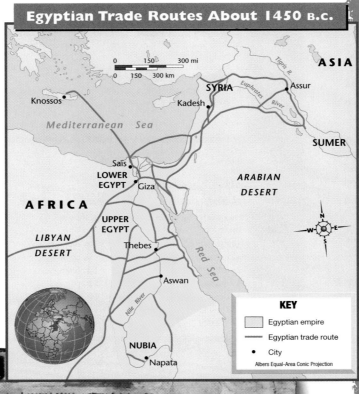

Egyptian Trade Routes About 1450 B.C.

KEY
- Egyptian empire
- Egyptian trade route
- • City

Albers Equal-Area Conic Projection

3 Teach

Students may **practice** the skill by carrying out the instructions given in Try It Out. You might provide students with photocopies of a community or neighborhood street map. Remind students that symbols should suggest their meaning. For example, a tiny drawing of your school could serve as the map key symbol for the school; a tree could indicate a park.

For reinforcement, students might use other colors to add a "scenic" route or a "short-cut" route to their maps.

4 Assess

Students should **apply** the skill by completing the last activity section. **Assess** their ability by having students, in turn, identify and explain each element's purpose. Give students several starting points and destinations and have them trace the routes the Egyptians would have used.

Answers to . . .

APPLY THE SKILL

1. Egyptian Trade Routes About 1450 B.C. shows Egypt and the surrounding regions. The map key indicates that the lines on the map are Egyptian trade routes, the dots are cities, and the yellow area is the Egyptian empire.
2. Dark red lines indicate routes.
3. Egyptian traders used more land routes. A trader would pass through Saïs. The distance between Assur and Giza is about 750 miles.

CHAPTER 3 Review and Activities

Reviewing Main Ideas

1. Life was centered around the annual flooding of the Nile, which was followed by planting the crops. Farming communities flourished near the Nile.

2. Answers may vary, but should indicate that the Nubians, with their iron weapons, controlled trade all the way to the Red Sea. They traded iron items for items from other parts of the world.

3. Strong pharaohs were able to keep peace throughout the kingdom. Egyptians believed that the pharaoh's power was absolute and obeyed the pharaoh.

4. Hatshepsut preserved the peace and encouraged trade. Thutmose III led the army in conquest and expanded the empire.

5. Egyptian religion explained nature. People tried to please the gods so that the gods would not harm them.

6. The pyramids were tombs for pharaohs.

7. The pharaoh was at the top. Below the pharaoh was a small group of priests, members of pharaoh's court, and nobles. Beneath them was a middle class of merchants and artisans. Beneath them were the peasants.

8. Students' answers will vary, but may include the hieroglyphic writing system; a measurement system; or achievements in astronomy and medicine. Students may say that hieroglyphics were important for communication and for keeping records.

9. Although Nubia and Egypt were rivals at times, through most of their history they were peaceful, friendly neighbors.

10. Kerma was near the Third Cataract of the Nile. Napata was near the Fourth Cataract of the Nile. Meroë was between the Fifth and Sixth Cataracts of the Nile. Students should describe one of the kingdoms.

Reviewing Key Terms

Sentences should show the correct meanings of terms through context.

Reviewing Main Ideas

1. Explain how the Nile affected everyday life in ancient Egypt.
2. How was trade important to Nubian civilization?
3. How did the pharaohs unify all of Egypt under their rule?
4. What were the main accomplishments of Hatshepsut and Thutmose III?
5. Why was religion so important to the people of ancient Egypt?
6. Explain the purpose of the pyramids.
7. Describe the levels of Egyptian society.
8. List four accomplishments of the ancient Egyptians. Then choose one of them and describe its importance.
9. Describe the relationship between Egypt and Nubia throughout their long history.
10. Name the three major Nubian kingdoms, and describe the location of each. Then choose one kingdom and describe it.

Reviewing Key Terms

Use each key term in a sentence that shows the meaning of the term.

1. cataract
2. delta
3. silt
4. pharaoh
5. dynasty
6. regent
7. afterlife
8. mummy
9. pyramid
10. hieroglyph
11. papyrus
12. astronomer
13. artisan

Critical Thinking

1. **Drawing Conclusions** Explain how Egyptian ideas about the afterlife have increased our knowledge of ancient Egypt.
2. **Making Comparisons** Compare the length of Egypt's civilization with that of the Assyrians and the Babylonians. How do you account for the differences?

Graphic Organizer

Copy the chart onto a sheet of paper and title it "Levels of Egyptian Society." Then fill in the empty spaces to complete the chart. Beside each space, describe briefly the group you wrote there.

Graphic Organizer

Pharaoh	Head of government, religion, and the military. He is "responsible" for the annual flooding of the Nile.
Nobles and Priests	Own and run large estates and are part of Pharaoh's court.
Merchants and Skilled Workers	Merchants trade crafts and articles made by artisans.
Peasants and Common Workers	Peasants farm the land; common workers build roads, temples, pyramids, and other buildings.

Map Activity

Place Location

Egypt and Nubia

For each place listed below, write the letter from the map that shows its location.

1. Nile River
2. Mediterranean Sea
3. Red Sea
4. Upper Nubia
5. Lower Nubia
6. Sahara
7. the Nile delta
8. Upper Egypt
9. Lower Egypt

Writing Activity

Writing a Poem

Sitting near the Nile waiting for it to flood, you think about the river and its importance to life. Write a poem expressing your thoughts and feelings.

Internet Activity

Use a search engine to find the site called **Egypt's CultureNet.** Click on Museums. Then click on Museums in Egypt. Select the Egyptian Museum. Explore the museum by selecting different links. Create a "What to See" list you would use if you visited the museum in person.

Skills Review

Turn to the Skills Activity.

Review the steps for understanding a route map. Then complete the following: (a) In your own words, explain what a route map is. (b) How is a route map different from other kinds of maps?

How Am I Doing?

Answer these questions to help you check your progress.

1. Can I describe the main geographic features of Egypt and Nubia?
2. Do I understand how Egyptian society was organized?
3. Can I identify the main historical periods of ancient Egypt?
4. Can I identify the important kingdoms of Nubia?
5. Can I describe the main features of Egyptian and Nubian culture?
6. What information in the chapter can I use in my book project?

Critical Thinking

1. Possible answer: The pyramids demonstrate the Egyptians' engineering skills. The artifacts found in the tombs are examples of items Egyptians used in everyday life.

2. Sample answer: The Assyrian and Babylonian empires together lasted about 250 years. The Egyptian civilization lasted nearly 2,000 years. Both the Assyrian and Babylonian rulers often ruled by force. The rulers of Egypt, viewed as divine, had the loyalty of the people.

Map Activity

1. F	4. I	7. B
2. A	5. G	8. E
3. H	6. D	9. C

Writing Activity

Students' poems should express their feelings of anticipation as they wait for the Nile to flood.

Skills Review

(a) It shows how to get from one place to another. (b) A route map shows the routes or paths that people follow.

Resource Directory

Teaching Resources

Chapter Tests Forms A and B are in the Tests booklet, pp. 14–19.

Program Resources

Writing Process Handbook includes Using Transitions, p. 30, to help students with the Writing Activity.

Media and Technology

Color Transparencies
Color Transparency 174
(Graphic organizer table template)
Prentice Hall Writer's Solution
Writing Lab CD-ROM
Computer Test Bank
Resource Pro™ CD-ROM

Internet Activity

If students are having difficulty finding this site, you may wish to have them use the following URL, which was accurate at the time this textbook was published:

http://www.idsc.gov.eg/ culture/index.htm

You might also guide students to a search engine. Four of the most useful are Infoseek, AltaVista, Lycos, and Yahoo. For additional suggestions on using the Internet, refer to the Prentice Hall Social Studies' Educator's Handbook "Using the Internet," in the *Prentice*

Hall World Explorer Program Resources.

For additional links to world history and culture topics, visit the Prentice Hall Home Page at:
http://www.phschool.com

How Am I Doing?

Point out to students that this checklist is a quick reminder of what they learned in the chapter. If their answer to any of the questions is *no* or if they are unsure, they may need to review the topic.

Ancient India

To help you plan instruction, the chart below shows how teaching resources correspond to chapter content. Use the resources to vary instruction, add activities, or plan block schedules. Where appropriate, resources have suggested time allotments for students. Time allotments are approximate.

Managing Time and Instruction

	The Ancient World Teaching Resources Binder		World Explorer Program Resources Binder	
	Resource	mins.	Resource	mins.
1 SECTION 1 **The Indus and Ganges River Valleys**	**Chapter and Section Support** Reproducible Lesson Plan, p. 60 ⓢ Guided Reading and Review, p. 61 ⓢ Section Quiz, p. 62 Critical Thinking Activity, p. 76	20 25	**Outline Maps** South Asia: Physical, p. 36 **Nystrom Desk Atlas** Ⓣ **Primary Sources and Literature** Readings **Writing Process Handbook** Organizing Material in a Logical Sequence, pp. 23–24	20 20 40 25
SKILLS ACTIVITY **Reading Tables**	**Social Studies and Geography Skills,** Reading a Table, p. 62	30		
2 SECTION 2 **The Beginnings of Hinduism**	**Chapter and Section Support** Reproducible Lesson Plan, p. 63 ⓢ Guided Reading and Review, p. 64 ⓢ Section Quiz, p. 65	20 25		
3 SECTION 3 **The Beginnings of Buddhism**	**Chapter and Section Support** Reproducible Lesson Plan, p. 66 ⓢ Guided Reading and Review, p. 67 ⓢ Section Quiz, p. 68	20 25	**Outline Maps** South Asia: Political, p. 37 Southeast Asia: Political, p. 43	20 20
4 SECTION 4 **The Golden Age of Maurya India**	**Chapter and Section Support** Reproducible Lesson Plan, p. 69 ⓢ Guided Reading and Review, p. 70 ⓢ Section Quiz, p. 71 ⓢ Vocabulary, p. 73 Reteaching, p. 74 Enrichment, p. 75 ⓢ Chapter Summary, p. 72 **Tests** Forms A and B Chapter Tests, pp. 20–25	20 25 20 25 25 15 40	**Outline Maps** South Asia: Political, p. 37 Ⓣ **Interdisciplinary Explorations** *India: Beyond the Golden Age*	20 40
LITERATURE FEATURE **The Envious Buffalo retold by Joseph Gaer**	**Social Studies and Geography Skills,** Determining If you Understood What you Read, p. 74	30	Ⓣ **Primary Sources and Literature** Readings	40

Block Scheduling Folder
PROGRAM TEACHING RESOURCES

Block Scheduling Program Support

- Activities and Projects
- Interdisciplinary Links
- Resource Pro™ CD-ROM
- Media and Technology

Media and Technology

Resource	mins.
📹 ⌘ Ⓢ World Video Explorer	20
▢ Color Transparencies 4, 94	20
▢ Color Transparency 167	20
⌘ Planet Earth CD-ROM	20
▢ Color Transparencies 74, 76	20
▢ Color Transparency 74	20
🎧 Ⓢ Guided Reading Audiotapes	20
▢ Color Transparency 174	
(Graphic organizer table template)	20
⌘ The Writer's Solution CD-ROM	30
💾 Computer Test Bank	30

Ⓣ Teaming Opportunity
This resource is especially well-suited for teaching teams.

Ⓢ Spanish
This resource is also in Spanish support.

- ⌘ CD-ROM
- 🖥 Laserdisc
- ▢ Transparency
- 💾 Software
- 📹 Videotape
- 🎧 Audiotape

Assessment Opportunities

From Guiding Questions to Assessment A series of Guiding Questions serves as an organizing framework for this book. The Guiding Questions that relate to this chapter are listed below. Section Reviews and Section Quizzes provide opportunities for assessing students' insights into these Guiding Questions. Additional assessments are listed below.

GUIDING QUESTIONS

- *How did physical geography affect the growth of ancient civilizations?*
- *How did the beliefs and values of ancient civilizations affect the lives of their members?*

ASSESSMENTS

Section 1

Students should be able to create a model showing how the people of Mohenjo-Daro planned their city.

▶ **RUBRIC** See the Assessment booklet for a rubric on assessing student performance on a project.

Section 2

Students should be able to write a brief report outlining the basic beliefs of Hinduism.

▶ **RUBRIC** See the Assessment booklet for a rubric on assessing a report.

Section 3

Students should be able to create a map of the spread of Buddhism.

▶ **RUBRIC** See the Assessment booklet for a rubric on assessing a map produced by a student.

Section 4

Students should be able to give an oral presentation revealing why Asoka is considered one of India's greatest leaders.

▶ **RUBRIC** See the Assessment booklet for a rubric on assessing an oral presentation.

Activities and Projects

Mental Mapping

Get Oriented Divide students into three teams. Explain that orienteering is a sport that involves using a compass to follow directions to get from one place to another. Have one team of students write out compass directions that would allow someone to travel from Babylon to the Nile delta and then to the Indus River.

Have another team make a large outline map of this region. The map should be very large. Babylon should be labeled as a starting point. Unlabeled markers (for example, large red dots) should be placed on the Nile delta and Mohenjo-Daro, a site on the Indus River about 200 miles north of Karachi, Pakistan. The map should include a compass rose.

Place the map on the floor. Ask volunteers from the third team to navigate from one spot to the next following the compass directions provided by the first team.

Links to Current Events

Population Density Divide students into pairs or small groups and supply each group with one and one half $8\frac{1}{2}''$ x $11''$ sheets of white paper and one and one half $8\frac{1}{2}''$ x $11''$ sheets of colored paper. Have them measure the colored paper into 1-inch squares and cut out the squares. They should end up with 132 squares.

Next, ask them to place 27 squares on the $8\frac{1}{2}''$ x $11''$ white paper and 88 squares on the half sheet of white paper. Tell them that the paper with the 27 squares represents the population density of the United States, and that the paper with 88 squares represents the population density of India.

Hands-On Activities

An Ancient Civilization Invite students to find objects in their environment that they could imagine are archaeological finds from the site of an ancient civilization. For example, students might find pieces of broken pottery, metal that could be tools, jewelry, or wood that has been carved or whittled. Ask each student to speak for a minute about the object he or she has found. Students should explain where they found their objects and how they think the objects might have been used by people of the imaginary ancient civilization.

Animal Symbols Tell students that archaeologists have found many square seals depicting animals in ancient Indus civilization sites. Scholars believe these animals may have represented certain families or groups of people of these ancient cities. Ask students to find examples of ways that animals are used to represent different groups of people in American culture. If they have trouble coming up with examples, suggest they think about political parties, professional sports teams, and college and university mascots. Have students make collages showing the use of some of these animal symbols. *English Language Learners*

Urban Planning Mohenjo-Daro was carefully planned with a sanitation system that included covered drains connected by chutes that went to most houses. It also included areas for storage of grain and water. Ask students to think about similar things a modern town or city needs. Allow them to draw a plan or diagram showing how these features would be incorporated into a new city that was being built. *Average*

Great Religions Ask students to research and report on the Hindu and Buddhist religions. Have them make charts that provide information about the major holidays, beliefs, and practices. *Challenging*

A Maurya Time Line As students read Section 4 of this chapter, have them create a time line listing major events that shaped the Maurya empire. *Basic*

F.Y.I.

This page can help you extend your own and students' understanding of the concepts in this chapter. You may want to browse through some of the suggestions in the **Bibliography. Interdisciplinary Links** can connect social studies understandings to areas elsewhere in the curriculum through the use of other Prentice Hall products. **National Geography Standards** reflected specifically in this chapter are listed for your convenience. Some hints about appropriate **Internet Access** are also provided. **School to Careers** provides insights into the practical uses of some of the concepts in this chapter as they might pertain to various careers.

BIBLIOGRAPHY

FOR THE TEACHER

Feverstein, Georg. *In Search of the Cradle of Civilization: New Light on Ancient India.* Quest Books, 1995.

Wangu, Madhu Bazas. *Buddhism: World Religions.* Facts on File, 1993.

Wangu, Madhu Bazas. *Hinduism: World Religions.* Facts on File, 1991.

FOR THE STUDENT

Easy
Shepard, Aaron. *Savitri: A Tale of Ancient India.* Albert Whitman & Company, 1992.

Average
Sharma, Rashmi. *Ashoka.* Vidya Books, 1991.

Sharma, Rashmi. *Siddhartha Gautama, "Buddha."* Vidya Books, 1990.

Challenging
Boisselier, Jean. *The Wisdom of the Buddha.* Harry N. Abrams, 1994.

LITERATURE CONNECTION

Gray, J.A.B. *East Indian Tales and Legends.* Oxford, 1989.

Madhur, Jaffrey. *Seasons of Splendor: Tales, Myths, and Legends from India.* Puffin, 1985.

INTERDISCIPLINARY LINKS

Subject	Theme: Movement
MATH	Middle Grades Math: Tools for Success *Course 1*, Lesson 1-7, **Decision Making: Polling Your Peers**
SCIENCE	Prentice Hall Science *Exploring Earth's Weather*, Lesson 1-3, **Winds**
LANGUAGE ARTS	Choices in Literature *Where Paths Meet*, **The Race**

NATIONAL GEOGRAPHY STANDARDS

Students explore the 18 National Geography Standards throughout *The Ancient World.* Chapter 4, however, concentrates on investigating the following standards: 2, 3, 4, 6, 8, 9, 10, 12, 13, 15. For a complete list of the standards, see the *Teacher's Flexible Planning Guide.*

SCHOOL TO CAREERS

In Chapter 4, Ancient India, students learn about the ancient civilizations and religions that developed in India. Additionally, they address the skill of reading tables. Understanding ancient India can help students prepare for careers in many fields such as history, international trade, diplomacy, and so on. Skill in reading tables is particularly useful for engineers, actuaries, accountants, and others. The curriculum presented in this book, as in all eight titles of Prentice Hall's *World Explorer* program, is designed to prepare students not only for careers but also for good citizenship—of the world as well as of this country.

INTERNET ACCESS

Many social studies teachers and students use Internet browsers, or search engines, to investigate particular topics. For the best results, use narrow rather than broad topics. Try these for Chapter 4: Himalaya Mountains, Hinduism, Asoka, Mohenjo-Daro. Finding age-appropriate sites is an important consideration when using the Internet. For links to age-appropriate sites in world studies and geography, visit the Prentice Hall Home Page at: **http://www.phschool.com**

CHAPTER 4

Ancient India

Connecting to the Guiding Questions

As students read this chapter, they will focus on early Indian civilizations. Content in this chapter corresponds to the following Guiding Questions:

● How did physical geography affect the growth of ancient civilizations?

● How did the beliefs and values of ancient civilizations affect the lives of their members?

Using the Map Activities

Suggest that students work in pairs to complete the map activities.

• India is surrounded on three sides by water and on nearly all sides by mountains, limiting the movement of people.

• Summer winds bring rain because they have crossed the ocean. Winter winds bring cool, dry air; they come from the north across a desert.

Heterogeneous Groups

The following Teacher's Edition strategies are suitable for heterogeneous groups.

Cooperative Learning

Interdisciplinary Connections

Critical Thinking

SECTION 1
The Indus and Ganges River Valleys

SECTION 2
The Beginnings of Hinduism

SECTION 3
The Beginnings of Buddhism

SECTION 4
The Golden Age of Maurya India

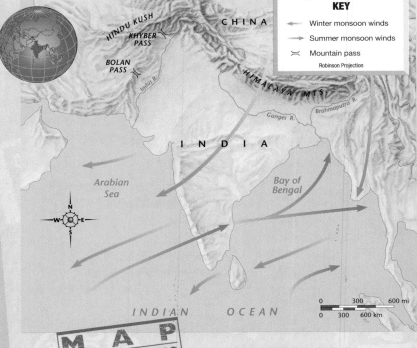

Important features of India are the mountains, the oceans, and the winds that blow across the region. They are shown on the map. To help you become acquainted with India's geography and climate, do the following activities.

Study the map
Describe the location of the mountains and oceans. What effect do you think these features had on the movement of people to and from India?

Follow the wind
Trace the wind arrows on the map with your finger. Which winds, winter or summer, do you think bring rain to India? Why? Which winds bring dry, cool air? Why?

Resource Directory

Media and Technology

Case Study: The Maurya Empire, from the World Video Explorer, enhances students' understanding of the Maurya empire and its lasting effects on India.

Chapter 6

The Indus and Ganges River Valleys

BEFORE YOU READ

Reach Into Your Background

People all around the world are affected by their environment. In what ways does your environment influence the way you live your everyday life? In what ways do you affect your environment?

Questions to Explore

1. How did geography influence the history of India?
2. How did people live in one of the early cities in the Indus River Valley?

Key Terms

subcontinent   migrate
monsoon   caste
citadel

Key Places

Himalaya Mountains
Indus River Valley
Mohenjo-Daro
Ganges River Valley

For thousands of years, India was cut off from the rest of the ancient world by a great wall. Rising along India's northern border, the wall was more than 1,500 miles (2,400 km) long and nearly 5 miles (8 km) high. The wall was not made of stone or bricks. It was a wall of snow-capped peaks and icy glaciers. This great barrier is the Himalaya Mountains, the highest mountain range in the world.

India's Geographic Setting

Stretching south from the Himalaya Mountains, the kite-shaped land of India bulges out from Asia into the Indian Ocean. Geographers refer to India as a **subcontinent**, or a large landmass that juts out from a continent.

For centuries, geography limited contact between the Indian subcontinent and the rest of the world. The Himalaya Mountains and the Hindu Kush separate India from Asia. Find

▼ At 29,028 feet (8,848 m), Mount Everest is not only the highest peak in the Himalaya Mountains, but the highest in the world.

Lesson Objectives

1. Identify major geographic features of India and how the features affected history.

2. Describe the ancient city of Mohenjo-Daro and its culture.

Lesson Plan

1 Engage

Warm-Up Activity

Give students two flat pieces of modeling clay. Have them slide these together until they collide, noting the fold that rises as the pieces collide. Explain that this is a model of how the Himalaya Mountains formed. Urge students to consider as they read the section how this huge physical barrier affected the lives of people in ancient India.

Activating Prior Knowledge

Ask students what an air conditioner, an umbrella, and a toboggan have in common. Help students understand that all three items are human-made objects devised in response to certain environmental conditions. Then have students read Reach Into Your Background in the Before You Read box.

Teaching Resources

📁 **Reproducible Lesson Plan** in the Chapter and Section Resources booklet, p. 60, provides a summary of the section lesson.

📁 **Guided Reading and Review** in the Chapter and Section Resources booklet, p. 61, provides a structure for mastering key concepts and reviewing key terms in the section. Available in Spanish in the Spanish Chapter and Section Resources booklet, p. 38.

Program Resources

Material in the **Primary Sources and Literature Readings** booklet extends content with a selection related to the concepts in this chapter.

Outline Maps South Asia: Physical, p. 36

2 Explore

As students read the section, ask them to consider the following questions. Why was farming possible for people of the Indus River Valley? What is one possible reason Mohenjo-Daro survived so long? How did life in the valley change after Aryans finally penetrated the Himalayan barrier?

3 Teach

Tell students that they have discovered two time capsules—one from the Indus River Valley civilization (Mohenjo-Daro) and one from the Ganges River Valley (when Aryans lived there). Have students describe the contents of each capsule. Then invite students to explain what the contents reveal about the civilizations' relationships with their physical environment. This activity should take about 25 minutes.

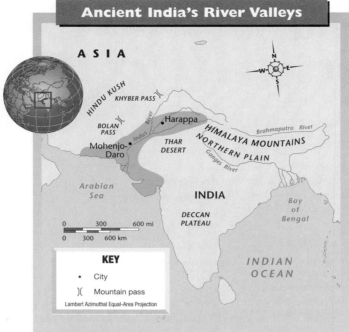

Ancient India's River Valleys

KEY
- City
)(Mountain pass

Lambert Azimuthal Equal-Area Projection

Map Study Passes through India's mountain ranges allowed people to move into and settle in two of India's fertile river valleys, the Indus and the Ganges. **Location** Invaders also used the mountain passes to get to the Indus River settlements. From what direction would such invaders have come?

TO SCIENCE

The Creation of the Himalaya Mountains
Millions of years ago, all of today's continents were part of a single continent called Pangaea (pan JEE uh). Then Pangaea slowly broke apart. Eventually, India broke loose from Africa and began moving northeast. About 55 million years ago, India began crashing into Asia. The force of the collision pushed up the earth to form the Himalaya Mountains.

them on the map at the beginning of the chapter. The Bay of Bengal, the Indian Ocean, and the Arabian Sea limit contact with lands to the east and west. These mountains and waters have been a major influence on the history and culture of the land.

A Climate of Monsoons India's climate is dominated by the **monsoons,** strong winds that blow across the region at certain times of year. Look again at the map on the first page of this chapter. From October to May, the winter monsoon blows from the northeast, spreading dry air across the country. Then, in the middle of June, the wind blows in from the Indian Ocean. This summer monsoon picks up moisture from the ocean. It carries rains that drench the plains and river valleys daily.

The people depend on summer monsoons to provide life-giving rain. If the monsoon is late or weak, crops die, causing famine. If it brings too much rain, overflowing rivers may cause deadly floods.

Barriers and Pathways Although the mountains isolate India from other lands, they do have openings. Find the passages on the map above. For thousands of years, passes through the Hindu Kush mountain range have served as highways for invading people. The earliest people of northern India probably entered the valley of the Indus River through these pathways.

Great rivers rise in the mountains. Fed by melting snows and rain, the Indus and Ganges (GAN jeez) rivers cut through the mountains. They flow across the plains of northern India and make farming possible in the river valleys.

Life in the Indus River Valley

From the rich soil of the Indus River Valley, early farmers harvested a surplus of wheat and other grains. With a surplus of food, the population grew. Some villages became cities. From around 2500 B.C. to 1500 B.C., well-planned cities flourished in the valley. One of these, Mohenjo-Daro (moh HEHN joh DAH roh), lay along the banks of the Indus River.

Resource Directory

Teaching Resources

📁 **Critical Thinking Activity** in the Chapter and Section Resources booklet, p. 76, helps students apply the skill of expressing problems clearly.

Media and Technology

📽 **Color Transparencies** 4, 94

Program Resources

Nystrom Desk Atlas

The World's Earliest City Planners   Mohenjo-Daro was a large city that needed careful planning. Because the Indus River often flooded, the city's rulers built Mohenjo-Daro on a high mound of earth. To make travel easier in the city, streets were laid out in squares. People built their homes and shops along these squares. At the center of the city was the **citadel,** or fortress. It was a group of public buildings enclosed by a high brick wall. One building held a huge bath with dressing rooms for bathers. Nearby stood a storehouse for the city's grain supply.

Mohenjo-Daro must have been much cleaner than most other cities of the time. Clay pipes ran under the brick streets. They carried waste from homes and public buildings away from the city. Outside the city, canals ran along the Indus River, which often flooded. The canals controlled the flooding and directed water where it was most needed.

READ ACTIVELY

Predict What do you think life would have been like in an Indus Valley city?

▼ The baked-brick ruins of Mohenjo-Daro and its citadel are in the present-day country of Pakistan.

Trading Partners Archaeologists believe that artisans from Mohenjo-Daro created elaborately decorated furniture, complete with bone and ivory inlays, which were then exported to faraway Mesopotamian cities. Trading also took place with the Kingdom of Elam (in southern Iran).

Interdisciplinary Connections

Art Because so many different seals have been discovered at Mohenjo-Daro, some archaeologists believe the seals were an individual's or a businessperson's mark. The picture (often an animal) and writing on the seal either told the owner's name or represented him or her pictorially. A hole at the back of the seal allowed a person to wear it on a strip of leather. Provide red clay and invite students to create their own signature seals. Encourage them to use classroom objects and tools to mark their seals in ways that represent them. Invite the class to match the seals to their makers if possible. *English Language Learner, Kinesthetic*

▶ Copper workers from Mohenjo-Daro forged this almost human-shaped weapon (below). Merchants may have used the seals (right) to identify their goods—much as businesses today use logos.

READ ACTIVELY

Connect How was Mohenjo-Daro similar to the Sumerian cities you read about?

Living in Mohenjo-Daro The city buzzed with activity. Merchants and artisans sold their wares from shops that lined the streets. Wagons loaded with grain rolled through the city. Traders came from as far away as Mesopotamia to buy and sell precious goods. The citizens of Mohenjo-Daro lived in homes that opened onto courtyards. Children played with toys and pets. Adults enjoyed games and music. Artisans fashioned jewelry and bright cotton clothing for the people to wear.

The language of the people is still a mystery. Their writings appear on square seals. But experts have not yet been able to figure out the writing. The form of government and the religion of Mohenjo-Daro are also unknown. No royal tombs or great temples have been found. But we do know they had a number of gods.

A Mysterious Decline About 2000 B.C., Indus River Valley farmers began to abandon their land. The climate may have changed, turning the fertile soil into desert. Or great earthquakes may have caused floods that destroyed the canals. Without enough food, people began to leave the cities of the Indus River Valley. Between 2000 B.C. and 1500 B.C., invaders from the north entered the valley. The people who remained at Mohenjo-Daro were too weak to resist them.

Conquest by the Aryans

The invaders called themselves Aryans (AIR ee uhnz), which in their language meant "noble" or "highborn." They **migrated,** or moved, from their homelands in central Asia. For several centuries, waves of these nomadic herders swept into India.

As the Aryans crossed the plains of northern India, the people of the Indus River Valley huddled behind the crumbling walls of their cities. They were no match for Aryan warriors armed with bows and arrows and axes. Especially terrifying were their chariots drawn by charging horses. Gradually, the Aryans conquered the people of the Indus River Valley. Many became slaves of the invaders.

The Forests of the Ganges River

Forests were once common along the banks of the Ganges River. Today, most forests are gone, but the river helps feed the people of India. People eat fish from the river and grow crops on the fertile land of the Ganges Valley. **Critical Thinking** How might this stretch of the river change if people settled nearby?

Aryans Occupy Northern India   After they had conquered the Indus River Valley people, the Aryans gradually moved into the Ganges River Valley to the east. By about 800 B.C., they had learned to make tools and weapons out of iron. With iron axes, the Aryans cleared areas of the thick rain forests of the northeast. Here they built farms, villages, and even cities.

Aryan Life   Most of what we know of early Aryan life comes from religious books called Vedas, which means "knowledge." At first, the Vedas were handed down from memory by Aryan priests. They were not written down for hundreds of years.

The Vedas tell us that the earliest Aryans were herders and warriors who lived in villages and tended flocks of cattle and sheep. Always on the move, these people did not build cities or spacious homes at first. For a long time, they had no written language. Priests, called Brahmins, performed religious services and composed hymns and prayers.

The Aryans organized their society around three classes. Priests guarded religious traditions, warriors fought, and ordinary people worked. Gradually, the Aryans drew the conquered people into their class system and made them a fourth class. This class included farmworkers, laborers, and servants.

By 500 B.C., there was a strict division of classes. Europeans later called it the caste system. Each **caste,** or class, had special work and duties to perform. Under the caste system, people always had to stay in the caste of their parents.

Over time, the caste system became more complicated. The main castes divided into hundreds of different groups, in which each person had the same occupation, or type of work. Shopkeepers, farmers, traders, barbers, and weavers each belonged to their own group. Since people could not leave their caste, they did the same work as their parents and other members of the group. A weaver's son would be a weaver. A barber's daughter would marry a barber.

SECTION 1 REVIEW

1. Define   (a) subcontinent, (b) monsoon, (c) citadel, (d) migrate, (e) caste.

2. Identify   (a) Himalaya Mountains, (b) Indus River Valley, (c) Mohenjo-Daro, (d) Ganges River Valley.

3. How did geography affect the way people lived in ancient India?

4. How did the leaders of Mohenjo-Daro plan their city?

Critical Thinking

5. Drawing Conclusions   The people of the Indus River Valley planned their cities with great care. What might this tell you about their form of government and their values?

Activity

6. Writing to Learn   List some words you think describe the city and the people of Mohenjo-Daro. Use these words to write a paragraph about life in the city.

The Beginnings of Hinduism

BEFORE YOU READ

Reach Into Your Background

Your beliefs and traditions are part of your life. They come from your family, your commu-nity, and your own ideas. Think about some of your beliefs and traditions. Consider where each came from.

Questions to Explore

1. How did the basic beliefs of the Hindu religion develop?
2. Explain the Hindu idea of reincarnation.

Key Terms

reincarnation
dharma
ahimsa

Key People

Brahma
Vishnu
Shiva

"**O** Lord of the storm gods, may your grace come down to us. . . . Do not hide the sun from our sight. O Rudra, protect our horseman from injury and may we have worthy children through your grace. . . . Your glory is unbounded, your strength unmatched among all living creatures. O Rudra, wielder (handler) of the thunder-bolt. Guide us safely to the far shore of existence where there is no sorrow."

This prayer was part of one of the early Aryan Vedas. It praised gods of nature and asked for protection against ill fortune. What, do you think, is the meaning of the plea "Do not hide the sun from our sight"?

The Roots of Hindu Belief

The Aryans passed such hymns honoring their gods from generation to generation. As Aryan culture mixed with that of the people they conquered, new ideas and beliefs became part of the Vedas. From this blending came the world's oldest living religion, Hinduism.

▼ Shiva is one of the Hindus' most important gods. Hindus believe that Shiva periodically destroys and re-creates the world.

Teaching Resources

📁 **Reproducible Lesson Plan** in the Chapter and Section Resources book-let, p. 63, provides a summary of the section lesson.

📁 **Guided Reading and Review** in the Chapter and Section Resources book-let, p. 64, provides a structure for mastering key concepts and reviewing key terms in the section. Available in Spanish in the Spanish Chapter and Section Resources booklet, p. 40.

Media and Technology

📽 **Color Transparency** 167

Lesson Objectives

1. Describe the develop-ment of Hinduism from ancient times.

2. Identify the basic beliefs and duties of Hindus.

Lesson Plan

1 Engage

Warm-Up Activity

Suggest to students that they consider the following sce-nario. All students' actions and behavior will be evaluated at the end of the year. The evaluation results will deter-mine where students will be placed for the next school year. Students who have exhibited good behavior might spend the next year as teachers' assistants or even teachers. Those who have behaved badly could be returned to a lower grade. There are no immediate con-sequences for bad behavior, only the certainty of moving downward in the future. Ask students how such a system might affect their behavior.

Activating Prior Knowledge

Ask volunteers to talk about some events they and their family or community cele-brate. (Examples might include Christmas, Passover, Fourth of July, or Founders' Day.) Ask: *Do you celebrate in the same way at the same time each year? Is the celebration related to religious beliefs?* Then have students read Reach Into Your Background in the Before You Read box.

2 Explore

As students read the section, ask them to look for answers to questions such as the following: How did Hinduism develop from several different ideas and beliefs? What are the names and roles of some Hindu gods and goddesses? What are the basic beliefs of Hinduism? What are the duties of a Hindu?

3 Teach

Have each student create two study cards for a test on this section using card headings such as *Hinduism—Main Ideas* and *Memorable Details of Hinduism.* (Students should write their names on the backs of the cards.) Collect and mix the cards. Then invite volunteers to draw cards. Use the cards as springboards for a discussion about the worldwide appeal of Hinduism. This activity should take about 25 minutes.

Background

Daily Life

Goddesses Goddesses have been important in Hinduism from its earliest origins. One goddess (Ganga) is represented by the Ganges River. Although all rivers are considered holy by the Hindus, the Ganges is the holiest. Each day, Hindus come from far away to bathe in the river and pray beside it. They believe its waters will purify their souls.

Answers to . . .

KRISHNA

The student has portrayed him as a child.

Krishna

Dhruv Khanna
age 12
India

Traditionally, artists' portrayals of the god Krishna show him as having blue skin. Other Hindu gods also have certain physical traits that help people identify them. For instance, paintings and sculptures of the god Shiva show him with four arms. **Critical Thinking** Krishna figures in many Hindu legends. He appears as a mischievous child, a cowherd, a chariot driver, and a hunter. In what role has the student artist shown Krishna?

Predict What are the Hindus' gods and goddesses like?

A Blend of Religions As Hinduism developed over 3,500 years, it absorbed many beliefs from other religions. This made Hinduism very complex. Many Hindus believe that since people are different, they need many different ways of approaching god. Thus, many different Hindu practices exist side by side.

Hinduism is more than one of the world's major religions. It is the national religion of modern India and a way of life for more than 700 million people today. Its beliefs have influenced people of many other religions. Yet Hinduism is unlike other major world religions. There is no one single founder, but Hindus have many great religious thinkers. Hindus worship many gods and goddesses, but they believe in one single spirit.

Hindu Gods and Goddesses The gods and goddesses of Hinduism stand for different parts of the single spirit. An ancient Hindu saying expresses this idea: "God is one, but wise people know it by many names." The most important Hindu gods are Brahma, the Creator; Vishnu, the Preserver; and Shiva, the Destroyer. These gods can take many different forms, both human and animal. Each of these gods is part of a single, all-powerful force called *brahman*.

Hindu teachings say that Brahma was born from a golden egg. He created the Earth and everything on it. However, he is not as widely worshipped as Vishnu and Shiva.

Hindus believe that Vishnu is a kindly god who is concerned with the welfare of human beings. Vishnu visits Earth from time to time in different forms. He does this to protect humans from disaster or to guide them.

Unlike Vishnu, Shiva is not concerned with human matters. He is very powerful. Shiva sometimes destroys the universe, but he also creates it again. Shiva developed from the god Rudra, the "wielder of the thunderbolt" in the prayer at the beginning of this section.

Hindu gods have their own families. Many Hindus, for example, worship Shiva's wife Shakti, who plays a role in human life. Like her husband, she is both a destroyer and a creator. She is both kind and cruel.

Basic Beliefs of Hinduism

All Hindus share certain central beliefs that are contained in religious writings or sacred texts.

The Upanishads One of the Hindu religious texts is the Upanishads (oo PAN uh shadz). *Upanishad* means "sitting near a teacher." Much of the Upanishads is in the form of questions by pupils and responses by teachers. For example: "Who," asks a pupil, "created the world?" The teacher replies, "Brahman is the creator, the universal soul."

When asked to describe brahman, the teacher explains that it is too complicated for humans to understand. Brahman has no physical form.

LINKS TO LANGUAGE ARTS

Common Roots The Hindu sacred books were written in a language called Sanskrit. It is one of the oldest known languages. Sanskrit is related to many other languages in the world, such as ancient Greek and Latin. Modern languages including Spanish, German, and English also have common roots with ancient Sanskrit.

▼ Special journeys to sacred places, such as this temple in southern India, are an important feature of Hindu life.

4 Assess

See the answers to the Section Review. You might also assess students' completed study cards.

Acceptable cards should include at least two of the basic beliefs of Hinduism and two important details.

Commendable cards should note the complexity of the beliefs of Hinduism. Cards should touch upon most of the basic beliefs and some of the details mentioned in the text.

Outstanding cards should note the complexity of the beliefs of Hinduism. Cards should thoroughly discuss the basic beliefs and should explain how some of the details are related to the basic beliefs.

Activity

Interdisciplinary Connection

Language Arts The relationships among many of the Hindu gods are explained in stories. Direct students to read a Hindu myth in a collection of world myths. (A possible source is *The Illustrated Book of Myths* by Neil Philip.) Then have students share the myth with the class in one of three ways: a captioned illustration, a puppet show, or an in-character retelling. *Kinesthetic*

Global Perspectives

Yoga Over the centuries, six schools of Hindu philosophy developed. Yoga, which means "union" in Sanskrit, is one of these. The yoga school teaches that the soul should be separate from the body and the mind. In order to free the soul, and thus attain freedom from the cycle of rebirth, people who practice yoga must pass through eight stages to discipline the mind and body. Some stages involve control of breathing and a complex series of physical exercises, *asanas,* that are meant to make the body flexible and healthy. These stages of yoga have become quite popular in the United States and Europe as means of achieving relaxation, physical fitness, and an overall improvement in health and well-being.

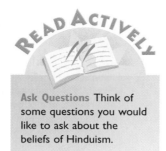

READ ACTIVELY

Ask Questions Think of some questions you would like to ask about the beliefs of Hinduism.

▼ In this scene from the ancient Hindu poem *Mahabharata,* the god Krishna drives the hero's chariot to victory. A major theme of the *Mahabharata* explores the proper conduct for different classes of people, including kings, warriors, and common folk.

Reincarnation One of the ideas in the Upanishads is **reincarnation,** or rebirth of the soul. The Hindus believe that a person may die, but the soul is reborn in the body of another living thing. Hindus believe that every living thing has a soul. This idea has been an important part of other Asian beliefs as well as Hinduism.

What body will the soul enter when it is reincarnated? According to Hindu belief, it is the actions of a person in this life that affect his or her fate in the next. Good behavior is always rewarded. Bad behavior is always punished. Faithful followers of Hinduism will be reborn into a higher position. Those whose acts have been bad may be born into a lower caste. They may even return as an animal. If a person leads a perfect life, he or she may be freed from this cycle of death and rebirth. The soul is then one with brahman.

A Hindu's Duties To become united with the one spirit and escape the cycle of death and rebirth, a person must obey his or her dharma (DAHR muh). **Dharma** are the religious and moral duties of each person. These duties depend on factors such as a person's class, occupation, and age. By obeying his or her dharma, a person comes closer to brahman.

Resource Directory

Teaching Resources

📁 **Section Quiz** in the Chapter and Section Resources booklet, p. 65, covers the main ideas and key terms in the section. Available in Spanish in the Spanish Chapter and Section Resources booklet, p. 41.

Honoring a Royal Guest

The *puja*, or ceremonial worship of a god as a royal guest, is part of all Hindus' daily lives. Pujas may include ritual bathing and feeding and the offering of flowers, incense, perfume, and other gifts. **Critical Thinking** The way Hindus perform puja varies throughout India. Why do you think this is so?

Another important idea of Hinduism is **ahimsa** (uh HIM sah), or nonviolence. To Hindus, all people and things are part of brahman. This means they must be treated with respect. For this reason, many Hindus do not eat meat and try to avoid hurting living things.

Many Paths to Truth

Hinduism teaches that there is more than one path to the truth. No matter how a person searches for truth, he or she is accepted as a Hindu.

Because of this view, Hinduism allows its followers to worship in different ways. One Hindu may present gifts to a personal god. His or her devotion to the god brings the soul closer to brahman. Another may practice special exercises and deep thinking to help free the soul from the cares of the world. Still others hope to be united with brahman by learning the sacred writings.

SECTION 2 REVIEW

1. Define (a) reincarnation, (b) dharma, (c) ahimsa.

2. Identify (a) Brahma, (b) Vishnu, (c) Shiva.

3. How did the early Aryan religion grow into Hinduism?

4. How are good and bad behavior related to reincarnation in Hinduism?

Critical Thinking

5. Identifying Central Issues What does "escaping the cycle of birth and death" mean to Hindus?

Activity

6. Writing to Learn Hindu teachers often taught their students in the form of questions and answers. Write a dialogue in which a student asks questions about Hindu beliefs, and the teacher responds.

Using the Writing Process

As a way to **introduce** the skill, write the following headings on the chalkboard: *Prewrite, Draft, Revise, Proofread, Publish*. Help students **practice** and **apply** the skill by discussing each step in the context of writing an essay about how a person can escape the cycle of death and rebirth. In prewriting, a writer might list words and phrases linked to the topic, for example, *moral duties* or *nonviolence*. During drafting, a writer shapes the ideas from prewriting into sentences and paragraphs focused on a main idea. During revision, writers take out unimportant ideas and rework any clumsy or awkward sentences. Stress that good writers then proofread their work, checking for spelling, grammar, and usage errors. Finally, writers publish or share their work. Many possibilities exist for sharing written work, including a school newspaper or a school computer network.

SECTION **3**

The Beginnings of Buddhism

Lesson Objectives

❶ Identify Buddha and describe his life and teachings.

❷ Summarize the main principles of Buddhism.

❸ Reconstruct the development of Buddhism in ancient India and how it spread to other countries.

Lesson Plan

1 Engage

Warm-Up Activity

Ask students to list—for their eyes only—five things they would like to change about school or their family. Urge students to focus on changes that reflect their approach to life—the issues or behaviors they feel are important in life. Ask students to think about why they believe each change needs to be made. Invite volunteers to share their ideas and discuss any common themes.

Activating Prior Knowledge

Have students read Reach Into Your Background in the Before You Read box. Point out that societies also adopt new ideas. For example, less than 100 years ago, American women were not allowed to vote in elections. Have students think about some of the ways societies make changes.

BEFORE YOU READ

Reach Into Your Background

Everyone experiences changes in life. You may move to another community or attend a new school. Your ideas can change as well. Think about events or ideas that have changed your life. How did you react to these changes? Did the changes seem hard to accept at first?

Questions to Explore

1. How did the Buddhist religion come about?
2. How did the teachings of Buddhism develop and spread?

Key Terms

meditate
nirvana
missionary

Key People

Siddhartha Gautama

▶ Countless different paintings and sculptures of the Buddha (Siddhartha Gautama) exist all over the world. This golden statue from India shows the young Buddha.

According to Buddhist tradition, a young Hindu prince once lived a life of luxury in his palace in northern India. Protected by the walls of the palace, he saw none of the unpleasant troubles that touch other peoples' lives. He was content with his life, for he had everything he wanted.

Then, around the age of 30, he took some rides that changed his life—and changed the history of Asia. On his rides, he saw things he never imagined. He met a bent and tired old man. The prince had never realized that people grow frail. For the first time, he saw a man who was very sick. Finally, he saw death when he saw a body being carried to a funeral.

This suffering troubled the young man greatly. He wanted to know why there was so much suffering and pain in the world. He decided to change his life to find the answer. He gave up his wealth, his family, and his life of ease in order to find the causes of human suffering. The young man was named Siddhartha Gautama (sihd DAHR tuh goh TUH muh). What he discovered after seven years of wandering led him to found a major world religion, Buddhism.

Resource Directory

Teaching Resources

📁 **Reproducible Lesson Plan** in the Chapter and Section Resources booklet, p. 66, provides a summary of the section lesson.

📁 **Guided Reading and Review** in the Chapter and Section Resources booklet, p. 67, provides a structure for mastering key concepts and reviewing key terms in the section. Available in Spanish in the Spanish Chapter and Section Resources booklet, p. 42.

Program Resources

Outline Maps South Asia: Political, p. 37
Southeast Asia: Political, p. 43

The Teachings of Buddhism

As Gautama traveled in the 500s B.C., he sought answers to the meaning of life. At first, Gautama studied with Hindu philosophers. But their ideas did not satisfy him. He could not accept the Hindu belief that only Brahmins could pass on knowledge.

Gautama decided to stop looking outwardly for the cause of suffering. Instead, he tried to find understanding within his own mind. He did this by meditating. **Meditating** is thinking deeply about sacred things. Buddhist tradition says that Gautama fasted and meditated under a fig tree. After 49 days, he found the answers he sought. Now he understood the roots of suffering.

For the next 45 years, Gautama traveled across India and shared his knowledge. Over the years, he attracted many followers. Because he could explain things that troubled people, his followers called him the Buddha (boo duh)—"The Enlightened One." His teachings became known as Buddhism.

The Middle Way Buddhism differed from earlier religions in one important way. Other religions worshipped many gods or one God. Buddha taught that the answer to human suffering lay not in worshipping gods, but in right thinking and self-denial.

READ ACTIVELY

Ask Questions What questions would you like to ask about the religion of Buddhism?

The Three Jewels of Buddhism

The Buddha (the teacher), *dharma* (the teaching), and *sangha* (the community of believers) are known as the three jewels of Buddhism. **Critical Thinking** How does this painting show the three jewels of Buddhism?

Media and Technology

 Color Transparencies 74, 76

2 Explore

Instruct students to read the section. Ask them to pay special attention to finding answers to the Questions to Explore. They may record their ideas in a reading log. Together, draft answers using the recorded ideas. The following questions can stimulate the process: How did Buddha's ideas grow from his experiences and Hindu beliefs? What was the appeal of Buddhism?

Background

Biography

Mahavira: Founder of Jainism Mahavira was born about the same time as Siddhartha Gautama. Like Gautama, he left behind a privileged life in a quest for spirituality and sought to modify rather than replace Hindu ideas. Mahavira said that each wrong act added an impurity to the soul. Good behavior could reverse this process. A completely pure soul would no longer need to be reborn.

The Jains, as followers of Mahavira are called, applied these ideas very strictly. They allowed themselves to be bitten by insects, preferring minor discomfort over taking the life of any creature. Mahavira followed his ideas so stringently that he gave up food, starving himself to death.

Answers to ...

THE THREE JEWELS OF BUDDHISM

The painting shows the Buddha teaching a group of followers.

3 Teach

Have students develop a layout for an Internet website about Buddhism. The layout should include text and graphics. Data should include a brief explanation of Buddhist ideas and history. Encourage students to include answers to four "frequently asked questions" about Buddhism.

4 Assess

See the answers to the Section Review. You might also assess students' website layouts.

Acceptable layouts include accurate historical and ideological information and several appropriate graphics.

Commendable layouts include accurate information and appropriate graphics. Layouts also identify and provide answers to frequently asked questions.

Outstanding layouts include accurate information, appropriate graphics, and answers to frequently asked questions. Additional information refers to Buddhism's worldwide appeal.

The Practice of Buddhism

Chart Study The Middle Way is also called the Eightfold Path. The chart shows the eight parts of the path and what they mean. Buddhists in Tibet use prayer wheels that contain a written holy verse. Each turn of the wheel is equivalent to saying the prayer aloud. **Critical Thinking** How do you think the prayer wheel helps the man follow the Eightfold Path?

The Eightfold Path

	Step	Meaning
1.	Right Understanding	Having faith in the Buddhist view of the universe
2.	Right Intention	Making a commitment to practice Buddhism
3.	Right Speech	Avoiding lies and mean or abusive speech
4.	Right Action	Not taking life, not stealing, not hurting others
5.	Right Livelihood	Rejecting jobs and occupations that conflict with Buddhist ideals
6.	Right Effort	Avoiding bad attitudes and developing good ones
7.	Right Mindfulness	Being aware of the body, feelings, and thoughts
8.	Right Concentration	Thinking deeply to find answers to problems

Adapted from *Encyclopaedia Britannica*.

READ ACTIVELY

Predict Why do you think some people might have been attracted to the religion of Buddhism?

Buddha taught that human suffering is caused by selfish desires for power, wealth, and pleasure. The way a person becomes free from suffering is by giving up these selfish desires. The way to do this is to follow the Middle Way. The Middle Way avoids two extremes—too much pleasure and too much worry about life.

Reaching Nirvana   To find this Middle Way, Buddha taught, people must act unselfishly toward others and treat people fairly. They must tell the truth at all times. People should also avoid violence and the killing of any living thing. If people followed Buddha's path, their sufferings would end. They would eventually find **nirvana,** or lasting peace. By reaching nirvana, people would be released from the endless wheel of reincarnation.

Followers of Buddhism   Buddhism also taught that all people are equal. Anyone, Buddha declared, could follow the path to nirvana, regardless of his or her social class. This idea appealed to many people.

Like other religions, Buddhism has priests. Anyone can become a Buddhist priest, or monk. Buddha encouraged his followers to establish monasteries. There they would learn, meditate, and teach. He also urged monks to become **missionaries,** or people who spread their religious beliefs to others.

Buddhism in India

After gaining the understanding of human suffering that he looked for, Buddha spent the rest of his life teaching. Followers flocked to hear his sermons. Rulers and ordinary people gathered around him. After his death, his teachings spread all over India. For many years, Buddhism and Hinduism existed side by side in India.

The Golden Age of Buddhism in India came during the rule of Asoka (uh SOH kuh), one of India's greatest rulers. You will read about him in the next section. However, Buddha's teachings did not last in the land of his birth. Over time, Buddhism died out almost completely in India.

At the same time, Hinduism absorbed many Buddhist ideas. Hindus came to believe in many of the teachings of Buddha. They accepted the idea that it is wrong to harm other living creatures. They accepted nonviolence. Many Hindus came to honor Buddha as a reincarnation of the god Vishnu. But, for many centuries, Hindus could not accept Buddha's ideas of equality.

▼ Sculptures often show Buddha in one of three poses—meditating, teaching, or lying down. These poses may be linked to the great events of Buddha's life, his enlightenment, his teaching, and his reaching Nirvana.

Background

Links Across Time

Worship at Home Buddhists worship at shrines. Today, many Buddhists have small shrines in their homes, with a small statue of Buddha, a candleholder, and a vessel in which to burn incense. Before meditating or performing other rituals, Buddhists light the candles to symbolize the light of Buddha's ideas. The incense symbolizes purity, wisdom, and compassion. Flowers are the other necessary component and represent unity and equality.

Activity

Interdisciplinary Connections

Art Check out some books on Indian or Buddhist art and show students examples of Buddhist art and architecture such as the cave temples of Ajanta, which were carved from a mountain. Invite students to talk about one example. Interested students might also try carving their own caves out of clay. *Visual, Kinesthetic*

SKILLS MINI LESSON

Distinguishing Facts From Opinions
You may **introduce** the skill by indicating that facts are statements that can be proved or disproved. Opinions cannot be proved or disproved. Help students **practice** the skill by writing the following sentences on the chalkboard: *Buddhism began in India,* and *It is wrong to harm another living creature.* Ask students to identify which sentence represents a fact and to explain why. (The first sentence is factual. Students can prove the statement is true.) Then ask students to explain why the remaining sentence presents an opinion. (It represents a *belief* of a person or a group. Not everyone would agree with the statement.) Suggest that students **apply** the skill by recording other facts and opinions as they read.

The Spread of Buddhism

Map Study Missionaries and traders carried Buddha's ideas and teachings throughout Asia. **Movement** Which place did Buddhism reach first, Burma or Korea?

ASIA

KOREA A.D. 300s
JAPAN A.D. 500s
AFGHANISTAN A.D. 100s
TIBET A.D. 600s
East China Sea
CHINA A.D. 100s
Arabian Sea
BURMA 1st century A.D.
INDIA 200s B.C.
Bay of Bengal
PACIFIC OCEAN
SOUTHEAST ASIA 1st century A.D.
South China Sea
SRI LANKA 200s B.C.
INDIAN OCEAN
SUMATRA A.D. 300s
JAVA A.D. 300s

KEY
Area where Buddhism originated
Spread of Buddhism
Robinson Projection

0   500   1,000 mi
0   500   1,000 km

Buddhism Spreads to Other Countries

Buddhism, however, was accepted by millions of people in other lands. Missionaries carried Buddha's message throughout Asia. It took root in China and grew there. Millions of Chinese became Buddhists. They mixed the ideas of Buddha with those of earlier teachers. Buddhist monasteries became centers of religious thought in China. From China, Buddhism spread to Korea and Japan. Today, Buddhism is part of the cultures of such countries as Japan, Korea, China, Tibet, and Vietnam.

SECTION 3 REVIEW

1. Define (a) meditate, (b) nirvana, (c) missionary.

2. Identify Siddhartha Gautama.

3. How did Buddha try to change the lives of people in India?

4. What happened to Buddhism in India?

Critical Thinking

5. Recognizing Cause and Effect According to Buddhism, how is human suffering connected to human desires?

Activity

6. Writing to Learn Write a journal entry that Siddhartha Gautama might have written after he discovered human suffering for the first time.

The Golden Age of Maurya India

Lesson Objectives

1. Outline the development of the Maurya empire.

2. Identify Emperors Chandragupta and Asoka and explain their roles in the Maurya empire.

3. State the importance of the Maurya empire in India's history.

BEFORE YOU READ

Reach Into Your Background

Think about someone you admire and respect. What traits does that person have?

How does she or he act? How could you be more like that person?

Questions to Explore

1. Why is the Maurya empire considered a golden age in India?
2. Why is Asoka considered one of India's greatest leaders?

Key Terms

absolute power
convert

Key People

Chandragupta
Asoka

1 Engage

Warm-Up Activity

Tell students that a new schoolwide student leader is about to be chosen. Invite volunteers to brainstorm some likely problems and issues that such a leader might face. Then ask students to consider and list the qualities a leader would need to successfully cope with these issues.

Activating Prior Knowledge

Have students read Reach Into Your Background in the Before You Read box. You might encourage students to organize their ideas about admirable traits in chart form.

A round 330 B.C., a new ruler came to the throne of a kingdom in northeastern India. Within 35 years, the tiny kingdom grew into the giant Maurya (MAH oor yuh) empire. The first king of this empire was Chandragupta (chuhn druh GUP tuh) Maurya.

Chandragupta lived in grand style. A Greek traveler described the impressive sight that greeted him at the king's court. The royal palace was supported by great wooden pillars coated with gold. In the park where the palace stood, fountains sprayed the air and fish splashed in ponds. Scores of servants waited on the king.

Chandragupta enjoyed luxuries from all parts of Asia. When the king appeared before his subjects, he was often seated in a golden chair carried on his servants' shoulders. Sometimes he rode on an elephant covered with jewels.

▼ This complex design shows the skill of Maurya artisans. One figure is part human and part dragon.

Teaching Resources

📁 **Reproducible Lesson Plan** in the Chapter and Section Resources booklet, p. 69, provides a summary of the section lesson.

📁 **Guided Reading and Review** in the Chapter and Section Resources booklet, p. 70, provides a structure for mastering key concepts and reviewing key terms in the section. Available in Spanish in the Spanish Chapter and Section Resources booklet, p. 44.

Program Resources

Outline Maps South Asia: Political, p. 37

2 Explore

As students read the section, have them refer to the list of leadership qualities created in the Warm-Up Activity. Urge students to evaluate both Chandragupta and Asoka against these qualities. Ask: *Why were these men so powerful? How did they use their power to both help and hurt India?*

3 Teach

Ask students to create a chart similar to the following:

Chandragupta		Asoka	
Actions	Results	Actions	Results

Students should complete the charts with information from the section, noting the importance of each action and result. This activity should take about 25 minutes.

4 Assess

See the answers to the Section Review. Completed charts can also serve as assessment tools.

Acceptable charts include three accurate entries in each column.

Commendable charts include at least three accurate entries and show a distinction between the two emperors.

Outstanding charts include at least three accurate entries and demonstrate recognition of the significance of each action.

Elephants in Battle

The people of India were the first to use elephants in war. During battles, the huge animals fearlessly charged toward men and horses, causing panic and chaos.

LINKS ACROSS THE WORLD

Chandragupta and Alexander the Great Chandragupta started life as a slave. One of his masters educated him. Then he met Alexander the Great, the Greek conqueror of the ancient world. Near the time of the meeting, legend says a lion awakened Chandragupta one night by licking his body. Chandragupta thought this meant he would become a great ruler, like Alexander. He made that idea a reality.

Building the Maurya Empire

India was made up of a number of warring states before Chandragupta came to power. Strong and ruthless, he founded the Maurya empire. His armies overthrew kingdoms along the Ganges River. Turning west, his armies advanced into the Indus River Valley. Only a few years later, his power extended over most of north and central India.

Chandragupta was guided by the basic belief that a ruler must have **absolute power,** or complete control over the people. This idea came from a book of advice called *The Science of Material Gain.* The book urged kings to control all their subjects and to maintain an army of spies to inform on them.

Chandragupta commanded a huge army. Thousands of foot soldiers and mounted troops were ready to maintain law and order and to crush any revolts. The army also had 9,000 war elephants, which struck fear into the hearts of opponents.

Prosperity and Poisoners Under Chandragupta, the empire enjoyed great success. Most of its wealth came from foreign trade. The Maurya empire built up a widespread trade with such faraway places as Greece, Rome, and China.

However, as his rule continued, Chandragupta became fearful for his life. Thinking poisoners were everywhere, he made servants taste his food. To avoid being murdered, he slept in a different room every night. One story says that he finally became a monk in south India. Fasting and praying, he starved himself to death.

Maintaining the Empire Chandragupta did not gain wealth for himself only. Though his rule was harsh, he used his wealth to improve his empire. New irrigation systems brought water to farmers. Forests were cleared, and more food was produced. Government officials promoted crafts and mining. A vast network of roads made it easier for Maurya traders to exchange goods with foreign lands. Chandragupta's leadership brought order and peace to his people.

Resource Directory

Media and Technology

 Color Transparency 74

Asoka: A Father to His People

When Chandragupta died, the empire passed to his son. When the son died, Chandragupta's grandson, Asoka, gained power. Asoka, whose name means "without sorrow," further expanded Chandragupta's empire. By the end of his rule in 232 B.C., Asoka had built the greatest empire India had ever seen.

The Battle of Kalinga   For more than 35 years, Asoka ruled an empire that included much of the subcontinent of India. During the first years of his rule, Asoka was as warlike as his grandfather. He conquered new territories to the east. Early in his rule, Asoka led his army south into the state of Kalinga. He won a bloody battle in 261 B.C. in which more than 100,000 people died. The great slaughter at Kalinga was a turning point in Asoka's life. He was filled with sorrow over the bloodshed. He gave up war and violence. He freed his prisoners and restored their land. Later, he converted, or changed his beliefs, to Buddhism.

▼ People believe that this Buddhist monument, the Great Stupa, was begun by Asoka. The massive dome represents heaven encircling the Earth.

Cooperative Learning

Plan a Vegetarian Meal
After becoming a Buddhist, Asoka gave up eating meat and encouraged all Indians to follow suit. Today, many Indians are vegetarian. Provide some vegetarian cookbooks for students. Have them read about vegetarian dietary restrictions and how to meet important nutritional needs when not eating meat. Invite students to plan and, if possible, prepare and sample a vegetarian dish. *English Language Learner*

Interdisciplinary Connections

Language Arts Ask students to compose messages in the style of Asoka's moral messages to his people. Emphasize that students' messages should not concern matters of religion but rather appropriate student behavior. Students may present their messages on posters, clay tablets, computer displays, or audio recordings. *English Language Learner, Visual*

Asoka Spreads Buddha's Message Asoka practiced and preached the teachings of Buddha. He did not allow the use of animals for sacrifices. He gave up hunting, the traditional sport of Indian kings.

Asoka thought of his people as his children. Like a father, he was concerned with their welfare. He had hospitals built throughout his kingdom. He even had wells dug every mile beside the roads so that travelers and animals would not go thirsty.

Asoka was also concerned with his people's moral and spiritual life. To carry Buddha's message throughout his vast empire, Asoka issued writings of moral advice. Some writings urged people to honor their parents. Others asked people not to kill animals. Still others encouraged people to behave with tolerance and with truthfulness. Asoka also issued laws that required people to be treated with humanity. His advice and laws were carved on pillars of stone 30 to 40 feet (9 to 12 meters) high throughout his empire. One pillar bore these words:

> "Both this world and the other are hard to reach, except by great love of the law, great self-examination, great obedience, great respect, great energy."

Asoka's tolerance for others allowed him to accept Hindus. Many of Buddha's teachings became part of Hinduism during Asoka's rule. Buddhism grew under Asoka. He sent missionaries far and wide to

Connect Think of an event in your life that caused you to make changes or rethink the way you do things. Why did the event make you want to change?

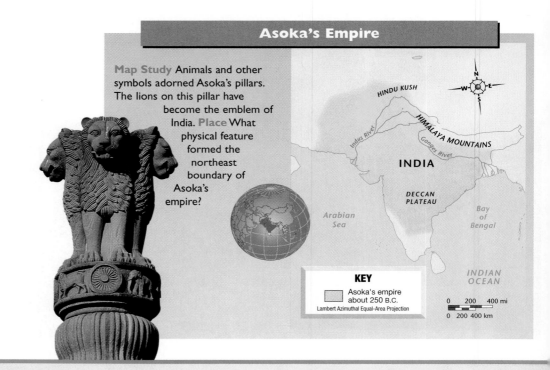

Asoka's Empire

Map Study Animals and other symbols adorned Asoka's pillars. The lions on this pillar have become the emblem of India. **Place** What physical feature formed the northeast boundary of Asoka's empire?

HINDU KUSH

HIMALAYA MOUNTAINS

Indus River

Ganges River

INDIA

DECCAN PLATEAU

Arabian Sea

Bay of Bengal

INDIAN OCEAN

KEY

Asoka's empire about 250 B.C.

Lambert Azimuthal Equal-Area Projection

0   200   400 mi

0   200 400 km

Teaching Resources

Section Quiz in the Chapter and Section Resources booklet, p. 71, covers the main ideas and key terms in the section. Available in Spanish in the Spanish Chapter and Section Resources booklet, p. 45.

Vocabulary in the Chapter and Section Resources booklet, p. 73, provides a review of key terms in the chapter.

Available in Spanish in the Spanish Chapter and Section Resources booklet, p. 47.

Reteaching in the Chapter and Section Resources booklet, p. 74, provides a structure for students who may need additional help in mastering chapter content.

Enrichment in the Chapter and Section Resources booklet, p. 75, extends chapter content and enriches students' understanding.

Buddhism Today

An orange-robed monk teaches the principles of Buddhism to these students in Bangkok, the capital of the modern-day country of Thailand. A gold statue of the Buddha occupies a place of honor.

Background

Links Across Time

Indian Flag Asoka and his laws are remembered in the modern Indian flag. The Dharma Chakra (Wheel of Law) symbol was on many of Asoka's pillars and is also the focal point of India's flag, which was adopted in 1947.

spread its message. It was missionaries sent by Asoka who spread Buddhism to China. Asoka's sister and brother went to Ceylon—today, the country of Sri Lanka—as Buddhist missionaries. He even sent teachers to Egypt, Greece, and North Africa.

At Asoka's death, India was united as never before. However, the great Maurya empire declined after his death. Without his strong rule, his territories divided. Small states began fighting with one another. Several centuries of invasion and disorder followed. It took almost 600 years before India was united again.

SECTION 4 REVIEW

1. Define (a) absolute power, (b) convert.

2. Identify (a) Chandragupta, (b) Asoka.

3. How did Chandragupta and Asoka build a great empire?

4. Why could Asoka be called a father to his people?

Critical Thinking

5. Recognizing Cause and Effect How did Buddhism in India influence the empire of Asoka?

Activity

6. Writing to Learn Asoka wrote many rules of conduct for himself and others to follow. Write down some rules of conduct that you would like to see leaders today follow. Do you think it is possible for today's leaders to follow these rules? Why or why not?

Section 4 Review

1. (a) complete control over people (b) to change beliefs

2. (a) founder of the Maurya empire (b) great ruler and builder of the Maurya empire

3. through military conquest and strict rule

4. He cared about his people and tried to guide their spiritual lives.

5. Answers may vary. Possible answers: Buddhism caused Asoka to stop focusing on war and conquest and focus instead on improving his people's spiritual lives.

6. Rules may vary, but may include a focus on respect for people of many cultures, peace, concern for the environment, and working well with other government leaders. Students should support their opinions with facts.

Spanish Glossary in the Spanish Chapter and Section Resources, pp. 85–89, provides key terms translated from English to Spanish as well as definitions in Spanish.

Chapter Summary in the Chapter and Section Resources booklet, p. 72, provides a summary of chapter content. Available in Spanish in the Spanish Chapter and Section Resources booklet, p. 46.

Cooperative Learning Activity in the Activities and Projects booklet, pp. 32–35, provides two student handouts, one page of teacher's directions, and a scoring rubric for a cooperative learning activity on making a map of Mohenjo-Daro.

Media and Technology

Guided Reading Audiotapes (English and Spanish)

SKILLS ACTIVITY

Reading Tables

Lesson Objectives

❶ Explain how a table works.

❷ Demonstrate how to make a table.

❸ Use a table to find information.

Lesson Plan

1 Engage

Warm-Up Activity

Pose the introductory situation to the class, allowing volunteers to role-play the scene. Work with students to brainstorm what information would be included on Mrs. Frankel's class's table of pizza choices.

Activating Prior Knowledge

Ask volunteers who have used tables before to name or describe the standard elements of a table (columns, rows, category labels, and so forth).

2 Explore

To **introduce** students to the skill, read the Get Ready text with them. Explain that the terms *chart* and *table* mean the same thing. Point out to students that columns are arranged vertically and rows horizontally.

"I want mushroom."

"I think we should have spinach."

"Mmmm, let's get pepperoni!"

The kids in Ms. Frankel's class were trying to figure out what kind of pizza to order for their party day. Ceretha and Ben were in charge of figuring out what to order.

"Wait!" said Ceretha. "We'll never be able to figure this out and remember what everyone wants."

"Let's just get organized," Ben said. "I'll make a table of all this information. That way, we can see at a glance who wants what kind, how many of us want the same kind, and so on."

Resource Directory

Teaching Resources

📁 **Reading a Table** in the Social Studies and Geography Skills booklet, p. 62, provides additional skill practice.

Get Ready

A chart or table can help you organize and compare information. It is a simple way to arrange facts in columns and rows to make them easy to understand. Charts and tables also provide information in a way that is easy to read and refer to.

Try It Out

To see how a table can work, try making one yourself. Find out what four of your classmates' favorite things are. Fill in a table like the one below.

Classmate	Favorite Food	Favorite TV Show	Favorite Sport
First person			
Second person			
Third person			
Fourth person			

Do several people like the same TV show? How are the first and third persons' favorites alike? How are they different?

Apply the Skill

In this book, you are reading about some of the world's major religions. A good way to understand some information about them is by reading the table below. Follow these steps.

1. **Determine the purpose of the table.** By reading the title and the headings of the columns, you will understand what the table is about. What kinds of information will this table give you?

2. **Use the table.** To locate facts in a table, look across a horizontal row (from left to right) and down a vertical column (from top to bottom) to the spot they intersect, or cross each other. Suppose you want to know where Judaism was founded. What column headings would you read? Which row would you look for? When was Judaism founded? (Remember that the abbreviation *c.* means "about.")

3. **Analyze the information.** Tables are especially useful for comparing information. Which religion was founded most recently? On which continent was each religion founded? Which religions were founded in India?

4. **Use the information.** How might this information be useful to you when reading about ancient history?

Major World Religions		
Religion	When Founded	Where Founded
Buddhism	c. 525 B.C.	India
Christianity	c. A.D. 30	Southwest Asia
Hinduism	c. 1500 B.C.	India
Islam	c. A.D. 622	Southwest Asia
Judaism	c. 1800 B.C.	Southwest Asia

Chapter Review 4

Reviewing Main Ideas

1. Mountains and oceans isolated India from other cultures.

2. The city was well planned, with great attention paid to cleanliness and hygiene.

3. Hinduism grew out of basic Aryan ideas, as expressed in documents such as the Vedas.

4. the religious or moral duties of each person; a person's class, occupation, gender, and age

5. The solution to human suffering is in each person's mind, not in worshipping a god.

6. Buddha's ideas made spiritual peace and insight accessible to all people, regardless of social class.

7. The Maurya empire united India more than ever before; its leaders improved farmlands and services; it brought prosperity and interaction with other cultures through trade.

8. expansion of the empire, writings of moral advice, improvement of public services, spread of Buddhism; These achievements united India.

Reviewing Key Terms

Sentences will vary, but should show correct meaning of each term through context.

Critical Thinking

1. Archaeologists have learned about Mohenjo-Daro by studying its ruins, which show a carefully planned city with highly developed services.

2. Gautama vowed to change his life when he saw that much suffering accompanies normal life. Asoka changed his life after realizing he was responsible for a great deal of bloodshed.

CHAPTER 4 Review and Activities

Reviewing Main Ideas

1. What was the effect of mountains and oceans on the history of India?
2. What made Mohenjo-Daro an advanced city?
3. Explain the connection between early Aryan religion and Hinduism.
4. What do Hindus mean by dharma? What does a person's dharma depend on?
5. Explain the central idea of Buddhism.
6. Explain why Buddha's ideas appealed to so many people.
7. Give three reasons why the Maurya empire was called India's golden age.
8. List four achievements of Asoka and explain their importance in ruling India.

Reviewing Key Terms

Use each key term below in a sentence that shows the meaning of the term.

1. subcontinent
2. monsoon
3. citadel
4. migrate
5. caste
6. reincarnation
7. dharma
8. ahimsa
9. meditate
10. nirvana
11. missionary
12. absolute power
13. convert

Critical Thinking

1. **Drawing Conclusions** Although the language of Mohenjo-Daro is a mystery, its people created a highly organized civilization. How do we know this?
2. **Making Comparisons** How does Gautama's life changing experience with suffering compare to Asoka's?

Graphic Organizer

Copy the chart onto a sheet of paper. Then fill in the empty boxes to complete the chart.

	Achievements	Effect on India's History
Indus Valley People		
Aryans		
Hinduism		
Buddhism		
Maurya Empire		

Graphic Organizer

	Achievements	Effects on India's History
Indus Valley People	city planning, drainage systems	created sophisticated culture
Aryans	Vedas, caste system	brought origins of Hinduism and caste system to India
Hinduism	reincarnation, tolerance	introduced reincarnation, dharma, ahimsa
Buddhism	meditation, the Middle Way, nirvana open to all, equality of all people	offset caste system with ideas of equality, opened worship to all individuals
Maurya Empire	unified India, improved lands and services, wealth from trade, spread of Buddhism, tolerance	irrigation systems, forests cleared for farming, vast network of roads

Map Activity

India

For each place listed below, write the letter from the map that shows its location.

1. Himalaya Mountains
2. Hindu Kush Mountains
3. Indus River
4. Ganges River
5. Mohenjo-Daro

Place Location

Writing Activity

Writing Inscriptions
Asoka helped spread Buddha's message by inscribing stone pillars with his teachings. Think about the beliefs of Hinduism.

Write inscriptions that could be put on pillars to spread the teachings of Hinduism. Keep in mind the beliefs of Hinduism, and how people worship.

Internet Activity

Use a search engine to find the site called **Alhamkara.** Select several links to explore in the Table of Contents. Then either write a "day-in-the-life" account of your life in the Maurya court, make a time line to track the changes of India's cuisine over time, or compare and contrast Hindu views of nature with Western views.

Skills Review

Turn to the Skills Activity.
Review the steps for reading a table. Then, briefly explain how a table makes it easy to compare information.

How Am I Doing?

Answer these questions to help you check your progress.

1. Can I describe the main geographic features of India?
2. Do I understand how the civilizations of ancient India compare to other ancient civilizations I've studied?
3. Can I identify historic events or movements that shaped the culture of India?
4. What information from this chapter can I use in my book project?

Map Activity

1. B   3. D   5. C
2. A   4. E

Writing Activity

Inscriptions should accurately reflect elements of Hinduism such as the many paths to truth, dharma, ahimsa, reincarnation, importance of priests, Brahma, and other gods.

Skills Review

In tables, facts are arranged in columns and rows in such a way as to make them easy to read, understand, and compare.

Internet Activity

If students are having difficulty finding this site, you may wish to have them use the following URL, which was accurate at the time this textbook was published:

**http://www.ncb.gov.sg/nhb/
alam/
Alamkarahome.html#
toc**

You might also guide students to a search engine. Four of the most useful are Infoseek, AltaVista, Lycos, and Yahoo. For additional suggestions on using the Internet, refer to the Prentice Hall Social Studies'

Educator's Handbook "Using the Internet," in the *Prentice Hall World Explorer Program Resources.*

For additional links to world history and culture topics, visit the Prentice Hall Home Page at:
http://www.phschool.com

How Am I Doing?

Point out to students that this checklist is a quick reminder of what they learned in the chapter. If their answer to any of the questions is *no* or if they are unsure, they may need to review the topic.

Resource Directory

Teaching Resources

Chapter Tests Forms A and B are in the Tests booklet, pp. 20–25.

Program Resources

Writing Process Handbook includes Organizing Material in a Logical Sequence, pp. 23–24, to help students with the Writing Activity.

Media and Technology

Color Transparencies
Color Transparency 174
(Graphic organizer table template)
Prentice Hall Writer's Solution
Writing Lab CD-ROM
Computer Test Bank
Resource Pro™ CD-ROM

Lesson Objectives

❶ Analyze and explain a traditional Indian fable.

❷ Relate the fable to the Buddhist traditions and ideas it reflects.

Lesson Plan

1 Engage

Building Vocabulary

Point out that the notes in the margins can help students understand certain words and can give helpful hints as students read. Vocabulary defined in the margins includes *harrow, chaff, husk, millet,* and *shabbily.*

Activating Prior Knowledge

Have students read Reach Into Your Background in the Before You Read box. Ask volunteers to share instructive stories that have been told to them. Discuss how these stories teach lessons.

2 Develop Student Reading

As a class, read and discuss the Questions to Explore. Also, point out the questions in the margin. Tell students to keep all of them in mind as they read the story. Students might jot down their responses to some of the questions in a literature log.

The Envious Buffalo

**A JATAKA STORY FROM *THE FABLES OF INDIA*
RETOLD BY JOSEPH GAER**

BEFORE YOU READ

Reach Into Your Background

Has anyone ever tried to teach you something by telling you a story? Have you ever given advice to a friend by telling an experience you had?

People around the world have always used stories to teach important lessons. The Jataka stories from India teach such lessons. They are part of Buddhism's sacred writings. They tell of the past lives of Buddha, before he was released from the wheel of reincarnation. In his earlier lives, he is called the Bodisat, or the Buddha-to-be. The Bodisat appears in the Jataka stories as a king, teacher, lion, monkey, or other creature.

Many of the Jataka stories are fables, like this one. A fable is a brief story with few characters. It teaches a simple lesson about life called a moral. Fables usually have one or more animal characters.

Questions to Explore

1. What can you learn from this story about the life of farmers in India?
2. Why is this story a good example of the beliefs of Buddhism?

Bubalus (BOO buhl us)

harrow *v.* to break up soil

chaff *n.* the coverings removed from seeds of grain before the grain is ground into flour

husk *v.* to remove the coverings from seeds of grain

millet (MIL it) *n.* a kind of grain

O n a small farm in southern India there lived a water buffalo named Big Red Bubalus with his younger brother named Little Red Bubalus. These two brothers did all the hard work on the farm. They plowed and they harrowed; they seeded; and they brought in the harvest for their owner. In between the crops they worked the water wheel which irrigated the farm and the garden; and they turned the pump to supply water for the house and pigpen.

When the crop was in, Big Red Bubalus and Little Red Bubalus were harnessed again to turn the grindstone which milled the flour for the family.

Yet for all their labors they were rarely rewarded. They were seldom allowed to bathe in the stream, which they loved to do. And all they were given to eat was grass and straw, or chaff when the grain was husked.

This same farmer owned a pig who did nothing but eat and wallow in the water pumped up for him by the buffaloes. Yet the hog was fed on rice and millet and was well taken care of by the farmer and his family.

Resource Directory

Teaching Resources

📁 **Determining If You Understood What You Read** in the Social Studies and Geography Skills booklet, p. 74, provides additional skill practice.

Program Resources

Material in the **Primary Sources and Literature Readings** booklet provides additional literature selections on the region under study.

► Again and again the younger buffalo would complain; and each time the older buffalo merely said: "Envy not the pig."

Little Red Bubalus complained to his brother: "We, who do all the hard work, are treated shabbily and our master gives us next to nothing to eat. Most of the time we have to go out into the pasture to find our own food. Yet this lazy pig is fed all the time and never does any work."

"Envy him not, little brother," said Big Red Bubalus (who was the Bodisat in the form of a buffalo). And he would say no more.

Again and again the younger buffalo would complain; and each time the older buffalo merely said:

"Envy not the pig."

One day the farmer's only daughter was engaged to be married. And as the wedding day drew near, the hog was slaughtered and roasted for the wedding feast.

Then Big Red Bubalus said to Little Red Bubalus: "Now do you see why a pig is not to be envied?"

And Little Red Bubalus replied: "Yes, now I understand. It is better to feed on straw and chaff, and to live out our lives, than to be fattened on rice only to end up on a roasting spit."

shabbily *adv.* unfairly, ungenerously

READ ACTIVELY

Connect Have you ever envied someone? How did it make you feel?

About the Selection

"The Envious Buffalo" is part of the *Jatakas,* or stories of the previous lives of the Buddha. In *Jataka* tales, the Buddha-to-be often appears in another form such as that of an elephant, a king, or an outcast. However, the tales always end with his revealing his true identity.

This version of "The Envious Buffalo" can be found in *The Fables of India* by Joseph Gaer, which was published by Little, Brown and Company in 1955.

3 Assess

Work through the Exploring Your Reading questions with students.

1. He envies the extra food, bathing, and care the pig gets.
2. Big Red Bubalus is the Bodisat.
3. Answers will vary. Students may say that the Bodisat might play roles in which he gives advice that reflects Buddhist beliefs.
4. They feel envy, they talk, and they give and take advice.
5. Big Red Bubalus wants Little Red Bubalus to learn the lesson on his own by watching what happens to the pig.
6. Answers will vary. Possible answer: Power, wealth, and pleasure may carry too high a price.
7. Acceptable fables will contain a recognizable lesson. Outstanding fables will contain vivid and lively characters.

EXPLORING YOUR READING

Look Back

1. Why does Little Red Bubalus envy the pig?

2. Which character is the Bodisat in this story?

Think It Over

3. From this fable and from what you know about Buddhism, what role do you think the Bodisat might play in other Jataka stories?

4. How are the animals in this story like humans?

5. Why doesn't Big Red Bubalus explain why Little Red Bubalus should not envy the pig?

Go Beyond

6. Restate the moral of this fable in a general way that fits people.

Ideas for Writing: Short Story

7. Think of a lesson about life you think people should be aware of. Using this story as a model, write a fable that teaches the moral you have chosen.

THE ANCIENT WORLD
Ancient China

To help you plan instruction, the chart below shows how teaching resources correspond to chapter content. Use the resources to vary instruction, add activities, or plan block schedules. Where appropriate, resources have **suggested time allotments** for students. Time allotments are approximate.

Managing Time and Instruction

	The Ancient World Teaching Resources Binder		World Explorer Program Resources Binder	
	Resource	**mins.**	**Resource**	**mins.**
1 SECTION 1 The Geography of China's River Valleys	**Chapter and Section Support** Reproducible Lesson Plan, p. 78		**Outline Maps** China and Neighboring Countries:	
	Ⓢ Guided Reading and Review, p. 79	20	Political, p. 41	20
	Ⓢ Section Quiz, p. 80	25	East Asia: Physical, p. 39	20
	Critical Thinking Activity, p. 94	30	**Nystrom Desk Atlas**	20
			Ⓣ **Primary Sources and Literature Readings**	40
			Writing Process Handbook Editing for Content, Clarity, and Style, pp. 35–36	25
SKILLS ACTIVITY Organizing Information	**Social Studies and Geography Skills,** Identifying the Main Idea, p. 41	30		
2 SECTION 2 Confucius and His Teachings	**Chapter and Section Support** Reproducible Lesson Plan, p. 81			
	Ⓢ Guided Reading and Review, p. 82	20		
	Ⓢ Section Quiz, p. 83	25		
	Social Studies and Geography Skills, Recognizing Ideologies, p. 48	30		
3 SECTION 3 Strong Rulers Unite Warring Kingdoms	**Chapter and Section Support** Reproducible Lesson Plan, p. 84		**Outline Maps** China and Neighboring Countries:	
	Ⓢ Guided Reading and Review, p. 85	20	Political, p. 41	20
	Ⓢ Section Quiz, p. 86	25		
4 SECTION 4 Achievements of Ancient China	**Chapter and Section Support** Reproducible Lesson Plan, p. 87		**Outline Maps** South Asia: Political, p. 37	20
	Ⓢ Guided Reading and Review, p. 88	20	China and Neighboring Countries, p. 41	
	Ⓢ Section Quiz, p. 89	25		
	Ⓢ Vocabulary, p. 91	20		
	Reteaching, p. 92	25		
	Enrichment, p. 93	25		
	Ⓢ Chapter Summary, p. 90	15		
	Tests Forms A and B Chapter Tests, pp. 26–31	40		
ACTIVITY SHOP: LAB Rivers That Flood	Activity Shop: Lab, p. 6	30		

Block Scheduling

Block Scheduling Folder
PROGRAM TEACHING RESOURCES

Activities and Projects

Interdisciplinary Links

Block Scheduling Program Support

Resource Pro™ CD-ROM

Media and Technology

Media and Technology	
Resource	**mins.**
◀■▶ ◢Ⓢ World Video Explorer	20
▭ Color Transparencies 31, 56, 57, 95	20
▭ Color Transparency 75	20
◢ Planet Earth CD-ROM	20
▭ Color Transparencies 74, 75	20
◠ Ⓢ Guided Reading Audiotapes	20
▭ Color Transparency 174	
(Graphic organizer table template)	20
◢ The Writer's Solution CD-ROM	30
▯ Computer Test Bank	30

Ⓣ **Teaming Opportunity**
This resource is especially well-suited for teaching teams.

Ⓢ **Spanish**
This resource is also in Spanish support.

◢ **CD-ROM**

◢ **Laserdisc**

▭ **Transparency**

▯ **Software**

◀■▶ **Videotape**

◠ **Audiotape**

Assessment Opportunities

From Guiding Questions to Assessment   A series of Guiding Questions serves as an organizing framework for this book. The Guiding Questions that relate to this chapter are listed below. Section Reviews and Section Quizzes provide opportunities for assessing students' insights into these Guiding Questions. Additional assessments are listed below.

GUIDING QUESTIONS

- *How did physical geography affect the growth of ancient civilizations?*

- *How did the beliefs and values of ancient civilizations affect the lives of their members?*

ASSESSMENTS

Section 1

Students should be able to create a chart showing how the early Chinese family household was organized.

▶ **RUBRIC**   See the Assessment booklet for a rubric on assessing charts.

Section 2

Students should be able to create a web of the values that Confucianism stress.

▶ **RUBRIC**   See the Assessment booklet for a rubric on assessing graphic organizers.

Section 3

Students should be able to write a paragraph explaining how the emperor Shi Huangdi helped unite China.

▶ **RUBRIC**   See the Assessment booklet for a rubric on assessing a writing assignment.

Section 4

Students should be able to give an oral presentation of an advancement of the Han dynasty.

▶ **RUBRIC**   See the Assessment booklet for a rubric on assessing an oral presentation.

Activities and Projects

Mental Mapping

Size It Up Distribute sheets of 8 1/2 x 11 inch paper that are blank except for a square measuring about 1.75 inches by 1.75 inches. This square roughly represents the land area of the fifty United States and the District of Columbia, about 3.5 million square miles.

Give students a few minutes to draw squares that they think might represent the sizes of Egypt, India, and China relative to the United States and to one another. As a class, discuss the relative sizes of these countries as compared to the United States. (Egypt is about one ninth the size of the United States with 385,229 square miles; India is about one third the size of the United States; China is slightly larger than the United States with about 3.7 million square miles.)

Links to Current Events

Two Billion Sold Tell students that China has about two billion people, making it by far the most populous country in the world. Many American and European countries would like to sell goods to all these people. There are many barriers to trade, however. Some are political, some are economic, and many are cultural. Chinese people do not necessarily want or need many of the goods manufactured in the West. Nonetheless, many western companies have been marketing goods in China.

Have students research an American product that is being sold in China. Has the product been altered to be more appealing to the Chinese? What problems has the company encountered in selling the product in China? How is the advertising and packaging similar to or different from advertising or packaging for the product in the United States?

Hands-On Activities

What Is It Like in China? Ask students to locate China on a globe. Point out that its eastern edge is bordered by water. Have students identify the East China Sea and South China Sea, then the countries that border China. Have them compare physical and climate maps of China to consider its many climates and landforms. You may want to have students describe how China's location and climate compare to those of the United States.

The Teachings of Confucius
Ask students to create a small booklet. Every left-hand page of the booklet should cite a principle of Confucianism. Every right-hand page should describe an example of how this principle might be applied to modern life in the United States. *Average*

River Valleys Point out that ancient Chinese civilization, like ancient Egyptian civilization, depended on the flood cycles of a major river. In China, the river was the Huang He. Suggest that students compare and contrast the Nile and Huang He rivers and the civilizations that grew up around them. *Basic*

Resolve a Dispute Tell students that rival kingdoms battled each other in China for many years. Eventually, powerful rulers ended these wars by conquering all of China. Ask students to discuss this method of resolving a dispute. What other ways can they think of for resolving such problems? How are disputes between countries over territory handled in the modern world? *Challenging*

Ancient Lands Have students locate major rivers, major cities of ancient China, the Great Wall of China, and other features on an outline map of China. *English Language Learners*

F.Y.I.

This page can help you extend your own and students' understanding of the concepts in this chapter. You may want to browse through some of the suggestions in the **Bibliography. Interdisciplinary Links** can connect social studies understandings to areas elsewhere in the curriculum through the use of other Prentice Hall products. **National Geography Standards** reflected specifically in this chapter are listed for your convenience. Some hints about appropriate **Internet Access** are also provided. **School to Careers** provides insights into the practical uses of some of the concepts in this chapter as they might pertain to various careers.

BIBLIOGRAPHY

FOR THE TEACHER

Cleary, Thomas. *The Essential Confucius: The Heart of Confucius' Teachings in Authentic I Ching Order.* HarperSanFrancisco, 1992.

Cotterell, Arthur. *Ancient China.* Knopf, 1994.

Hoobler, Thomas. *Confucianism.* Facts on File, 1993.

Martell, Hazel. *The Ancient Chinese.* New Discovery Books, 1993.

Reid, Straun. *The Silk and Spice Routes: Inventions and Trade.* New Discovery Books, 1994.

FOR THE STUDENT

Easy

Major, John S. *The Silk Route: 7,000 Miles of History.* HarperCollins, 1995.

Average

Williams, Brian. *Ancient China.* Viking, 1996.

Challenging

Confucius. *The Wisdom of Confucius.* American Classical College Press, 1982.

LITERATURE CONNECTION

Fang, Linda. *The Ch'i-Lin Purse: A Collection of Ancient Chinese Stories.* Farrar, Straus and Giroux, 1994.

Rappaport, Doreen. *The Journey of Meng.* Dial, 1991.

INTERDISCIPLINARY LINKS

Subject	Theme: Continuity
MATH	Middle Grades Math: Tools for Success *Course 2,* Lesson 9-5, **Exploring Maps and Scale Drawings**
LANGUAGE ARTS	Choices in Literature *Communication Explosion,* **Hailibu the Hunter** Prentice Hall Literature *Copper,* **The Living Kuan-yin**

NATIONAL GEOGRAPHY STANDARDS

Students explore the 18 National Geography Standards throughout *The Ancient World.* Chapter 5, however, concentrates on investigating the following standards: 6, 10, 11, 13, 14, 15. For a complete list of the standards, see the *Teacher's Flexible Planning Guide.*

SCHOOL TO CAREERS

In Chapter 5, Ancient China, students learn about the early history and culture of that country. Additionally, they address the skill of organizing information. Understanding ancient China can help students prepare for careers in many fields such as international trade, foreign relations, history, and so on. Organizing information is a skill particularly useful for writers, editors, scientists, and others. The curriculum presented in this book, as in all eight titles of Prentice Hall's *World Explorer* program, is designed to prepare students not only for careers but also for good citizenship—of the world as well as of this country.

INTERNET ACCESS

Many social studies teachers and students use Internet browsers, or search engines, to investigate particular topics. For the best results, use narrow rather than broad topics. Try these for Chapter 5: Huang He, Shang dynasty, Confucius, Great Wall of China. Finding age-appropriate sites is an important consideration when using the Internet. For links to age-appropriate sites in world studies and geography, visit the Prentice Hall Home Page at: **http://www.phschool.com**

Connecting to the Guiding Questions

As students complete this chapter, they will focus on the accomplishments of early Chinese civilization. Content in this chapter corresponds to the following Guiding Questions:

● How did physical geography affect the growth of ancient civilizations?

● How did the beliefs and values of ancient civilizations affect the lives of their members?

Using the Map Activities

Help students use the map activities to learn how geography affected early Chinese civilization.

• Students may say that the Gobi Desert and Himalaya Mountains probably kept China relatively isolated.

• Students will probably choose areas near the Huang He or Chang Jiang rivers.

Heterogeneous Groups

The following Teacher's Edition strategies are suitable for heterogeneous groups.

Cooperative Learning
Critical Thinking
Interdisciplinary Connections

CHAPTER 5 — Ancient China

SECTION 1
The Geography of China's River Valleys

SECTION 2
Confucius and His Teachings

SECTION 3
Strong Rulers Unite Warring Kingdoms

SECTION 4
Achievements of Ancient China

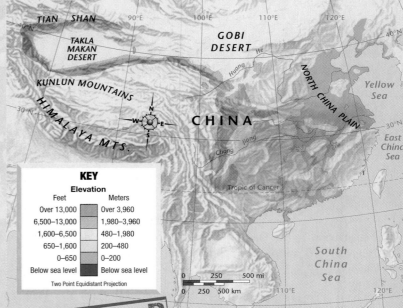

KEY

Elevation

Feet	Meters
Over 13,000	Over 3,960
6,500–13,000	1,980–3,960
1,600–6,500	480–1,980
650–1,600	200–480
0–650	0–200
Below sea level	Below sea level

Two Point Equidistant Projection

MAP ACTIVITIES

Ancient China was the location of one of the world's first civilizations. Get to know this region by completing the following activities.

Study the map
From looking at the map, do you think it was easy or hard for the people of China to make contact with people of other civilizations? Explain your answer.

Choose a place
You know that ancient civilizations in Egypt, Mesopotamia, and India started in river valleys. Pick a place on the map where you think Chinese civilization might have started, and explain your choice.

Resource Directory

Media and Technology

Spotlight On: Buddhism Yesterday and Today, from the World Video Explorer, enhances students' understanding of Buddhism and its spread throughout China.

Chapter 7

The Geography of China's River Valleys

Section 1

Lesson Objectives

1. Explain the importance of physical geography in the development of Chinese civilization.

2. Summarize how the structure of families may have influenced the development of Chinese society.

Lesson Plan

1 Engage

Warm-Up Activity

Ask students to imagine that the class has been stranded on a desert island. How would they organize themselves in order to survive? If they discovered an indigenous group of hunters living on the far side of the island, would they make contact? Why or why not?

Activating Prior Knowledge

Have students read Reach Into Your Background in the Before You Read box. Help students identify some regions of the United States that are prone to hurricanes or earthquakes. Point out that often these areas are quite populous. Discuss whether there are certain benefits or reasons for living in such areas and, if so, are the benefits worth the risk?

BEFORE YOU READ

Reach Into Your Background

Is the area where you live subject to natural dangers, such as earthquakes, floods, or severe storms? If so, what steps has your community taken to protect the people from such natural disasters?

Questions to Explore

1. How did geography help shape China's view of the world?
2. How was the early Chinese family household organized?

Key Terms

loess
dike
extended family

Key Places

North China Plain
Huang He
Chang Jiang River

What words would you use to describe dragons like this one? You may think of these imaginary beasts as being fierce and scary. People of some cultures would agree with you. But to the Chinese people, the dragon is a respected spirit, not a terrible monster. In China, dragons are friendly beasts that bring good luck. They are also connected with the rain that makes the fields fertile.

The Chinese also use this respected spirit to show the importance of their rivers. They traditionally describe their rivers as dragons. The dragon's limbs are the smaller streams. They flow into the dragon's body, or main river. The dragon's mouth is the delta, where the river flows into the sea.

▼ This colorful dragon gazes at a statue of the Buddha in the Cave of the Thousand Buddhas in Dunhuang, China.

The Geographic Setting of Ancient China

Rivers were important to the development of civilization in China. Other landforms and climate played a role, too.

Teaching Resources

📁 **Reproducible Lesson Plan** in the Chapter and Section Resources booklet, p. 78, provides a summary of the section lesson.

📁 **Guided Reading and Review** in the Chapter and Section Resources booklet, p. 79, provides a structure for mastering key concepts and reviewing key terms in the section. Available in Spanish in the Spanish Chapter and Section Resources booklet, p. 49.

Program Resources

Material in the **Primary Sources and Literature Readings** booklet extends content with a selection related to the concepts in this chapter.

Outline Maps China and Neighboring Countries: Political, p. 41
East Asia: Physical, p. 39

2 Explore

Ask students to read the section. Then discuss the rise of civilization in China. Ask: *Why did the people of the Middle Kingdom settle along the Huang He, despite the dangers of flooding? Why might a rigidly organized family unit have been an asset in early societies?*

3 Teach

Help students use a branching graphic organizer chart to show the cause-and-effect chain of events that led to the development of Chinese civilization. Tell students to place the Huang He at the top of the chart. Have students use information in the section to complete the chart. This activity should take about 25 minutes.

4 Assess

See the answers to the Section Review. You may also use students' completed charts as an assessment.

Acceptable charts include at least three cause-and-effect relationships.

Commendable charts include at least three cause-and-effect relationships plus opinions, supported by facts, about the relative importance of certain events.

Outstanding charts include at least three cause-and-effect relationships plus inferences regarding the importance of family organization in ancient Chinese society.

Answers to ...

MUDDY RIVER

People could use water from the river for drinking, cooking, and farming.

Muddy River

Large ships cannot travel on the Huang He. Large amounts of loess are deposited on the river's bottom, making it too shallow for safe passage. **Critical Thinking** How could being near a river help people who live in a dry climate?

READ ACTIVELY

Visualize Visualize the shape of a river as a dragon.

Contrasting Climate and Landforms Locate the North China Plain on the map on the opening page of this chapter. The climate and vegetation of this northern region of China are very different from those in the south. Monsoons from the South China Sea bring rains to the southern half of China. This area is warm and wet. The monsoon rains don't reach the cooler, northern part of China and the North China Plain. This area doesn't get much rain at other times, either. As a result, the climate is very dry. To survive in this dry land, people have always depended on rivers.

The "Middle Kingdom" Geographic barriers such as mountains and seas cut China off from other lands. As a result, the Chinese knew only of the nomadic peoples to the north and west of them. They had no knowledge of the powerful civilizations half a world away: Egypt, India, Greece, and Rome. In fact, the Chinese did not call their land "China." They were so sure that they lived at the center of the world that they called themselves the "Middle Kingdom."

Rivers, the Birthplace of Civilization Several of the world's earliest civilizations—in Mesopotamia, Egypt, and India—grew up near major rivers. In China, the same forces were at work. Identify on the map the Huang He (hwahng hay) and the Chang Jiang (chahng jee AHNG), sometimes called the Yangzi River. Civilization began in

China along the Huang He and later spread to the wetter south along the Chang Jiang River, the longest river in China.

Like rivers in other parts of the world, China's rivers overflowed their banks each spring. They brought fresh, fertile topsoil to the land. Because of this, China's first farming villages developed along its rivers.

The Huang He, or "Yellow River," begins in the highlands of Tibet. From there, it flows for more than 3,000 miles (4,800 km) until it empties into the Yellow Sea. It is the second-longest river in China.

The Huang He is the muddiest river in the world. In fact, it is called the "Yellow" River because of the **loess** (lehs), or yellow-brown soil, that its waters carry along. When the Huang He floods, it deposits loess on the surrounding plain. After thousands of years and countless floods, the Huang He has carpeted the North China Plain with a thick layer of soil. This makes the land perfect for growing crops, especially a grain called millet. For thousands of years, millet was an important part of the Chinese diet because it grew so well on the northern plain.

China's Sorrow　The Chinese people also call the Huang He "China's Sorrow." The river was unpredictable and sometimes dangerous. It brought life to the land. But frequently it also took life away. Destructive floods could come without warning, sometimes as often as

▼ The staircaselike platforms on this hillside above the Huang He are called terraces. These platforms increase the amount of land available for farming. They also prevent soil from washing away during heavy rains.

Teaching Resources

📁　**Critical Thinking Activity** in the Chapter and Section Resources booklet, p. 94, helps students apply the skill of recognizing cause and effect.

Activity

Cooperative Learning

Dragon River　In Chinese mythology, the Ti Lung, or Earth Dragon, was believed to control rivers and other waterways. Invite students to create a class mural of the Huang He. Have the class work in small groups, making each group responsible for a section of the river. Encourage groups to use bright colors and to picture the river in the form of a dragon, with the mouth as the delta and the limbs as the streams. Some group members may color or decorate the dragon and others can locate and label major cities. *English Language Learner, Visual*

Background

Global Perspectives

Raging Rivers　The people of China's Middle Kingdom were not alone in being at the mercy of a mighty river. People in Sumer in Mesopotamia also experienced the recurring destruction of floods. The Sumerians created a complex system of irrigation canals to control their flood waters. Even so, stories of floods are found throughout Sumerian literature. Many scholars believe that the biblical account of the great flood in Genesis is based in part on the Sumerians' experiences.

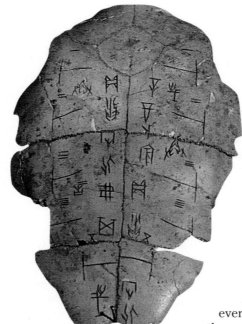

◄Today, we have paperback books, but the ancient Chinese read "turtlebacks." Even though the symbols on this turtle shell are about 4,000 years old, they are quite similar to modern Chinese symbols.

LINKS ACROSS TIME

Writing in China The earliest examples of Chinese writing appear on turtle shells and animal bones. These were done by the Shang people between 1750 B.C. and 1120 B.C. Then, each symbol, or character, stood for a thing or idea. Over the years, each character in Chinese writing has come to stand for a word or part of a word. Now there are about 50,000 characters in all! Some characters have been in use for almost 4,000 years.

every two years. Sometimes a flood drowned thousands of people. At times, the river flooded with such force that the water cut an entirely new path over the land. The course of the river could change by hundreds of miles.

To help control the flooding, early Chinese people built dikes along the banks of the Huang He. A **dike** is a protective wall that holds back the waters. But these dikes only worked for a while. As the river water flowed along, some of the loess settled to the bottom. This raised the level of the river. Eventually, the river rose high enough to burst through the dikes, causing even more deadly floods. Despite such dangers, the early Chinese people continued to settle along the banks of the Huang He.

Sowing the Seeds of Civilization

Historians do not know exactly when the first farming settlements developed in the Huang He Valley. Some think it was as early as 5000 B.C. Before that, the people of the North China Plain were probably nomads who moved from place to place to hunt and gather food.

The Shang dynasty was the first known civilization in China. It arose some time after 1700 B.C. The Shang people built China's first cities. Among their many accomplishments is some of the finest bronze work of ancient China.

The Shang people also produced the first Chinese writing. Like Mesopotamia's cuneiform and our own alphabet, the Chinese system of writing could be used for different languages. This was helpful for communications, because China had many regional languages.

The Bonds of Family

The family was the center of early Chinese society. It was far more important than the individual or the nation. For each person, the family was the chief source of well-being. A person's first responsibility was always to the family.

Traditional Families A household in ancient China might contain as many as five generations living together. This meant that small children lived with their great-great-grandparents as well as their parents, uncles and aunts, cousins, brothers and sisters, and so on. These closely related people are called an **extended family.** In rich families, the members might live together in one big home. But most of China's people were poor. In farming villages, members of the extended family might live in separate one-room cottages. The cottages were within easy walking distance from one another.

The status of each person in a Chinese extended family depended on age and sex. The center of authority was usually the oldest man. He had

◀ The elegance of this Chinese family's silk robes shows that they were quite wealthy.

Background

Daily Life

A Peasant's Lot Ancient Chinese society was largely agricultural. Most commoners were peasants who worked for a feudal lord. A poem of the Zhou period (1122 B.C.–256 B.C.) describes a year in the life of a peasant and his family: In the first seven months, the peasant, his wife, and daughter work constantly—repairing tools, plowing, and planting seeds—while the lord's steward strolls by periodically to see how the work is progressing. During the eighth through twelfth months, the peasant trains as a warrior to serve the lord in battle while his family makes clothes for the lord's children, brews wine for the lord's birthday, and hunts foxes for the lord's winter coat.

Section I Review

1. (a) yellow-brown soil carried by a river (b) protective wall built to hold back river waters (c) all of one's relations, in addition to one's immediate family

2. (a) an area in northern China made fertile by loess deposits from the flooding of the Huang He (b) China's second-longest river, which flows from Tibet to the Yellow Sea (c) China's longest river, lying south of the Huang He

3. Loess deposits from the river made the North China Plain fertile for farming. People settled along the banks because the land was good for farming.

4. The household might contain as many as five generations. Status depended upon age and gender. The center of authority was the oldest male, and women had less status than men.

5. Answers may vary. Students should answer that all of these civilizations began in river valleys and had economies based on farming.

6. Descriptions may vary. However, students' descriptions should correspond to their own age and gender.

◀ Girls in ancient China rarely received a formal education. Instead, they learned household tasks such as weaving and cooking. At the age of 15, girls took part in special ceremonies during which their hair was pinned up, as in the photograph. This was a sign that they had entered adulthood.

the most privileges and power in the family. He decided who his children and grandchildren would marry. When children were disrespectful, he punished them strictly. After the oldest male died, by tradition all his lands were divided among his sons. Each son then started his own household.

Women's lives were usually governed by men. According to tradition, they obeyed their fathers in youth, their husbands in middle age, and their sons in old age. When a woman married, she left her household and became part of her new husband's family.

Family Names The Chinese were the first people known to use two names. One name was for the family, which was passed down from father to son. The other was for the individual. Of course, people in the United States also use two names. In Chinese society, however, the family name comes first. If this system were used in American society, you would know the first President of the United States as Washington George, not George Washington. Think of other famous people in American history. What would their names be in the Chinese naming style?

The fact that the family name comes first in China shows how important the family is. This tradition in Chinese society dates back to the very earliest times. Centuries later, a great philosopher, Confucius (kuhn FYOO shuhs), added a new meaning to the importance of one's family.

Connect What would your name be if the Chinese naming system were used in the United States?

SECTION 1 REVIEW

1. Define (a) loess, (b) dike, (c) extended family.

2. Identify (a) North China Plain, (b) Huang He, (c) Chang Jiang.

3. How did the Huang He affect ancient Chinese civilization?

4. How was the early Chinese family household organized?

Critical Thinking

5. Making Comparisons What do you think ancient China might have in common with other great ancient civilizations of Mesopotamia, Egypt, and India?

Activity

6. Writing to Learn Imagine what your life would have been like in an early Chinese household. Write a description.

Confucius and His Teachings

BEFORE YOU READ

Reach Into Your Background

Why should you do your homework? How should you act toward other people? Must you always obey your parents? Must you always respect the President of the United States? How would you answer these questions? Early Chinese thinkers asked themselves similar questions in an effort to establish a system of rules for their society.

Questions to Explore

1. What values did Confucianism stress?
2. How did Confucius' ideas help shape Chinese society?

Key Terms

philosophy   civil service

Key People

Confucius

One day, the teacher Confucius and his students were walking through the countryside. In the distance they heard a woman crying. As they came around a bend in the road, they saw the woman kneeling at a grave. "Why are you crying?" they asked her. "Because," she answered, "a tiger killed my husband's father. Later, the tiger also killed my husband. Now, the tiger has killed my son as well."

They then asked the woman, "Why do you stay in this place after these terrible things have happened?" The woman answered, "Because there are no cruel rulers here." Confucius turned to his students and said, "Remember this. A cruel ruler is fiercer and more feared than a tiger."

The Life of Confucius

Confucius was the most famous—and important—of the early Chinese thinkers. The Chinese, who regarded Confucius as a great teacher, called him Kong Fu Zi (kahng FOO zuh), or "Master Kong." *Confucius* is the Western version of this name. After his death, Confucius' followers told many stories about him. Most of them were like the story of the woman and the tiger.

▼ Little detail exists about Confucius' life. No one really knows what he looked like. An artist made this portrait more than 1,000 years after Confucius' death.

Teaching Resources

📁 **Reproducible Lesson Plan** in the Chapter and Section Resources booklet, p. 81, provides a summary of the section lesson.

📁 **Guided Reading and Review** in the Chapter and Section Resources booklet, p. 82, provides a structure for mastering key concepts and reviewing key terms in the section. Available in Spanish in the Spanish Chapter and Section Resources booklet, p. 51.

Lesson Objectives

1 Describe the problems in Chinese society that Confucianism tried to address.

2 Specify the principles emphasized by Confucianism.

3 Explain the effects of Confucianism on Chinese government and society.

Lesson Plan

1 Engage

Warm-Up Activity

Ask each student to write down a rule that they have found to be valuable. Have volunteers read their rules aloud. Start a discussion about why families, schools, communities, and nations have rules. Ask students to consider how rules serve to keep a group of people together. Should rules ever be changed? Why or why not? Should rules be made by a group of people, or should one person make all the rules?

Activating Prior Knowledge

Have students read Reach Into Your Background in the Before You Read box. Ask them to recall what they learned about the status of different family members in ancient China. Have students think of a rule that might have existed in ancient China. For example, "A son must obey his father." Discuss some of the potential problems with these rules.

2 Explore

Have students read through the section and discuss Confucius and Confucianism. Why did the rulers of Confucius' time have little interest in following his teachings? What ideas did Confucius have about how people should treat each other? How did Confucius' ideas help some poor people obtain government offices?

3 Teach

Invite students to make a booklet entitled *The Teachings of Confucius*. Encourage students to illustrate each rule or lesson that they include in their booklet. This activity should take about 30 minutes.

4 Assess

See the answers to the Section Review. You may also use students' completed booklets as an assessment.

Acceptable booklets include rules about loyalty, respect, family, and order.

Commendable booklets include rules about loyalty, respect, family, and order and include illustrations.

Outstanding booklets include rules about loyalty, respect, family, and order and include illustrations that show the rules being practiced.

READ ACTIVELY

Ask Questions What questions might you ask Confucius about human relationships?

Confucius was born in 551 B.C. to a noble but poor family of the North China Plain. When he was three years old, his father died. His mother raised him alone. He loved learning and was largely self-taught. Confucius hoped to advance to an important government office, but he never did.

Instead, Confucius decided to try teaching. He charged students a fee to take classes. Many historians think that he was China's first professional teacher. Confucius taught his students his views of life and government. Some of his students went on to hold important government posts.

In Confucius' time, only the rich could afford an education. But Confucius also accepted students who truly wanted to learn, even if they were poor. As he noted:

> "From the very poorest upward . . . none has ever come to me without receiving instruction. I instruct only a student who bursts with eagerness. Only one who bubbles with excitement do I enlighten."

Later in his life, Confucius wandered about North China. He looked for a ruler who would follow his teachings, but was unsuccessful. Confucius returned home a disappointed man. He died in 479 B.C. at the age of 72. By the time of his death, he believed his life had been a failure. He was wrong.

Confucius and His Students

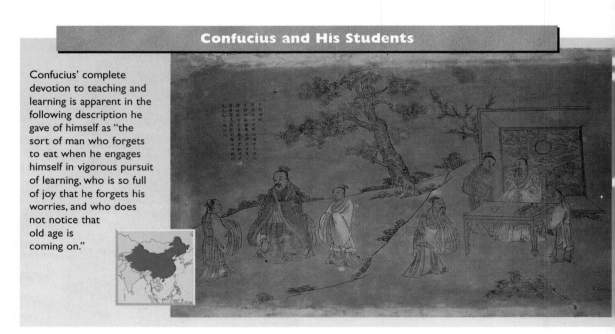

Confucius' complete devotion to teaching and learning is apparent in the following description he gave of himself as "the sort of man who forgets to eat when he engages himself in vigorous pursuit of learning, who is so full of joy that he forgets his worries, and who does not notice that old age is coming on."

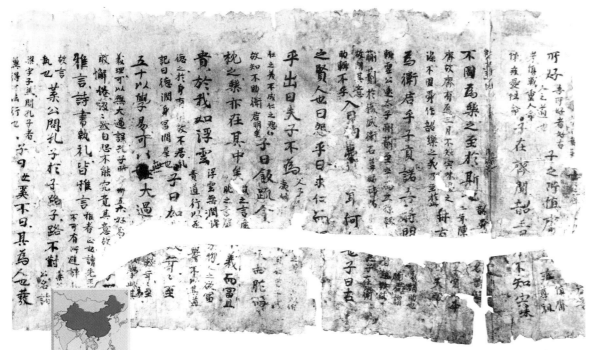

▲ This manuscript is at least 1,000 years old. In it are preserved the teachings of Confucius, known as the *Analects*. The *Analects* formed the basis of Chinese education for more than 2,000 years.

The Teachings of Confucius

Confucius did not claim to be an original thinker. He felt that his role was to pass on the forgotten teachings of wise people from an earlier age. Many of his teachings focused on persuading rulers to reform. He also aimed to bring peace, stability, and prosperity to their kingdoms.

Confucius himself never wrote down his teachings. Instead, his students gathered a collection of his sayings after his death. Together, these writings made up a **philosophy,** or system of beliefs and values. It became known as Confucianism. Confucianism was one of several important philosophies of ancient China. Over time, it began to guide many aspects of life there.

Confucius lived in a period known as the "Time of the Warring States." Powerful rulers of several Chinese states, or kingdoms, fought each other for the control of land. They seemed more interested in getting power than in ruling wisely. Confucius hoped to persuade these rulers to change their ways and bring peace to China.

Confucius' goal was order in society. He believed that if people could be taught to behave properly to one another, order and peace would return. Society would prosper. Confucius said people should know their place in the family and society. They should respect people above and below them. Everyone must treat others justly. He described people in

The Five Classics
Confucianism was based on the Five Classics, which were works of ancient Chinese literature. One, the *Book of Songs,* contains 305 poems. Some were written as early as 1000 B.C. Their subjects include war, love, and loss. In one, a wife speaks fondly of her husband who has gone to war: "My lord is on service;/ How can I not be sad?"

Activity

Interdisciplinary Connections

Language Arts Explain to students that Confucians often interpreted poems in order to derive a moral. For example, a poem about undying devotion to a sweetheart could be seen as a pledge of loyalty to the king. Invite students to write a short poem about love, family life, school, or work. Then have students exchange poems with a partner and write an interpretation of their partner's poem from a Confucian perspective.

Resource Directory

Teaching Resources

📁 **Recognizing Ideologies** in the Social Studies and Geography Skills booklet, p. 48, provides additional skill practice.

Another Golden Rule
Hundreds of years after Confucius' death, the Golden Rule was also proposed by Jesus of Nazareth in his Sermon on the Mount. Matthew 7:12 quotes Jesus as saying, "So always treat others as you would like them to treat you; that is the meaning of the Law and the Prophets." Historians note that Jesus' version is stated in the positive, while Confucius' is in the negative.

Daily Life

The Poor Shall Rise Civil service exams sometimes allowed a poor but talented man to surpass his so-called betters. However, China was still a class-conscious society, as the following story shows. Two friends, one wealthy and one poor, were about to depart for the imperial examinations. The local prefect held a farewell dinner but did not invite the poor student. A year later, the poor man returned to his hometown with top honors. The prefect was humiliated when all the town's high officials came out to welcome the poor man's return.

READ ACTIVELY

Predict Whom do you think Confucius meant by "those in authority"?

various relationships: ruler and ruled; father and son; husband and wife; older brother and younger brother; and friend and friend. Then he explained how they should behave. Confucius said people in authority—princes or parents—must set a good example. If a ruler was good, his people would follow his example and become good, too. Confucius summarized his ideas about relationships in a simple sentence. It is similar to what Christians and Jews call the Golden Rule: "Do not do to others what you would not want done to yourself."

The Impact of Confucius

Confucius' teachings had a major impact on Chinese government. They became the basic training for members of the civil service. The **civil service** is the group of people who carry out the work of government.

Before Confucius' ideas took hold, government posts were generally given to the sons of important people. Afterward, any male could hold a government post on merit—that is, how well he did his job. People who receive a reward on merit have shown, in some way, that they deserve that reward. Candidates for government jobs had to pass official examinations. To advance, they had to pass more exams. These exams were based on Confucius' teachings.

▶ The lantern this statue holds symbolizes faithfulness. According to Confucianism, wives were to show faith and devotion to their husbands.

Resource Directory

Teaching Resources

📁 **Section Quiz** in the Chapter and Section Resources booklet, p. 83, covers the main ideas and key terms in the section. Available in Spanish in the Spanish Chapter and Section Resources booklet, p. 52.

Landing a Government Job

In this painting, a Chinese emperor watches over eager scholars taking the civil service examination. Those who passed had their names placed on a waiting list for government jobs in such areas as census taking, taxation, justice, and road building.

The examination system did bring more able young men into government service. However, it did not open government jobs to everyone. Candidates still had to know how to read. This made it difficult for a poor man to advance. But it was not impossible. Many talented but poor young men rose to high government positions.

Confucius would have been surprised at the impact he had on China. He did not consider himself particularly wise or good. In fact, he felt that he was a failure. But Confucius left his mark on Chinese life as perhaps no one before or after has.

SECTION 2 REVIEW

1. **Define** (a) philosophy, (b) civil service.
2. **Identify** Confucius.
3. What are some basic ideas of Confucianism?

4. How did Confucius' teachings change the way civil servants were chosen in ancient China?

Critical Thinking
5. **Drawing Conclusions** What do you think Confucius would say about government in the United States today? Would he feel that it followed his ideas? Why or why not?

Activity
6. **Writing to Learn** You are a government official in a small state in northern China. One day, a wandering teacher named Confucius comes to your court. Write a journal entry that describes what Confucius said and how your ruler reacted to him.

Section 2 Review

1. (a) a system of beliefs and values (b) the group of people who perform the work of government

2. early Chinese philosopher who taught about order in society and personal relationships

3. There is a proper order in the family and society, and each person should know his or her place. People should respect and treat people both above and below them as they would wish to be respected and treated.

4. Civil service examinations were given so that choices were based on merit instead of family connections.

5. Students may suggest that our government follows certain Confucian ideas because officeholders are supposedly chosen on merit and members of our bureaucracy must take civil service examinations.

6. Students' journal entries may have the following theme: Confucius suggests that the ruler treat his subjects fairly and appoint advisers based on merit, but the ruler rejects his advice because he is ruthless and ambitious.

SKILLS MINI LESSON

Assessing Your Understanding
You may **introduce** the skill by indicating to students that in order to be sure they understand an entire section of text, they need to make sure they understand each part of the section. Help students **practice** the skill by working with them to find the main ideas of Confucius' teachings. First, have students identify the part of the section that discusses Confucius' ideas. Next, instruct them to find key words, such as *summarized*, that point to the underlying principles of Confucian thought. Ask students to **apply** the skill by identifying the principles and writing short explanations of them.

SECTION 3
Strong Rulers Unite Warring Kingdoms

Lesson Objectives

1 Describe the methods Shi Huangdi used to unify China.

2 Explain the effect Shi Huangdi had on Chinese culture.

3 Summarize the reasons for the long reign of the Han dynasty.

Lesson Plan

1 Engage

Warm-Up Activity

Ask students to think about team sports and to imagine two different types of coaches. One coach shouts at the players when the team loses and threatens to remove players who make mistakes. The other coach gives the team pep talks and advice when they lose. Ask students to decide which team would be more successful and to explain their reasoning.

Activating Prior Knowledge

Have students read Reach Into Your Background in the Before You Read box. You might point out to students that there are some countries in the world in which the governments *do* make decisions about what residents can and cannot read. Discuss with students why a government might take such actions. Ask students how they would feel about living in such a country.

BEFORE YOU READ

Reach Into Your Background
How would you feel if your government leaders removed many books from the library and burned them? Who do you think is the best judge of what you should read? Why?

Questions to Explore
1. How did the emperor Shi Huangdi help unite China?
2. How did Han rulers build a powerful empire that reunited China for more than 400 years?

Key Terms
currency
warlord

Key People
Shi Huangdi
Liu Bang
Wudi

▼ This life-size, armor-clad, terra-cotta warrior appears ready to defend Shi Huangdi's empire.

In 1974, a group of farmers was digging a well in a grove of trees in northern China. Six feet down, they found some pottery made of a clay-like material called terra cotta. Another five feet down, they unearthed the terra-cotta head of a man. Archaeologists began digging—and discovered more than 8,000 life-sized statues of horses, chariots, and men. It was a terra-cotta army. For more than 2,000 years, these buried soldiers had kept watch at the tomb of the great Chinese emperor, Shi Huangdi (shee hoo ahng DEE).

Today, visitors to the tomb of Shi Huangdi are stunned by the sight of this army. No two statues are identical. Each statue is carefully made, down to the smallest detail of clothing. There are even royal chariots pulled by life-sized terra-cotta horses.

With his underground army, Shi Huangdi planned to rule a second empire in the afterlife. He also had grand plans for the real-life empire he created in China. His dynasty, he boasted, would last for 10,000 generations.

Resource Directory

Teaching Resources

📁 **Reproducible Lesson Plan** in the Chapter and Section Resources booklet, p. 84, provides a summary of the section lesson.

📁 **Guided Reading and Review** in the Chapter and Section Resources booklet, p. 85, provides a structure for mastering key concepts and reviewing key terms in the section. Available in Spanish in the Spanish Chapter and Section Resources booklet, p. 53.

Program Resources

Outline Maps China and Neighboring Countries: Political, p. 41

One China, One Ruler

Actually, Shi Huangdi's dynasty lasted for only two generations. But he is still a major figure in Chinese history. He is the ruler who unified China.

The Qin Dynasty   Shi Huangdi's original name was Zheng (juhng). He ruled a fierce people, the Qin (cheen), who lived along China's western edge. A Chinese poet described Zheng this way: "Cracking his long whip, he drove the universe before him. . . . His might shook the four seas."

Marching Across Time

Flakes of paint still cling to some of Shi Huangdi's warriors (below), indicating that they were once brilliantly colored. This kneeling soldier (right) shows the attention to detail artists paid as they made the terra-cotta figures. A craftsman uses ancient techniques to make a model of a terra-cotta soldier (left).

Media and Technology

 Color Transparency 75

2 Explore

Have students read the section. Then discuss the Qin and Han dynasties. How did Shi Huangdi organize the government? Why was Shi Huangdi so ruthless in his treatment of enemies and of those who disagreed with him? How did Wudi help strengthen and stabilize the government of the Han dynasty?

3 Teach

Invite students to make compare-and-contrast charts with three columns and three rows. In the first column, ask students to label the rows *Character*, *Accomplishments*, and *Failures*. They should label the second and third columns *Shi Huangdi* and *Liu Bang*. Have students fill in the boxes with information from the section. For each ruler, students may also suggest how the attributes are related. This activity should take about 25 minutes.

4 Assess

See the answers to the Section Review. You may also use students' completed charts as an assessment.

Acceptable charts include at least two facts per box.

Commendable charts include at least two facts per box and include some explanations of how the rulers' characters are related to their accomplishments and failures.

Outstanding charts include more than two facts per box and include thorough explanations of how the rulers' characters are related to their accomplishments and failures.

Background

Daily Life

Writing Standards One of Shi Huangdi's best reforms was the standardization of written script. In 221 B.C., the government proclaimed one script to be the country's standard. The use of any other script was made illegal. This proclamation had the added benefit (or perhaps main purpose) of eliminating any excuses for misunderstanding the written law.

Background

Links Across Time

Great Walls The Great Wall of China is actually a series of walls built over many centuries. In the A.D. 500s and 600s, the Sui dynasty constructed Great Walls. During the Ming dynasty, these walls were rebuilt and inner Great Walls were built as second lines of defense. It is these inner walls that can be seen in northern China today.

READ ACTIVELY

Connect Why do modern people know about other civilizations, even though ancient people did not?

By 221 B.C., Zheng had extended his rule over most of the land that makes up modern-day China. After seizing power, Zheng took his new title of Shi Huangdi, which means "First Emperor." He expected his sons and grandsons would number themselves Second Emperor, Third Emperor, and so on. His dynasty is named after the people of his homeland. It is the Qin dynasty.

Strengthening the Empire

Shi Huangdi set about changing China through strong and harsh rule. One of his first tasks was to protect the new empire from its enemies.

The Great Wall Throughout history, Chinese rulers had to worry about the nomads that lived along China's huge northern border. Shi Huangdi had a plan to end these border wars. He ordered the largest construction project in Chinese history. It is called the Great Wall of China. Locate the wall on the map on page 138.

▶ The Great Wall has not always looked as it does today. Parts of the Great Wall have been destroyed and rebuilt many times. Further changes were made to meet the military needs of various emperors. For example, one emperor had watchtowers built so that guards could send news of enemy activities with smoke or fire signals. **Regions** What part of his empire did Shi Huangdi hope the Great Wall would protect?

Previous rulers had built walls along the border. Shi Huangdi decided to connect them. He ordered farmers from their fields and merchants from their stores to form an army of 300,000 workers. When it was finished, the wall stretched for 1,400 miles (2,240 km). That is about the distance from Washington, D.C., to Denver, Colorado.

Organizing the Government   To put down rebellions from within the empire, Shi Huangdi put thousands of farmers to work building roads. The new roads enabled his armies to rush to the scene of any uprisings.

The emperor dealt swiftly with local rulers who opposed him by having them killed or put in prison. Shi Huangdi divided all China into areas called districts. Each district had a government run by the emperor's most trusted officials.

Unifying the Culture

Shi Huangdi was not content to unify the government of China. He also wanted the many peoples of these united kingdoms to have one economy and one culture.

Connect Would you have liked to live in China when Shi Huangdi ruled it? Why or why not?

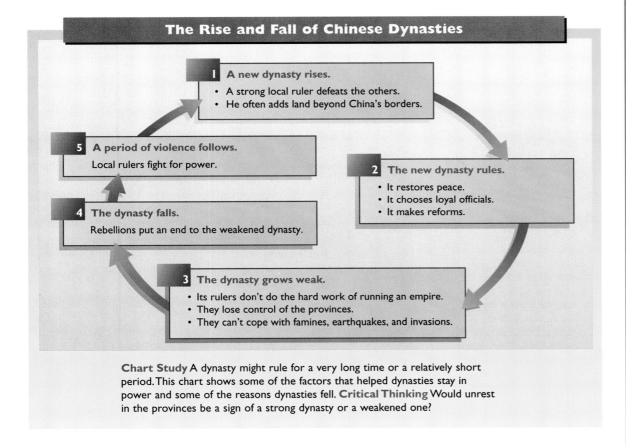

The Rise and Fall of Chinese Dynasties

1 A new dynasty rises.
- A strong local ruler defeats the others.
- He often adds land beyond China's borders.

2 The new dynasty rules.
- It restores peace.
- It chooses loyal officials.
- It makes reforms.

3 The dynasty grows weak.
- Its rulers don't do the hard work of running an empire.
- They lose control of the provinces.
- They can't cope with famines, earthquakes, and invasions.

4 The dynasty falls.
Rebellions put an end to the weakened dynasty.

5 A period of violence follows.
Local rulers fight for power.

Chart Study A dynasty might rule for a very long time or a relatively short period. This chart shows some of the factors that helped dynasties stay in power and some of the reasons dynasties fell. **Critical Thinking** Would unrest in the provinces be a sign of a strong dynasty or a weakened one?

Biography

Lü Hou The first woman to rule China was Liu Bang's wife, Lü Hou (also called Gao Hou). She was an extremely ambitious woman and was instrumental in her husband's rise to power. When Liu Bang died, Lü Hou and Liu Bang's son ruled for a brief time. Lü Hou then appointed a child as emperor and seized power. She issued royal orders under her own name and hoped to begin her own dynasty by distributing important government jobs to members of her own family. Lü Hou was not ultimately successful—after her death (in 180 B.C.), power returned to her husband's family—but she did establish a precedent. Whenever an emperor died and there was no heir, the surviving empress (acting as a mouthpiece for senior statesmen) issued royal orders until a new ruler was chosen.

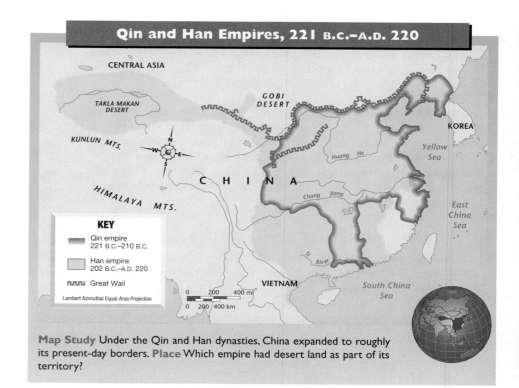

Qin and Han Empires, 221 B.C.–A.D. 220

KEY

- Qin empire 221 B.C.–210 B.C.
- Han empire 202 B.C.–A.D. 220
- Great Wall

Lambert Azimuthal Equal-Area Projection

0 200 400 mi
0 200 400 km

Map Study Under the Qin and Han dynasties, China expanded to roughly its present-day borders. **Place** Which empire had desert land as part of its territory?

Han Dynasty Bronze Work The Han dynasty was a time when the arts flourished. Skilled artisans made beautiful objects of bronze decorated with gold, silver, and gems. They also created fine bronze mirrors. These were discs polished on one side. On the back, they were decorated with borders, animal symbols, and writing. Mirrors were important in China because they symbolized self-knowledge.

He ordered that one **currency,** or type of money, be used throughout China. The new currency was a round coin with a square hole in the middle. A common currency made it easier for one region of China to trade goods with another. He also ordered the creation of common weights and measures, an improved system of writing, and a law code.

Shi Huangdi also tried to control the thoughts of his people. In 213 B.C., he outlawed the ideas of Confucius and other thinkers. Instead, he required that people learn the philosophies of Qin scholars. He commanded that all books in China be burned except those about medicine, technology, and farming. Hundreds of scholars protested the order. Shi Huangdi had them all killed.

Shi Huangdi's death in 210 B.C. started four years of chaos and civil war that ended in the murder of his son. Shi Huangdi's grandson could not hold China together. Rebellions broke out. The dynasty that was supposed to last "for 10,000 generations" lasted for only 15 years.

The Han Dynasty

One of the rebels who helped overthrow the Qin dynasty was a talented ruler named Liu Bang (LEE oo bahng). By 202 B.C., he won out over his rivals and became emperor of China. Liu Bang was the first emperor of a new dynasty: the Han (hahn). He was also the first ruler in Chinese history who was born a peasant. Liu Bang created a stable government. His rule was less harsh than Shi Huangdi's.

Stable governments were a feature of the Han dynasty, which lasted for about 400 years. Han rulers realized that they needed educated people to work in the government. So they set up the civil service system based on Confucianism.

Wudi: The Warrior Emperor   The Han dynasty reached its peak under Wudi (woo dee), Liu Bang's great-grandson. Wudi came to power in 140 B.C., when he was only 14 years old. He remained in power for more than 50 years.

Wudi's main interest was war and military matters. In fact, his name means "Warrior Emperor." He made improvements to Shi Huangdi's Great Wall. He also strengthened the army. By the end of Wudi's reign, Chinese rule stretched west into Central Asia, north into present-day Korea, and south into what today is the country of Vietnam. Locate the Han empire on the map on the opposite page.

The End of the Han Empire   The great emperor Wudi died in 87 B.C. After that, the Han dynasty slowly started to fall apart. The process took more than two centuries. Over time, roads and canals fell into disrepair. **Warlords,** leaders of armed local bands, gained power.

The last Han emperor was kept in power by a warlord who tried to control the empire through him. When that warlord died in A.D. 220, the emperor gave up power. The Han dynasty had ended. China broke up into several smaller kingdoms.

▼ These bronze jars from the Han dynasty show the degree of excellence and skill of Chinese bronze-workers. These jars were probably used only during important ceremonies.

SECTION 3 REVIEW

1. Define   (a) currency, (b) warlord.

2. Identify   (a) Shi Huangdi, (b) Liu Bang, (c) Wudi.

3. How did Shi Huangdi strengthen the central government of China?

4. Why did the Han dynasty last much longer than the Qin dynasty?

Critical Thinking

5. Recognizing Bias   Most information about the emperor Shi Huangdi comes from the writings of Confucian historians who lived during the Han dynasty. Remember, the Han dynasty began when Liu Bang defeated Shi Huangdi's grandson. How might this fact affect what we know about Shi Huangdi?

Activity

6. Writing to Learn   The farmers who discovered Shi Huangdi's terra-cotta army made one of the most important archaeological finds in history. You have been called in to examine the find. Write a journal entry about the wonders the farmers have shown you.

SECTION 4

Achievements of Ancient China

BEFORE YOU READ

Reach Into Your Background

What will future historians call the time we live in? Will they think it was a great age? Will they praise its scientific advances, such as the computer and space flight? What do you think?

Questions to Explore

1. What role did Confucianism play in China during the Han dynasty?

2. What important advances in technology were made in China during the Han dynasty?

Key Terms

silk

Key People and Places

Sima Qian
Silk Road

▼ Camels are undoubtedly better equipped than humans to endure a sandstorm. Double rows of protective eyelashes and the ability to close their nostrils help them survive sandstorms.

The caravan slowly plods across the hot sand of the Takla Makan Desert. Weary travelers wearing long robes sway on top of camels. Riderless camels are heaped high with heavy loads.

Suddenly, the camels stop, huddle together, and snarl viciously. An old man riding the lead camel turns around and shouts. No one can hear him because the screaming wind drowns out his words. The man jumps from his camel and quickly wraps a strip of felt around his nose and mouth. The other travelers rush to dismount and cover their faces, too. Just then, the sandstorm hits with full force.

Then, as quickly as it came, the sandstorm is gone. The travelers wipe sand from their eyes and tend to their camels. They have survived just one of the many challenges of traveling on the long and treacherous trade route known as the Silk Road.

The Silk Road: China Meets the West

The Emperor Wudi's conquests in the west brought the Chinese into contact with the people of Central Asia. Trade with these people introduced the Chinese to such new foods as grapes, walnuts, and garlic. This exchange of goods gave rise to a major new trade route. Called the Silk Road, it ran all the way from China to the Mediterranean Sea. Follow the route of the Silk Road on the map below.

The Silk Road was not one continuous road. Rather, it was a series of routes covering more than 4,000 miles (6,400 km), a little less than the distance from Chicago to Hawaii. Travel along the Silk Road was hard and dangerous. The Silk Road began in northern China and went west along the Great Wall of China. Then, it entered a narrow fringe of land between the barren Gobi Desert and the towering Nan Shan, or Southern Mountains. More dangerous land loomed to the west, where the Silk Road edged around the fringes of the dangerous Takla Makan Desert. Here, as you have read, travelers faced the peril of sudden, blinding sandstorms.

READ ACTIVELY

Predict What effect do you think the Silk Road had on China?

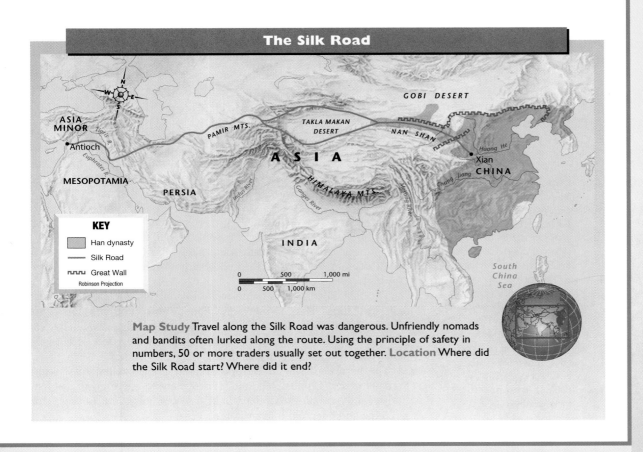

The Silk Road

KEY
- Han dynasty
- Silk Road
- Great Wall

Robinson Projection

0   500   1,000 mi
0   500   1,000 km

ASIA MINOR · Antioch
MESOPOTAMIA
PERSIA
PAMIR MTS.
TAKLA MAKAN DESERT
NAN SHAN
GOBI DESERT
ASIA
HIMALAYA MTS.
INDIA
Xian
CHINA
Huang He
Chang Jiang
Mekong River
Ganges River
Indus River
Euphrates R.
Tigris R.
South China Sea

Map Study Travel along the Silk Road was dangerous. Unfriendly nomads and bandits often lurked along the route. Using the principle of safety in numbers, 50 or more traders usually set out together. **Location** Where did the Silk Road start? Where did it end?

Media and Technology

 Planet Earth CD-ROM includes World Wonders, Cultural: The Great Wall which enhances students' understanding of ancient China.

Color Transparencies 74, 75

2 Explore

After students have read through the section, discuss the achievements of the Han dynasty. Ask students why the arts flourished during this dynasty and why people in China today call themselves "the children of Han." Students might also discuss the reasons for technological advancement in early China.

3 Teach

Suggest that students create word webs that show a cause-and-effect relationship between the adoption of Confucian principles and the advancement of Chinese civilization. This activity should take about 20 minutes.

Answers to ...

MAP STUDY

It started in Xian, China, and ended in Antioch in Asia Minor.

4 Assess

See the answers to the Section Review. You may also use students' completed webs as an assessment.

Acceptable webs identify Confucianism as a starting point and show at least three developments that can be related to its adoption by the Han dynasty.

Commendable webs identify Confucianism as a starting point and show at least five developments that can be related to its adoption by the Han dynasty. Webs also account for intervening causes.

Outstanding webs identify Confucianism as a starting point and show that many developments can be related to the adoption of Confucianism by the Han dynasty. Webs also indicate more minor cause-and-effect relationships.

LINKS TO SCIENCE

Cloth from Caterpillars
Silk is spun by a type of caterpillar called a silkworm. The silkworm winds a cocoon of fine thread around itself. Before the caterpillar can change to a moth, the fine thread—as much as a mile of it—is carefully unwound from the cocoon. This thread is joined with others to form one thick enough to weave into beautiful cloth. The Chinese knew how to make silk by 1000 B.C.

The Art of Silk Making

Fine silk is actually the product of worms (below center) that eat nothing but mulberry leaves. In ancient China, women tended these silkworms until they spun cocoons. Then the women carefully unwound the cocoons and wove the threads into silk cloth. One of the last steps was to pound the silk to soften it—the task shown at the left. Only wealthy people could afford fine silk robes such as the one below.

Once the road crossed the Pamir Mountains, travel was easier. The road passed through Persia and Mesopotamia. Finally, it turned north to the city of Antioch (AN tee ahk), in what today is Syria. From here, traders shipped goods across the Mediterranean to Rome, Greece, Egypt, and other lands that bordered the Mediterranean.

A Route for Goods Few travelers journeyed the entire length of the Silk Road. Generally, goods were passed from trader to trader as they crossed Asia. With each trade along the route, the price of the goods went up. By the time the goods arrived at the end of their journey, they were very expensive.

The Silk Road got its name from **silk,** a valuable cloth first made only in China. Han farmers developed new methods for raising silkworms, which made the silk. Han workers found new ways to weave and dye the silk. These methods were closely guarded secrets. The penalty for revealing them was death.

The arrival of silk in Europe created great excitement. Wealthy Romans prized Chinese silk and were willing to pay high prices for it. And wealthy people in China would pay well for glass, horses, ivory, woolens, and linen cloth from Rome.

A Route for Ideas More than goods traveled the road. New ideas did, too. For example, missionaries from India traveled to China along a section of the road and brought the religion of Buddhism with them. By the time the Han dynasty ended, Buddhism was becoming a major religion in China.

Old Traditions, New Accomplishments

Traditional Chinese ideas flourished during the Han dynasty. Han rulers realized that during troubled times in the past, people had lost respect for tradition. To bring back this respect, rulers encouraged people to return to the teachings of Confucius. It is also why rulers during the Han and later dynasties required members of the civil service to be educated in Confucian teachings.

Language and Literature Under the Han dynasty, the arts and scholarship flourished. Chinese poets wrote excellent poetry. Chinese scholars put together the first dictionary of the Chinese language. But the greatest advance was in the field of history.

Until the time of the Han, the Chinese people had only a shadowy knowledge of their own history. They knew only myths that had been passed down from generation to generation. But often these stories were in conflict with each other. No one was sure just when Chinese rulers had lived or what they accomplished.

Predict Why would Han dynasty rulers want to bring back Confucian ideas of respect for authority and tradition?

Han Fine Art

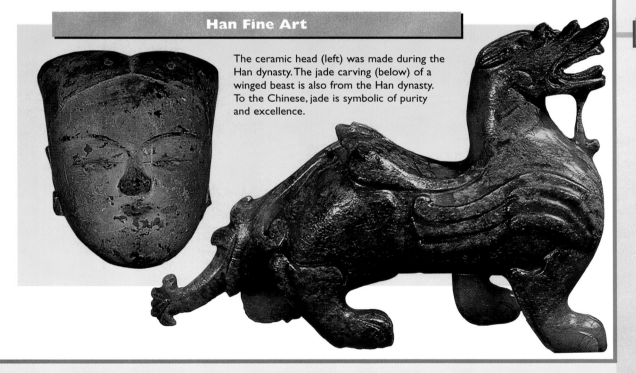

The ceramic head (left) was made during the Han dynasty. The jade carving (below) of a winged beast is also from the Han dynasty. To the Chinese, jade is symbolic of purity and excellence.

The scholar Sima Qian (soo MAH chen) decided to solve the problem. He spent his life writing a history of China from mythical times to the emperor Wudi. His work, called *Historical Records,* is a major source of our information about ancient China. Sima described his work:

> **❝** I wish to examine all that encircles heaven and man. I want to probe the changes of the past and present.**❞**

Background

Global Perspectives

An Explosive Mixture
During the A.D. 900s, Chinese alchemists mixed sulfur and nitrates with carbon and developed a kind of gunpowder. However, it was deemed ineffective for military purposes, and the Chinese used it only for fireworks. The Arabs, however, formulated a more effective gunpowder that they employed in military actions. By the 1350s, gunpowder was in wide use throughout Europe.

Chinese Achievements

Achievements of Ancient China

Technology	Medicine	The Arts
• Paper made from wood pulp	• Acupuncture—treatment of disease using needles	• Silk weaving
• Iron plow for breaking up soil	• Anesthetics—substances that put patients to sleep for surgery	• Jade carving
• Rudder—a device used to steer ships		• Bronze working
• Wheelbarrow	• Herbal remedies—discovery of plants useful as medicines	• Temples and palaces
• Fishing reel		• Poetry and history
• Compass	• Circulatory system—discovery that blood travels through the body	

Chart Study This chart shows just a few of the achievements of the ancient Chinese. **Critical Thinking** Which two Chinese inventions were helpful for farmers?

This wheelbarrow allowed one worker to move loads once carried by two. A mixture of chopped plants, water, and other materials was dried on mesh to form sheets of paper. Over 3,000 years ago, the Chinese learned to carve beautiful objects from jade like this ax blade. The Chinese made the first magnetic compasses. Because a compass needle always points north and south, Chinese sailors referred to compasses as "south-pointing fish."

Answers to . . .

CHART STUDY

The iron plow and wheelbarrow helped farmers.

Resource Directory

Teaching Resources

📁 **Section Quiz** in the Chapter and Section Resources booklet, p. 89, covers the main ideas and key terms in the section. Available in Spanish in the Spanish Chapter and Section Resources booklet, p. 56.

📁 **Vocabulary** in the Chapter and Section Resources booklet, p. 91, provides a review of key terms in the chapter. Available in Spanish in the Spanish Chapter and Section Resources booklet, p. 58.

📁 **Reteaching** in the Chapter and Section Resources booklet, p. 92, provides a structure for students who may need additional help in mastering chapter content.

📁 **Enrichment** in the Chapter and Section Resources booklet, p. 93, extends chapter content and enriches students' understanding.

📁 **Spanish Glossary** in the Spanish Chapter and Section Resources, pp. 85–89, provides key terms translated from English to Spanish as well as definitions in Spanish.

Advances in Technology During the Han dynasty, China became the most advanced civilization in the world. Its government was stable, so the Chinese could turn their attention to improving their society. Some accomplishments of the Han dynasty are shown in the chart. For example, Chinese artisans began making iron farming tools. These were a great improvement over the stone hoes and plows that farmers had traditionally used. Under Han leadership, workers constructed vast irrigation systems. They developed new ways of farming. They also developed something the world still depends on every day—paper.

Paper To keep records, Mesopotamians had to carve their cuneiform characters in stone or press them into clay tablets. The Chinese had similar problems. The Chinese used wood scrolls. Later, they wrote messages and even whole books on silk. Then, around A.D. 105, the Chinese made one of their greatest discoveries. They invented paper. The first paper was made from tree bark, hemp, and old rags. It was strengthened with starch and then coated with gelatin, a gooey substance that gave it strength.

This invention influenced learning and the arts in China. After several centuries, the use of paper spread across Asia and into Europe. Eventually paper replaced papyrus from Egypt as the material for scrolls and books.

Other Practical Inventions During the Han dynasty, the Chinese invented many practical devices that did not reach Europe until centuries later. Among them were the wheelbarrow, the fishing reel, the rudder (for steering boats), and the collar and harness that allowed animals to pull heavy loads.

The Han dynasty came to an end in the 200s A.D. But its accomplishments were not forgotten. People in China today call themselves "the children of Han."

SECTION 4 REVIEW

1. **Define** silk.

2. **Identify** (a) Sima Qian, (b) Silk Road.

3. Why did the influence of Confucius grow during the Han dynasty?

4. Name three accomplishments of the Chinese during the Han dynasty.

Critical Thinking

5. **Recognizing Cause and Effect** What do you think was the most important achievement of ancient China? Why?

Activity

6. **Writing to Learn** You are a historian in A.D. 2150. Write a brief description of the accomplishments of the United States in the late 1900s. Use these categories: Trade, Culture, Technology.

📁 **Chapter Summary** in the Chapter and Section Resources booklet, p. 90, provides a summary of chapter content. Available in Spanish in the Spanish Chapter and Section Resources booklet, p. 57.

📁 **Cooperative Learning Activity** in the Activities and Projects booklet, pp. 36–39, provides two student handouts, one page of teacher's directions, and a scoring rubric for a cooperative learning activity on making a map of the Silk Road.

Media and Technology

🎧 **Guided Reading Audiotapes** (English and Spanish)

SKILLS ACTIVITY

Organizing Information

"**C**hris, what is wrong with your hand?" Chris's mother found him shaking his hand back and forth.

"It hurts, Mom. I've been copying this chapter for hours, taking notes for my report about Confucianism," said Chris.

"Are you really copying every word?" Chris nodded. "Well, you should be writing down only the main ideas and supporting details," she said.

Chris protested. "But it all seems important!"

"I know," said his mother. "But when you read carefully, you will see that some ideas are more important than others. When you figure that out, you will understand the chapter better."

Get Ready

Taking notes is an excellent way to organize information, or arrange facts in a way that makes sense to you.

When you take notes from a book, you should record main ideas and the details that support them. You do this by writing down key words, or the most important words and phrases. It is important to write them in a way that shows how the ideas represented by the key words are related. Usually, you write main ideas as headings and list the details that support them below the headings.

Try It Out

The paragraph in the box on the next page gives information about Confucius. Practice organizing information by reading it carefully and completing the steps that follow.

A. Use key words and phrases to record the main idea. The main idea is often stated in a single sentence. What sentence in the paragraph states the main idea? Using key words, write it down. Don't copy the whole sentence. Write the main idea as a heading.

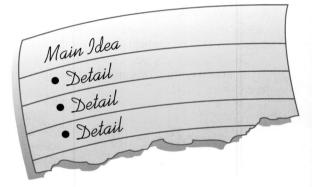

B. Use key words and phrases to record details. Usually, most of the sentences in a paragraph support, or tell more about, the main idea. What details in the passage support the main idea? Record them under the main idea heading, to show that they support it. Remember, you're taking notes, not copying. Use key words and phrases.

Exchange notes with a partner to compare them. Did you identify the same main idea? The same details? Do your notes organize information in a way that is easy to understand? What could you do to improve your work?

Apply the Skill

Look through Section 1 of Chapter 5 in this book. Organize the information in it.

① **Use key words and phrases to record the main idea of the section.** One helpful hint is to look at the headings within the section.

② **Use key words and phrases to record details.** How can you identify some of these?

The Chinese philosoper Confucius taught his students to live a life of virtue and respect for wisdom. Three parts of his teachings are especially important. First, he taught people to behave toward others as they would like to be treated themselves. Second, he had many sayings about the 'person with integrity,' and he spoke of this person as a model of virtue for his students. Third, he said that people should respect social rules and treat others according to those rules. Confucius also collected and edited poetry, music, and other writings from a time that he called the golden age. His own teachings and sayings were later written down in a book called the *Analects*.

③ **Double-check your notes.** Compare them to the section. Decide whether your notes give a clear picture of the whole section.

3 Teach

Students can use the Try It Out paragraph to **practice** the skill. Remind them to focus on key words and phrases and to use their own words when taking notes. As a class, share and discuss the notes students took.

For additional reinforcement, have students offer examples of key words drawn from written material posted in your classroom.

4 Assess

Have students **apply** their information-organizing skills in the last part of the activity. **Assess** students' skills by comparing their written notes with the section Lesson Objectives and Section Review questions.

Answers to ...
APPLY THE SKILL

1. Students' notes should contain key words and phrases from headings.
2. Key words are often in dark type or may be parts of titles or headings.

Reviewing Main Ideas

1. The family was the basic unit of society. A person's first responsibility was always to the family. Family was more important than the state or the individual.

2. Geographic barriers such as mountains and deserts prevented contact with other civilizations.

3. Answers may vary, but might include the following: there is an order to all things; loyalty and respect are essential; maintaining the correct values in the family will translate to the larger society; people should know their place in society and respect those above and below them; those in authority should set a good example; and people should practice the Golden Rule.

4. The rulers in Confucius' time were not interested in his teachings. It took more enlightened leaders and the promotion of his ideas by his students before Confucius was honored.

5. Answers may vary. Students may answer that Shi Huangdi built the Great Wall to keep out invaders, standardized currency, and killed or imprisoned local rulers who opposed him, replacing them with trusted officials.

6. Answers will vary. Students may suggest the following reason: Han rulers realized that they needed educated people to work in the government, so they set up the civil service based on the principles of Confucianism.

7. Answers may vary. Possible answers: The invention of paper promoted the spread of learning and cultivation of the arts. The recording of history helped unify China under a common heritage.

Reviewing Key Terms

1. e   **4.** a   **7.** c
2. d   **5.** f   **8.** g
3. b   **6.** h

CHAPTER 5 Review and Activities

Reviewing Main Ideas

1. Explain the importance of the extended family in early Chinese life.
2. Why were the early Chinese unaware of other ancient civilizations in Egypt, Mesopotamia, and India?
3. Give two examples of the teachings of Confucius.
4. Describe why Confucius died a disappointed man, but was honored by the Chinese more after his death.
5. Describe three actions the emperor Shi Huangdi took to unite China.
6. Why did the Han dynasty promote the ideas of Confucius?
7. Name two achievements of the Han dynasty, and explain their importance.

Reviewing Key Terms

Match the definitions in Column I with the key terms in Column II.

Column I	Column II
1. a kind of money	**a.** extended family
2. a fine yellow soil	**b.** dike
3. protective wall built along rivers to hold back the waters	**c.** civil service
4. several generations of closely related people	**d.** loess
5. a system of beliefs and values	**e.** currency
6. a valuable cloth made in China	**f.** philosophy
7. group of people who carry out the government's work	**g.** warlord
8. local leader of armed bands	**h.** silk

Critical Thinking

1. Recognizing Cause and Effect How did the harsh rule of Shi Huangdi help Liu Bang come to power?
2. Drawing Conclusions From what you know about the teachings of Confucius, do you think he would approve of the way people live today in the United States? Why or why not?

Graphic Organizer

Copy the chart onto a sheet of paper. Then fill in the empty boxes to complete the chart.

	Qin Dynasty	Han Dynasty
Important Emperors		
Impact of Dynasty on China		

Graphic Organizer

	Qin Dynasty	Han Dynasty
Important Emperors	Shi Huangdi	Liu Bang, Wudi
Impact of Dynasty on China	unified China	stability through adoption of Confucianism; arts flourish; empire expands; technological advances

Map Activity

Place Location

Ancient China
For each place listed below, write the letter from the map that shows its location.

1. Huang He

2. Chang Jiang

3. North China Plain

4. Great Wall of China

5. Silk Road

Writing Activity

Creating a Legend
Many legends about Confucius, such as the story about the woman grieving by her son's grave in Section 2, were written by Confucian scholars long after his death. Use what you know about Confucius and China to write a similar brief story. Use his ideas about family or government to write the moral, or lesson, of the story.

Internet Activity

Use a search engine to find **The Ancient China Home Page.** Click on Anthology. Then click on The Analects or The Tao Te Ching and read several chapters. Choose a section of one of the works that relates to your own life and explain the connection. Then make a booklet in which you can collect favorite teachings from different cultures.

Skills Review

Turn to the Skills Activity. Review the directions for organizing information. Then answer the following: (a) Define key terms. (b) Why should you not copy everything you read as you take notes?

How Am I Doing?

Answer these questions to help you check your progress.

1. Can I describe the important geographic features of ancient China?

2. Do I understand the impact of the teachings of Confucius on Chinese society?

3. Can I name at least two emperors who were important in Chinese history?

4. Can I describe the cultural advances made during the Han dynasty?

5. What information from this chapter can I use in my book project?

Internet Activity

If students are having difficulty finding this site, you may wish to have them use the following URL, which was accurate at the time this textbook was published:

http://eawc.evansville.edu/chpage.htm

You might also guide students to a search engine. Four of the most useful are Infoseek, AltaVista, Lycos, and Yahoo. For additional suggestions on using the Internet, refer to the Prentice Hall Social Studies' Educator's Handbook "Using

the Internet," in the *Prentice Hall World Explorer Program Resources.*

For additional links to world history and culture topics, visit the Prentice Hall Home Page at:
http://www.phschool.com

How Am I Doing?

Point out to students that this checklist is a quick reminder for them of what they learned in the chapter. If their answer to any of the questions is *no* or if they are unsure, they may need to review the topic.

Critical Thinking

1. The abuses of Shi Huangdi made more people dissatisfied with and disrespectful of the Qin government.

2. Answers may vary. Students may suggest that Confucius would not approve of people being disrespectful of others.

Map Activity

1. C   4. B
2. E   5. A
3. D

Writing Activity

Students' stories should reflect daily life in early Chinese civilization and include a Confucian moral. Some stories might even use the family as a metaphor for government.

Skills Review

(a) the most important words and phrases (b) It would take too much time; taking notes saves you from having to read everything over again because you just write down main ideas and key terms.

Resource Directory

Teaching Resources

Chapter Tests Forms A and B are in the Tests booklet, pp. 26–31.

Program Resources

Writing Process Handbook includes Editing for Content, Clarity, and Style, pp. 35–36, to help students with the Writing Activity.

Media and Technology

Color Transparencies
Color Transparency 174
(Graphic organizer table template)
Prentice Hall Writer's Solution
Writing Lab CD-ROM
Computer Test Bank
Resource Pro™ CD-ROM

Lesson Objectives

1 Describe dikes and identify their purpose.

2 Explain how dikes can be used to prevent uncontrolled river flooding.

Lesson Plan

1 Engage

Warm-Up Activity

Show students photographs of flooded lands. You can find these in books about rivers, newspaper files, or in encyclopedias. Together, list some problems that flooding causes. Then discuss how important it is for people living near a river to control its floods.

Activating Prior Knowledge

Have students write a short, descriptive paragraph about a flood. Encourage them to paint a vivid picture of the flood's sights, smells, and sounds. Ask students to explain what people could build to control those floods. Record their explanations on the chalkboard.

2 Explore

Have students read the entire Activity Shop before beginning work. Tell students that river flooding today is often controlled by dams that are built across a river's flow. You might point out that there are some negative aspects to dikes and dams. For example, soils that were once enriched by annual flooding lose much of their fertility. Dams and dikes also interfere with the natural flow of waters, which has resulted in a loss of habitat for certain plants and animals.

ACTIVITY SHOP

Rivers That Flood

In early history, people had no control over flooding rivers. The Huang He, or Yellow River, in China, is sometimes called "China's Sorrow" because its yearly floods cause so much damage. In time, the Chinese people learned to use dikes, or walls made of earth, to hold back the flood waters.

Purpose

In this activity, you will find out how dikes made from dirt can help protect people and the land from floods.

Materials

- large pan (about 9″ x 13″)
- dirt
- beaker of water
- collection bucket

Procedure

STEP ONE

Set up a flood box like the one shown in the first picture. First, pour dirt in the pan so it is about half full. Pat the dirt into the pan so that it is flat and firm, but not hard. Then, dig a small riverbed in the dirt with your finger. The riverbed should go from one narrow end of the pan to the other.

STEP TWO

Create a model of a river. Put something under one of the narrow ends of the pan so that the pan is on a slight angle. Slowly pour some water into the riverbed at the higher end. This model represents a normally flowing river. Notice how the water is held in place by the sides of the "riverbank." Pour the water out of the pan into a collection bucket. If some of the dirt slips out, rebuild your riverbed.

STEP THREE

Create a model of a flood. Put your pan of dirt on an angle again and refill your beaker of water. Now pour the water quickly into the

Resource Directory

Teaching Resources

Activity Shop: Lab in the Activities and Projects booklet, p. 6, provides a structure that helps students complete the lab activity.

riverbed so that some of the water spills over the riverbank. Notice what happens to the low-lying areas surrounding the river. Pour the water out of the pan into a collection bucket.

STEP FOUR

Build dikes out of dirt to contain the flood water. Make small hills out of dirt to run lengthwise along your model river. These dikes will run completely along the river on both sides of the river. Make one row about 1 inch from each side of the river. Make another row about 2 inches from each side of the river (1 inch from the first row you made).

STEP FIVE

See how the dikes can prevent flooding. Create another flood in your river by pouring water quickly into the riverbed. What happens when the water reaches the first dike? Repeat the activity with more water until the first dike is overflowed or washes away.

▲ **Flood Control** These ancient dikes made of earth help prevent flooding in the Hubei province of China.

Observations

1️⃣ When the river is running slowly, how well does the riverbank contain the water?

2️⃣ What happens to the plains surrounding the river when the river rises above its banks?

3️⃣ How did the second dike help protect the land?

ANALYSIS AND CONCLUSION

1. How might flooding affect a large civilization living along the banks of a river?

2. How might dikes help civilizations near rivers grow and develop?

3 Teach

Before beginning, protect the floor and students' clothing. Place collection buckets in accessible locations.

Organize students into small groups to build the models. Individual students can take turns carrying out each step. Read aloud the questions under Observations. Ask groups to look for answers to these questions as they work.

Observations

1. It contains water quite well.
2. Water covers them.
3. It held back water when the first dike was washed away or became covered by water.

4 Assess

Have students build on their earlier explanations of how dikes work by writing short explanatory captions for their group's model. Evaluate the captions and individual demonstrations for clarity and accuracy. You may also use students' answers to Analysis and Conclusion to assess their understanding.

Answers to . . .

ANALYSIS AND CONCLUSION

1. Possible answer: They would probably try to invent some way to control floodwaters, so they could enjoy the benefits of living near a river without risking periodical destruction.
2. A civilization that built dikes could control flooding and would probably thrive. It would be able to enjoy the benefits of living near a river (fertile land, access to water for drinking, transportation, and irrigation).

Ancient Greece

To help you plan instruction, the chart below shows how teaching resources correspond to chapter content. Use the resources to vary instruction, add activities, or plan block schedules. Where appropriate, resources have **suggested time allotments** for students. Time allotments are approximate.

Managing Time and Instruction

	The Ancient World Teaching Resources Binder		World Explorer Program Resources Binder	
	Resource	mins.	Resource	mins.
SECTION 1 **The Rise of Greek Civilization**	**Chapter and Section Support** Reproducible Lesson Plan, p. 96 ⑤ Guided Reading and Review, p. 97 ⑤ Section Quiz, p. 98	20 25	**Outline Maps** Mediterranean Europe: Political, p. 21 Western Europe: Physical, p. 17 **Nystrom Desk Atlas** Ⓣ Primary Sources and Literature Readings **Writing Process Handbook** Writing an Introduction, p. 29	20 20 20 40 25
SKILLS ACTIVITY **Drawing Conclusions**	**Social Studies and Geography Skills,** Drawing Conclusions, p. 52	30		
SECTION 2 **Greek Religion, Philosophy, and Literature**	**Chapter and Section Support** Reproducible Lesson Plan, p. 99 ⑤ Guided Reading and Review, p. 100 ⑤ Section Quiz, p. 101 Critical Thinking Activity, p. 115	20 25 30		
SECTION 3 **Daily Life of the Ancient Greeks**	**Chapter and Section Support** Reproducible Lesson Plan, p. 102 ⑤ Guided Reading and Review, p. 103 ⑤ Section Quiz, p. 104	20 25		
SECTION 4 **Athens and Sparta: Two Cities in Conflict**	**Chapter and Section Support** Reproducible Lesson Plan, p. 105 ⑤ Guided Reading and Review, p. 106 ⑤ Section Quiz, p. 107	20 25	**Outline Maps** The Middle East and North Africa: Political, p. 29	20
SECTION 5 **The Spread of Greek Culture**	**Chapter and Section Support** Reproducible Lesson Plan, p. 108 ⑤ Guided Reading and Review, p. 109 ⑤ Section Quiz, p. 110 ⑤ Vocabulary, p. 112 Reteaching, p. 113 Enrichment, p. 114 ⑤ Chapter Summary, p. 111 **Tests** Forms A and B Chapter Tests, pp. 32–37	20 25 20 25 25 15 40	**Outline Maps** The Middle East and North Africa: Physical, p. 29	20
ACTIVITY SHOP: INTERDISCIPLINARY **Hold an Ancient Greek Festival**	Ⓣ Activity Shop: Interdisciplinary, p. 7	30		
LITERATURE **The Sirens retold by Bernard Evslin**	**Social Studies and Geography Skills,** Giving Yourself a Purpose for Reading, p. 69	30	Ⓣ Primary Sources and Literature Readings	40

Block Scheduling Folder
PROGRAM TEACHING RESOURCES

Activities and Projects

Block Scheduling Program Support

Interdisciplinary Links

Resource Pro™ CD-ROM

Media and Technology

Media and Technology

Resource	mins.
World Video Explorer	20
Planet Earth CD-ROM	20
Color Transparencies 4, 89, 168	20
Color Transparency 127	20
Planet Earth CD-ROM	20
Color Transparency 70	20
Color Transparency 70	20
Guided Reading Audiotapes	20
Color Transparency 174	20
(Graphic organizer table template)	
The Writer's Solution CD-ROM	30
Computer Test Bank	30

T **Teaming Opportunity**
This resource is especially well-suited for teaching teams.

S **Spanish**
This resource is also in Spanish support.

CD-ROM

Laserdisc

Transparency

Software

Videotape

Audiotape

Assessment Opportunities

From Guiding Questions to Assessment A series of Guiding Questions serves as an organizing framework for this book. The Guiding Questions that relate to this chapter are listed below. Section Reviews and Section Quizzes provide opportunities for assessing students' insights into these Guiding Questions. Additional assessments are listed below.

GUIDING QUESTIONS

- *How did the beliefs and values of ancient civilizations affect the lives of their members?*
- *What accomplishments is each civilization known for?*

ASSESSMENTS

Section 1

Students should be able to write a glossary of the key terms in this section.

▶ **RUBRIC** See the Assessment booklet for a rubric on assessing a glossary.

Section 2

Students should be able to create a web of the major accomplishments of the Golden Age.

▶ **RUBRIC** See the Assessment booklet for a rubric on assessing graphic organizers.

Section 3

Students should be able to role-play a scene portraying daily life of the ancient Greeks.

▶ **RUBRIC** See the Assessment booklet for a rubric on assessing a role-playing activity.

Section 4

Students should be able to create a time line of major events in classical Greece from 500 B.C. to 400 B.C.

▶ **RUBRIC** See the Assessment booklet for a rubric on assessing a time line.

Section 5

Students should be able to create a map of the spread of Greek culture.

▶ **RUBRIC** See the Assessment booklet for a rubric on assessing a map produced by a student.

Activities and Projects

Mental Mapping

Mediterranean Geography List the following names on the chalkboard: Spain, Egypt, Italy, Greece, Libya, Portugal, Lebanon, Tunisia, France, Israel, Turkey, Algeria, Albania, Syria, Yugoslavia, and Morocco.

Tell students that all of these countries have a coastline on the Mediterranean Sea. Give students an outline map of the Mediterranean region. Allow them to have a few minutes to match the labels on the chalkboard to the outlines of the countries. Then give students a chance to check their work and correct it, if necessary, against a published map.

Tell students that the Mediterranean was the site of many ancient empires.

Links to Current Events

It's All Greek Tell students that many words in our language come from ancient Greek. List the following examples on the chalkboard: encyclopedia, chorus, cornucopia, cynic, delta, echo, fate, fury, fraternity, giant, grace, hyacinth, iota, labyrinth, mask, mentor, mime, nectar, nemesis, Nike, odyssey, Olympian, orchestra, protagonist, psyche, rhapsody, siren, skeptic, sophisticated, sorority, stadium, sphinx, stoic, titan, and weird.

Many of the words were names of characters in Greek myths or are from Greek theater, philosophy, or mathematics. Have each student choose an interesting word. Ask them to research the word with a dictionary or encyclopedia to find out its Greek origin. Ask each student to give a one-minute oral report explaining the Greek use of the word and its modern English meaning.

Hands-On Activities

Porches, Columns, and Stadiums Many American structures have been influenced by the architecture of the ancient Greeks. Provide, or have students locate, pictures of ancient Greek theaters, temples, and other structures. Point out the use of columns, porches, covered colonnades, arena-style seating, and other features.

Ask students to think of buildings they may have seen in their town that have some of these features. If there are not many buildings in the local area with classical features, have students look for pictures of buildings in Washington, D.C., their state capital, and other cities. Have them identify structures that resemble the ancient Greek buildings.

Ask students why they think people still use the styles of architecture of a civilization that is more than 2,000 years old.

Debate of Two City-States Have students stage a debate between citizens of Sparta and citizens of Athens. There may be up to three contestants on each side. Ask them to debate the question of which city offered a better way of life. *Average*

Mythical Dramatics Have a group of students choose one story from Greek mythology. Ask them to stage it for the class, using costumes and props as appropriate. *Challenging*

Graphic Organizer Have students create a graphic organizer with columns labeled Religion, Philosophy, and Literature. Tell them to list the names of Greeks who made a contribution to each of these areas in the appropriate column. *Basic*

Frieze of a Golden Age Tell students that the frieze, a long band decorating the entire length of one or more walls, was an important art form of ancient Greece. A frieze could depict historical or mythological events. It was usually sculpted in low relief, but could also be painted. Have students work together to create a frieze for one or more walls of the classroom showing daily life in ancient Greece. *English Language Learners*

F.Y.I.

This page can help you extend your own and students' understanding of the concepts in this chapter. You may want to browse through some of the suggestions in the **Bibliography. Interdisciplinary Links** can connect social studies understandings to areas elsewhere in the curriculum through the use of other Prentice Hall products. **National Geography Standards** reflected specifically in this chapter are listed for your convenience. Some hints about appropriate **Internet Access** are also provided. **School to Careers** provides insights into the practical uses of some of the concepts in this chapter as they might pertain to various careers.

BIBLIOGRAPHY

FOR THE TEACHER
Descamps-Lequime, Sophie, and Denise Vernerey. *The Ancient Greeks: In the Land of the Gods.* Millbrook, 1992.

Loverance, Rowena. *Ancient Greece.* Viking, 1993.

Macdonald, Fiona. *A Greek Temple.* Bedrick, 1992.

FOR THE STUDENT
Easy
Powell, Anton, and Philip Steele. *The Greek News.* Candlewick Press, 1996.

Average
Clare, John D., ed. *Ancient Greece.* Gulliver, 1994.

Sutcliff, Rosemary. *The Wanderings of Odysseus: The Story of* The Odyssey. Delacorte, 1996.

Challenging
Fleischman, Paul. *Dateline: Troy.* Candlewick Press, 1996.

Theulé, Fréderic. *Alexander and His Times.* Henry Holt and Company, 1996.

LITERATURE CONNECTION
Household, Geoffrey. *The Exploits of Xenophon.* Linnet Books, 1989.

King, Perry Scott. *Pericles.* Chelsea House, 1988.

Osborne, Mary Pope. *Favorite Greek Myths.* Scholastic, 1989. Also available on CD-ROM, Scholastic Smart Books, 1994.

INTERDISCIPLINARY LINKS

Subject	Theme: Achievement
MATH	Middle Grades Math: Tools for Success *Course 1,* Lesson 6-4, **Exploring** π *Course 2,* Lesson 5-6, **Exploring the Pythagorean Theorem**
SCIENCE	Prentice Hall Science *Exploring the Universe,* Lesson 2-2, **Motions of the Planets**
LANGUAGE ARTS	Choices in Literature *It's Up to You,* **The Golden Apples** *Joining Hands,* **Anna, Age 17, Greek** Prentice Hall Literature *Bronze,* **Demeter and Persephone** *Copper,* **The Gorgon's Head**

NATIONAL GEOGRAPHY STANDARDS

Students explore the 18 National Geography Standards throughout *The Ancient World.* Chapter 6, however, concentrates on investigating the following standards: 4, 6, 9, 10, 14, 15, 17. For a complete list of the standards, see the *Teacher's Flexible Planning Guide.*

SCHOOL TO CAREERS

In Chapter 6, Ancient Greece, students learn about the roots of some elements of our own civilization. Additionally, they address the skill of drawing conclusions. Understanding ancient Greece can help students prepare for careers in many fields such as architecture, philosophy, history, art, archaeology, and so on. Drawing conclusions is a skill particularly useful for news commentators, journalists, police officers, and others. The curriculum presented in this book, as in all eight titles of Prentice Hall's *World Explorer* program, is designed to prepare students not only for careers but also for good citizenship—of the world as well as of this country.

INTERNET ACCESS

Many social studies teachers and students use Internet browsers, or search engines, to investigate particular topics. For the best results, use narrow rather than broad topics. Try these for Chapter 6: Trojan War, Acropolis, Homer, Parthenon. Finding age-appropriate sites is an important consideration when using the Internet. For links to age-appropriate sites in world studies and geography, visit the Prentice Hall Home Page at: **http://www.phschool.com**

CHAPTER 6

Ancient Greece

Connecting to the Guiding Questions

In this chapter, students will focus on the achievements of ancient Greece. Content in this chapter corresponds to the following Guiding Questions:

● How did the beliefs and values of ancient civilizations affect the lives of their members?

● What accomplishments is each civilization known for?

Using the Map Activities

As students describe the land shown on the map, introduce geographic terms such as *peninsula*.

• Greece consists of peninsulas and islands. It is small compared to the United States.

• Ancient Greeks probably fished and traded. Greeks probably built cities abroad to establish trade.

Heterogeneous Groups

The following Teacher's Edition strategies are suitable for heterogeneous groups.

Interdisciplinary Connections
Language Arts   p. 155
Language Arts   p. 178
Critical Thinking
Recognizing Cause
and Effect   p. 157
Drawing Conclusions   p. 163
Cooperative Learning
Presenting Myths   p. 163
Planning a Festival   p. 167

SECTION 1
The Rise of Greek Civilization

SECTION 2
Greek Religion, Philosophy, and Literature

SECTION 3
Daily Life of the Ancient Greeks

SECTION 4
Athens and Sparta
TWO CITIES IN CONFLICT

SECTION 5
The Spread of Greek Culture

MACEDONIA
Mt. Olympus
9,570 ft.
(2,917 m) ▲
Troy
Aegean Sea
GREECE
Marathon
Olympia
Athens
Sparta

KEY
• City
▲ Mountain peak
Lambert Conic Conformal Projection

Mediterranean Sea
Crete

0   50   100 mi
0   50   100 km

MAP ACTIVITIES

The land of ancient Greece extended south into the Mediterranean Sea. It was a mountainous land. Ancient Greece also included a large number of islands in the Mediterranean. The ancient Greeks built colonies in places outside of Greece, such as the coast of Asia Minor, or modern-day Turkey. To help you get to know this region, carry out the following activities.

Describe the region
How would you describe the land of Greece? How would you compare the land of Greece to that of the United States?

Think about the people
From the map, make some guesses about how the people of ancient Greece earned their livelihood. What role did the sea probably have in their lives? Why do you think some Greeks left ancient Greece to build cities elsewhere?

Resource Directory

Media and Technology

Culture: Greek Theater, from the World Video Explorer, enhances students' understanding of Greek theater and its influences.

Chapter 8

The Rise of Greek Civilization

Section 1

BEFORE YOU READ

Reach Into Your Background

What makes the community where you live special? What makes it a community? Does it have traditions and customs of its own? What are they? What does your community share with its neighbors?

Questions to Explore

1. How did geography influence the development of civilization in Greece?
2. How did democracy develop in Athens?

Key Terms

peninsula
epic
acropolis
city-state

aristocrat
tyrant
democracy

Key People and Places

Homer
Solon
Troy

First there was nothing. Then came Mother Earth. The gods of Night and Day appeared next, and then starry Sky. Earth and Sky created the Twelve Titans (TYT unz). These great gods rebelled against their father Sky and took away his power. The youngest of the Titans, Cronos, ruled in his father's place. In time, Cronos had six children. The youngest, mighty Zeus (zoos), toppled Cronos from his throne.

With such words, the people of ancient Greece described the struggles of their gods. Like their gods, the people of Greece had to struggle for power and independence. Their struggles began with the land itself.

Greece's Geographic Setting

The land of Greece looks as if the sea had smashed it to pieces. Some pieces have drifted away to form small, rocky islands. Others barely cling to the mainland. Greece is a peninsula made up of peninsulas. A **peninsula** is an area of land surrounded by water on three sides. Look at the map. As you can see, no part of Greece is very far from the sea.

Mountains are the major landform of Greece. Greece's islands are mostly mountain peaks. Mountains wrinkle the mainland, so there are only small patches of farmland. Only about one fifth of Greece is good for growing crops. No wonder the Greeks became traders and sailors. At times, they even left Greece to found colonies far away.

What was life like for people living in Greece 3,000 years ago? In a way, the ancient Greeks were all islanders. Some lived on real islands completely surrounded by water or on small peninsulas. Others lived on

▼ The sea was an important part of life in ancient Greece. It inspired an artist to decorate this clay pot with soldiers riding dolphins.

Teaching Resources

📁 **Reproducible Lesson Plan** in the Chapter and Section Resources booklet, p. 96, provides a summary of the section lesson.

📁 **Guided Reading and Review** in the Chapter and Section Resources booklet, p. 97, provides a structure for mastering key concepts and reviewing key terms in the section. Available in Spanish in the Spanish Chapter and Section Resources booklet, p. 60.

Program Resources

Material in the **Primary Sources and Literature Readings** booklet extends content with a selection related to the concepts in this chapter.

Outline Maps Mediterranean Europe: Political, p. 21 Western Europe: Physical, p. 17

Lesson Objectives

1 Describe Greece's geographic setting.

2 Explain the significance of Greek myths.

3 Identify different forms of government that developed in Greek city-states.

Lesson Plan

1 Engage

Warm-Up Activity

Tell the class to imagine that they live in a valley surrounded by mountains. Another community lives in a valley on the other side of these mountains. Encourage students to discuss differences that might occur, over time, in language, customs, and beliefs, as well as in attitudes toward the other community.

Activating Prior Knowledge

Have students read Reach Into Your Background in the Before You Read box. Ask students who have lived in other communities, states, or countries to describe how your community differs from other places they have lived. Suggest that students consider schools, entertainment, clothing, and slang. Invite the class to speculate on reasons for the differences.

2 Explore

After students have read the section, discuss how geography influenced the development of many small city-states that traded and waged war against one another. What did these groups have in common? How do we know about the Trojan War? How do we know Troy existed? How was Greek heritage preserved?

3 Teach

Ask students to create a chart for the three systems of government: *Rule by Aristocrats*; *Rule by Tyrants*; and *Rule by the People* (democracy). For each system, have students describe the form of government, one of its benefits, and one of its problems. Share the information on the charts. This activity should take about 20 minutes.

4 Assess

See the answers to the Section Review. You may also use students' charts for assessment.

Acceptable charts complete the assignment as stated.

Commendable charts contain opinions backed by facts from the text.

Outstanding charts show an understanding of how these forms of government evolved.

▶ Several typical geographic features appear in this picture of the northwestern coast of Greece. These features include a rocky coastline and rugged mountains. **Critical Thinking** How did the geographic features shown affect the way ancient people lived in this area?

Predict What effect do you think the geography of Greece had on the kind of communities that developed?

"land islands." Mountains cut off these small communities from each other. The geography of Greece made it hard for people from different communities to get together.

For this reason, it is no surprise that ancient Greek communities thought of themselves as separate countries. Each one developed its own customs and beliefs. Each believed its own land, traditions, and way of life were the best. And each was more than ready to go to war to protect itself. In fact, for most of their history, the Greeks were so busy fighting among themselves that it is easy to forget that they shared a common heritage, spoke the same language, and worshipped the same gods.

Greek Beginnings

All Greeks shared a wealth of stories and myths about their origins. The myths explained the creation of the universe and the features of nature. They described the adventures of Greek heroes and gods. Various stories told how cities and traditions came to be.

The most important stories told about the Trojan War, a long struggle between Greece and the city of Troy on the west coast of Asia Minor. All the great heroes from both regions joined in the war.

The Trojan War The story of the Trojan War has everything a story should have—great battles, plots and schemes, loyalty and betrayal. According to the myths, a prince named Paris, from the wealthy city of Troy, was the guest of a Greek chieftain named Menelaus (men uh LAY us). Breaking the law of the gods, Paris kidnapped Menelaus' wife, Helen, and took her to Troy. To get Helen back, the Greek chieftains sent a huge army to attack Troy.

For ten long years, the war dragged on. Many heroes on both sides perished. At last, the Greeks conquered Troy by a trick—the Trojan Horse. The Greeks burned and looted Troy and then returned home.

Two **epics,** or long poems, about the Trojan War survive today. They are the *Iliad* and the *Odyssey*. The *Iliad* tells about a quarrel between Greek leaders in the last year of the war. The *Odyssey* describes the adventures of the hero Odysseus (oh DIS ee us) as he struggles to return to his homeland from Troy.

These epics may have been composed by many people, but they are credited to a poet called Homer. The poems were important to the Greeks. They taught them what their gods were like and how the noblest of their heroes behaved. Today, people think these poems came from stories memorized by several poets and passed down by word of mouth through many generations. Homer may have been the last and greatest in this line of poets who told about the Trojan War.

Ask Questions What would you like to know about the Trojan War?

Trojan Horse

Sissy Pachiadaki
age 12
Greece

This picture shows how the Trojan Horse helped the Greeks conquer Troy. Greek warriors hid inside a huge wooden horse. The horse was rolled to the city gates. The Trojans thought it was a gift to the gods, so they brought it into their city. During the night, the Greek soldiers climbed out of the horse and let the rest of their army into Troy.

Writing for a Purpose
To **introduce** the skill to students, point out that writing can be used to inform, entertain, or persuade. Also indicate that one way to help people remember history is to make it entertaining—myths accomplish that goal. Tell students that myths are often stories about characters with supernatural powers. Myths can be about adventures, battles between good and evil, or explanations for natural phenomena, such as how the world was created. Have students **practice** and **apply** the skill by working in pairs to create their own myths. Suggest that they decide what subject their myth will present, who they will be writing for (their peers), and the purpose of their myth (to entertain).

Links Across Time

City-States in the Renaissance In Italy, from the 1000s on, some cities grew in independence, wealth, and power. Florence, Genoa, Milan, Pisa, and Venice became centers of trade and banking and developed into states with the same powers as nations. In the 1300s and 1400s, these Italian city-states were the centers of the Renaissance—a revival of learning and art spurred by a renewed interest in the achievements of ancient Greece and Rome. The free exchange of ideas in the city-states led to great advances in science, philosophy, mathematics, and the arts.

◀These warriors decorate a vase from the 500s B.C. The background is the natural color of the baked clay. The black figures were painted on.

Troy Discovered Over the years, people came to believe that Troy and the Trojan War were fiction. An amateur archaeologist, Heinrich Schliemann, disagreed. In the late 1800s he used clues in the *Iliad* to pinpoint the location of Troy. When he and later archaeologists dug there, they found nine layers of ruins from ancient cities. One was possibly the Troy of the *Iliad* and the *Odyssey*.

The Dark Ages of Greece Not long after the end of Troy, civilization in Greece collapsed. No one knows exactly why. Life went on, but poverty was everywhere. People no longer traded for food and other goods beyond Greece. They had to depend on what they could raise themselves. Some were forced to move to islands and to the western part of Asia Minor. The art of writing disappeared.

These years, from the early 1100s B.C. to about 750 B.C., have been called Greece's Dark Ages. Without writing, people had to depend on word of mouth to keep their traditions and history alive. Old traditions were remembered only in the myths that were told and retold.

Greece's Dark Ages were not completely bleak, however. During this time, families gradually began to resettle in places where they could grow crops and raise animals. Some of these family farms may have developed into villages. When they chose places to build their farms, people favored places near rocky, protected hills where they would be safe from attack. The name for such a place was **acropolis,** meaning "high city."

Governing the City-States

Sometime around 750 B.C., villages in a small area probably joined together to form a city in the shadow of an acropolis. At that time, each city began to develop its own traditions and its own form of government and laws. Each one was not only a city, but also a separate independent state. Today, we call these tiny nations **city-states.** Each included a city and the villages and fields surrounding it. Hundreds of Greek city-states grew up, each more or less independent.

Aristocracy: Nobles Rule   The earliest rulers of city-states were probably chieftains or kings who were military leaders. By the end of Greece's Dark Ages, most city-states were ruled by **aristocrats,** members of the rich and powerful families. Aristocrats controlled most of the good land. They could afford horses, chariots, and the best weapons to make themselves stronger than others.

A New Type of Ruler   As the Greeks sailed to foreign ports trading olive oil, marble, and other products, the city-states became richer. A middle class of merchants and artisans developed. They wanted some say in the government of their cities. These people could not afford to equip themselves with horses and chariots for war. However, they could afford armor, swords, and spears. With these weapons, large groups of soldiers could fight effectively on foot. Gradually, military strength in the cities shifted from aristocrats to merchants and artisans.

As a result of these changes, aristocratic governments were often overthrown and replaced by rulers called tyrants. A **tyrant** was a ruler who seized power by force. Tyrants were usually supported by the middle and working classes. Today, we think of tyrants as being cruel and violent. That was true of some Greek tyrants, but others ruled wisely and well.

Democracy: Rule by the People   Eventually, the people of many city-states overthrew tyrants who were too harsh. A few cities moved to a form of government called **democracy.** In a democracy, citizens govern themselves. The city-state in which democracy was most fully expressed was Athens.

▼ The Acropolis in Athens was known for its beautiful temples. It was also a fortress. During wartime, people moved to the Acropolis where the enemy could not easily reach them.

Activity

Critical Thinking

Recognizing Cause and Effect   *Suitable as either a whole class or an individual activity.* Ask students to read *A New Type of Ruler.* Then have students identify two causes that led to the development of rule by tyrants. Help students recognize that the merchants' and artisans' desire for a voice in government and their ability to pay for arms to overthrow the aristocrats led to the development of this kind of government. Point out to students that phrases in the text like *as a result* often signal the description of a cause-and-effect relationship.

Background

Links Across Time

A Citizen's Lot   In Athenian democracy, all male citizens voted in the Assembly. From this group, 500 were chosen by lot to serve for one year on the Council, a decision-making body. Jury members for court trials were also chosen by lot. But, as in modern democracies, some officials were elected. The 10 generals who formed the Board of Generals were elected by the Assembly.

SKILLS MINI LESSON

Using Distribution Maps

You might **introduce** the skill by reading the following quote from the Greek philosopher Plato, which illustrates the importance of the sea to the Greeks: "We live around the sea like frogs around a pond." Explain that by 750 B.C., rapid increases in population forced many Greeks to move away from the Greek islands and form settlements elsewhere. Then tell students to turn to the map in the Activity Atlas entitled Greek Settlements From About 1100 B.C. to 500 B.C. Tell them that distribution maps show where something is located. This distribution map, for example, shows where Greek settlements developed. Help students **practice** using the skill by asking them to identify something that all the settlements have in common. (All are very close to a coast and have access to the sea.) Ask students to **apply** the skill by using the distance scale and the compass rose to locate the city and settlement farthest west from Greece. (Maenace is about 1,500 miles west of Greece.)

1. (a) land surrounded on three sides by water (b) a long poem that tells a story (c) a high, rocky place (d) a city that is an independent nation (e) a member of a rich and powerful family (f) a ruler who seized power by force (g) a form of government in which citizens govern themselves

2. (a) poet who wrote about the Trojan War (b) reformer who helped form the democracy of Athens (c) an ancient city in Asia Minor

3. At first, aristocrats who controlled most of the good land ruled. Aristocracies were often overthrown by tyrants; usually the middle classes supported tyrants. Eventually, the people of many city-states overthrew harsh tyrants and formed democracies in which the people govern themselves.

4. Men who were citizens of Athens benefited most. They had a say in debating important laws and were allowed to participate in the government.

5. Mountains isolated communities from one another and contributed to the need of each community to be self-sufficient.

6. Answers may vary. Students' answers should indicate that the Dark Ages of Greece were characterized by widespread poverty, little trade, and the disappearance of writing.

Symbols of Democracy

In this carving (right), the woman stands for democracy. She is crowning a man seated on a throne. He stands for the Athenian people. The carving reminded the people of Athens of their duty to take part in government. Greek citizens served on juries at trials. Bronze plates like this one (below) were used to identify and choose members of juries.

READ ACTIVELY

Connect Would you like to have lived under the democracy in Athens? Why or why not?

About 594 B.C., a wise Athenian leader called Solon won the power to reform the laws. Solon was well known for his fairness. His laws reformed both the economy and the government of Athens. One of his first laws canceled all debts and freed citizens who had been enslaved for having debts. Another law allowed any male citizen of Athens aged 18 or older to have a say in debating important laws. These laws and others allowed Athens to become the leading democracy of the ancient world.

However, not everyone living in ancient Athens benefited from democracy. Only about one in five Athenians was a citizen. Some of the people living in Athens were enslaved. These people did not take part in democracy. Nor did women and foreigners. But the men who were citizens of Athens were free and self-governing.

SECTION 1 REVIEW

1. Define (a) peninsula, (b) epic, (c) acropolis, (d) city-state, (e) aristocrat, (f) tyrant, (g) democracy.

2. Identify (a) Homer, (b) Solon, (c) Troy.

3. Describe the three kinds of governments that developed in the Greek city-states after the Dark Ages.

4. What group of Athenians benefited most from democracy? Why?

Critical Thinking

5. Recognizing Cause and Effect How did the mountains in Greece contribute to the rise of city-states?

Activity

6. Writing to Learn Describe conditions in Greece during the period between the 1100s B.C. and the 700s B.C. Why are these years referred to as Greece's Dark Ages?

Resource Directory

Teaching Resources

Section Quiz in the Chapter and Section Resources booklet, p. 98, covers the main ideas and key terms in the section. Available in Spanish in the Spanish Chapter and Section Resources booklet, p. 61.

Greek Religion, Philosophy, and Literature

SECTION 2

BEFORE YOU READ

Reach Into Your Background
Think about the things that make the United States a good place to live. What do you like about living here? How would you describe life in the United States to someone from another country? What would you say were the most important achievements of the United States?

Questions to Explore
1. What were some accomplishments of the Golden Age?

2. How did Greek philosophers try to understand the world?

Key Terms
tribute   philosopher
immortal   tragedy

Key People and Places
Pericles
Parthenon
Socrates

> **"O**ur constitution does not copy the laws of neighboring states. We are a pattern to other cities rather than imitators. Our constitution favors the many instead of the few. That is why it is called a democracy. If we look at the laws, we see they give equal justice to all . . . . Poverty does not bar the way, if a man is able to serve the state. . . . In short, I say that as a city we are the school for all Greece.**"**

These are the words of the Athenian leader Pericles (PEHR ih kleez). He was reminding the citizens that Athens was special. Pericles' words had special meaning: They were spoken during the first year of a war with Sparta, another Greek city-state. Eventually, it was Sparta that ended Athens' Golden Age of accomplishment.

▶ Pericles led the Athenians in peace and war. The helmet he wears reminds us that he was a skilled general.

Lesson Objectives

1. Describe important Greek contributions to art, architecture, and drama.

2. Outline the development of Greek religion and philosophy.

3. Explain the roles of Pericles and Socrates.

Lesson Plan

1 Engage

Warm-Up Activity

Ask students why we admire great athletes. Discuss how athletes represent what the human body can achieve. Go on to discuss attributes other than athleticism that we admire: beauty, intelligence, moral strength, and so on. Tell students that the ancient Greeks' admiration for these qualities is evident in their democratic government, philosophy, and artistic renderings of the human form.

Activating Prior Knowledge

Have students read Reach Into Your Background in the Before You Read box. Write the following headings on the chalkboard: *Art, Government, Literature, Architecture, Drama* (theater and movies). Ask students to name some examples of outstanding American achievements in each category.

Teaching Resources

📁 **Reproducible Lesson Plan** in the Chapter and Section Resources booklet, p. 99, provides a summary of the section lesson.

📁 **Guided Reading and Review** in the Chapter and Section Resources booklet, p. 100, provides a structure for mastering key concepts and reviewing key terms in the section. Available in Spanish in the Spanish Chapter and Section Resources booklet, p. 62.

2 Explore

Have students read the section. Discuss the achievements of Pericles, of the architects and sculptors of the Parthenon, of the philosophers Democritus and Socrates, and of Greek playwrights. Discuss how democracy helped spur these great achievements.

3 Teach

After students have read the section, organize them into several teams. Direct each team member to write one quiz question that can be answered with information from the section. Quizzes should have at least one question for each subheading. Have teams exchange quizzes and answer questions. This activity will take about 30 minutes.

4 Assess

See the answers to the Section Review. You may also use teams' quizzes for assessment.

Acceptable quizzes include at least one question addressing each subheading.

Commendable quizzes include at least one question addressing each subheading, one or two of which require higher-level thinking.

Outstanding quizzes include at least one question addressing each subheading, three of which require higher-level thinking.

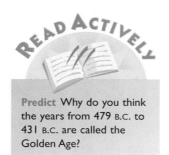

READ ACTIVELY

Predict Why do you think the years from 479 B.C. to 431 B.C. are called the Golden Age?

The Golden Age of Athens

The years from 479 B.C. to 431 B.C. are called the Golden Age of Athens. During the Golden Age, Athens grew rich from trade and from silver mined by slaves in regions around the city. **Tribute,** or payments made to Athens by its allies, added to its wealth.

Athenians also made amazing achievements in the arts, philosophy, and literature. And democracy reached its high point. For about 30 years during the Golden Age, Pericles was the most powerful man in Athenian politics. This well-educated and intelligent man had the best interests of his city at heart. When he made speeches to the Athenians, he could move and persuade them.

Pericles was a member of an aristocratic family, but he supported democracy. Around 460 B.C., he became leader of a democratic group. He introduced reforms that strengthened democracy. The most important change was to have the city pay a salary to its officials. This meant that poor citizens could afford to hold public office.

The Flourishing Arts

Today, Pericles is probably best known for making Athens a beautiful city. In 480 B.C., during one of the city's many wars, the Acropolis of Athens had been destroyed. Pericles decided to rebuild the Acropolis

In Honor of Athena

and create new buildings to glorify the city. He hired the Greek world's finest architects and sculptors for the project.

Magnificent Architecture The builders of the new Acropolis brought Greek architecture to its highest point. Their most magnificent work was the Parthenon, a temple to the goddess Athena. The temple was made of fine marble. Rows of columns surrounded it on all four sides. Within the columns was a room that held the statue of Athena, made of wood, ivory, and gold. The statue rose 40 feet (12 m), as high as a four-story building.

Lifelike Sculpture The great statue of Athena disappeared long ago. However, much of the sculpture on the inside and outside of the temple still exists. Many of the scenes that decorate the Parthenon have three important characteristics. First, they are full of action. Second, the artist carefully arranged the figures to show balance and order. Third, the sculptures are lifelike and accurate. However, they are ideal, or perfect, views of humans and animals. These characteristics reflect the goal of Greek art. This goal was to present images of human perfection in a balanced and orderly way. Real people and animals would not look like these sculptures.

The Golden Rectangle
Greek architects based the design of their buildings on a figure called the Golden Rectangle. A Golden Rectangle is one with the long sides about one and two thirds times the length of the short sides. The Greeks thought Golden Rectangles made buildings more pleasing to look at. Modern architects have also used the Golden Rectangle.

It took the Athenians 15 years to build the Parthenon (left), considered the home on Earth of the goddess Athena. Its beauty still crowns the city of Athens. The graceful riders (far left, on facing page) are part of a sculptured procession. They were carved on the inner wall of the Parthenon.

Background

Links Across Time

Influence of Greek Art
Greek art had a strong influence on Roman and Hellenistic art. But by the Middle Ages, the Greek influence was no longer apparent in European painting and sculpture. Art during the Middle Ages was almost exclusively devoted to Christian religious themes. Portrayals of human figures were stiff, stylized, and not very realistic. This style of art remained the norm until the 1300s, when the works of the Italian painter Giotto heralded a return to the Classical ideals. In Giotto's paintings, human beings look more lifelike and are shown to be expressive and emotional.

Plato (427 B.C.–347 B.C.)
One of Socrates' most famous followers was Plato, an aristocrat from a powerful family. Plato founded a school called the Academy, which is considered by some to be the first university. Plato is best known for his philosophical works called dialogues. In many of the dialogues, Socrates appears as a character asking what other people's ideas of "truth," "justice," or "beauty" might be. In others, Plato seems to use Socrates as a spokesman for his own ideas, such as that living a virtuous life leads to happiness.

Background

Links Across Time

A Cynic's View Today, people use the word *cynic* to describe someone who is jaded or distrustful. The Cynics, however, were not necessarily the ancient counterparts of today's curmudgeons. These Cynics belonged to a school of philosophy that developed in the 300s B.C. Cynics advocated moral virtue and a renunciation of worldly things, which were deemed to be the source of evil and unhappiness. To attain "freedom," Cynics reduced their possessions, relationships with other people, and pleasures as much as possible. Antisthenes, a founder of the Cynic school of philosophy and a student of Socrates, summarized the Cynic's goal when he said, "I would rather go mad than enjoy myself."

Predict What kind of gods do you think the Greeks worshipped?

The Search for Knowledge

Greeks worshipped a family of gods and goddesses called the Twelve Olympians. Each ruled different areas of human life. The chart on the next page gives you more information about the Olympians.

Greek Religion Wherever the Greeks lived, they built temples to the gods. Since the gods had human forms, they also had many human characteristics. The main difference between gods and humans was that the gods were perfect in form and had awesome power. Also, the gods were **immortal,** which meant they lived forever.

In addition to the 12 great gods led by Zeus, the Greeks worshipped many lesser ones. They also honored mythical heroes like Achilles (uh KIL eez), who had done great deeds during the Trojan War. The story of Achilles is told in the *Iliad.*

Greek Science and Philosophy Most Greeks believed that their gods were the source of all natural events. But a few thinkers disagreed. About 150 years before the Golden Age of Athens, some people thought about ways besides myths to understand the world.

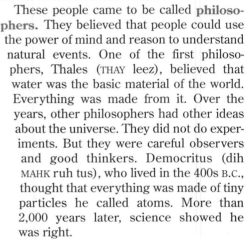

▶ The ancient Greeks worshipped many gods. One of them was Athena, the goddess of wisdom.

These people came to be called **philosophers.** They believed that people could use the power of mind and reason to understand natural events. One of the first philosophers, Thales (THAY leez), believed that water was the basic material of the world. Everything was made from it. Over the years, other philosophers had other ideas about the universe. They did not do experiments. But they were careful observers and good thinkers. Democritus (dih MAHK ruh tus), who lived in the 400s B.C., thought that everything was made of tiny particles he called atoms. More than 2,000 years later, science showed he was right.

During the Golden Age and later, several important philosophers taught in Athens. One was a man called Socrates (SOCK ruh teez). People in the marketplace of Athens could not help but notice this sturdy, round-faced man. He was there at all hours of the day, eagerly discussing wisdom and goodness.

Socrates wanted people to consider the true meaning of qualities such as justice and courage. To do this, he asked

Resource Directory

Teaching Resources

Critical Thinking Activity in the Chapter and Section Resources booklet, p. 115, helps students apply the skill of distinguishing fact from opinion.

A Family of Gods

God or Goddess	Description
Zeus (zoos)	King of the gods and goddesses. Ruler of the sky and storms. Lord of the thunderbolt. Protector of the law.
Hera (HIR uh)	Wife and queen to Zeus. Goddess of marriage and women.
Apollo (uh PAHL oh)	Son of Zeus. Handsome young god of poetry, music, and medicine.
Athena (uh THEE nuh)	Zeus' wise daughter. Goddess of crafts. War goddess who defended her cities, including Athens.
Poseidon (poh SY duhn)	Zeus' brother. Ruler of the sea and cause of earthquakes. Lord of horses.

Chart Study The Greeks considered these five gods to be the most powerful of the Twelve Olympians. **Critical Thinking** Which of these gods were concerned with the way people lived? Which were related to natural events?

▼ This bronze statue of the god Poseidon was made about 460 B.C.

questions that made others think about their beliefs. Sometimes they became angry, because Socrates often showed them that they didn't know what they were talking about. "Know thyself," was his most important lesson.

Socrates' questions frightened many Athenians. This man challenged all the values of Athens. In 399 B.C., Socrates was brought to trial. The authorities accused him of dishonoring the gods and misleading young people. He was condemned to death. Friends visited Socrates in prison and urged him to flee. He replied that escape would be unacceptable behavior. He calmly drank poison and died.

Connect How would you feel toward Socrates if he questioned your values?

Greek Drama

What do today's plays, movies, and television shows have in common with Athens? The answer is surprising. The Athenians were the first people to write dramas. Among the city's greatest achievements were the plays written and produced there in the 400s B.C., during the Golden Age. These plays soon became popular all over the Greek world.

Tragedy Some of the most famous Greek plays were tragedies. A **tragedy** is a serious story that usually ends in disaster for the main character. Often, tragedies told of fictional humans who were destroyed when forced to make impossible choices. A Greek tragedy consisted of

Activity

Critical Thinking

Drawing Conclusions *Suitable as either a whole class or an individual activity.* Discuss with students what they think "knowing yourself" means. Remind them to use what they have just read about Socrates along with their own experiences to draw a conclusion about what "know thyself" means. Have students write an essay in which they tell why knowing yourself is an important goal.

Activity

Cooperative Learning

Presenting Myths Have students work in groups to present a myth about a Greek god or goddess. One group member may appear dressed as a god or goddess and may tell the myth. Remaining group members can act as a Greek chorus, presenting the location and background of the myth and reciting any additional commentary necessary to the story. *English Language Learner, Kinesthetic*

Answers to . . .

CHART STUDY

Zeus, Hera, Apollo, and Athena were concerned with the way people lived. Zeus and Poseidon were related to natural events.

1. (a) a payment made to Athens by its allies (b) able to live forever (c) a person who uses the power of the mind to understand natural events (d) a serious story that usually ends in disaster for the main character

2. (a) an Athenian leader who introduced reforms that strengthened democracy (b) a temple to Athena (c) a great Greek philosopher who wanted people to think about their beliefs

3. Possible response: People built impressive temples to honor their gods and godesses.

4. Natural events could be understood using the power of mind, reason, and careful observation.

5. Answers may vary, but should indicate that Athens, with its government, its art and architecture, and its philosophers, was a model for the Greek city-states that followed.

6. Students' essays should reflect an understanding of how democracy and freedom fostered the individual expression of ideas and encouraged the development of artists, writers, and philosophers.

several scenes that featured the characters of the story. Between the scenes, a chorus chanted or sang poems. In most plays, the author used the chorus to give background information, comment on the events, or praise the gods.

Performances of tragedies were part of contests held during religious festivals. At the main festival at Athens in the spring, three playwrights entered four plays apiece in the contest. The city chose wealthy citizens to pay the bills for these dramatic contests.

Comedy   Comic writers also competed at the dramatic festivals. During the 400s B.C. in Athens, these poets wrote comedies that made fun of well-known citizens and politicians and also made jokes about the customs of the day. Because of the freedom in Athens, people accepted the humor and jokes.

▶ **Theater at Epidaurus** This is the most famous of ancient Greek theaters. The seating area, which held 14,000 people, is built into a hillside. The round space, or orchestra, was where the action took place and the chorus danced and sang. The theater is still used for plays today. It is so well constructed that everyone can easily hear the words of the play.

SECTION 2 REVIEW

1. Define   (a) tribute, (b) immortal, (c) philosopher, (d) tragedy.

2. Identify   (a) Pericles, (b) Parthenon, (c) Socrates.

3. What part did religion play in Athenian achievements during the Golden Age?

4. According to Greek philosophers, how could people understand natural events?

Critical Thinking

5. Drawing Conclusions Why do you think Pericles called Athens "the school of all Greece"?

Activity

6. Writing to Learn   Write a brief essay describing the achievements that Athenians made during the Golden Age.

Teaching Resources

Section Quiz in the Chapter and Section Resources booklet, p. 101, covers the main ideas and key terms in the section. Available in Spanish in the Spanish Chapter and Section Resources booklet, p. 63.

Daily Life of the Ancient Greeks

Lesson Objectives

1. Describe everyday life in ancient Greece.

2. Compare the daily lives of Athenian men, women, and slaves.

BEFORE YOU READ

Reach Into Your Background

Ask yourself the following questions about your daily life at home and at school. How does the climate of your region affect your daily life? Who does the work in your home to keep things running?

Questions to Explore

1. What was life like during the Golden Age of Greece?

2. What was the difference between the daily lives of men, women, and slaves in Athens?

Key Terms

agora

Key Places

Athens

Lesson Plan

1 Engage

Warm-Up Activity

Have students work with a partner to create a Know–Want to Know–Learned chart. In the first column, they will list what they know about everyday life in ancient Greece. In the second, they will write questions that they hope to answer by reading the section. As they read, they will write new information in the Learned column.

Activating Prior Knowledge

Have students read Reach Into Your Background in the Before You Read box. Prompt students' responses by asking them how climate might affect their choice of outdoor sports. Have students list who is responsible for keeping their home running smoothly.

The light from the courtyard was still gray when the young boy awoke. The boy sat up on his hard bed and felt the air on his face. He had to get up for school. The boy swallowed his breakfast, pulled his cloak around him, and left the house. Others inside were just beginning to stir. Soon, the household would be starting the day's weaving and other chores.

On the way to school, the boy met other students. All were carrying wooden tablets covered with wax. They would write their lessons on the tablets. They talked about their lesson, a long passage of history that they had to memorize.

The best part of the day came after school. Then, the boy spent the afternoon at the training ground. All the boys exercised and practiced wrestling and throwing a flat plate called a discus. They might watch older athletes training to compete in the Olympic Games, held in honor of Zeus.

In the Marketplace

On their way to school, the boys passed through the Agora (AG uh ruh) of Athens. The Acropolis was the center of Athens' religious life, and the Agora was the center of its public life. It was not far from the Acropolis, which rose in splendor above it. All Greek

▼ This statue captures a Greek athlete as he throws a discus. This event is still part of the Olympic Games.

Teaching Resources

 Reproducible Lesson Plan in the Chapter and Section Resources booklet, p. 102, provides a summary of the section lesson.

Guided Reading and Review in the Chapter and Section Resources booklet, p. 103, provides a structure for mastering key concepts and reviewing key terms in the section. Available in Spanish in the Spanish Chapter and Section Resources booklet, p. 64.

Media and Technology

Color Transparency 127

2 Explore

Ask students to read the section. Discuss with students some typical activities of people in ancient Greece. Ask students what they learned about why slavery existed in Greece. Talk about why the lives of men and women were different.

3 Teach

Ask students to write a short story about a day in the life of a family in ancient Greece. Students should include characters that are men, women, children, and slaves and should use several settings in their story. Encourage students to use vivid details to make their stories come to life. This activity should take about 25 minutes.

4 Assess

See the answers to the Section Review. You may also use students' stories for assessment.

Acceptable stories include male and female characters and slaves and distinguish between the duties and activities of the different characters.

Commendable stories include male and female characters and slaves and feature several different settings, such as the agora, a private home, or a temple.

Outstanding stories include male and female characters and slaves and feature several different settings. Stories include vivid descriptions and details that reflect the content of the section.

READ ACTIVELY

Visualize Try to visualize people talking and carrying on their business in the Athenian Agora.

cities had **agoras,** or public market and meeting places. Athens' Agora was probably the busiest and most interesting of them all.

In the morning, many Athenian men wandered to the Agora. They liked being outdoors. The mild climate of Athens made it possible to carry on business in the open. In the Agora, the men talked of politics and philosophy. Sometimes they just gossiped.

As they talked, they heard the cries of vendors, or sellers of goods, and the haggling over prices. Some people came eager to find bargains. The streets were lined with shops. Farmers and artisans also sold their

The Agora of Athens Today

For archaeologists, the Agora is a rich source of information about ancient Athens.
1. The temple of Hephaistos, god of metalworking
2. Buildings important to Athenian democracy. They include the Bouleterion, where laws were written, and the round Tholos, the workplace for citizens who ran the government.
3. The Middle Stoa. Stoas were long buildings lined with columned walkways. Behind the columns were shops and offices.

wares from stands set up under shady trees. Just about any food an Athenian would want could be found in the Agora. Everyday goods were also for sale—sheep's wool, pottery, hardware, cloth, and books.

Temples and government buildings lined the Agora. One building was headquarters for Athens' army. Another was a prison. A board displayed public notices such as new laws and upcoming court cases.

Life at Home

The splendor of public buildings in Athens contrasted with the simplicity of people's houses, even in the Golden Age. Throughout Greece, private homes were plain. Made of mud bricks, they consisted of rooms set around an open courtyard hidden from the street. The courtyard was the center of the household. Other rooms might include a kitchen, storerooms, a dining room, and bedrooms. Some homes even had bathrooms. But water had to be carried from a public fountain.

Like homes, Greek food was simple. Breakfast might be just bread. For midday meals, the Athenian might add cheese or olives to the bread. Dinner would be a hot meal that was more filling. It might consist of fish and vegetables followed by cheese, fruit, and even cakes sweetened with honey. Most Athenians ate little meat. Even wealthy families only ate meat during religious festivals.

Slavery in Ancient Greece

It was the job of Greek women to spin thread and weave it into cloth. If these women were wealthy, they owned slaves to help them. Slaves did a great deal of work throughout the city-states of Greece. No one knows for sure, but historians

Greek Vase Painting The Athenians were known for their beautiful pottery. They decorated vases, jars, and cups with black or reddish-tan figures. Many scenes were mythological, but others showed Athenian daily life.

▶ In this school scene, a teacher holds a scroll showing the first words of the *Odyssey*. The boy may be reciting them from memory.

Activity

Cooperative Learning

Planning a Festival
Mention to students that festivals were eagerly awaited by the ancient Greeks and attracted large crowds. Some Greek festivals celebrated the harvest while others honored gods or goddesses. Celebratory activities included grand processions, athletic contests, banquets, poetry readings, and plays. Ask small groups to research ancient Greek festivals. Students may present their findings in a "schedule of events" for a festival. Encourage students to include descriptions or drawings of specific sports, foods, and activities that will be part of the festival. *Visual*

Slavery in Ancient Times
Most slaves in ancient times
were people captured in war,
but others were criminals or
people in debt. The ancient
Egyptians, Sumerians, Babylonians, and Persians all had
slaves. The Aztecs of ancient
Mexico also enslaved prisoners of war; some were sacri-
ficed in religious ceremonies.

Connect If you were a
ruler, how would you
change Greek society so
everyone had equal rights?

estimate that as many as 100,000 slaves may have lived in Athens. That
is almost one third of the population. Today, we consider slavery a
crime. But almost no one questioned it in ancient times, even in democratic Athens.

Many free people became enslaved when they were captured by
armies during war or by pirates while traveling on ships. Some slaves
were the children of slaves. A large number in Greece were foreigners,
because some Greeks were uncomfortable owning other Greeks.
Enslaved people did many kinds of work. Some provided labor on farms.
Others dug silver and other metals in the mines. Still others assisted
artisans by making pottery, constructing buildings, or forging weapons
and armor. Most Greek households could not run without slaves. They
cooked and served food, tended children, and wove cloth.

It is hard to make general statements about how enslaved people
were treated. Household slaves may have had the easiest life. Often they

▶ This carved grave marker,
or stele, shows Hegeso, an
Athenian woman, choosing a
jewel from a box held by an
enslaved girl.

were treated like members of the family. The slaves who worked in the mines suffered the most. The work was not only physically tiring, but also extremely dangerous. Slaves in the mines did not live long.

Women in Athens

If you had walked through the Agora, you might have been surprised to see that most of the people there were men. If you had asked where the women were, an Athenian man might have replied, "At home."

Home was where most Athenian women spent their days. They had almost none of the freedom their husbands, sons, and fathers took for granted. They could not take any part in politics. Nor could they vote. They could not own property. About the only official activity allowed them was to be priestesses in religious groups.

Running the home and family was the job of women. In some wealthy families, men and women had completely separate quarters. Women organized the spinning and weaving, looked after supplies of food and wine, and cared for young children. They also kept track of the family finances. If a family was wealthy enough to have slaves, they were the woman's responsibility as well. She directed them, trained them, and cared for them when they were sick.

Women throughout Greece did important work. No Greek man would have denied it. Yet women were expected to be almost invisible. As Pericles said: "The greatest glory will belong to the woman who is least talked about by men, whether they praise her or find fault with her."

▼ Making clothing for the family was the job of the Greek wife and her enslaved servants. The women wove woolen cloth on large standing looms like the one pictured on this vase from the 500s B.C.

SECTION 3 REVIEW

1. **Define** agora.

2. **Identify** Athens.

3. What place was the center of activity for men during the Golden Age?

4. How did the lives of men, women, and slaves in Athens differ?

Critical Thinking

5. **Identify Central Issues** What do you think was the most important aspect of life in Athens? Why?

Activity

6. **Writing to Learn** Write a journal entry about your day at school that covers the same events as those discussed in this section. Discuss who wakes you up, what you eat for breakfast, and what you do after school. How does your day compare with that of the Greek boy you read about at the beginning of this section?

Resource Directory

Teaching Resources

📁 **Section Quiz** in the Chapter and Section Resources booklet, p. 104, covers the main ideas and key terms in the section. Available in Spanish in the Spanish Chapter and Section Resources booklet, p. 65.

Section 3 Review

1. public market or meeting place where government buildings were located

2. city-state whose government was a democracy

3. the agora; men met at the agora to do business, to buy and sell goods, and to discuss politics and philosophy

4. Answers may vary. Answers should show an awareness that only men had the rights of citizens, such as voting and holding office. Men also owned property and were given an education. These things were denied to women. Women were expected to stay at home and run the household. Slaves did a great deal of the work in the Greek city-states. They worked for artisans, farmers, and in the mines.

5. Answers may vary. Some students may cite the separate lives and roles of men, women, and slaves.

6. Answers may vary. Students will likely point out that they do not have to get up as early and that they use different methods to learn their lessons. Like the Greek boy, some students may practice sports after school.

❶ Compare and contrast life in Athens and Sparta.

❷ Explain the significance of the Greek victory over the Persians.

❸ Summarize the reasons for the conflict between Athens and Sparta and for Athens's defeat.

Lesson Plan

1 Engage

Warm-Up Activity

Ask a volunteer to read aloud the story in the opening three paragraphs of the section. Begin a discussion about what the story indicates about the lives and values of the Spartans. Work with students to generate a list of words that describe traits valued by the Spartans. Have students discuss how those traits compare with what they know about the Athenians. Ask students to make some predictions about the likelihood of the peoples of Sparta and Athens getting along with each other.

Activating Prior Knowledge

Explain to students that *values* are a person's beliefs or principles. Tell students that they might think of their values as their personal set of rules to live by. Then have students read Reach Into Your Background in the Before You Read box.

SECTION 4
Athens and Sparta
TWO CITIES IN CONFLICT

BEFORE YOU READ

Reach Into Your Background

All people are different. Because of their backgrounds, people place different values on different things. How are some of your values different from those of some of your friends?

Questions to Explore

1. How did Athens differ from Sparta?

2. What was the result of the war between Athens and Sparta?

Key Terms
plague
blockade

Key Places
Sparta
Persia
Marathon

▶ This mysterious bronze warrior from Sparta is wrapped in a cloak and wears a helmet that hides his face.

The boy stood still and straight beside his companions as their trainer approached. "You," the trainer barked. "Are you sick? Don't think you'll get out of sword practice—and why are you holding your belly? Hiding something?"

The trainer gave the boy's cloak a sharp tug. It fell to the ground, freeing a fox that streaked off into the underbrush. The boy sank down to the ground, shaking. His cloak was a crimson red. His side was shredded with deep cuts and bites. The boy had stolen the fox and hidden it beneath his cloak.

Later, the boy died from his wounds. The people of his city, Sparta, celebrated his life. He had endured terrible pain without giving any sign of his distress. To the Spartans, this was the sign of true character.

A Spartan Life

This Spartan story of the boy and the fox may be true or not. Yet it tells us much about the people of Sparta, a city-state in southern Greece.

If the life of the citizens of Athens was free and open, the life of the citizens of Sparta was the opposite. Life in Sparta was harsh and even cruel. The Spartans themselves were tough, silent, and grim. Sparta's army easily equaled Athens' in the 400s B.C. However, Sparta never came close to equaling Athens' other achievements.

Resource Directory

Teaching Resources

📁 **Reproducible Lesson Plan** in the Chapter and Section Resources booklet, p. 105, provides a summary of the section lesson.

📁 **Guided Reading and Review** in the Chapter and Section Resources booklet, p. 106, provides a structure for mastering key concepts and reviewing key terms in the section. Available in Spanish in the Spanish Chapter and Section Resources booklet, p. 66.

Program Resources

Outline Maps The Middle East and North Africa: Political, p. 29

Like the warrior on the previous page, Sparta's sheer mountains sometimes wear a cloak of mystery. The city lies in a fertile valley with mountains on three sides. Sparta spent its money and energy on its army instead of fine buildings. Today, few ruins remain to tell us about this important city-state.

A Different Kind of City   In its early days, Sparta seemed to be developing as the other Greek cities were. Then, in the 600s B.C., wars inside and outside the city led to changes in government and the way people lived. The changes turned Sparta into an awesome war machine. The city-state made one basic rule: Always put the city's needs above your own.

Early in its history, the Spartans conquered the land around their city. They turned the conquered people into helots, or slaves. Helots (HEL uts) did all the farm work on the land owned by Spartan citizens. This left the Spartans free to wage war. However, the helots far outnumbered the Spartans. Living in fear of a helot revolt, the Spartans turned their city into an armed camp. They treated the helots very harshly.

Growing Up in Sparta   The life of every Spartan was in the hands of the government from the first moment of life. Only the healthiest children were raised. This was because the Spartans wanted only the healthiest males as its soldiers. Training began early. At seven, a Spartan boy left his mother to live in barracks with other boys. His training continued for the next 13 years.

By the age of 12, a boy had spent long hours practicing with swords and spears. He had only one cloak and a thin mat to sleep on. He could hardly live on the food he was given, so he was urged to steal. This was to help him learn how to live off the land during a war. However, if the boy was caught, he was severely punished. After all, if a soldier was caught stealing, he would probably be killed. Boys were expected to bear pain, hardship, and punishment in silence.

Media and Technology

Planet Earth CD-ROM includes World Wonders, Cultural: Acropolis which enhances students' understanding of ancient Greece.

Color Transparency 70

2 Explore

Have students read the section. Then direct students' attention to the time line and discuss the main events shown. Ask: *Why was the Greek victory against the Persians important? Why did Sparta go to war against Athens? Could Athens have prevented its own destruction?*

Background

Daily Life

Spartan Personalities
Young children of Sparta were often cared for by helot nurses who were instructed not to hold or comfort the children when they were upset. Not surprisingly, many Spartan children grew up to be grim, stern, and silent. One story tells of an Athenian ambassador who delivered this message to the Spartan government: "If we come to your city, we will destroy it." The Spartans replied with one word: "If."

3 Teach

Instruct students to compare and contrast Athens and Sparta in an essay of at least two paragraphs. Have them tell which city they think was a greater civilization and why. This activity should take about 15 minutes.

4 Assess

See the answers to the Section Review. You may also use students' completed essays for assessment.

Acceptable essays point out the differences in government, education, and philosophy.

Commendable essays elaborate on the differences in government, education, and philosophy and support opinions with facts.

Outstanding essays elaborate on the differences between Athens and Sparta and are well written, well organized, and contain original ideas.

Activity

Journal Writing

Students in Sparta If students are keeping an Explorer's Journal, you may wish to do this writing activity as part of that journal. Ask students to imagine that they are visiting Sparta. Have them write a journal entry about their impressions of the education and training of Spartans who are their age.

Working Together In one of the wars against the Persians, some 6,000 Greeks had to defend a mountain pass leading into southern Greece. They faced almost 200,000 Persians. Most of the Greeks retreated, but 300 Spartan soldiers stood their ground. All died in the battle. They didn't hold back the Persians. But they earned undying praise for their brave sacrifice.

Like their brothers, girls also trained and competed in wrestling and spear throwing. No one expected the girls to become soldiers. But Spartans did believe that girls who grew up strong and healthy would have strong, healthy children. Spartan women had a somewhat better life than women in other Greek city-states. They were allowed to own land and even take some part in business.

Spartan life lacked the beauty and pleasures found in Athens and some other Greek cities. But Spartan warriors were known for their skill and bravery. The Spartan fighting force played a key role in the Greek wars against the Persians, a people who lived across the Aegean Sea, east of Greece.

The Persians Invade

Much of the history of the Greeks tells of wars they fought among themselves. But near the beginning of the 400s B.C., a new threat loomed. This was the growing might of Persia. By 520 B.C., the Persians had already gained control of the Greek colonies on the west coast of Asia Minor.

In the fall of 490 B.C., a huge force of thousands of Persians landed in Greece itself. They gathered at Marathon, about 25 miles (40 km) north of Athens. The Athenians hastily put together a small army. The Persians outnumbered them by at least two to one. For several days the armies stared tensely at each other across the plain of Marathon.

Then, without warning the Athenians rushed the Persians, who were overwhelmed by the furious attack. By the time the battle was over, the Athenians had killed 6,400 Persians and lost only 192 soldiers themselves. In a few hours, this tiny state had defeated the giant that had come to destroy it.

◀ A Persian duels with a Greek warrior (left) on this vase from the 500s B.C. To the left is the hand of another Persian raising a bow.

Classical Greece, 500 B.C. to 400 B.C.

490 B.C.–
479 B.C.
Persian War

479 B.C.–431 B.C.
Greece's "Golden Age"

431 B.C.–404 B.C.
Peloponnesian Wars

| 500 B.C. | 480 B.C. | 460 B.C. | 440 B.C. | 420 B.C. | 400 B.C. |

479 B.C.
Greeks drive
Persians from
Greece.

460 B.C.
Pericles becomes
leader of democratic
group in Athens.

432 B.C.
Parthenon is
finished.

429 B.C.
Pericles dies of
the plague.

404 B.C.
Athens
surrenders
to Sparta.

480 B.C.
Persians burn
the Acropolis
in Athens.

▲ The time line shows important events in the 400s B.C., the high point in ancient Greece's history.

Greece and the Persian Empire

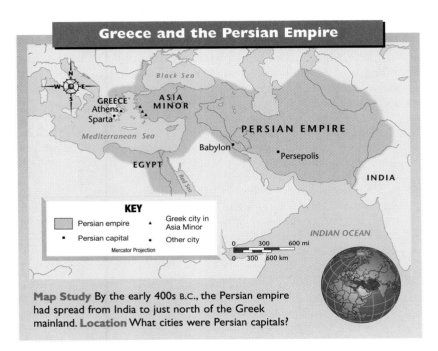

KEY

▢ Persian empire	▲	Greek city in Asia Minor
▪ Persian capital	●	Other city

0   300   600 mi

0   300   600 km

Mercator Projection

Map Study By the early 400s B.C., the Persian empire had spread from India to just north of the Greek mainland. **Location** What cities were Persian capitals?

ACROSS TIME

A Run from Marathon
After Marathon, the Athenians sent their fastest runner to tell the people of Athens of the victory. His chest heaving, the runner covered the distance to the city and shouted to the people "Rejoice! We have won." Then he dropped dead. This valiant run is still honored today every time anyone runs the 26.2 miles of a marathon race.

After Persia: Athenian Empire

After several more battles, the Persians were finally defeated. The influence of Athens spread over much of eastern Greece. Athens joined itself with other city-states and supported democratic groups within them. In time, these cities became more like subjects than allies.

Background

Links Across Place

Marathon Races In today's marathons, runners cover 26.2 miles (42.2 km). Originally, however, the marathon was 25 miles, the distance from Marathon to Athens. In 1908, when the Olympics were held in London, King Edward VII wanted to watch the start of the race from his home at Windsor Castle. The marathon was changed to the distance from the castle to the royal box at the Olympic stadium in London— 26.2 miles—and has remained that distance ever since.

Background

Daily Life

Spartan Music Before Spartans turned their attention completely to war, they were believed to have invented music. Music of harps and pipes was played at feasts and festivals. The Spartans even trained for battle to the sound of pipes. It has been said that the Spartans destroyed Athens's walls to the music of flutes.

Answers to . . .

MAP STUDY

Both Babylon and Persepolis were Persian capitals. Accept either answer.

◄ The Athenians put great faith in their fleet of warships. These ships played a huge role in defeating Persia.

Connect If you lived in another city-state, how would you feel about the power of Athens? Why?

Sparta and Athens at War Athens may have been a democracy at home. But it began to act unfairly toward the other city-states. At first the allies had paid tribute to Athens for protection in case the Persians caused more trouble. But later Athens used this money for the Parthenon and other projects. In response, the people of these city-states began to fear and resent Athens' power. They looked to Sparta, which had not joined the alliance, to protect them. In 431 B.C., Athens and Sparta went to war. The conflict lasted for 27 years. It is called the Peloponnesian War, because Sparta was located in the Peloponnesus, or southern part of Greece.

The Fall of Athens Early in the war, Athens was struck by a **plague,** or widespread disease. By the time the plague ended five years later, about one third of Athens's people had died from it. Among the dead was Pericles.

Athens never recovered from its losses during the plague. In 405 B.C., the Spartans staged a **blockade,** in which they surrounded and closed the harbor where Athens received food shipments. Starving and beaten, the Athenians surrendered in 404 B.C. The victorious Spartans knocked down Athens' walls. Athens never again dominated the Greek world.

SECTION 4 REVIEW

1. Define (a) plague, (b) blockade.

2. Identify (a) Sparta, (b) Persia, (c) Marathon.

3. How was the life of citizens of Athens more free and open than the life of citizens of Sparta?

4. What events led to the war between Athens and Sparta?

Critical Thinking

5. Recognizing Cause and Effect How did the attitude of the people of Athens lead to their own downfall?

Activity

6. Writing to Learn Pretend you are the trainer in the story that begins this section. Write a report explaining the event to other Spartan officers. Be sure to write the story from the Spartan point of view.

The Spread of Greek Culture

Reach Into Your Background

Who are your heroes? Are there people living today or in the past whom you admire? Why are they your heroes?

What can you do to become more like them?

Questions to Explore

1. What role did the conquests of Alexander the Great play in spreading Greek culture?

2. What advances in science did the Greeks make after Alexander's death?

Key Terms

barbarian
assassinate
Hellenistic

Key People and Places

King Philip
Alexander the Great
Euclid
Archimedes
Macedonia
Alexandria

King Philip of Macedonia (mas uh DOH nee uh) had not wasted the money he spent on Greek tutors for his son. Young Alexander was a fine student— and an eager one. The boy wanted to learn as much as he could, especially about the ideas and deeds of the Greeks.

The kingdom of Macedonia lay just north of Greece. Alexander thought of himself as Greek and spoke the Greek language. But people who lived to the south in such cities as Athens and Sparta did not really accept the Macedonians as Greeks. They thought the Macedonians were **barbarians,** or wild, uncivilized people.

Alexander's tutor was the Greek philosopher Aristotle (AIR uh staht ul). Aristotle taught the boy Greek literature, philosophy, and science. Aristotle also passed on his strong feelings that the Greeks were far better than other people and, therefore, deserved to rule.

Alexander loved his tutor, but his role model was Achilles, the warrior hero of the *Iliad.* One day, Alexander vowed, he would visit the site of Troy and lay a wreath on the tomb of his hero.

◀▼ This carving of King Philip of Macedonia (left), illustrates his strength and energy. The silver coin (below) is stamped with a portrait of his son, Alexander.

Recognizing Bias

You may **introduce** the skill by explaining to students that *bias* is judgement based on personal feelings and opinions rather than on facts. Tell students that it is important to recognize bias, or prejudice, in what they read and hear. Point out that a common form of bias is name-calling. As an example, use the Greeks' calling the Macedonians "barbarians." Have students **practice** and **apply** the skill by making a list of the words or phrases that come to mind when they hear the term *barbarian.* Ask which terms they think imply bias and which, if any, are fair terms to apply to the people of Macedonia. Discuss why the Greeks wanted to belittle the Macedonians.

Lesson Objectives

❶ Summarize the achievements of Alexander the Great.

❷ Explain how Alexander's conquests spread Greek culture.

❸ Describe Hellenistic achievements in architecture, mathematics, and science.

Lesson Plan

1 Engage

Warm-Up Activity

Invite students to work with a partner to list American products that people all over the world (especially young people) like and buy. Share lists as a class. Lists will probably include American pop and rock music, soft drinks, blue jeans, movies, and TV programs. Remind students that throughout history, some cultures have been more influential than others.

Activating Prior Knowledge

Have students read Reach Into Your Background in the Before You Read box. Ask students what qualities they would expect someone called Alexander the Great to have had. Point out that *great* can mean "large," "wonderful," "important," "famous," or "grand." Ask each student to think of an appropriate title for one of his or her heroes. Ask volunteers to share their titles.

2 Explore

Have students read the section. Ask them what King Philip, Alexander's father, achieved. What were Alexander's conquests? In what way was Alexander responsible for the spread of Greek culture? Discuss what is meant by Hellenistic culture, and ask students to describe some Hellenistic achievements.

3 Teach

Direct students to create a biographical encyclopedia entry for Alexander the Great. They should include a history of his life and at least three important achievements of Hellenistic culture related to Alexander's conquests. Encourage students to explain the significance of the events they write about. This activity should take about 25 minutes.

Answers to ...

MAP STUDY

about 1,400 miles (2,240 km)

176   CHAPTER 6

Alexander Builds an Empire

Before King Philip seized power in 359 B.C., Macedonia was poor and divided. Philip united Macedonia and built an army even stronger than Sparta's. With such an army and with his talent for waging war, Philip captured one Greek city-state after another. By 338 B.C., Philip controlled all of Greece. No one had ever done this.

Alexander Comes to the Throne   Philip then planned to attack Persia. But in 336 B.C., before he could carry out his plan, he was **assassinated,** or murdered, by a rival. At just 20 years old, Alexander became king. This was his chance to be as great as his hero Achilles.

Alexander the Great   One of Alexander's first actions was to invade the Persian Empire. Within 11 years, he had conquered Persia, Egypt, and lands extending beyond the Indus River in the east. He earned the right to be called "Alexander the Great."

Alexander's energy and military genius helped him succeed. He drove himself and his army hard, advancing across vast lands at lightning speed. His soldiers grumbled, but they obeyed him. Wherever

READ ACTIVELY

Ask Questions Think of some things you would like to know about Alexander the Great and his deeds.

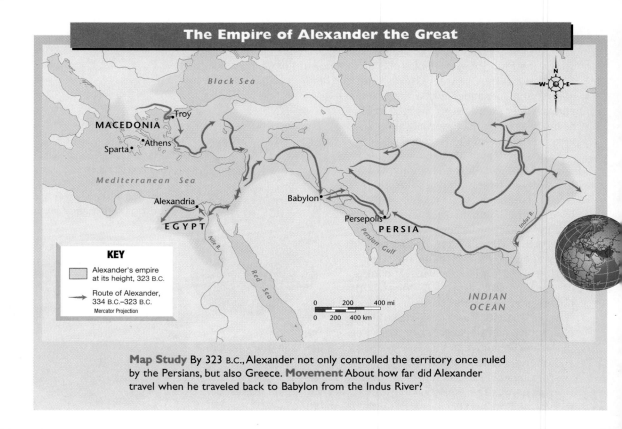

The Empire of Alexander the Great

KEY

Alexander's empire at its height, 323 B.C.

→ Route of Alexander, 334 B.C.–323 B.C.
Mercator Projection

0   200   400 mi

0   200   400 km

Map Study By 323 B.C., Alexander not only controlled the territory once ruled by the Persians, but also Greece. **Movement** About how far did Alexander travel when he traveled back to Babylon from the Indus River?

Resource Directory

Teaching Resources

📁 **Reproducible Lesson Plan** in the Chapter and Section Resources booklet, p. 108, provides a summary of the section lesson.

📁 **Guided Reading and Review** in the Chapter and Section Resources booklet, p. 109, provides a structure for mastering key concepts and reviewing key terms in the section. Available in Spanish in the Spanish Chapter and Section Resources booklet, p. 68.

Program Resources

Outline Maps The Middle East and North Africa: Physical, p. 29

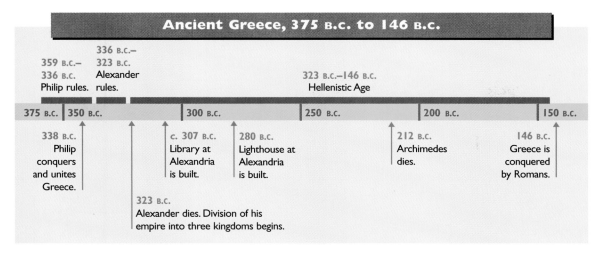

Ancient Greece, 375 B.C. to 146 B.C.

359 B.C.–336 B.C.
Philip rules.

336 B.C.–323 B.C.
Alexander rules.

323 B.C.–146 B.C.
Hellenistic Age

| 375 B.C. | 350 B.C. | | 300 B.C. | | 250 B.C. | 200 B.C. | | 150 B.C. |

338 B.C.
Philip conquers and unites Greece.

c. 307 B.C.
Library at Alexandria is built.

280 B.C.
Lighthouse at Alexandria is built.

212 B.C.
Archimedes dies.

146 B.C.
Greece is conquered by Romans.

323 B.C.
Alexander dies. Division of his empire into three kingdoms begins.

▲ The Hellenistic Age began with the death of Alexander. How long did it last?

Alexander went, he established cities. Many of them he named after himself. Even today, there are numerous cities named Alexandria or Alexandropolis throughout western Asia. Alexander never stayed very long in his cities. He quickly pushed on. He never lost a battle.

At last, not far beyond the Indus River, his weary troops refused to go another step east. Alexander was angry, but he turned back. Alexander got as far as Babylon, where he came down with a fever. In 323 B.C., only 13 years after he came to the throne, Alexander died. Like the legendary warrior Achilles, he had died young. But he had gone far beyond the deeds of his hero. He had conquered practically all of the known world.

Greek Culture Spreads

Alexander's death spelled death for his empire. Within 50 years, the empire had broken into three main kingdoms. Each one was ruled by a family descended from one of his commanders. Although the empire broke apart, Greek culture remained alive and well in these new kingdoms.

The Hellenistic Kingdoms When Alexander took control of lands, he tried not to destroy the cultures of the defeated people. Instead, he hoped that in his new cities the local cultures would mix with Greek culture. Unfortunately, this did not happen in the three **Hellenistic** kingdoms, as they came to be called. Hellenistic comes from the word Hellas—the name Greeks gave their land.

The cities of the Hellenistic world were modeled after Greek cities. Greek kings ruled, and Greeks held the most important jobs. There were Greek temples and agoras. Citizens gathered at large theaters for performances of old Greek tragedies. The Greek language was spoken in the cities, though people in the countryside spoke local languages.

Media and Technology

  Color Transparency 70

Language Arts Tell students that many English words have Greek origins. Provide students with copies of the following examples of Greek roots and their meanings:

mono-	one or single
photo-	light
micro-	small
phono-	sounding
tele-	far off
astro-	star
-graph or -graphy	writing
-gram	writing or record
-scope	for viewing or observing
-meter or -metry	measure
-nomy	knowledge
-logy	the science or theory of something

Show students how familiar words such as *microscope* are formed from Greek roots. Challenge students to use the list to form other familiar words. Students may also propose unfamiliar words and their probable definitions. Have students consult a dictionary to verify unfamiliar words and check definitions. *English Language Learner*

Hellenism in Egypt The greatest of all Hellenistic cities was Alexandria in Egypt. Alexander had founded this city in 332 B.C. at the edge of the Nile delta. Alexandria became the capital of Egypt. Over the years, it grew famous as a center for business and trade. Its double harbor was dominated by a huge lighthouse that rose about 400 feet (122 m) in the air. The tower was topped by a flame that guided ships safely into port.

The important Hellenistic cities were centers of learning. But Alexandria was greater than any of the rest. It boasted the largest library in the world, with half a million book rolls. Alexandria was the learning capital of the Greek world. Scholars and writers from all over came to use the huge library.

Mathematics and science also flourished at Alexandria. Around 300 B.C., a mathematician named Euclid (YOO klid) developed the branch of mathematics called geometry. He started with accepted mathematical laws. Then, he wrote carefully thought out, step-by-step proofs of mathematical principles. The proofs helped explain the qualities of such figures as squares, cubes, angles, triangles, and cones. Mathematicians today still use Euclid's system.

READ ACTIVELY

Visualize Try to visualize the huge, scroll-filled library at Alexandria.

▶ The great lighthouse at Alexandria, called the Pharos, was considered one of the Seven Wonders of the World.

Teaching Resources

📁 **Section Quiz** in the Chapter and Section Resources booklet, p. 110, covers the main ideas and key terms in the section. Available in Spanish in the Spanish Chapter and Section Resources booklet, p. 69.

📁 **Vocabulary** in the Chapter and Section Resources booklet, p. 112, provides a review of key terms in the chapter. Available in Spanish in the Spanish Chapter and Section Resources booklet, p. 71.

📁 **Reteaching** in the Chapter and Section Resources booklet, p. 113, provides a structure for students who may need additional help in mastering chapter content.

📁 **Enrichment** in the Chapter and Section Resources booklet, p. 114, extends chapter content and enriches students' understanding.

📁 **Spanish Glossary** in the Spanish Chapter and Section Resources, pp. 85–89, provides key terms translated from English to Spanish as well as definitions in Spanish.

Levers and Pulleys

Ancient people had used levers and pulleys for centuries. A Greek scientist named Archimedes discovered new ways to use them. He invented the compound pulley, a combination of the fixed pulley and the moveable pulley shown here.

Pulleys

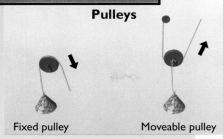

Fixed pulley · Moveable pulley

Lever

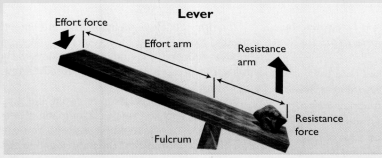

Effort force
Effort arm
Resistance arm
Resistance force
Fulcrum

Have you ever heard that people of Christopher Columbus' time believed the Earth was flat? This is not accurate. In Hellenistic times, many scientists knew the Earth was round. A scientist named Eratosthenes (ehr uh TAHS thuh neez) even calculated the distance around the Earth. His answer, 24,662 miles (39,679 km), was very close.

Probably the greatest scientist of the times was Archimedes (ar kuh MEE deez). Archimedes discovered that people can use pulleys and levers to lift very heavy objects. One story says that he hoisted up a loaded ship with these devices. Once he boasted: "Give me a lever long enough and a place to stand on, and I will move the Earth."

LINKS TO SCIENCE

The Earth and the Sun
One scientist of the 200s B.C. rejected the idea that the Earth was the center of the universe. Aristarchus of Samos believed that the sun is at the center and that the Earth revolves around it. His idea did not catch on. Astronomers continued to believe in an Earth-centered universe until the A.D. 1500s.

SECTION 5 REVIEW

1. **Define** (a) barbarian, (b) assassinate, (c) Hellenistic.
2. **Identify** (a) King Philip, (b) Alexander the Great, (c) Euclid, (d) Archimedes, (e) Macedonia, (f) Alexandria.
3. What features of Greek culture could be seen in the Hellenistic kingdoms?
4. Describe the contributions of Euclid, Eratosthenes, and Archimedes.

Critical Thinking
5. **Identifying Central Issues** Why do you think Alexander the Great named so many cities after himself?

Activity
6. **Writing to Learn** Think of someone you consider a hero or a role model. Write a description of that person. Is he or she more like King Philip and Alexander or like Aristotle and Archimedes? Explain your answer.

📁 **Chapter Summary** in the Chapter and Section Resources booklet, p. 111, provides a summary of chapter content. Available in Spanish in the Spanish Chapter and Section Resources booklet, p. 70.

📁 **Cooperative Learning Activity** in the Activities and Projects booklet, pp. 40–43, provides two student handouts, one page of teacher's directions, and a scoring rubric for a cooperative learning activity on writing a radio play of a Greek myth or story.

Media and Technology

🎧 **Guided Reading Audiotapes** (English and Spanish)

Drawing Conclusions

The teacher looked right at Lisa when she asked, "How did the people of Athens feel about drama?"

Lisa swallowed hard. She had read the assignment, but there wasn't anything in the book about how Athenians felt about drama. She did remember a few facts, though. "They had a lot of theaters and put on a lot of plays. Sometimes they had contests to see who could write the best plays." Lisa hoped her answer was good enough.

"And so from all of that, can you tell how they felt about drama?" her teacher asked.

Lisa took a shot. "Well, I guess if they had so much of it they must have liked it ."

"Right! Good!"

Lisa breathed a sigh of relief. Of course the Athenians felt drama was important. And Lisa felt good about herself, having answered a tough question—about something that wasn't even in the book.

Get Ready

Lisa could answer the question because she drew a conclusion from what she read. Drawing conclusions means learning something more from what you read than just what is written. Drawing conclusions is a skill that will help you get the most from your schoolwork or any reading you do.

You draw conclusions by making intelligent, educated guesses. You base your conclusion on clues, or evidence, you find in what you read. By adding these clues to what you already know, you draw a conclusion.

You draw conclusions in everyday life, too. For example, suppose you see a long line of people waiting to buy tickets to a concert. You can draw the conclusion that the singer giving the concert is very popular, even if you do not know anything else about that performer.

Try It Out

Practice drawing a conclusion from this sentence.

All Spartan men served in the army.

You can draw the conclusion that the military was a central part of Spartan society. Notice that this conclusion is directly related to what you read, even though it is not stated in the sentence. The conclusion goes beyond what is written. You use what you already know to add to what you read. You already know that if half the population of a society does something, it must be an important part of that society.

Clues from what you read + **What you already know** = **Conclusions about what you read**

Resource Directory

Teaching Resources

📁 **Drawing Conclusions** in the Social Studies and Geography Skills booklet, p. 52, provides additional skill practice.

Apply the Skill

Read again the part of Section 1 in this chapter that tells about the Trojan War. Draw some conclusions.

1 **Look for clues.** The first sentence of the part about the war says, "The story of the Trojan War has everything a story should have—great battles, plots and schemes, loyalty and betrayal."

2 **Think about what you already know.** Think about stories you like to read or watch in the movies or on television.

3 **Draw a conclusion based on what you read and what you already know.** Why has the history of the Trojan War been so interesting to so many people through the years?

Explain how the conclusion you drew was based on clues in what you read plus what you already know. What other conclusions can you draw about the Trojan War?

The clue in this sentence tells me that the story of the Trojan War is about great battles.

I already know that I like stories about great battles.

What's my conclusion?

The Trojan War

3 Teach

Have students **practice** the skill on the Try It Out sentence. Explain that it is important to carefully search one's personal knowledge for information that is relevant. You might model removing the specific context (Spartan) from the sentence. The resulting sentence—*All men served in the army*—is easier to check against students' own experiences.

For additional reinforcement, have students complete diagrams about a possible event such as an upcoming test or project, noting clues and a conclusion.

4 Assess

Encourage students to **apply** their skill by completing the final part of the activity. To **assess**, invite students to list text clues and personal knowledge/experience in a two-column table and to use the table to draw conclusions. Evaluate their tables along with the conclusions they suggest.

Answers to . . .

APPLY THE SKILL

1. Students might conclude that the story will be exciting and action-packed.
2. Students might think about action films or films about famous battles.
3. Students might answer that the idea of the Trojan Horse is so unlike any other battle tactic ever used that it has remained vivid throughout history.

Chapter 6 Review

Reviewing Main Ideas

1. Greece was bordered by the Mediterranean and Aegean seas, and fishing and trading with other areas naturally developed. In addition, Greece is a mountainous country, and communities developed in isolation from each other.

2. Aristocracy was rule by powerful families. Tyranny was rule by a tyrant supported by middle-class merchants and artisans. Democracy was rule by citizens.

3. Student answers may include the ideas that gods and goddesses caused all natural events and ruled the lives of humans.

4. Answers may vary, but should include the ideas that Greek art showed humans in ideal or perfect form, that Greek philosophy was based on an examination of how human beings should live, and that Greek democracy expressed faith in the intelligence of people.

5. Students may say that life was very different for men, women, and slaves. Only free men could participate in government and business and move about the city freely.

6. Women spent a lot of time in the home, where they trained and supervised slaves. Slaves might work for farmers, in households, or in mines.

7. Spartan life was centered around military training. The government kept its residents busy training for and waging war, so there was little time or support for developing the arts or sciences.

8. Athens surrendered to Sparta and no longer dominated the Greek world.

9. Greek culture was spread by Alexander the Great as he made conquests in Persia, Egypt, and Southwest Asia.

10. Students answers should include the discovery that the Earth was round, the computation of the distance around the Earth, and the invention of the pulley and the lever.

Reviewing Key Terms

Sentences will vary, but should show correct meaning through context.

Reviewing Main Ideas

1. What role did the sea and mountains play in the development of ancient Greece?
2. Explain the difference between aristocracy, tyranny, and democracy in ancient Greece.
3. List two ideas that governed Greek religions.
4. From what you have read about Greek art, history, religion, and philosophy, how would you describe the Greek attitude towards the achievements of human beings?
5. What was everyday life like in the Golden Age of Athens?
6. Describe the roles of women and slaves in Athenian life.
7. How did life in Sparta keep this city-state from achieving the kinds of things Athens achieved?
8. Describe the relationship of Athens to Sparta after their long war.
9. How did Greek culture spread from Greece to parts of Europe, Africa, and Southwest Asia?
10. Describe some advances made in science during the Hellenistic period.

Reviewing Key Terms

Use each key term below in a sentence that shows the meaning of the term.

1. peninsula
2. epic
3. acropolis
4. city-state
5. aristocrat
6. tyrant
7. democracy
8. tribute
9. immortal
10. philosopher
11. tragedy
12. agora
13. plague
14. blockade
15. barbarian
16. assassinate
17. Hellenistic

Critical Thinking

1. **Identifying Central Issues** What did the Greek city-states have in common? What kept them separate?
2. **Making Comparisons** Compare the way most ancient Greeks would have explained their world to the way the philosophers did.
3. **Cause and Effect** Athenians were proud of their culture and their city. How do you think that view was influenced by Athens' defeat by the Spartans?

Graphic Organizer

Copy the chart onto a separate sheet of paper. Then fill in the boxes to complete the chart.

Important Wars and Their Results	
Important People and What They Did	
Governments	
Culture/Literature/ Art/Science	

Graphic Organizer

Important Wars and Their Results	• Trojan War: Greeks defeated Troy. • Battle of Marathon: Greeks defeated the Persians and ended their rule. • Peloponnesian War: Sparta defeated the Athenians and Athens never again dominated the Greek world.
Important People and What They Did	• Solon: reformed economy and government of Athens • Pericles: introduced reforms that strengthened democracy • Alexander the Great: conquered Persia, Egypt, and parts of Western Asia; helped spread Greek culture to these lands; established library in Alexandria
Governments	• aristocracy, tyranny, and then democracy
Culture/Literature/ Art/Science	• Culture: Socrates challenged the values of Athenians. Greek drama flourished. • Literature: Homer wrote the *Iliad* and the *Odyssey*. • Art: Lifelike sculpture was perfected. • Science: Archimedes developed the pulley and the lever. Euclid invented geometry.

Map Activity

The Greek World
For each place listed below, write the letter from the map that shows its location.

1. Athens
2. Sparta
3. Macedonia
4. Marathon
5. Troy

Place Location

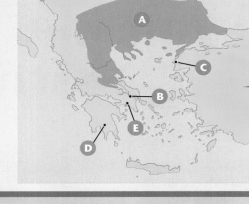

Writing Activity

Writing a Dialogue
Imagine that the Athenian boy from Section 3 met the Spartan boy from Section 4. The time is the Golden Age of Athens. Write a dialogue, or conversation, between them. Have each young man tell the other about how he was raised and educated. Have each defend the way of life and form of government in his own city.

Internet Activity

Use a search engine to find **The Ancient Greece Home Page.** Click on GreekQuest 1996. Read about Athens and Sparta. Then scroll down to Gender Issues and explore the links. Write a report or give a presentation describing what life was like for women in ancient Greece.

Skills Review

Turn to the Skills Activity.
Think again about the steps for drawing conclusions. Why is it important to consider what you already know as you are reading?

How Am I Doing?

Answer these questions to help you check your progress.

1. Do I understand how the geographical features of Greece affected life there in ancient times?
2. Can I describe ancient Greek religion, types of government, and cultural achievements?
3. Can I identify some events that shaped the history of the ancient Greek world?
4. What information from this chapter could I use in my book project?

Internet Activity

If students are having difficulty finding this site, you may wish to have them use the following URL, which was accurate at the time this textbook was published:
http://www.unl.edu/tcweb/ altc/staffpages/Greece.html

You might also guide students to a search engine. Four of the most useful are Infoseek, AltaVista, Lycos, and Yahoo. For additional suggestions on using the Internet, refer to the Prentice Hall Social Studies' Educator's Handbook "Using the Internet," in the *Prentice Hall World Explorer Program Resources*.

For additional links to world history and culture topics, visit the Prentice Hall Home Page at:
http://www.phschool.com

How Am I Doing?

Point out to students that this checklist is a quick reminder of what they learned in the chapter. If their answer to any of the questions is *no* or if they are unsure, they may need to review the topic.

Critical Thinking

1. The Greek city-states had a common heritage, language, and religion but had rivalries in trade and different forms of government.

2. Most ancient Greeks would have attributed natural events and occurrences in human lives to the actions of the gods. Philosophers would have attributed natural events to the rules of nature and the occurrences in human lives to the actions of people.

3. Students should point out that the Athenians thought that they were superior to all other peoples. This view changed after Athens' defeat by Sparta.

Map Activity

1. E	3. A	5. C
2. D	4. B	

Writing Activity

Student dialogues should be written from the correct point of view and reflect knowledge of each city-state's government, way of life, and education.

Skills Review

It allows you to connect your own experiences to what you are reading and helps you understand.

Resource Directory

Teaching Resources

Chapter Tests Forms A and B are in the Tests booklet, pp. 32–37.

Program Resources

Writing Process Handbook includes Writing an Introduction, p. 29, to help students with the Writing Activity.

Media and Technology

Computer Test Bank Resource Pro™ CD-ROM

Color Transparencies Color Transparency 174 (Graphic organizer table template)

Prentice Hall Writer's Solution Writing Lab CD-ROM

Lesson Objectives

1. Identify and describe some elements of an ancient Greek festival.

2. Plan and research festival activities.

3. Use interdisciplinary skills to stage an ancient Greek festival.

Lesson Plan

1 Engage

Warm-Up Activity

Invite students to briefly write or tell about a recent visit to a festival, perhaps a neighborhood cultural festival or an agricultural fair. Have volunteers write descriptive words about these festivals on the chalkboard. Organize the words into common positive and negative festival qualities.

Activating Prior Knowledge

Ask students whether they have ever participated in or helped to plan a festival, perhaps entering an animal in competition or cooking for a food fair. Invite volunteers to share lessons from those experiences with the class.

Hold an Ancient Greek Festival

The ancient Greeks held many religious festivals. One festival included an athletic competition known as the Olympics. Contests such as wrestling and footraces were often part of a larger festival that included plays and feasts.

Purpose

To learn more about the culture of ancient Greece, plan a festival to share information about ancient Greek games, food, drama, art, and mathematical and scientific discoveries.

Resource Directory

Teaching Resources

Activity Shop: Interdisciplinary in the Activities and Projects booklet, p. 7, provides a structure that helps students complete the interdisciplinary activity.

Plan a Festival

Read the five festival presentations described here and divide into groups to organize them.

PUT ON A PLAY

Act out an ancient Greek myth such as the story of Perseus and Medusa or Orpheus and the underworld. To tell the story, you might choose a narrator as well as actors. Introduce your performance with background information on each character in the myth.

PRESENT AN ART SHOW

Collect pictures of ancient Greek art. Find out what people or events the pictures represent. If possible, also find out how each kind of art was made. Write a caption for each picture and hang the picture in a "gallery" on your classroom wall.

DISCOVER ANCIENT KNOWLEDGE

Ancient Greeks contributed many ideas to the fields of math and science. Find out what kind of math they helped invent. Also, research one of their scientific ideas. For example, you might find out what the Greek astronomer Ptolemy thought about the universe. Create a poster that shows your findings in a way that people can understand. Add the poster to your classroom's gallery.

PLAN A FEAST

Write a menu for an ancient meal that includes some of the foods the Greeks might have eaten. How were each of the foods on your menu grown or produced in ancient Greece? Who grew the food? Who prepared it?

Links to Other Subjects

Performing a scene from a Greek drama	**Language Arts**
Researching Greek art	**Art**
Explaining contributions from ancient Greek mathematicians or scientists	**Math, Science**

SPEAK ABOUT THE OLYMPICS

Research the Olympic Games in ancient Greece. Here are a few of the questions you should answer: Why were the Olympics held? What games did the spectators see? Could anyone compete in the games? Brainstorm for some other questions to answer. Then give a presentation about what you have learned. You can give your presentation by yourself or with a group.

ANALYSIS AND CONCLUSION

Write a summary describing what you learned from the festival. Be sure to answer the following questions in your summary.

1. What was the most interesting idea or fact you learned from each presentation?

2. Did the festival make you think of any new questions about ancient Greek drama, art, math, science, food, or athletic competitions? Think of at least three questions.

---

2 Explore

As a class, take turns reading parts of the Activity Shop aloud. Then have students contribute to a list of necessary materials. Also ask students to write down at least one reference source they might use to gather information (for instance, books on ancient Greece, art references, sports histories, encyclopedias, or the Internet).

3 Teach

Help students form groups to plan and research the festival activities. Students within each group should identify tasks and decide on assignments for each member. Some members may want to work with a partner on related tasks.

4 Assess

Let groups perform or present their festival activity. Invite other classes to enjoy the festival. You might place a response box at the classroom door for students' comments. Assess students' work on the basis of quality and accuracy of research as well as creativity and clarity of presentation. You may also use students' summaries of what they learned as an assessment.

Lesson Objectives

① Describe the characteristics of an ancient Greek myth.

② Relate the ideas presented in a Greek myth to knowledge of ancient Greek life and culture.

Lesson Plan

1 Engage

Building Vocabulary

Point out that the notes in the margins can help students understand certain words and can give helpful hints as students read. Vocabulary defined in the margins includes *Thrinacia, strait, islet, caulk, strain, surge, rail, lap, purl, spume, hawser, appall, aspect, Scylla,* and *Charybdis.* Read through the definitions with students. Point out that many of the words are vivid—highly descriptive—verbs that help readers picture the action or understand the mood of a story. Have students choose one of these verbs with which to write a descriptive sentence. Ask volunteers to read their sentences aloud.

Activating Prior Knowledge

Have students read Reach Into Your Background in the Before You Read box. Talk about the feeling of being torn between better judgment and pleasure or beauty.

LITERATURE

The Sirens

A GREEK MYTH
FROM *THE ADVENTURES OF ULYSSES*
RETOLD BY BERNARD EVSLIN

Reach Into Your Background

Do television commercials make you want to buy the things they advertise? Have you ever been persuaded to do something because someone made it sound fun or exciting? Sometimes messages like this can make things appear better than they are.

Such messages can lead people in the wrong direction.

The Sirens (SY ruhnz) in this myth are creatures who use their songs to lead sailors to destruction. The hero Ulysses (yoo LIS eez) is warned about the Sirens as he tries to sail to his island home in Greece after the Trojan War. The clever and curious Ulysses had expected an easy journey home. Instead, he was delayed by adventures that tested his mind and spirit.

The tale of Ulysses and the Sirens comes from Homer's *Odyssey.* Ulysses is the name

the Roman people gave to the Greek hero Odysseus. Like Homer himself and other storytellers, Bernard Evslin has retold the ancient story of the Sirens in his own words. The events are the same as those in the *Odyssey.* But the author has added many details to make the story his own.

Questions to Explore

1. What does this story tell you about the technology of the Greeks?

2. What can you learn about the Greek idea of a hero from this story?

In the first light of morning Ulysses awoke and called his crew about him.

"Men," he said. "Listen well, for your lives today hang upon what I am about to tell you. That large island to the west is Thrinacia, where we must make a landfall, for our provisions run low. But to get to the island we must pass through a narrow strait. And at the head of this strait is a rocky islet where dwell two sisters called Sirens, whose voices you must not hear. Now I

shall guard you against their singing, which would lure you to shipwreck, but first you must bind me to the mast. Tie me tightly, as though I were a dangerous captive. And no matter how I struggle, no matter what signals I make to you, *do not release me,* lest I follow their voices to destruction, taking you with me."

Thereupon Ulysses took a large lump of the beeswax that was used by the sail mender to slick his heavy thread and kneaded it

Thrinacia (thrih NAY shee uh) *n.* mythological island that might have been Sicily
strait n. narrow ocean passage between two pieces of land
islet n. small island

Resource Directory

Teaching Resources

📁 **Giving Yourself a Purpose for Reading** in the Social Studies and Geography Skills booklet, p. 69, provides additional skill practice.

Program Resources

Material in the **Primary Sources and Literature Readings** booklet provides additional literature selections on the region under study.

◀ This Siren is part of a scene on a Greek vase made about 470 B.C. She flies over Ulysses' ship while he is tied to the mast.

in his powerful hands until it become soft. Then he went to each man of the crew and plugged his ears with soft wax; he caulked their ears so tightly that they could hear nothing but the thin pulsing of their own blood.

Then he stood himself against the mast, and the men bound him about with rawhide, winding it tightly around his body, lashing him to the thick mast.

They had lowered the sail because ships cannot sail through a narrow strait unless there is a following wind, and now each man of the crew took his place at the great oars. The polished blades whipped the sea into a froth of white water and the ship nosed toward the strait.

Ulysses had left his own ears unplugged because he had to remain in command of the ship and had need of his hearing. Every sound means something

upon the sea. But when they drew near the rocky islet and he heard the first faint strains of the Sirens' singing, then he wished he, too, had stopped his own ears with wax. All his strength suddenly surged toward the sound of those magical voices. The very hair of his head seemed to be tugging at his scalp, trying to fly away. His eyeballs started out of his head.

For in those voices were the sounds that men love:
Happy sounds like birds railing, sleet hailing, milk pailing. . . .
Sad sounds like rain leaking, trees creaking, wind seeking. . . .
Autumn sounds like leaves tapping, fire snapping, river lapping. . . .
Quiet sounds like snow flaking, spider waking, heart breaking. . . .

caulk *v.* to stop up and make tight
strain *n.* tune
surge *v.* to rise or swell suddenly
rail *v.* to scold
lap *v.* to splash in little waves

READ ACTIVELY

Predict How will Ulysses keep his men from hearing the voices of the Sirens?

2 Develop Student Reading

Point out and discuss the Questions to Explore and margin questions. Explain that this myth is a retold story and that it may be presented in a different way from the original. Be sure that students understand, however, that it retains the main characters and message of the original story.

Background

About the Author

Homer Although "The Sirens" is retold here by Bernard Evslin, it was made famous by Homer. Homer was a Greek poet who lived around 700 B.C. Scholars believe he wrote the epic poems the *Odyssey* and the *Iliad* for the educated upper class of ancient Greek society.

About the Selection

"The Sirens," as well as many other tales from Homer's *Odyssey,* can be found in *The Adventures of Ulysses* by Bernard Evslin. The book was published by Scholastic in 1969.

READ ACTIVELY

Predict What do you think Ulysses will do when he hears the Sirens' song?

purl *v.* to make a soft murmuring sound like a flowing stream
spume *n.* foam
hawser (HAW zur) *n.* a large rope

▶ The rocky shore of Sicily where Greek myths said the Sirens lived.

It seemed to him then that the sun was burning him to a cinder as he stood. And the voices of the Sirens purled in a cool crystal pool upon their rock past the blue-hot flatness of the sea and its lacings of white-hot spume. It seemed to him he could actually see their voices deepening into a silvery, cool pool and must plunge into that pool or die a flaming death.

He was filled with such a fury of desire that he swelled his mighty muscles, burst the rawhide bonds like thread, and dashed for the rail.

But he had warned two of his strongest men—Perimedes (pehr ih MEE deez) and Eurylochus (yoo RIHL uh kus)—to guard him close. They seized him before he could plunge into the water. He swept them aside as if they had been children. But they had held him long enough to give the crew time to swarm about him. He was overpowered—crushed by their numbers—and dragged back to the mast. This time he was bound with the mighty hawser that held the anchor.

The men returned to their rowing seats, unable to hear the voices because of the wax corking their ears. The ship swung about and headed for the strait again.

Louder now, and clearer, the tormenting voices came to Ulysses. Again he was aflame with a fury of desire. But try as he might he could not break the thick anchor line. He strained against it until he bled, but the line held.

The men bent to their oars and rowed more swiftly, for they saw the mast bending like a tall tree in a heavy wind, and they

feared that Ulysses, in his fury, might snap it off short and dive, mast and all, into the water to get at the Sirens.

Now they were passing the rock, and Ulysses could see the singers. There were two of them. They sat on a heap of white bones—the bones of shipwrecked sailors—and sang more beautifully than senses could bear. But their appearance did not match their voices, for they were shaped like birds, huge birds, larger than eagles. They had feathers instead of hair, and their hands and feet were claws. But their faces were the faces of young girls.

When Ulysses saw them he was able to forget the sweetness of their voices because their look was so fearsome. He closed his eyes against the terrible sight of these bird-women perched on their heap of bones. But when he

closed his eyes he could not see their ugliness, then their voices maddened him once again, and he felt himself straining against the bloody ropes. He forced himself to open his eyes and look upon the monsters, so that the terror of their bodies would blot the beauty of their voices.

But the men, who could only see, not hear the Sirens, were so appalled by their aspect that they swept their oars faster and faster, and the black ship scuttled past the rock. The Sirens' voices sounded fainter and fainter and finally died away.

When Perimedes and Eurylochus saw their captain's face lose its madness, they unbound him, and he signaled to the men to unstop their ears. For now he heard the whistling gurgle of a whirlpool, and he knew that they were approaching the narrowest part of the strait, and must past between Scylla and Charybdis.

appall *v.* to horrify
aspect *n.* the way something looks
Scylla (SIL uh) *n.* a monster who ate sailors passing through the Straits of Messina between Italy and Sicily
Charybdis (kuh RIB dis) *n.* a monster in the form of a deadly whirlpool near Scylla

READ ACTIVELY

Visualize Try to picture the Sirens on their rocky islet.

EXPLORING YOUR READING

Look Back
1. What does Ulysses fear will happen if he is not tied to the mast and his companions do not have wax in their ears?

Think It Over
2. Do you think Ulysses is a good leader? Why or why not?

3. Ulysses "left his own ears unplugged" so he could still be in command. What do you think might be another reason that he listened to the Sirens?

4. Why do you think that the Sirens are birds with human faces?

Go Beyond
5. What do you think people mean when they describe something as a Siren song?

Ideas for Writing: Retelling in a Different Form
6. "The Sirens" is in the form of a short story. Use another form of writing to retell it. You might choose to make it into a poem. Or you could write a play or movie script, with dialogue, stage directions, and descriptions of the scenes. You might even want to draw it as a comic strip.

Activity

Critical Thinking

Drawing Conclusions
Suitable as a whole class activity. Discuss with the class the characteristics Ulysses displays (bravery, willpower, sensitivity to beauty, concern for others). Then ask students to suppose that Ulysses can no longer serve as the ship's captain. As a class, develop a job description that describes the personal and professional qualifications required of the new captain of Ulysses' ship.

3 Assess

Work through the Exploring Your Reading questions with students.

1. He fears they will steer the ship toward the Sirens' song and thus destroy it on the rocks.
2. Answers will vary. Possible answers: Yes, because he is willing to take the most risk to protect his ship. No, because he puts himself and his men at risk.
3. Answers will vary. Students may suggest that he was curious about the Sirens' beautiful song.
4. Answers will vary. Accept any reasonable answer.
5. Something very desirable, but possibly dangerous, that is hard to resist.
6. Acceptable retellings should retain the essential message of "The Sirens" (sometimes beauty, or other things you want badly, can lure you onto the wrong path). Outstanding writing should show creativity in the choice of genre and in the retelling of the story.

Ancient Rome

To help you plan instruction, the chart below shows how teaching resources correspond to chapter content. Use the resources to vary instruction, add activities, or plan block schedules. Where appropriate, resources have **suggested time allotments** for students. Time allotments are approximate.

Managing Time and Instruction

	The Ancient World Teaching Resources Binder		World Explorer Program Resources Binder	
	Resource	**mins.**	**Resource**	**mins.**
1 SECTION 1 **The Roman Republic**	**Chapter and Section Support** Reproducible Lesson Plan, p. 117 Ⓢ Guided Reading and Review, p. 118 Ⓢ Section Quiz, p. 119	 20 25	**Outline Maps** Mediterranean Europe: Political, p. 21 Western Europe: Physical, p. 17 **Nystrom Desk Atlas** Ⓣ **Primary Sources and Literature** **Readings** **Writing Process Handbook** Proofreading, p. 37	 20 20 20 40 25
SKILLS ACTIVITY **Reading Actively**	**Social Studies and Geography Skills,** Asking Questions While You Read, p. 70	30		
2 SECTION 2 **The Roman Empire**	**Chapter and Section Support** Reproducible Lesson Plan, p. 120 Ⓢ Guided Reading and Review, p. 121 Ⓢ Section Quiz, p. 122	 20 25	Ⓣ **Interdisciplinary Explorations** *The Glory of Ancient Rome*	
3 SECTION 3 **Daily Life Among the Romans**	**Chapter and Section Support** Reproducible Lesson Plan, p. 123 Ⓢ Guided Reading and Review, p. 124 Ⓢ Section Quiz, p. 125 Critical Thinking Activity, p. 136 **Social Studies and Geography Skills,** Distinguishing Fact From Opinion, p. 43	 20 25 30 30		
4 SECTION 4 **A New Religion: Christianity**	**Chapter and Section Support** Reproducible Lesson Plan, p. 126 Ⓢ Guided Reading and Review, p. 127 Ⓢ Section Quiz, p. 128	 20 25	**Outline Maps** Western Europe: Political, p. 18 The Middle East and North Africa: Political, p. 29	 20 20
5 SECTION 5 **The Fall of Rome**	**Chapter and Section Support** Reproducible Lesson Plan, p. 129 Ⓢ Guided Reading and Review, p. 130 Ⓢ Section Quiz, p. 131 Ⓢ Vocabulary, p. 133 Reteaching, p. 134 Enrichment, p. 135 Ⓢ Chapter Summary, p. 132 **Tests** Forms A and B Chapter Tests, pp. 38–43	 20 25 20 25 25 15 40	**Outline Maps** Mediterranean Europe: Political, p. 21	 20

Activities and Projects

Block Scheduling Program Support

Interdisciplinary Links

Resource Pro™ CD-ROM

Media and Technology

Media and Technology

Resource	mins.
⬤ 🖉 Ⓢ **World Video Explorer**	20
🖵 **Color Transparency 89**	20
🖉 **Planet Earth CD-ROM**	20
🖵 **Color Transparency, Historical Map Set 1**	20
🖵 **Color Transparencies 67, 70**	20
🖵 **Color Transparencies 67, 70**	20
🎧 Ⓢ **Guided Reading Audiotapes**	20
🖵 **Color Transparency 174**	
(Graphic organizer table template)	20
🖉 **The Writer's Solution CD-ROM**	30
🖬 **Computer Test Bank**	30

Ⓣ **Teaming Opportunity**
This resource is especially well-suited for teaching teams.

Ⓢ **Spanish**
This resource is also in Spanish support.

🖉 **CD-ROM**

🖉 **Laserdisc**

🖵 **Transparency**

🖬 **Software**

⬤ **Videotape**

🎧 **Audiotape**

Assessment Opportunities

From Guiding Questions to Assessment A series of Guiding Questions serves as an organizing framework for this book. The Guiding Questions that relate to this chapter are listed below. Section Reviews and Section Quizzes provide opportunities for assessing students' insights into these Guiding Questions. Additional assessments are listed below.

GUIDING QUESTIONS

- *How did the beliefs and values of ancient civlizations affect the lives of their members?*
- *How did civilizations develop a government and an economic system?*

ASSESSMENTS

Section 1

Students should be able to write an explanation of what caused the Roman Republic to collapse.

▶ **RUBRIC** See the Assessment booklet for a rubric on assessing cause-and-effect statements.

Section 2

Students should be able to create a chart of Roman advances in architecture, technology, or science.

▶ **RUBRIC** See the Assessment booklet for a rubric on assessing charts.

Section 3

Students should be able to role-play a scene demonstrating how slaves were treated in ancient Rome.

▶ **RUBRIC** See the Assessment booklet for a rubric on assessing a role-playing activity.

Section 4

Students should be able to write a glossary of the key terms in the section.

▶ **RUBRIC** See the Assessment booklet for a rubric on assessing a glossary.

Section 5

Students should be able to write a short report on the decline of the Roman Empire.

▶ **RUBRIC** See the Assessment booklet for a rubric on assessing a report.

Activities and Projects

Mental Mapping

A Mighty Empire Divide students into teams. Give each team a map of present-day Europe. Have the class locate Rome. Then ask them to speculate about the extent of the Roman Empire at its height.

Each team will try to name the present-day countries whose territory was at least partially included in the Roman Empire.

Give students three to five minutes to play. Using the map at the beginning of the chapter, have the class work as a whole to evaluate the answers and determine each team's score. Answers should include England (or Britain), Portugal, Spain, France, Germany, Switzerland, Brussels, Luxembourg, Austria, Hungary, the Czech Republic, Slovakia, Albania, Rumania, the former Yugoslavia, Bulgaria, Greece, Turkey, Ukraine, Russia (very small portion), Georgia, Iraq, Syria, Lebanon, Israel, Jordan, Egypt, Libya, Tunisia, Algeria, and Morocco.

Links to Current Events

Republican Government Explain that while most democratic governments of today are far more democratic than the Roman Republic was, some of the forms of government in ancient Rome are the basis of government in the United States and other democracies.

Have students create a large chart to display on a wall or bulletin board of the classroom. As they learn about the government of the Roman Republic in this chapter, have them list the characteristics of that government in one column. In another column, have them list the corresponding characteristics of the government of the United States in the twentieth century.

For example, both systems of government allowed voting. Both also had a senate. But the people who were allowed to vote and people who could serve in the senate were quite different in ancient Rome than they are in the present-day United States.

Hands-On Activities

In the Forum Have students create a Roman forum. Depending on the space and resources of your classroom, this could take the form of a table-top model made of clay, balsa wood, foam, and similar materials. If space allows, however, encourage students to create a forum they can walk around in to stage meetings and public events. Large pieces of paper could be cut and painted to simulate building facades on the classroom walls. Desks and seats could be rearranged to create a large forumlike open area in the classroom.

As students work through this chapter, encourage them to use their forum as a setting for the staging of skits that dramatize key events in the history of ancient Rome.

Time Line of a New Religion Have students create a time line listing important dates and events in the development of Christianity during the Roman Empire. *English Language Learners*

Laurels Tell students that in ancient Greece and Rome, people who had achieved honors as poets, athletes, or military leaders were often given a crown of laurels to wear. Invite volunteers to nominate great Romans at an awards ceremony. Each volunteer will choose an individual, research the biography of that person, and then present the biography orally to the rest of the class. Encourage students to present the biographies as dramatically as possible, using visual aids when appropriate. You might ask students who are going to participate in this project to tell you in advance who they are choosing to prevent duplicate nominations. After the biographies are presented, allow the class to vote (or indicate approval through applause or cheering) for the Romans they think should win laurels. *Challenging*

Who Destroyed Rome? Ask students to write a radio play called "Who Destroyed Rome?" The play should focus on a private eye who is trying to understand what caused the fall of the Roman empire. *Average*

F.Y.I.

This page can help you extend your own and students' understanding of the concepts in this chapter. You may want to browse through some of the suggestions in the **Bibliography. Interdisciplinary Links** can connect social studies understandings to areas elsewhere in the curriculum through the use of other Prentice Hall products. **National Geography Standards** reflected specifically in this chapter are listed for your convenience. Some hints about appropriate **Internet Access** are also provided. **School to Careers** provides insights into the practical uses of some of the concepts in this chapter as they might pertain to various careers.

BIBLIOGRAPHY

FOR THE TEACHER
Freeman, Charles. *The World of the Romans.* Oxford, 1993.

McKeever, Susan. *Ancient Rome.* Dorling Kindersley, 1995.

Rome: Echoes of Imperial Glory. Time-Life Books, 1994.

FOR THE STUDENT
Easy
Langley, Andrew, and Philip de Souza. *The Roman News.* Candlewick Press, 1996.

Average
James, Simon. *Ancient Rome.* Viking, 1992.

Morley, Jacqueline. *Roman Villa.* Bedrick, 1992.

Challenging
Bernard, Charlotte. *Caesar and Rome.* Henry Holt and Company, 1996.

Ochoa, George. *The Assassination of Julius Caesar.* Silver, 1991.

LITERATURE CONNECTION
Connolly, Peter. *Tiberius Claudius Maximus: The Cavalryman.* Oxford, 1989.

Connolly, Peter. *Tiberius Claudius Maximus: The Legionary.* Oxford, 1989.

Speare, Elizabeth. *The Bronze Bow.* Houghton, 1961.

Yarbro, Chelsea. *Four Horses for Tishtry.* Harper & Row, 1985.

INTERDISCIPLINARY LINKS

Subject	Theme: Expansion
MATH	Middle Grades Math: Tools for Success *Course 2,* Chapter 2, **Math and Architecture: Three Dimensional Figures**
SCIENCE	Prentice Hall Science *Dynamic Earth,* Lesson 2-3, **Volcano and Earthquake Zones, Connections: The Vault of the Earth** *Exploring the Universe,* Lesson 2-3, **A Trip Through the Solar System**

NATIONAL GEOGRAPHY STANDARDS

Students explore the 18 National Geography Standards throughout *The Ancient World.* Chapter 7, however, concentrates on investigating the following standards: 1, 2, 3, 4, 6, 9, 10, 11, 13, 14, 15, 17. For a complete list of the standards, see the *Teacher's Flexible Planning Guide.*

SCHOOL TO CAREERS

In Chapter 7, Ancient Rome, students learn about another ancient civilization that has influenced modern Western civilization. They also learn the skill of reading actively. These understandings can help students prepare for careers in fields such as religion, history, government, education, and so on. Reading actively is a skill particularly useful for writers, educators, researchers, and others. The curriculum presented in this book, as in all eight titles of Prentice Hall's *World Explorer* program, is designed to prepare students not only for careers but also for good citizenship—of the world as well as of this country.

INTERNET ACCESS

Many social studies teachers and students use Internet browsers, or search engines, to investigate particular topics. For the best results, use narrow rather than broad topics. Try these for Chapter 7: Julius Caesar, Tiber River, Colosseum, Constantinople. Finding age-appropriate sites is an important consideration when using the Internet. For links to age-appropriate sites in world studies and geography, visit the Prentice Hall Home Page at: **http://www.phschool.com**

Connecting to the Guiding Questions

As students complete this chapter, they will focus on the history of ancient Rome, from its earliest beginnings through the time of the republic to the fall of the western Roman Empire. Students will study the empire's expansion throughout the Mediterranean and its eventual collapse due to economic, political, and social disorder. Content in this chapter thus corresponds to the following Guiding Questions:

● How did the beliefs and values of ancient civilizations affect the lives of their members?

● How did civilizations develop a government and an economic system?

Using the Map Activities

On a sheet of paper, have students write the names of the ancient cities and Roman provinces shown on the map. Then ask them to write the correct modern place name next to each.

- Londinium—London
  Burdigala—Bordeaux
  Toletum—Toledo
  Gades—Cadiz
  Athenae—Athens
  Roma—Rome
  Byzantium—Istanbul
  Alexandria—Alexandria
  Carthago—Carthage or
  Tunis

- Gaul—France; Numidia—
  Algeria and Tunisia;
  Judea—Israel; Syria—
  Syria; Asia Minor—Turkey;
  Thrace—Turkey, Bulgaria,
  and Greece; Dacia—
  Romania

CHAPTER 7
Ancient Rome

MAP ACTIVITIES

The Roman Empire was huge. It set boundaries, built cities, and gave names to places that are used today. To get to know the effect of the Roman Empire on the modern world, complete the following activities.

What city is it today?

Look at the major cities of the Roman Empire at its height. Check the location of the cities against the maps of Europe, Asia, and Africa in the Atlas. Study the names of the cities. Compare the locations and names. What are the names of these cities today?

Name that country

Study the same maps, and tell which of today's countries match the following areas ruled by Rome: Gaul, Numidia, Judea, Syria, Asia Minor, Thrace, and Dacia.

Resource Directory

Media and Technology

  Spotlight On: Building an Empire, from the World Video Explorer, enhances students' understanding of the growth of the Roman Empire and its far-reaching influence.

Chapter 9

The Roman Republic

BEFORE YOU READ

Reach Into Your Background

Remember when you started the school year? What did it feel like to be in a new class, perhaps in a new school, and to begin new subjects? Was it exciting? Was it scary? What is it like to face a new world, with new challenges and new responsibilities?

Questions to Explore

1. Why did the early Romans form a republic?
2. Why did the Roman Republic collapse?

Key Terms

republic   consul
patrician   veto
plebeian   dictator

Key People and Places

Romulus and Remus
Etruscans
Julius Caesar   Italy
Octavian   Carthage
Tiber River   Gaul
Rome

Americans learn about the founding of their nation as young people. They read about the 13 British colonies, the battles of Lexington and Concord, and the leadership of George Washington. They learn about the final victory of the new nation, the United States of America.

In ancient times, young Romans also learned about the founding of their state. But it was a story that mixed a little fact with a great deal of legend. The main characters in the story were twin brothers, Romulus and Remus. They were the children of a princess and Mars, the Roman god of war. A jealous king feared that the twins would someday seize power from him. He ordered them to be drowned. However, the gods protected the infants. A female wolf rescued them. Then a shepherd found the twins and raised them as his own. The twins grew up, killed the king, and went off to build their own city. At a place where seven hills rise above the Tiber River, they founded the city of Rome.

▼ This bronze statue honors the wolf that rescued and cared for Romulus and Remus in the legend of Rome's founding.

Teaching Resources

📁 **Reproducible Lesson Plan** in the Chapter and Section Resources booklet, p. 117, provides a summary of the section lesson.

📁 **Guided Reading and Review** in the Chapter and Section Resources booklet, p. 118, provides a structure for mastering key concepts and reviewing key terms in the section. Available in Spanish in the Spanish Chapter and Section Resources booklet, p. 73.

Program Resources

Material in the **Primary Sources and Literature Readings** booklet extends content with a selection related to the concepts in this chapter.

Outline Maps Mediterranean Europe: Political, p. 21
Western Europe: Physical, p. 17

Heterogeneous Groups

The following Teacher's Edition strategies are suitable for heterogeneous groups.

Cooperative Learning

Conquering Carthage   p. 195
Touring the Provinces   p. 199
Arches Stand Stronger   p. 200

Critical Thinking

Drawing Conclusions   p. 205
Identifying Central
  Issues   p. 209
Recognizing Cause
  and Effect   p. 216

Interdisciplinary Connections

Language Arts   p. 211

Lesson Objectives

1. Explain the importance of Rome's geographic setting.

2. Describe Roman government during the republic.

3. Identify the consequences of expansion on economic and social conditions in Rome.

Lesson Plan

1 Engage

Warm-Up Activity

Ask students to imagine living during early Roman times. Explain that for boys and young men, learning to fight to defend your people was a way of life. For girls and young women, daily chores took up much of their time.

Activating Prior Knowledge

Have students read Reach Into Your Background in the Before You Read box. Discuss different ways people adapt to new circumstances.

2 Explore

Have students read the section and discuss the early history of Rome. What was the relationship between the patricians and the plebeians? What were some results of the friction between the two classes? What were some of Julius Caesar's accomplishments?

3 Teach

Ask student teams to stage a debate between patricians and plebeians shortly after the assassination of Julius Caesar. Teams should debate this question: Should plebeians and patricians have equal rights? Students should support their statements with information from the section. This activity should take about 25 minutes.

4 Assess

See the answers to the Section Review. You may also use students' debate performances as an assessment.

Acceptable debate performances include at least three facts from the section.

Commendable debate performances use more than three facts from the section to support arguments and to counter arguments.

Outstanding debate performances use more than three facts from the section to support arguments and also use facts to counter all arguments from the opposing team.

Answers to ...
MAP STUDY

the west coast

READ ACTIVELY

Predict From the story of Romulus and Remus, what do you think the Roman people valued?

Rome's Geographic Setting

We can learn much from the story of Rome's founding—even if it is mostly legend. We learn that the Romans valued loyalty and justice. People who broke the law would be severely punished, just as the king was punished. We also learn that the Romans believed that the favor of the gods was important.

The first settlers on Rome's seven hills were not thinking about building a great empire. They chose that site because it seemed to be a good place to live. The hills made it easy to defend. The soil was fertile. There was a river. But as centuries passed, the people of Rome discovered that the location of their city gave them other advantages. Rome was at the center of the long, narrow peninsula we now call Italy. Italy was at the center of the Mediterranean Sea. And the Mediterranean Sea was at the center of the known Western world.

Ancient Italy About 600 B.C.

Map Study Look at the map. Notice that Roman civilization arose on the Italian peninsula in southern Europe. The fertile soil of Italy's countryside (below) supported the olive trees and grape vines that fed a growing population. **Location** Which of Italy's coasts is Rome closest to?

Resource Directory

Program Resources

Nystrom Desk Atlas

Media and Technology

Color Transparency 89

Rome's Beginnings

We know very little about the people who actually founded Rome. However, we do know that their first settlements date from about the 900s B.C. Rome grew slowly, as the Romans fought their neighbors for land.

About 600 B.C., a mysterious people, the Etruscans (ee TRUHS kuhnz), took power in Rome. They spoke a language totally unlike any other in Italy. Although we have many examples of their writing, we can read very little of it. Where had they come from? Even today, no one is sure. For a time, Etruscans ruled as kings of Rome. However, in 509 B.C., the Romans revolted and drove the Etruscans from power.

Although the Romans defeated the Etruscans, the victors adopted Etruscan ideas. For example, many of the Roman gods were originally Etruscan. The Romans also borrowed the Greek alphabet that the Etruscans used. The Roman garment called the toga came from the Etruscans.

LINKS TO SCIENCE

The Roman Arch Roman architects made great use of the curved structure called the arch. Arches span openings in buildings. An arch can hold great weight above it. The Romans probably learned about arches from the Etruscans. Beginning in the 300s B.C., Romans used arches for water channels, bridges, and later for monuments.

Background

Links Across Place

The Etruscan Mystery
Archaeologists and linguists think that the Etruscans may have come from the northern part of Asia Minor. Etruscans also seem to have lived on the island of Lemnos in the Aegean Sea. They probably settled in Italy between 1100 B.C. and 900 B.C. Although the Etruscans used the Greek alphabet to represent words in their language, the Etruscan language was in no way related to Greek. There has been limited success in deciphering the language of the Etruscans. Perhaps their language was spoken in parts of Asia Minor before the arrival of early Greeks migrating from central Europe.

◀ Time has faded the painted colors but not the grace of this Etruscan tomb sculpture, which was made around 510 B.C.

Legal Language Roman law has greatly influenced law systems in the United States, Canada, and Europe. In fact, many familiar legal terms have Latin origins. The Latin word for "law," *lex* or *legis*, is the root of such English words as *legal*, *legislation*, and *legitimate*. Other English legal terms that have Latin ancestors include *judicial* and *judgment*, which are derived from the Latin *judex*, meaning "judge."

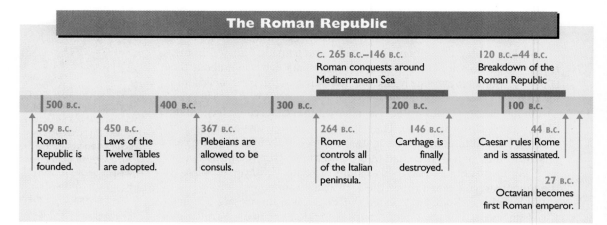

The Roman Republic

▲ The Roman Republic lasted for almost 500 years. By what year did Rome control all of the Italian peninsula?

Read Actively

Ask Questions What would you like to know about the differences between patricians and plebeians?

Rome Becomes a Republic

After driving the last Etruscan king from the throne, the Romans vowed never again to put so much trust in kings. They created a new form of government, a republic. In a **republic,** citizens who have the right to vote select their leaders. The leaders rule in the name of the people.

In the Roman Republic, the most powerful part of the government was a group called the senate. At first, the senate was made up only of 300 upper-class men called **patricians.** Ordinary citizens were known as **plebeians.** In the early republic, plebeians could not hold office or be senators. The government was led by two men called **consuls.** Before 367 B.C., plebeians could not be consuls. The senate advised the consuls on foreign affairs, laws, and finances, among other things.

Consuls almost always did what the senate wanted. Consuls ruled for one year only. Power was divided equally between them. Both had to agree before the government could take any action. If only one consul said "Veto" ("I forbid it"), the matter was dropped. Today, we use the word **veto** to mean the rejection of a bill by the President.

The Romans knew that their government might not work if the two consuls disagreed in an emergency. For this reason, Roman law held that a dictator could be appointed to handle an emergency. A **dictator** was an official who had all the powers of a king but could hold office for only six months.

Patricians Versus Plebeians Through wars of conquest, the Roman Republic extended its control across Italy. Within about 250 years, Rome had conquered almost all of Italy. This caused growing troubles between patricians and plebeians.

Patricians and plebeians had different attitudes. Patricians thought of themselves as leaders. They fought hard to keep control over the government. Plebeians believed they had a right to be respected and treated fairly. Plebeians did not trust the actions of the patrician senate.

They felt the senate was often unfair to the plebeians. Therefore, plebeians formed their own groups to protect their interests.

Many patricians grew wealthy because of Rome's conquests. They took riches from defeated people. Then, they bought land from small farmers and created huge farms for themselves. Plebeians did not work on these farms. Rather, the work was done by slaves brought back from conquests. Many plebeian farmers found themselves without work. The cities, especially Rome, were filled with jobless plebeians.

Eventually, angry plebeians refused to fight in the Roman army. Then the patricians gave in to one of their main demands. This was a written code of laws called the Laws of the Twelve Tables. The Twelve Tables applied equally to all citizens. They were hung in marketplaces so everyone could know what the laws were. Despite this victory, the plebeians never managed to gain power equal to the patricians.

Master of the Mediterranean   While patricians and plebeians fought for power in Rome, Roman armies were conquering new territories. Roman armies invaded the North African empire of the city of Carthage. After a series of bloody wars, they destroyed the empire of Carthage. They also seized control of Spain. Other Roman armies conquered Greece. Then, the Romans turned their attention to the warlike tribes of Gaul, which is now France.

The End of the Republic

Even though it ruled a large area, by 120 B.C. Rome was in trouble. Some leaders tried to break up estates and give land to the plebeians. The patricians fought back, and plebeian leaders were murdered.

In the next 75 years, a number of the most successful generals gathered private armies around them and fought for power. Consuls no longer respected each other's veto power. Rome dissolved into civil war, with private armies roaming the streets and murdering their enemies. As Rome seemed about to break up, Julius Caesar arose as a strong leader.

▼ Carthage had a formidable weapon—the elephant. War elephants easily smashed through enemy lines. They also terrified enemy soldiers. Little wonder, then, that the powerful Roman army took so long to conquer Carthage.

Activity

Cooperative Learning

Conquering Carthage
Point out Carthage on the map at the beginning of the chapter. Have students predict why the Romans might have wanted to conquer Carthage. Then, ask them to work in groups to check their predictions by researching ancient Carthage. Assign one of the following questions to each group: How did Carthage benefit from its geographic location? How did Carthage expand its empire, and how big was the empire? How was Carthage governed? Why were the Punic Wars (the wars between Carthage and Rome) fought? Ask groups to present their findings.

Background

Biography

Cleopatra (69 B.C.–30 B.C.)
Cleopatra was queen of Egypt, but she wanted to rule the world. To attain this goal, she formed an alliance with Julius Caesar, but he was killed before she could fully realize her ambitions. Following Caesar's death, Cleopatra married Mark Antony, the apparent heir to power. The marriage angered Octavian. In about 32 B.C., Octavian went to war and defeated Antony and Cleopatra. Cleopatra then tried to win over Octavian but failed. Realizing that Octavian meant to ruin her, Cleopatra chose to kill herself. According to legend, she allowed herself to be bitten by an asp, a snake symbolic of divine royalty.

1. (a) a type of government with a leader elected by citizens (b) an upper-class citizen of Rome (c) an ordinary citizen of Rome (d) a leader of Rome who served for one year (e) the rejection by one Roman consul of a measure proposed by the other (f) a leader granted the powers of a king for six months to deal with an emergency

2. (a) the legendary founders of Rome (b) a group of people who conquered the Romans about 600 B.C. (c) the Roman general who became dictator for life in 44 B.C. (d) the adopted son of Julius Caesar, who became Rome's first emperor (e) river along which Rome was founded (f) city located on seven hills above Tiber River (g) long, narrow peninsula stretching into the Mediterranean Sea (h) North African empire (i) area which is now France

3. They did not want one person to have absolute power.

4. He was the strongest leader available in a time when civil war between private armies convinced the Romans that they needed one strong man as dictator.

5. Answers may vary. Students' answers should indicate that the Roman senate would oppose Caesar's power because they feared that he would take away their power.

6. Journal entries should relate the basic circumstances of Caesar's assassination.

READ ACTIVELY

Predict Why do you think many Romans feared Julius Caesar?

▶ Julius Caesar was a powerful dictator of the Roman Empire. Later Roman leaders adopted his name as a title. In time, *Caesar* came to mean "emperor."

The Rise of Julius Caesar Caesar was a smart leader, eager for power. From 58 B.C. to 51 B.C., he led his army in conquering Gaul. He killed, enslaved, and uprooted millions of Gauls. He captured huge amounts of gold. His strong leadership won him the loyalty of his troops. They would follow him anywhere—even back to Rome to seize power. In 49 B.C., Caesar returned to Italy. War broke out between Caesar and the senate. Caesar won the war and became dictator of the Roman world in 48 B.C.

The Death of a Dictator For four years, Caesar took over important public offices. In 45 B.C., he became the only consul. In 44 B.C., he became dictator for life. Caesar took many useful steps to reorganize the government. But it seemed to many senators that Rome once again had a king. They hated this idea.

On March 15, 44 B.C., Caesar attended a meeting of the senate. His wife had urged him not to go, fearing danger. But Caesar insisted on going. At the meeting, a group of senators gathered around Caesar. Suddenly, they pulled out knives and began stabbing him. He fell to the ground, dead. Caesar had been a great leader. However, many Romans felt that he had gone too far, too fast, in gathering power.

Civil war followed Caesar's death. When war ended 13 years later, Caesar's adopted son, Octavian, held power. In 27 B.C., the senate awarded Octavian the title Augustus, which means "highly respected." He was the first emperor of Rome.

SECTION 1 REVIEW

1. Define (a) republic, (b) patrician, (c) plebeian, (d) consul, (e) veto, (f) dictator.

2. Identify (a) Romulus and Remus, (b) Etruscans, (c) Julius Caesar, (d) Octavian, (e) Tiber River, (f) Rome, (g) Italy, (h) Carthage, (i) Gaul.

3. Why did the Romans want the republic to have two leaders rather than one?

4. What factors enabled Julius Caesar to come to power?

Critical Thinking

5. Drawing Conclusions Why would the Roman senate be likely to lead the opposition to Caesar's growing power?

Activity

6. Writing to Learn You are sitting in the senate on March 15, 44 B.C., when Julius Caesar enters the chamber. Write a journal entry noting what happened next, including the reasons for the action.

Teaching Resources

Section Quiz in the Chapter and Section Resources booklet, p. 119, covers the main ideas and key terms in the section. Available in Spanish in the Spanish Chapter and Section Resources booklet, p. 74.

The Roman Empire

BEFORE YOU READ

Reach Into Your Background

This section might have been called "The Glory of Rome." What do you think that means? What makes a country "glorious"?

Questions to Explore

1. How did the Romans establish sound government to rule their empire?
2. What advances did the Romans make in the fields of architecture, technology, and science?

Key Terms

province   aqueduct

Key People and Places

Augustus   Greece
Hadrian   Colosseum

Lesson Objectives

1. Explain how Rome gained and ruled its empire.

2. Describe achievements made during the reign of the five "good emperors."

3. Interpret the influence of Greek culture on Rome.

Lesson Plan

1 Engage

Warm-Up Activity

Ask students to think of famous people who serve as role models. Then have students think of some celebrities that have "let their fans down." Ask: *Is being the center of attention always a good thing? How can fame have both positive and negative consequences?*

Activating Prior Knowledge

Allow students to preview the section by skimming it. Encourage them to pay special attention to the photographs and illustrations. Then have students read Reach Into Your Background in the Before You Read box.

2 Explore

Have students read the section and find answers to the following questions: What did Augustus gain by saying he wanted to restore the republic? How did the Romans benefit by being tolerant of the customs of conquered peoples? Why might Hadrian and Justinian have shown more concern for the rights of individuals than had emperors before them?

"Then the captured weapons passed. There were bronze helmets, shields, . . . and glittering steel swords piled on wagons. Then followed 3,000 men carrying 750 trays heaped with silver coins. . . . Next came the king's small children, now slaves, and the king himself in a dark robe. Some in the crowd wept for the children, but not for the king. Suddenly our great consul himself, in a golden chariot. . . . The crowd broke into a roar. . . . It was he who brought all this wealth and glory to Rome."

Rome's armies brought much wealth and glory to Rome in the years after Augustus came to power. When these armies returned to Rome, they were greeted with a magnificent parade, known as a "triumph."

Ruling an Empire

When Augustus came to power after Caesar's death, Roman control had already spread far beyond Italy. Under Augustus and the emperors who followed, Rome gained an even greater empire. Look at the map at the

▼ The Arch of Constantine, erected in Rome about A.D. 315, honors Constantine, the first emperor of Rome to become a Christian. In the background stands the Colosseum, Rome's huge stadium.

Teaching Resources

📁 **Reproducible Lesson Plan** in the Chapter and Section Resources booklet, p. 120, provides a summary of the section lesson.

📁 **Guided Reading and Review** in the Chapter and Section Resources booklet, p. 121, provides a structure for mastering key concepts and reviewing key terms in the section. Available in Spanish in the Spanish Chapter and Section Resources booklet, p. 75.

3 Teach

Organize students into groups. Ask groups to create a children's picture book entitled *The Glory of the Roman Empire*. Each group member should choose one of the main headings in the section and draw a picture or diagram that illustrates a key point made in the paragraphs following that heading. Group members should work together to write informational captions for each page of their book. This activity should take about 30 minutes.

4 Assess

See the answers to the Section Review. You might also assess students' completed picture books.

Acceptable books contain five illustrations that relate to key points under each of the main headings. Captions describe the illustration.

Commendable books contain at least five illustrations that relate to key points under each of the main headings. Captions explain how the illustration demonstrates the glory of Rome.

Outstanding books contain at least five illustrations that relate to key points under each of the main headings. Captions provide an organized narrative for the book.

READ ACTIVELY

Ask Questions What questions do you have about how the Romans governed their vast empire?

▼ Augustus ruled the Roman Empire from 27 B.C. to A.D. 14. He issued new coins to promote trade, and he set up a postal service. He also ordered a census, or population count, to improve tax collection.

beginning of this chapter. The Roman Empire stretched from Britain to Mesopotamia. Rome controlled all the lands around the Mediterranean. This gave the Romans great pride. In fact, they called the Mediterranean *mare nostrum* (MAH ray NOHS truhm), or "our sea."

Augustus, the Senate, and the People Augustus was an intelligent ruler. When he was struggling for power, he often ignored the senate and its laws. But after he won control, he changed his manner. He showed great respect for the senate and was careful to avoid acting like a king. He did not want to have the same fate as Julius Caesar. Augustus often said that he wanted to share power with the senate. He even said he wanted to restore the republic.

What really happened, however, was quite different. The senate and the people were so grateful for Rome's peace and prosperity that they gave Augustus as much power as he wanted.

Governing Conquered Peoples The Romans treated conquered peoples wisely. The Romans took some slaves after a conquest, but most of the conquered people remained free. To govern, they divided their empire into areas called **provinces**. Each province had a Roman governor supported by an army. Often, the Romans built a city in a new province to serve as its capital.

Generally, the Romans did not force their way of life on conquered peoples. They allowed these people to follow their own religions. Local rulers were allowed to run the daily affairs of government. As long as there was peace, Roman governors did not interfere in conquered peoples' lives. Rather, they kept watch over them. Rome wanted peaceful provinces that would supply it with the raw materials it needed. It also wanted the conquered people to buy Roman goods and to pay taxes. Many of the conquered people adopted Roman ways. Many learned to speak Latin, the language of the Romans, and to worship Roman gods.

The Five Good Emperors

Augustus died in A.D. 14. For 82 years after his death, Roman history was a story of good, bad, and terrible emperors. Two of the worst were Caligula (kuh LIG yuh luh) and Nero. They both may have been insane. Caligula

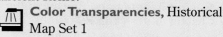

◀ Marcus Aurelius was the last of the five "good emperors." In this stone sculpture, he pardons the barbarians whose attacks weakened the Roman Empire.

proclaimed himself a god and appointed his favorite horse consul. Nero murdered his half-brother, his mother, and his wife.

In A.D. 96, Rome entered what is called the age of the five "good emperors." Only the last of these emperors had a son. Each of the others adopted the best young man he could find to be the next emperor.

Perhaps the greatest was the emperor Hadrian (HAY dree uhn). He worked hard to build a good government. His laws protected women, children, and slaves. He issued a code of laws so that all laws were the same throughout the empire. Hadrian reorganized the army so that soldiers were allowed to defend their home provinces. This gave them a greater sense of responsibility. Hadrian also encouraged learning.

The Greek Influence on Rome

The Romans had long admired Greek achievements. People said that Hadrian spoke Greek better than he spoke Latin. The last of the "good emperors," Marcus Aurelius (aw REE lee uhs), wrote a famous book of philosophy in Greek. Many Romans visited Greece to study Greek art, architecture, and ideas about government.

There was a major difference between Greek and Roman views of learning. The Greeks were interested in ideas. They sought to learn

READ ACTIVELY

Predict How does the civilization of Rome compare to that of Greece?

Cooperative Learning

Arches Stand Stronger
The Romans made great use of arches in the structures they built. Have students work in groups to demonstrate that arches are stronger than lintels. Challenge students to find a simple way to show how an arch works using pieces of cardboard. For example, you might give students two strips of cardboard about 2 inches wide and 11 inches long. Have students curve one strip into an arch, securing both ends with tape, and find how much weight it will support. Then, ask groups to lay the other strip flat across an open space equal to the span of the arch and try the same weights. Discuss the results of the demonstration.
English Language Learner, Visual, Kinesthetic

truths about the world through reason. They developed studies such as mathematics, philosophy, and astronomy, which is the study of the stars and planets. The Romans were more interested in using these studies to build things. Under the Romans, architecture and engineering blossomed. With these skills, they built their empire.

Architecture and Technology

Early Roman art and architecture copied the Etruscans. Later, the Romans studied and copied Greek sculpture and architecture. However, Roman statues and buildings were heavier and stronger in style than those of the Greeks. Using arches, Romans were able to build larger structures. They could create large open spaces inside buildings with wide arched ceilings supported by heavy walls.

Most large buildings were built of bricks covered with thin slabs of white marble. However, one important development was a new building material—concrete. Concrete was a mix of stone, sand, cement, and water that dried as hard as a rock. Concrete helped the Romans put up buildings that were far taller than any built before.

The greatest Roman building was the Colosseum, a giant arena that held 50,000 spectators. Its walls were so well built that the floor of the arena could be flooded for mock naval battles using real people in real boats. Stairways and ramps ran through the building. There were even elevators to carry wild animals from dens below the floor to the arena.

Roman engineers built roads from Rome to every part of the empire. This road system covered a distance equal to twice the distance around the Earth at the Equator. Do you know the saying, "All roads lead to Rome"? In Roman times, it was true. No matter what road travelers started out on, they would eventually arrive in Rome.

The Pantheon in Rome

Built during the reign of Emperor Hadrian, the Pantheon was first used to hold statues of the Roman gods. Later, it became a Christian church. Now it serves as the burial place of many famous Italians. At its highest point, the Pantheon's majestic dome rises 144 feet (47 m) above the floor. Light streams in from the opening at the top of the dome.

A Roman Road

Roman roads were built to allow the speedy movement of troops and communication around the empire. The first road built was the Appian Way. Begun in 312 B.C., it connected Rome with southern Italy. Roman roads were built as straight as possible and sometimes included tunnels. These roads were rugged and strong— some even have survived to today. The diagram below shows a typical Roman road.

Milestones were placed along Roman roads. Each was marked with the number of miles to Rome. A Roman mile was 1,000 paces. Each pace was two steps long, about 5 feet.

1 After surveyors laid out the road, workers dug parallel ditches. These ditches were lined with a row of curbstones.

5 The road was paved with tightly fitted flat stones. The surface was higher in the center to allow rainwater to run off into the side ditches.

4 Then came a layer of gravel, sand, and mortar about 1 foot thick.

2 Workers dug a deep ditch between the two rows of curbstones. They added a layer of broken flat stones 10 to 24 inches deep.

3 The next layer, about 9 inches thick, was made up of smaller stones mixed with lime mortar.

Exploring Technology

A Roman Road Allow students to examine the diagram. Then have them think about how weather affects an unpaved or poorly maintained road. You might have students consider what riding a bicycle over such surfaces is like. How do standing water, mud, and an uneven and slippery surface affect ease and speed of travel? Point out that the Romans carefully designed their roads so that they would still be serviceable during bad weather. Ask students to identify two features on the diagram that helped prevent flooding. (The higher surface in the center of the road allowed water to flow off the road; side ditches caught excess water.)

The snugly fitted flat stones provided a smooth surface for swift travel. Although some horse-drawn chariots carried loads of up to 725 pounds (330 kg), the superior condition of Roman roads allowed vehicles to travel anwhere from 15 miles (24 km) to 75 miles (120 km) per day.

The Romans used the same basic techniques as illustrated in the diagram to build more than 50,000 miles (80,000 km) of roads throughout Italy as well as in Greece, Spain, Asia Minor, North Africa, Gaul, and Britain. Suggest that students locate these places on the map at the beginning of the chapter. After the decline of the Roman Empire, the roads in these far-flung former provinces suffered neglect but remained in good enough repair to serve as transportation routes throughout the Middle Ages.

Romans were famous for their **aqueducts,** structures that carried water over long distances. The aqueducts were huge lines of arches, often many miles long. A channel along the top carried water from the countryside to the cities. Roman aqueducts tunneled through mountains and spanned valleys. Some are still being used today.

Roman Law

Roman law followed Roman roads throughout the empire. The great Roman senator Cicero (SIS uh roh) expressed Roman feeling about law.

Connect From what you know about law in the United States, how is it similar to Roman law?

> "What sort of thing is the law? It is the kind that cannot be bent by influence, or broken by power, or spoiled by money."

A later ruler named Justinian (juh STIHN ee uhn) used Roman law to create a famous code of justice. Here are a few laws from that code.

> "No one suffers a penalty for what he thinks. No one may be forcibly removed from his own house. The burden of proof is upon the person who accuses. In inflicting penalties, the age and inexperience of the guilty party must be taken into account."

Roman law continued to be passed down to other cultures, including our own. Think of our Bill of Rights. Do any of Justinian's laws appear there? Other Roman ideas of justice are also basic to our system of laws. For example, persons accused of crimes had the right to face their accusers. If there was doubt about a person's guilt, he or she would be judged innocent.

SECTION 2 REVIEW

I. Define (a) province, (b) aqueduct.

2. Identify (a) Caligula, (b) Hadrian, (c) Greece, (d) Colosseum.

3. Why did the Romans give Augustus so much power?

4. Why is Roman law important to us today?

Critical Thinking

5. Drawing Conclusions The "good emperor" Marcus Aurelius chose his son Commodus to follow him. Commodus was one of the worst emperors in Roman history. Why do you think a good emperor might make such a bad choice?

Activity

6. Writing to Learn Write down a few ideas for guidelines that you would give to every new governor of a Roman province. How should the governor treat the people of the province? What should the governor do about the religion and existing government of the conquered people?

Daily Life Among the Romans

Section 3

Lesson Objectives

1 Describe aspects of the daily life of the rich, the poor, and the slaves in ancient Rome.

2 Explain the status of women in Roman society.

BEFORE YOU READ

Reach Into Your Background

How would you describe your daily life? Have you ever thought that people in earlier times might have lived very differently? How do you think a person from another period in history would describe your life? What would they think was strange? What might be familiar?

Questions to Explore

1. How were the lives of the rich and the poor different in ancient Rome?

2. How were slaves treated in ancient Rome?

Key Terms

circus

Key People

Martial
Seneca

A t the height of its glory, Rome had the most beautiful monuments and public buildings in the world. Wealth and goods flowed into Rome from all parts of the empire. Tourists and merchants flocked to the city. Its marketplaces and shops had more goods than any other city. Not everyone was thrilled with the excitement. One Roman complained of narrow streets "jammed with carts and their swearing drivers." Another writer, the poet Martial (MAR shuhl), complained of the noise:

> "Before it gets light, we have the bakers. Then it's the hammering of the artisans all day. There's no peace or quiet in this city!"

The Rich, the Poor, and the Slaves

Roman society was made up of the few rich people, the many poor people, and the slaves. Most citizens had nothing like the luxuries of the wealthy. In fact, there was a huge difference between the lives of rich and poor. A majority of Romans were not only poor, they were jobless. Most of these survived only by handouts from the government.

▼ A scene from daily life in ancient Rome is shown in this faded 2,000-year-old fresco— a painting on a plaster wall. It shows customers buying fresh bread in a bakery.

Lesson Plan

1 Engage

Warm-Up Activity

Ask students to think about things that they take for granted, such as television, central heating, telephones, and modern plumbing. Explain that daily life in ancient Rome was very different. Tell students that life revolved around direct relationships with family members and servants and around loyalty to popular leaders. Ask students to think about how certain aspects of their lives would be different had they lived in ancient Rome.

Activating Prior Knowledge

Have students read Reach Into Your Background in the Before You Read box. Ask students to look around the classroom. What items do they see that would be unfamiliar to people from an earlier time period? What items would be familiar?

Teaching Resources

📁 **Reproducible Lesson Plan** in the Chapter and Section Resources booklet, p. 123, provides a summary of the section lesson.

📁 **Guided Reading and Review** in the Chapter and Section Resources booklet, p. 124, provides a structure for mastering key concepts and reviewing key terms in the section. Available in Spanish in the Spanish Chapter and Section Resources booklet, p. 77.

📁 **Critical Thinking Activity** in the Chapter and Section Resources booklet, p. 136, helps students apply the skill of making comparisons.

2 Explore

As students read the section, ask them to find answers to the following questions: How did the poor people of Rome live? What did the government do to help the poor? Why did women who had wealthy husbands have an advantage over poorer women? How did the duties of slaves vary?

3 Teach

Ask students to suppose that they are students living in ancient Rome. Have them write a paragraph about a typical day in their lives. Tell them that they should base their writing on what they have learned about daily life in Rome from reading the section. Have them include as many aspects of that life into their writing as they can manage in a paragraph. This activity should take about 20 minutes.

4 Assess

See the answers to the Section Review. You might also assess students' paragraphs.

Acceptable paragraphs describe a minimum of two events that could have occurred in the life of an ancient Roman student.

Commendable paragraphs describe a minimum of three events that could have occurred in the life of an ancient Roman student.

Outstanding paragraphs include at least five events or situations that could have occurred in the life of an ancient Roman student.

New Hairdo or Old?
People today are not the first to use makeup and to style their hair. The Romans and earlier people spent time and money on their looks. Rich Roman women used powdered minerals to paint their faces, make up their eyes, and redden their lips. Fancy hairdos were created with curling irons, dyes, and the work of slaves.

▼ Wealthy Roman families lived in villas like this one. In this drawing, the roof is cut away to show the inside. Find the dining room. Notice how the wealthy ate while lying on couches.

A Life of Luxury   The rich often had elegant homes in the city. They also had country estates called villas. Some wealthy families had huge estates in the provinces where much of the food for the empire was grown. Wealthy Romans were famous for overdoing things, especially concerning food. A Roman historian describes the eating habits of Aulus Vitellius (OW luhs vuh TEL ee uhs), emperor for only six months in A.D. 69.

> "He used to have three, or four, heavy meals a day. . . . He had himself invited to a different house for each meal. The cost to the host was never less than 400,000 coins a time."

Of course, few Romans could afford to eat like an emperor. Still, the wealthy were known for their feasts. Often they served game, perhaps partridge or wild boar. For very special occasions, they might also serve exotic dishes such as flamingo or ostrich. A special treat was dormouse cooked in honey. Roman feasts often had entertainment, including musicians, dancers, and performers reciting poems.

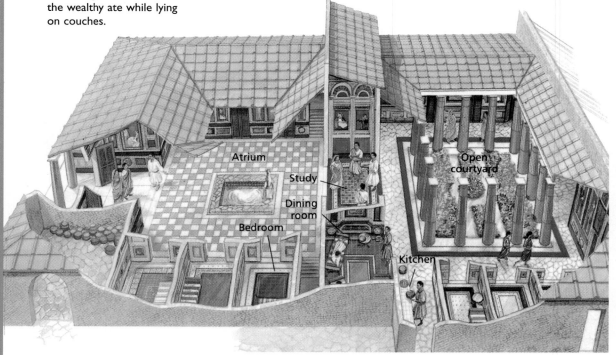

Atrium

Study

Dining room

Bedroom

Kitchen

Open courtyard

Roman Pots and Pans

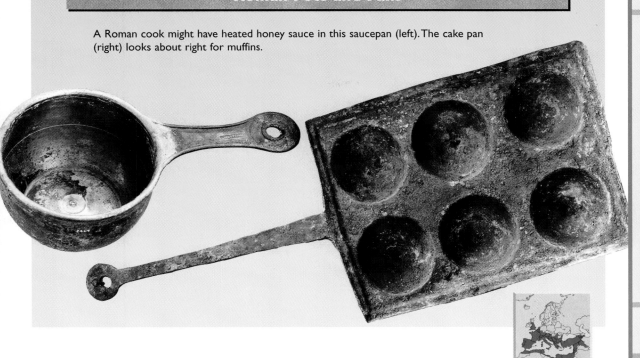

A Roman cook might have heated honey sauce in this saucepan (left). The cake pan (right) looks about right for muffins.

Another Way of Life for the Poor The world of the poor was a far cry from the feasts of the wealthy. In Rome, most people lived in poor housing. Many lived in tall apartment houses with no running water, toilets, or kitchens. All food and drink had to be carried up the stairs. Rubbish and human waste had to carried down, or—as frequently happened—dumped out the window. Because most houses were made of wood, fires were frequent and often fatal. The worst, in A.D. 64, destroyed most of the city.

Bread and Circuses Poor citizens needed wheat to survive. When wheat harvests were bad, or when grain shipments from overseas were late, the poor often rioted. To prevent this, the emperors provided free grain to the poor. They also provided spectacular shows. They were held in the Colosseum or in arenas called **circuses,** so the shows came to be called circuses, too.

The circuses could be violent. Romans, rich and poor, packed the arenas to watch the events. These included animals fighting other animals, animals fighting humans, and humans fighting humans. Clowns might also entertain, or there might even be a public execution of a criminal. The highlights of the day were the fights between gladiators, men who fought to the death. Most gladiators were slaves who had been captured in battle. However, a few were free men—and some women—who enjoyed the fame and fortune they could gain.

READ ACTIVELY

Visualize Visualize a feast at the home of a rich Roman. Then visualize a meal with poor Romans.

Activity

Critical Thinking

Drawing Conclusions
Suitable as an individual activity. Ask students to read *Another Way of Life for the Poor.* Then tell students that in Rome, the average man lived to the age of 26 and the average woman lived to the age of 23. Have students write a paragraph in which they draw some conclusions about why Romans had such short lives. Students should base their conclusions on what they have read.

Background

Daily Life

Job Security in Ancient Rome Although the emperor officially provided each Roman family with a monthly ration of grain, in reality only about one third of the families received the ration. In addition, there was a severe job shortage because much of the unskilled and skilled labor was performed by slaves. The Roman workers who did have jobs set up guilds to keep their jobs secure. These guilds established set salaries and protected members from some forms of competition. Even the lowliest occupations, such as sewer cleaners and public bath attendants, had their own guilds.

Journal Writing

A Call for Freedom Tell students to suppose that they are Roman citizens who believe that slavery is cruel and unfair and should be abolished. Ask students to write a journal entry calling for the end of slavery. Students should use the descriptions of the harsh conditions slaves endured to support their arguments for the ending of slavery in Rome.

Background

Biography

Epictetus (c. A.D. 55–135) The philosopher Epictetus began life as a slave. The name *Epictetus* is derived from a Greek word meaning "acquired." His real name is not known. Epictetus eventually became a freedman and an influential philosopher. Two of his central ideas perhaps resulted from his experiences as a slave: the recognition that a person's will, or purpose, is the only thing that truly belongs to that person and the belief that the accumulation of possessions leads to unhappiness.

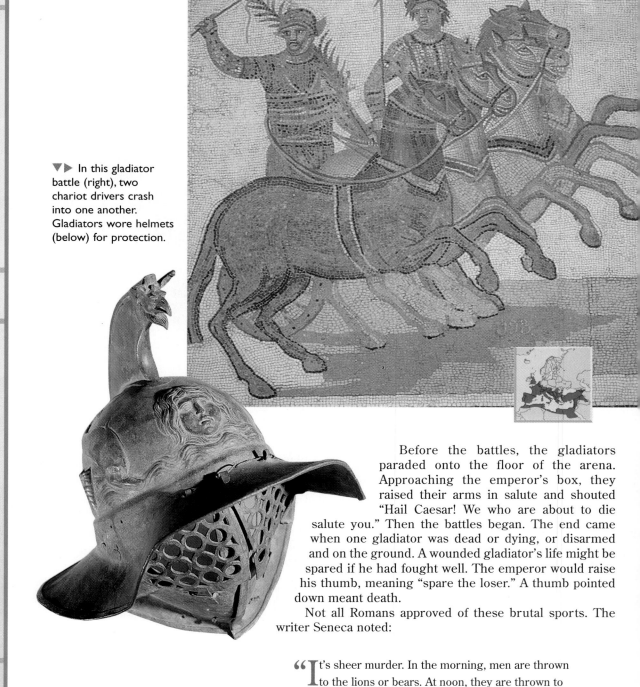

▼ ▶ In this gladiator battle (right), two chariot drivers crash into one another. Gladiators wore helmets (below) for protection.

Before the battles, the gladiators paraded onto the floor of the arena. Approaching the emperor's box, they raised their arms in salute and shouted "Hail Caesar! We who are about to die salute you." Then the battles began. The end came when one gladiator was dead or dying, or disarmed and on the ground. A wounded gladiator's life might be spared if he had fought well. The emperor would raise his thumb, meaning "spare the loser." A thumb pointed down meant death.

Not all Romans approved of these brutal sports. The writer Seneca noted:

> ❝It's sheer murder. In the morning, men are thrown to the lions or bears. At noon, they are thrown to the spectators.❞

Resource Directory

Teaching Resources

📁 **Distinguishing Fact From Opinion** in the Social Studies and Geography Skills booklet, p. 43, provides additional skill practice.

Roman Family Life

Despite these brutal sports, many Romans had a strong sense of values. Most of all, they valued family life. Roman writings are filled with stories of happy families and dedication and love.

The Roman government rewarded parents who had many children. Under Roman law, the father had absolute power over the entire household. He owned the household—wife, children, slaves, and furniture. In the early days, he could sell a son or daughter into slavery. Later, this power was reduced.

The amount of freedom a woman in ancient Rome enjoyed depended on her husband's wealth and status. Wealthy women had a great deal of independence. Women had a strong influence on their families, and some wives of famous men became famous themselves. The mothers or wives of some Roman emperors gained great political power.

Slavery in Rome

Slavery was common in ancient Rome. Almost every wealthy family owned slaves. Even poor families might own one. While few owners paid slaves for their work, they often took good care of household slaves. Slaves had almost no rights. Yet relationships between household slaves and their owners were sometimes trusting and tender. These slaves helped raise children and provided companionship. Sometimes they rose to important positions in the households of wealthy owners.

Household slaves were more fortunate. Other kinds of slaves often led short, brutal lives. Slaves who worked on farms sometimes worked chained together during the day and slept in chains at night. Slaves in copper, tin, and iron mines worked in terrible conditions. Gladiators risked death every time they fought. Roman warships were powered by slaves trained as rowers.

Some slaves were able to save tips or wages and buy their freedom. These might be slaves with very special skills, such as chariot racers. These sports heroes sometimes became famous and wealthy.

READ ACTIVELY

Ask Questions What do you want to know about the status of women and slaves in Rome?

SECTION 3 REVIEW

1. **Define** circus.

2. **Identify** (a) Martial, (b) Seneca.

3. How were the lives of rich and poor Romans different?

4. What was the difference in the treatment a household slave and a mine slave received?

Critical Thinking

5. **Recognizing Cause and Effect** How do you think abolishing slavery would have affected Roman family life?

Activity

6. **Writing to Learn** In this section, you read the reaction of the writer Seneca to a circus. Write a journal entry telling of your reactions to what you might have seen at a Roman circus.

Teaching Resources

Section Quiz in the Chapter and Section Resources booklet, p. 125, covers the main ideas and key terms in the section. Available in Spanish in the Spanish Chapter and Section Resources booklet, p. 78.

Section 3 Review

1. entertainment held in an outdoor arena

2. (a) a Roman poet who complained about the noise in Rome (b) a Roman writer who criticized the brutality of circuses

3. The rich had luxuries and more than they needed to live a good life, while the poor often had very little and lived on handouts from the government.

4. Household slaves were often treated fairly well and had good relationships with their owners; mine slaves worked under terrible conditions and often had short, miserable lives.

5. Answers may vary. Students will probably say that abolishing slavery would have had a huge affect on Roman family life. The wealthiest of Romans might employ and pay people to do the jobs once done by slaves. Former slaves would likely flock to the cities looking for work, causing an increased number of unemployed people and increasing the numbers of people that depended on government handouts. Businesses that used slave labor would have to pay workers, thereby lowering profits.

6. Students' journal entries should vividly reflect the contrast between the value of circuses as entertainment and the brutality that many witnesses observed in them.

1. Identify the basic principles of Jesus' teachings.
2. Describe how Christianity spread to various areas of the Roman Empire.
3. Explain how the Roman government viewed the rise of Christianity.

1 Engage

Warm-Up Activity

Ask students to recall the harsh realities of life for the poor and the enslaved in Rome. Then, have volunteers tell what they know about some of the basic beliefs of Christianity. Discuss with students whether they think Christianity might have appealed to many Romans. Ask students to predict how emperors and other powerful Romans would react to a set of beliefs that could be seen as a threat to their authority.

Activating Prior Knowledge

Have students read Reach Into Your Background in the Before You Read box. Discuss with students the fear of the unknown. Talk about why people sometimes feel threatened by new ideas, people, or places.

SECTION 4 · A New Religion: Christianity

BEFORE YOU READ

Reach Into Your Background

How would you feel if people teased or criticized you for a belief that you held? What would you do? Would you defend your belief? If so, how would you do this?

Questions to Explore

1. What ideas did Jesus teach?
2. How did the Roman government attack Christianity? How did the religion finally triumph?

Key Terms

messiah
disciple
Gospel
epistle
martyr

Key People and Places

Jesus
Paul
Nero
Judea

▼ In this Roman sculpture, Jesus restores sight to a blind man. Belief in Jesus' powers helped early Christians face cruel persecution.

"**B**lessed are the poor in spirit, for theirs is the kingdom of heaven.

Blessed are those who mourn, for they shall be comforted.

Blessed are the lowly, for they shall inherit the earth.

Blessed are those who hunger and thirst for what is right, for they shall be satisfied.

Blessed are the merciful, for they shall be treated with mercy.

Blessed are the pure in heart, for they shall see God.

Blessed are the peacemakers, for they shall be called children of God.

Blessed are those who are persecuted in the cause of right, for theirs is the kingdom of heaven."

—*The Sermon on the Mount, Matthew 5:1–10*

According to the Bible, Jesus, a Jewish religious teacher, spoke these words to his followers and others in the first century A.D. These words are an important part of the religion called Christianity. In the beginning, its followers were mainly the poor and slaves. Roman rulers tried to stamp out Christianity by killing its followers. But over time, it spread throughout the entire Roman Empire.

Teaching Resources

📁 **Reproducible Lesson Plan** in the Chapter and Section Resources booklet, p. 126, provides a summary of the section lesson.

📁 **Guided Reading and Review** in the Chapter and Section Resources booklet, p. 127, provides a structure for mastering key concepts and reviewing key terms in the section. Available in Spanish in the Spanish Chapter and Section Resources booklet, p. 79.

Program Resources

Outline Maps Western Europe: Political, p. 18
The Middle East and North Africa: Political, p. 29

The Beginnings of Christianity

Christianity was one of many religions in the vast Roman Empire. The empire contained many lands with different languages, customs, and religions. The Romans were tolerant toward the people in these lands. They allowed them to follow their own religions. But the conquered people had to show loyalty to Roman gods and to the emperor.

The Romans conquered the Jewish homeland of Judea in 63 B.C. At first, they respected the Jews' right to worship their God. But, many Jews resented foreign rule. Some believed that a **messiah,** or savior, would come to bring justice and freedom to the land. As opposition to Roman rule grew, the Romans struck back with harsh punishment. In 37 B.C., the Roman senate appointed a new ruler of Judea named Herod (HAIR uhd). It was during Herod's reign that a man named Jesus was born in the Judean town of Nazareth.

Most of what we know about Jesus' life is found in the New Testament, a part of the Christian Bible. After Jesus died, his **disciples,** or followers, told stories about his life and teaching. Between 40 and 70 years after his death, four stories of his life were written from these oral traditions. People came to believe that four disciples—Matthew, Mark, Luke, and John—had each written one story. These writings are called the **Gospels.**

We know little of Jesus' childhood and youth except that he grew up in Nazareth. He learned to be a carpenter and began teaching when he was about 30 years old. For three years, Jesus traveled from place to place, preaching to Jews who lived in the countryside. Much of what he taught was part of the Jewish tradition into which he had been born. Like all Jewish teachers, Jesus preached that there was only one true God.

According to the Gospels, Jesus taught that God was loving and forgiving. He said that a person had the responsibility to "love the Lord your God with all your heart and your neighbor as yourself." Jesus also said he

READ ACTIVELY

Ask Questions What questions do you have about Jesus and his beliefs?

▼ This scene, painted on a wall of a catacomb in Rome, shows Jesus with his disciples.

Media and Technology

Color Transparencies 67, 70

See the answers to the Section Review. You might also assess students' biographies.

Acceptable biographies identify two persons and state each person's role in attempting to promote or defeat Christianity.

Commendable biographies identify at least two persons and state each person's role in attempting to promote or defeat Christianity.

Outstanding biographies identify at least three persons, state each person's role in attempting to promote or defeat Christianity, and give reasons for the person's view.

was the Son of God and the Messiah. He promised that people who believed in him and followed his teachings would have everlasting life.

Jesus' teachings alarmed many people. Some complained to the Romans that Jesus was teaching that God was greater than the emperor. The Romans feared that he would lead an armed revolt against Roman rule, so the Roman governor condemned Jesus to death. He was crucified, or put to death by being nailed to a large wooden cross. According to the Gospels, Jesus rose from the dead and spoke to his disciples, telling them to spread his teachings.

Christianity Spreads

The Greek equivalent of the word *messiah* was *christos*. Many educated people of that day spoke Greek. As these people accepted Jesus' teachings, they began calling him Christ. After his death, his followers, called Christians, spread the new religion from Jerusalem to Antioch in Syria, and finally to Rome itself.

One of Jesus' most devoted disciples was a Jew named Paul. Paul was well educated and spoke both Greek and Latin. According to the

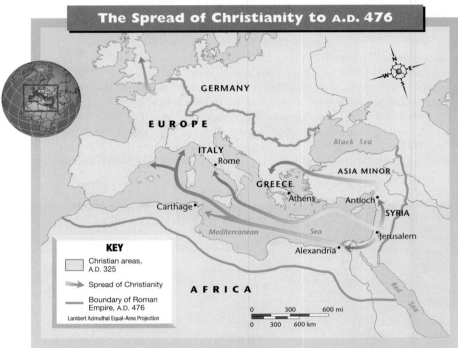

The Spread of Christianity to A.D. 476

KEY
- Christian areas, A.D. 325
- → Spread of Christianity
- — Boundary of Roman Empire, A.D. 476

Lambert Azimuthal Equal-Area Projection

0   300   600 mi
0 300 600 km

Map Study Paul and other apostles carried the Christian message to far-flung places. From its beginning in Jerusalem, the new religion eventually extended throughout the Roman Empire. **Location** Christianity spread out from Jerusalem. To which North African cities did it spread? To which Italian city did it spread?

Answers to ...

MAP STUDY

Christianity spread to the North African cities of Alexandria and Carthage, and the Italian city of Rome.

210 CHAPTER 7

Gospels, Paul at first rejected the Christian message. One day as he approached the Syrian city of Damascus, he had a vision that Jesus spoke to him. After this experience, Paul decided to travel to spread the word of Jesus. He persuaded Jesus' followers that his teachings should be spread to Greeks and Romans, and not just to Jews. Paul carried Christianity to the cities around the Mediterranean.

Paul's writings also helped turn the Christian faith into an organized religion. Paul wrote many **epistles** (ee PIS uhlz), or letters, to Christian groups in distant cities. Many of these epistles became a part of the Christian Bible.

The fast-growing new religion soon alarmed the Roman government. Christians refused to worship the Roman gods or the emperor. Many Roman officials began to view them as enemies of the empire. Under the emperor Nero, the first official campaign against the Christians began in A.D. 64. One night, a fire started in some shops in Rome. The fire burned for nine days and left much of the city in ruins.

Nero blamed the Christians. He watched with pleasure as Christians were sent to their deaths. Some were forced to fight wild animals in the Colosseum. Others were soaked with oil and burned alive. Others, like the disciple Paul, were crucified.

LINKS TO LANGUAGE ARTS

Sign of the Fish A secret sign that Christians used to identify one another was a simple image of a fish. How did a fish come to be an early Christian symbol? Each letter of the Greek word for fish, *ichthys*, was the first letter of a word in a Greek phrase. The phrase meant "Jesus Christ, Son of God, Savior."

Christian Catacombs

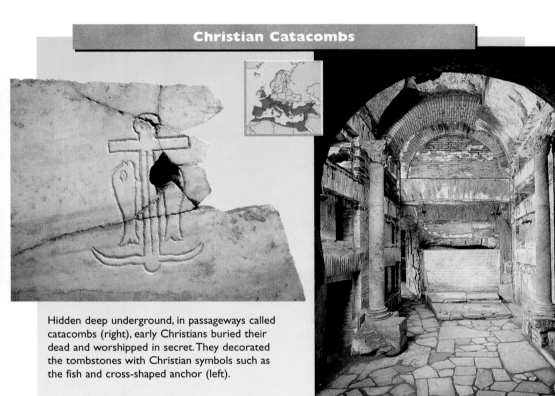

Hidden deep underground, in passageways called catacombs (right), early Christians buried their dead and worshipped in secret. They decorated the tombstones with Christian symbols such as the fish and cross-shaped anchor (left).

◀ Statues and paintings showing Jesus as a shepherd borrowed a popular pre-Christian symbol for gentleness and charity.

The Romans tormented Christians off and on for another 250 years. During these years, the Roman Empire began to lose its power. To explain the decline, Romans looked for people to blame. They found them among the followers of the new religion. As one Roman wrote:

> ❝If the Tiber River reaches the walls, if the Nile fails to rise to the fields, if the sky doesn't move or the Earth does, if there is famine or plague, the cry is at once: "The Christians to the Lions."❞

Still, Christianity spread throughout the empire. Its message of hope for a better life after death appealed to many. The help that Christian communities gave to widows, orphans, and the poor also attracted people. Not even the emperor Diocletian (dy uh KLEE shuhn) could stop its growth. Diocletian outlawed Christian services, imprisoned Christian priests, and put many believers to death.

However, these actions did the opposite of what Diocletian wanted. Many Romans admired the Christians. They saw them as martyrs and heroes. **Martyrs** are people who choose to die for a cause they believe in. By the A.D. 300s, about one in every ten Romans had accepted the Christian faith.

CITIZEN HEROES

To Be a Leader Fabiola was a rich Roman noblewoman. Near the end of the 300s, she gave up her comfortable life and became a Christian. She gave money to support her religion. Fabiola founded and worked in a hospital where anyone could come for care. It was the first public hospital in Western Europe.

SECTION 4 REVIEW

1. Define (a) messiah, (b) disciple, (c) Gospel, (d) epistle, (e) martyr.

2. Identify (a) Jesus, (b) Paul, (c) Nero, (d) Judea.

3. What ideas of Jesus attracted followers?

4. Why did Christianity seem threatening to the Roman government?

Critical Thinking

5. Drawing Conclusions Why do you think the Christians refused to worship the Roman gods and the emperor?

Activity

6. Writing to Learn You are a Roman official at the time of Jesus. Write a journal entry that describes your feelings about the new religion.

The Fall of Rome

BEFORE YOU READ

Reach Into Your Background

Have you ever thought about what you would do if you had all the money you could want?

Would you spend it wisely? Would you help others? Would you save some, or would you spend until the money began to run out?

Questions to Explore

1. Why did Rome begin to lose its power?
2. How did Constantine try to restore Rome's greatness?

Key Terms
mercenary
inflation

Key People and Places
Constantine
Diocletian
Constantinople

Lesson Objectives

1. Summarize the problems that led up to the decline of the Roman Empire.

2. Explain the effect of the acceptance of Christianity on the Roman Empire.

3. Describe how Rome fell to invaders.

Lesson Plan

1 Engage

Warm-Up Activity

Have students study the map of the Roman Empire at the beginning of the chapter. Ask them to estimate what percentage of the Earth's land was under the rule of Rome's emperor. Remind students that one man was the ruler of all this territory. Start a discussion of problems related to the size of the empire with questions such as: *How could an emperor really control such a large area? Why would it be difficult to defend such a large area against attack?*

Activating Prior Knowledge

Have students read Reach Into Your Background in the Before You Read box. Ask students to recall how some of Rome's emperors (particularly the bad emperors) spent money. Have students consider whether Rome spent its money wisely.

One day in the year A.D. 312, the emperor Constantine (KAHN stuhn teen) stood with his troops under a cloudy sky near a bridge across the Tiber River. He was filled with doubts. A battle was about to begin. His enemies were waiting on the other side of the river.

While Constantine was hoping for victory, the sun broke through the clouds. According to Constantine, the sun had a cross on it. And above the cross was written in Latin: "Under this sign you will conquer!"

The next morning, Constantine had his artisans put the Christian symbol of the cross on his soldiers' shields. In the battle, they won an overwhelming victory. Constantine believed that the victory had come from the Christian God. Constantine vowed to become a Christian.

Historians today debate whether this event ever happened. But we know that as emperor from A.D. 312 to A.D. 337, Constantine strongly encouraged the spread of Christianity throughout the Roman Empire. As he lay dying, he may have converted to Christianity.

◀ This statue of Emperor Constantine originally towered over 30 feet (9 m). Today, only the head remains.

Teaching Resources

📁 **Reproducible Lesson Plan** in the Chapter and Section Resources booklet, p. 129, provides a summary of the section lesson.

📁 **Guided Reading and Review** in the Chapter and Section Resources booklet, p. 130, provides a structure for mastering key concepts and reviewing key terms in the section. Available in Spanish in the Spanish Chapter and Section Resources booklet, p. 81.

Program Resources

Outline Maps Mediterranean Europe: Political, p. 21

2 Explore

As students read the section, have them analyze some of the reasons behind the fall of Rome. Why was the dependence on mercenaries to defend the empire a bad idea? How did the size of the Roman Empire increase its chances of being attacked? What kinds of economic problems did Rome have? What measures did Diocletian take to try to save the Roman Empire from decline?

3 Teach

Ask students to prepare a plan to rescue the Roman Empire from its downward spiral. Tell them that they will organize a temporary government to rule the empire until Rome can get back on its feet. Have them list the problems Rome faced and think of a possible solution for each of the problems. This activity should take about 25 minutes.

4 Assess

See the answers to the Section Review. You might also assess students' plans for Roman recovery based on the accuracy of their perception of the problems.

Acceptable plans identify a minimum of two problems and suggest solutions that demonstrate an accurate understanding of the problems.

Commendable plans identify a minimum of three problems and suggest solutions that demonstrate an accurate understanding of the problems.

Outstanding plans identify four or more problems and suggest solutions that constitute a coherent reform plan.

Ask Questions What questions do you have about the fall of Rome?

The Empire Crumbles

The Christian Church provided comfort and authority at a time when the mighty Roman Empire was on the edge of disaster. By the time Constantine took power, he could do little to stop the empire's fall.

The trouble started 125 years before. That's when the last of the "good emperors"—Marcus Aurelius—died. The emperor, known for his wisdom, left his son Commodus in power in A.D. 180. Commodus was not a wise choice. He was a savage ruler who loved the bloodshed of the gladiators. He ruled by bribing the army to support him.

The rule of Commodus began the decline of the Roman Empire. Historians do not agree on any one cause for this decline. Generally, they believe that the following problems together led to Rome's end.

Weak, Corrupt Rulers After Commodus, emperors were almost always successful generals and not politicians. They often stole money from the treasury. They used the money to enrich themselves and pay off the soldiers. Under these emperors, the government and the economy fell to pieces. The senate lost its power. During this time, even emperors were not safe. Between A.D. 180 and A.D. 284, Rome had 29 emperors. Most were murdered.

▼ These time line entries show the decline and collapse of the Roman Empire.

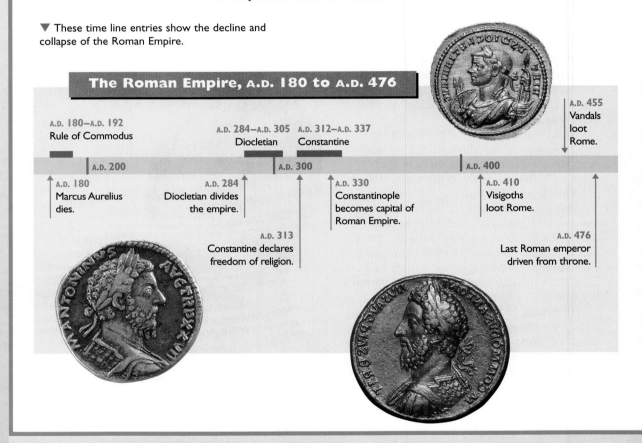

The Roman Empire, A.D. 180 to A.D. 476

A.D. 180–A.D. 192
Rule of Commodus

A.D. 284–A.D. 305
Diocletian

A.D. 312–A.D. 337
Constantine

A.D. 455
Vandals loot Rome.

A.D. 200

A.D. 300

A.D. 400

A.D. 180
Marcus Aurelius dies.

A.D. 284
Diocletian divides the empire.

A.D. 330
Constantinople becomes capital of Roman Empire.

A.D. 410
Visigoths loot Rome.

A.D. 313
Constantine declares freedom of religion.

A.D. 476
Last Roman emperor driven from throne.

Resource Directory

Media and Technology

 Color Transparencies 67, 70

Invasions of the Roman Empire to A.D. 476

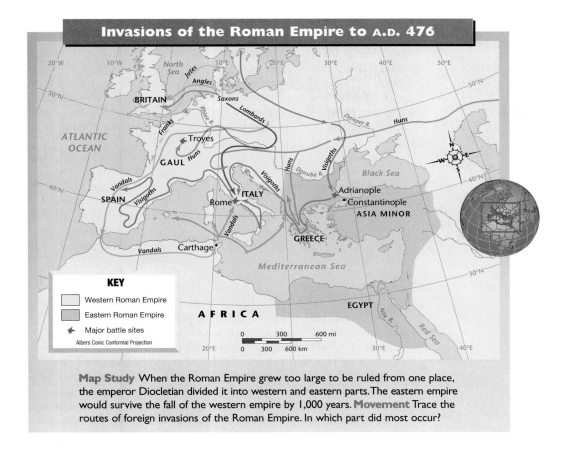

Map Study When the Roman Empire grew too large to be ruled from one place, the emperor Diocletian divided it into western and eastern parts. The eastern empire would survive the fall of the western empire by 1,000 years. **Movement** Trace the routes of foreign invasions of the Roman Empire. In which part did most occur?

A Mercenary Army Once, the Roman army had been made up of citizen soldiers ready to defend their land. Now the army was filled with **mercenaries,** foreign soldiers who serve only for pay. The problem with mercenaries is that they do not fight for any cause. They often switch sides if it is to their personal advantage. Rome's strength depended on a strong army loyal to the nation. Such an army was now just a memory.

The Size of the Empire The Roman Empire had grown too big to be ruled from one place. All over the empire, in Asia, Africa, and northern Europe, the enemies of Rome attacked. Tribes that the Romans had earlier conquered now poured over the empire's borders. This caused the empire to shrink.

Serious Economic Problems When Rome stopped conquering new lands, no new sources of wealth were available. This meant that taxes grew heavier. Further, the resources of the empire were being drained to pay an army that often would not fight. There was severe unemployment throughout the empire.

Expressing Problems Clearly
You may wish to **introduce** the skill by indicating that expressing a problem clearly is the most important step in solving it. Help students **practice** the skill by having them list reasons for the decline of the Roman Empire. Write their responses on the chalkboard. Encourage students to **apply** the skill by using the list to compose a paragraph that describes the reasons for the decline.

Answers to . . .
MAP STUDY

Most of the invasions took place in the western empire.

Critical Thinking

Recognizing Cause and Effect *Suitable as a whole class activity.* Present the following partially completed chart to students. Ask them to supply the missing causes and effects.

Cause	Effect
scarce food	
	less silver in each coin
Rome stopped conquering new lands.	
	Diocletian improved tax-collection system.
Diocletian improved tax-collection system.	More money was available to pay army.

Background

Links Across Place

The Visigoths The Visigoths, who had settled in what is now Romania, were one of the largest of the Germanic tribes that invaded the Roman Empire. Though deemed "barbaric" by the Romans, the Visigoths farmed and herded cattle, had their own language, and were fairly skilled metal workers. In response to a threat from other invaders, the Visigoths asked Rome for protection. The Romans allowed the Visigoths to settle in the empire but treated them cruelly. The Visigoths revolted in 378 and defeated the Roman army in battle. In 410, they captured and sacked Rome.

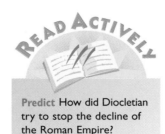

Predict How did Diocletian try to stop the decline of the Roman Empire?

Food was scarce. That made the price of food go up. To pay for this food, the government decided to produce more money in the form of coins. The value of those coins depended on the amount of silver in them. But since the government did not have much silver, it put less in each coin. So there was more money, but the money had less value. This situation is called **inflation.** If inflation is not controlled, money continues to buy less and less. Roman coins soon became worthless.

Trying to Stop the Decline Some emperors made strong efforts to stop the steady decline of the Roman Empire. While Diocletian persecuted Christians, he also worked to strengthen Rome. He enlarged the army and built new forts at the borders. He also improved the system of collecting taxes. This brought in more money to pay the army. Diocletian divided the empire into two parts to make it easier to rule. He ruled over the more wealthy east and appointed a co-emperor to rule over the west.

The Romans Accept Christianity

Diocletian and his co-emperor retired in A.D 305. A struggle for power followed. For seven years, generals fought each other for power until one—Constantine—came out the winner. As you read earlier, Constantine reported that the Christian God had helped his army win the battle for the control of Rome. A year later, Constantine proclaimed freedom of worship for people in the empire. No longer would Rome persecute the Christians. Christianity soon became the official religion of the Roman Empire—the one accepted by the government.

During Constantine's 25 years as emperor, he worked to strengthen the Christian church. In 330, Constantine moved his capital to the city of Byzantium (biz AN tee uhm). In his honor, the city was renamed Constantinople.

The Fall of Rome

Constantine had struggled to keep the empire together. But the forces pulling it apart were too great. After his death, invaders swept across Rome's borders and overwhelmed the empire. The invaders belonged to tribes from the north. Today, we call them Germanic tribes. The Romans called them barbarians. In the past, the Roman army had been able to defeat these

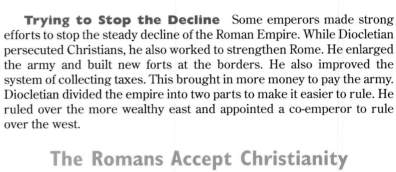

▼ This shows a Roman-style viaduct in Constantinople, the capital of the eastern Roman Empire. Today Constantinople is known as Istanbul, Turkey.

Resource Directory

Teaching Resources

📁 **Section Quiz** in the Chapter and Section Resources booklet, p. 131, covers the main ideas and key terms in the section. Available in Spanish in the Spanish Chapter and Section Resources booklet, p. 82.

📁 **Vocabulary** in the Chapter and Section Resources booklet, p. 133, provides a review of key terms in the chapter. Available in Spanish in the Spanish Chapter and Section Resources booklet, p. 84.

📁 **Reteaching** in the Chapter and Section Resources booklet, p. 134, provides a structure for students who may need additional help in mastering chapter content.

📁 **Enrichment** in the Chapter and Section Resources booklet, p. 135, extends chapter content and enriches students' understanding.

📁 **Spanish Glossary** in the Spanish Chapter and Section Resources, pp. 85–89, provides key terms translated from English to Spanish as well as definitions in Spanish.

◄ The Anglo-Saxons who invaded Roman England buried their kings in ships. At a site discovered in England in 1939, the ancient ship had rotted. Yet many solid gold items, including this helmet, remained.

tribes. Now, however, they could not stop the northerners. In the 400s, the Germanic tribes overran the empire. They captured and looted Rome in 410 and 455. The Roman emperor was almost powerless.

The last Roman emperor was 14-year-old Romulus Augustulus. His name recalled more than 1,000 years of Roman glory. But the boy emperor did not win glory for himself. In 476, a German general took power and sent him to work on a farm. After Romulus Augustulus, no emperor ruled over Rome and the western part of the empire.

However, even after Rome fell, the eastern part of the empire remained strong. Its capital, Constantinople, remained the center of another empire, the Byzantine empire, for another thousand years.

LINKS ACROSS TIME

Vandals Today, we call someone who destroys property and valuable things a *vandal*. The Vandals were one of the Germanic tribes that invaded the Roman Empire. They looted Rome in A.D. 455. They were no worse than the other Germanic tribes. But their name came to be connected to this kind of damaging behavior.

SECTION 5 REVIEW

1. **Define** (a) mercenary, (b) inflation.

2. **Identify** (a) Constantine, (b) Diocletian, (c) Constantinople.

3. Why did Roman money finally become worthless?

4. What did Diocletian do to make governing the Roman Empire easier?

Critical Thinking

5. **Expressing Problems Clearly** Summarize in two or three sentences the causes of the fall of the Roman Empire.

Activity

6. **Writing to Learn** Today, we think of the fall of the western Roman Empire in A.D. 476 as a great turning point in history. However, some historians think most people in those days hardly noticed any change. Why do you think that might be true?

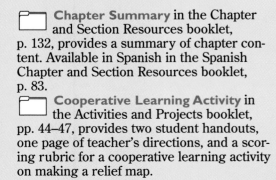

Chapter Summary in the Chapter and Section Resources booklet, p. 132, provides a summary of chapter content. Available in Spanish in the Spanish Chapter and Section Resources booklet, p. 83.

Cooperative Learning Activity in the Activities and Projects booklet, pp. 44–47, provides two student handouts, one page of teacher's directions, and a scoring rubric for a cooperative learning activity on making a relief map.

Media and Technology

Guided Reading Audiotapes (English and Spanish)

Reading Actively

Joji loved to read mystery stories. He was halfway through one when he thought to himself, "I want to know why this guy is going to the haunted house alone. What does he think he'll find there? Why doesn't he take someone with him?"

As he continued to read the story, Joji got excited again. "Wow!" he thought. "I bet the police will be there when the robber turns the corner. I can just see that robber's face when he gets caught. It will be just like that movie I saw once."

Get Ready

Joji was reading actively. He was enjoying what he was reading because he was actively participating in the story as he read. You can learn to do that, too. You can do it with everything you read, not just stories. You have been reading actively as you read this book, especially if you have paid attention to the hints in the margins labeled Read Actively.

Try It Out

Here are some strategies you can use to read actively.

A. Ask questions while you read. Joji did this when he asked himself why the hero was going into the haunted house alone. That helped Joji read to find out the answer. If you are reading a textbook, you might turn the headings into questions to ask yourself what you will find out as you read.

B. Connect what you read to your own life. Think about similar experiences you have had that can help you understand what you are reading. Joji's book reminded him of a movie he had seen. You can connect what you have read about ancient history in this book to your own life because you know something about what people need and how they act. And maybe you have read myths or stories or seen movies about the same topics.

C. Predict what you will find out. As you read, predict what will happen and why. Or think ahead to figure out how you think one fact you are reading might affect something else. See how your predictions match what you find out. What did Joji predict?

D. Visualize what things look like. As you read, form pictures in your mind. You can think about the expression on someone's face, as Joji did. You can also extend this strategy to think about how something smells or sounds or feels. This strategy can help you feel as though you are part of what you are reading.

Apply the Skill

Now practice by reading actively the boxed paragraphs about daily life in the streets of Rome. Use the strategies.

> The streets of Rome were very narrow and difficult to walk through, but that did not stop people from gathering there. Shops and their customers spilled out onto the streets. Butchers chopped meat and barbers shaved their customers right out in the open.
>
> Many Romans spent most of the day on the streets, rather than stay in their tiny, uncomfortable apartments. Children recited their lessons. People chatted with their friends and ran their businesses. Countless noises filled the air. Anyone walking through had to struggle with heavy crowds, full of shoving people.

1 Ask questions. Right after you read the first sentence, you might ask yourself why people could not succeed if they tried to hurry through the streets of Rome. What other questions did you ask yourself as you read?

2 Connect. What did you read in the paragraphs that made you think of something you have experienced or read about? Perhaps you have been in a crowd where you felt pushed from all sides.

3 Predict. Did you predict that the busy Roman streets would also be very noisy? What other predictions did you make? How did your predictions match what the paragraphs said?

4 Visualize. What would this street scene look like? What would it sound like? How might it smell?

Chapter 7 Review

Reviewing Main Ideas

1. Experience with kings made Romans want to limit their rulers' power.

2. Because its geographic setting was so favorable and its people so dedicated to its success, Rome conquered much of the known world and governed it fairly successfully.

3. Students' responses may include the development of concrete, aqueducts, the Roman arch, and the Roman system of roads. Aqueducts allowed Romans to bring water from the countryside to the cities.

4. Many poor people were unemployed and relied on handouts of grain from the government. Poor people lived in apartment buildings that frequently burned down.

5. Household slaves were often treated well, almost as though they were members of the family, while other slaves, working on farms or in mines or galleys, led short, miserable lives.

6. (a) God was loving and forgiving. (b) He promised that people who followed his teachings would have everlasting life.

7. Because Christians would not worship Roman gods, the Roman people suspected that Christians were trying to destroy the Roman state.

8. Mercenaries were working for pay, not out of loyalty to Rome, and paying for them helped ruin the economy.

9. Answers will vary. Answers may include references to the series of corrupt emperors who stole money from the treasury; Rome's army of unreliable mercenaries; the vast and unwieldy size of the empire; and the economic problems: high taxes, high food prices, and inflation.

10. Diocletian thought the empire was too big for one emperor to govern and that it could be better governed by two rulers.

Reviewing Key Terms

Sentences should show the correct meanings of words through context.

CHAPTER 7 Review and Activities

Reviewing Main Ideas

1. How did the experience with kings shape Romans' attitudes toward their republic?

2. Why was the Roman Empire successful?

3. List three major Roman advances in the field of technology. Then, choose one of them and describe its importance.

4. Give two examples of the way poor people lived in ancient Rome.

5. How were household slaves treated differently from other slaves?

6. (a) What were some teachings of Jesus?
(b) What did Jesus promise to his followers?

7. Why did the Romans persecute the early Christians?

8. What did mercenaries have to do with the decline of the Roman Empire?

9. Describe two possible reasons why the Roman Empire declined in power.

10. How was the division of Rome into two parts an attempt to restore its greatness?

Reviewing Key Terms

Use each key term below in a sentence that shows the meaning of the term.

1. republic
2. patrician
3. plebeian
4. consul
5. veto
6. dictator
7. province
8. aqueduct
9. circus
10. messiah
11. disciple
12. Gospel
13. epistle
14. martyr
15. mercenary
16. inflation

Critical Thinking

1. Recognizing Cause and Effect What good and bad effects resulted from the great size of the Roman Empire?

2. Drawing Conclusions Why did poor Romans and slaves find Christianity appealing?

Graphic Organizer

Copy the chart onto a sheet of paper. Then fill in the empty boxes to complete the chart.

	Roman Republic	Roman Empire	Christianity	Fall of Rome
Events				
People				
Achievements				

Graphic Organizer

	Roman Republic	Roman Empire	Christianity	Fall of Rome
Events	conquest of much of Italy and other lands, civil wars	first emperor, many years of peace	birth of Jesus, death of Jesus, persecution of Christians	series of bad rulers, economic problems, empire divided into two parts, Germanic invaders capture Rome
People	Julius Caesar	Augustus Caesar, Hadrian, Marcus Aurelius, Justinian	Jesus, Paul	Diocletian, Constantine
Achievements	brought stability and order, the Laws of the Twelve Tables	developments in mathematics, philosophy, architecture, law, and technology	spread of Christianity, writing of the Gospels and epistles	army enlarged, tax system improved, Christianity declared official religion

Map Activity

The Roman World
For each place listed below, write the letter from the map that shows its location.

1. Rome
2. Mediterranean Sea
3. Gaul
4. Judea
5. Britain
6. Greece
7. Constantinople

Place Location

Writing Activity

Writing a Short Story
Write a two-page fictional short story on one of the episodes that you read about in this chapter. Make your leading character a participant in the event you choose.

Skills Review

Turn to the Skills Activity. Then complete the following: (a) List the Read Actively strategies that can help you understand better what you read. (b) Briefly explain how to use each strategy.

Internet Activity
Use a search engine to find **The Ancient Rome Home Page.** Click on Chronology. Choose a time period and click on it. Use the Chronological Space/Time Index to travel to ancient Rome. Type a date in the box to see what was happening at that time. Then click on Quizzes to test your knowledge of the Roman emperors.

How Am I Doing?

Answer these questions to help you check your progress.

1. Can I describe how Rome's central location helped make it a powerful force in ancient times?

2. Do I understand something about the achievements of the ancient Romans?

3. Can I identify some events that shaped the history of the ancient Roman world?

4. Do I understand something about the beliefs of Christianity?

5. What information from this chapter could I use in my book project?

Internet Activity

If students are having difficulty finding this site, you may wish to have them use the following URL, which was accurate at the time this textbook was published:

http://eawc.evansville.edu/ropage.htm

You might also guide students to a search engine. Four of the most useful are Infoseek, AltaVista, Lycos, and Yahoo. For additional suggestions on using the Internet, refer to the Prentice Hall Social Studies' Educator's Handbook "Using the Internet," in the *Prentice Hall World Explorer Program Resources.*

For additional links to world history and culture topics, visit the Prentice Hall Home Page at:
http://www.phschool.com

How Am I Doing?

Point out to students that this checklist is a quick reminder of what they learned in the chapter. If their answer to any of the questions is *no* or if they are unsure, they may need to review the topic.

Critical Thinking

1. Answers will vary. One benefit was that a large empire provided a great source of revenue. One disadvantage was that it was difficult to govern.

2. Christianity implied the promise of salvation and relief from a poor and difficult life.

Map Activity

1. C	4. G	6. D
2. F	5. A	7. E
3. B		

Writing Activity

Students' stories will vary. Accept stories that accurately retell an event from the chapter and include a main character as a participant in the event.

Skills Review

(a) ask questions, connect, predict, visualize (b) Ask questions—turn headings into questions to ask yourself what you will find out as you read. Connect—think about how something is similar to experiences you have had. Predict—try to figure out what might happen and then match your predictions with what you find out. Visualize— form pictures in your mind as you read.

① Demonstrate knowledge of the ancient world through travel guides, posters, debates, and fairs.

② Explain key facts and ideas about the ancient world.

③ Apply knowledge of the text to creative presentations.

Lesson Plan

1 Engage

Warm-Up Activity

Review the Guiding Questions with the class. Ask students which question they found the most interesting when they began studying ancient civilizations. Which question gave them the most surprising answers? Then explain that the Project Menu offers several project options centered on the ancient world that will help them further explore a topic that interests them.

Activating Prior Knowledge

Ask students for examples of long-term projects they have worked on. Prompt the discussion by naming categories such as school projects, athletic or musical training, home projects, or scouting badge efforts. Ask students to recall challenges and strategies from these experiences.

THE ANCIENT WORLD
PROJECT POSSIBILITIES

The chapters in this book have some answers to these important questions.

☛ **What methods do people use today to try to understand cultures of the past?**

☛ **How did physical geography affect the growth of ancient civilizations?**

☛ **How did the beliefs and values of ancient civilizations affect the lives of their members?**

☛ **How did civilizations develop a government and an economic system?**

☛ **What accomplishments is each civilization known for?**

Doing projects is another way of answering the Guiding Questions in this book. Show what you know about the ancient world!

GEO CLEO

Project Menu

Now it's time for you to find your own answers by doing projects on your own or with a group. Here are some ways to make your own discoveries about the ancient world.

Ancient World Travel Guide As you study each civilization in this book, write a chapter for a travel guide to the world of ancient times. Create a map for each place, and write about its geography and history.

Include a picture of a special place or interesting feature of each civilization that travelers "must see." When you have finished all of the chapters, combine them to make a book.

Resource Directory

Teaching Resources

📁 **Book Projects** in the Activities and Projects booklet, pp. 8–19, provide a guide to completing the projects described on these two pages. Each project is supported by three pages of structured guidance.

From Questions to Careers

ARCHAEOLOGIST

Sometimes it seems amazing that we know so much about people and places that existed long ago. Since there were no cameras, no one took pictures of how it was back then. Often, there is no written record, either. The bits and pieces that we find out are like a jigsaw puzzle. Archaeologists are people who specialize in solving these puzzles.

Archaeologists study the past. They hunt for artifacts, such as pottery and tools. They examine very old, large structures like buildings and bridges. Archaeologists also study the natural objects that are found around these items such as bones, stones, and seeds. These ancient natural objects are called ecofacts.

Archaeologists may find artifacts and ecofacts in a variety of places. Some places, or sites, are easy to find, such as pyramids. Others are underground, underwater, or in caves.

Archaeologists make careful records of the items they find on a site. Often, they test the items to see how old they are.

Archaeologists study archaeology, history, languages, mathematics, and sciences. They work in excavation sites; in schools, teaching and researching; in museums; and in government jobs.

The Hall of Ancient Heritage Many ancient customs and activities such as games, sports, or celebrations still exist today. Choose one custom or activity from three or four civilizations in this book. Compare it with a modern custom or activity that seems similar to you. How are the versions alike? How are they different? What might be some reasons for those differences? To share your findings, create a poster with pictures and captions. Display this poster by itself or with others in a "Hall of Ancient Heritage" in your school.

Ancient Debate Which of the civilizations in this book made the greatest contributions to the modern world? Stage a debate with representatives from each civilization. To prove why your civilization is the best, you might research its form of government, art, inventions, language, science, literature, and other accomplishments. Visual aids such as pictures and posters could make your arguments more convincing. Rehearse your debate before presenting it to the class.

Life in the Ancient World Organize and hold an Ancient World Fair. Represent each of the civilizations in this book in your fair. You might have booths where students sell baked or fresh foods that represent each civilization. Other students can enact drama or sports that were popular in these civilizations. Include an art table, where visitors can make artwork or jewelry like that of the civilization. Other students can make or collect costumes for the participants to wear that look like the clothing of these civilizations.

2 Explore

Have students read Project Possibilities. Discuss archaeology as a career. List places where archaeologists work, such as universities and museums. If possible, ask an archaeologist to visit your class or arrange E-mail correspondence via the Internet.

3 Teach

Let students select a project. If you wish, assign projects to students. Group students according to their project selections. Suggest that students discuss research ideas and plan realistic schedules before getting started. If students are working cooperatively, help them clarify task assignments.

4 Assess

Designate a week as Project Week. Let students display or present their work.

Rubric

Acceptable projects follow the directions given in the Project Menu and include accurate facts and information.

Commendable projects reflect insightful comparisons of ancient and modern life, show evidence of careful research, and present knowledge of ancient civilizations.

Outstanding projects build on thorough research, showing originality and creativity and demonstrating thoughtful responses to the Guiding Questions.

Reference

TABLE OF CONTENTS

MAP AND GLOBE HANDBOOK

This Map and Globe Handbook is designed to help you develop some of the skills you need to be a world explorer. These can help you whether you explore from the top of an elephant in India or from a computer at school.

You can use the information in this handbook to improve your map and globe skills. But the best way to sharpen your skills is to practice. The more you practice, the better you'll get.

GEO CLEO and GEO LEO

Table of Contents

MAP AND GLOBE HANDBOOK

Using the Map and Globe Handbook

You may choose to present the Map and Globe Handbook as a special unit of study at the beginning of the year or at another point in the school year. As an alternative, you might prefer to choose among the activities in the Map and Globe Handbook to meet the specific needs of your class or of individual students.

Point out to students that they already know a great deal about maps. Ask them to sketch a quick map of the route from their house to school. Discuss the map elements that students include on their maps.

Read through the page with students.

Identify and define the five themes of geography.

Lesson Plan

1 Engage

Warm-Up Activity

Work with students to define the word *theme*. (An underlying idea built into or expanded upon in a work of art or study.)

Activating Prior Knowledge

Have students work in small groups for five minutes to write a definition of *geography*. Discuss their definitions. Then write the five themes on the chalkboard and ask students to break up their definitions, putting phrases under the proper headings. For example, if students wrote "studying where other countries are," that would fall under the theme of location. Add to students' definitions as needed.

2 Explore

Read the first verse of the poem "Midwest Town" by Ruth De Long Peterson to the class:

Farther east it wouldn't be on
    the map—
Too small—but here it rates a
    dot and a name.
In Europe it would wear a
    castle cap
Or have a cathedral rising like
    a flame.

Ask students to identify the geography themes in the verse (location and place).

Five Themes of Geography

Studying the geography of the entire world can be a huge task. You can make that task easier by using the five themes of geography: location, place, human-environment interaction, movement, and regions. The themes are tools you can use to organize information and to answer the where, why, and how of geography.

1 Location answers the question, "Where is it?" You can think of the location of a continent or a country as its address. You might give an absolute location such as "22 South Lake Street" or "40°N and 80°W." You might also use a relative address, telling where one place is by referring to another place. "Between school and the mall" and "eight miles east of Pleasant City" are examples of relative locations.

2 Place identifies the natural and human features that make one place different from every other place. You can identify a specific place by its landforms, climate, plants, animals, people, or cultures. You might even think of place as a geographic signature. Use the signature to help you understand the natural and human features that make one place different from every other place.

1. Location
Chicago, Illinois, occupies one location on the Earth. No other place has exactly the same absolute location.

2. Place
Ancient cultures in Egypt built distinctive pyramids. Use the theme of place to help you remember features that exist only in Egypt.

226

3 **Human-Environment Interaction** focuses on the relationship between people and the environment. As people live in an area, they often begin to make changes to it, usually to make their lives easier. For example, they might build a dam to control flooding during rainy seasons. Also, the environment can affect how people live, work, dress, travel, and communicate.

4 **Movement** answers the question "How do people, goods, and ideas move from place to place?" Remember that, often, what happens in one place can affect what happens in another. Use the theme of movement to help you trace the spread of goods, people, and ideas from one location to the next.

5 **Region** is the last geographic theme. A region is a group of places that share common features. Geographers divide the world into many types of regions. For example, countries, states, and cities are political regions. The people in these places live under the same type of government. Other features can be used to define regions. Places that have the same climate belong to a particular climate region. Places that share the same culture belong to a cultural region. The same place can be found in more than one region. The state of Hawaii is in the political region of the United States. Because it has a tropical climate, Hawaii is also part of a tropical climate region.

PRACTICE YOUR WORLD EXPLORER SKILLS

1 What is the absolute location of your school? What is one way to describe its relative location?

2 What might be a "geographic signature" of the town or city you live in?

3 Give an example of human-environment interaction where you live.

4 Name at least one thing that comes into your town or city and one that goes out. How is each moved? Where does it come from? Where does it go?

5 What are several regions you think your town or city belongs in?

3. Human-Environment Interaction
Peruvians have changed steep mountain slopes into terraces suitable for farming. Think how this environment looked before people made changes.

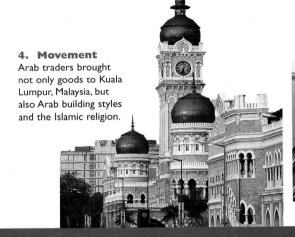

4. Movement
Arab traders brought not only goods to Kuala Lumpur, Malaysia, but also Arab building styles and the Islamic religion.

5. Regions
Wheat farming is an important activity in Kansas. This means that Kansas is part of a farming region.

Understanding Movements of the Earth

Planet Earth is part of our solar system. The Earth revolves around the sun in a nearly circular path called an orbit. A revolution, or one complete orbit around the sun, takes 365 1/4 days, or a year. As the Earth revolves around the sun, it is also spinning around in space. This movement is called a rotation. The Earth rotates on its axis—an invisible line through the center of the Earth from the North Pole to the South Pole. The Earth makes one full rotation about every 24 hours. As the Earth rotates, it is daytime on the side facing the sun. It is night on the side away from the sun.

The Earth's axis is tilted at an angle. Because of this tilt, sunlight strikes different parts of the Earth at certain points in the year, creating different seasons.

Earth's Revolution and the Seasons

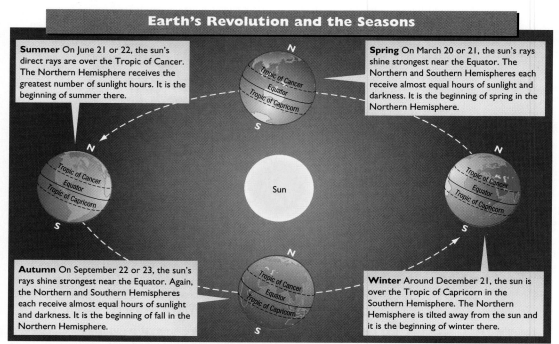

Summer On June 21 or 22, the sun's direct rays are over the Tropic of Cancer. The Northern Hemisphere receives the greatest number of sunlight hours. It is the beginning of summer there.

Spring On March 20 or 21, the sun's rays shine strongest near the Equator. The Northern and Southern Hemispheres each receive almost equal hours of sunlight and darkness. It is the beginning of spring in the Northern Hemisphere.

Autumn On September 22 or 23, the sun's rays shine strongest near the Equator. Again, the Northern and Southern Hemispheres each receive almost equal hours of sunlight and darkness. It is the beginning of fall in the Northern Hemisphere.

Winter Around December 21, the sun is over the Tropic of Capricorn in the Southern Hemisphere. The Northern Hemisphere is tilted away from the sun and it is the beginning of winter there.

▲ **Location** This diagram shows how the Earth's tilt and orbit around the sun combine to create the seasons. Remember, in the Southern Hemisphere the seasons are reversed.

PRACTICE YOUR WORLD EXPLORER SKILLS

① What causes the seasons in the Northern Hemisphere to be the opposite of those in the Southern Hemisphere?

② During which two months of the year do the Northern and Southern Hemispheres have about equal hours of daylight and darkness?

228   MAP AND GLOBE HANDBOOK

Maps and Globes Represent the Earth

Globes

A globe is a scale model of the Earth. It shows the actual shapes, sizes, and locations of all the Earth's landmasses and bodies of water. Features on the surface of the Earth are drawn to scale on a globe. This means a smaller unit of measure on the globe stands for a larger unit of measure on the Earth.

Because a globe is made in the true shape of the Earth, it offers these advantages for studying the Earth.

- The shape of all land and water bodies are accurate.
- Compass directions from one point to any other point are correct.
- The distance from one location to another is always accurately represented.

However, a globe presents some disadvantages for studying the Earth. Because a globe shows the entire Earth, it cannot show small areas in great detail. Also, a globe is not easily folded and carried from one place to another. For these reasons, geographers often use maps to learn about the Earth.

Maps

A map is a drawing or representation, on a flat surface, of a region. A map can show details too small to be seen on a globe. Floor plans, mall directories, and road maps are among the maps we use most often.

While maps solve some of the problems posed by globes, they have some disadvantages of their own. Maps flatten the real round world. Mapmakers cut, stretch, push, and pull some parts of the Earth to get it all flat on paper. As a result, some locations may be distorted. That is, their size, shape, and relative location may not be accurate. For example, on most maps of the entire world, the size and shape of the Antarctic and Arctic regions are not accurate.

PRACTICE YOUR WORLD EXPLORER SKILLS

1. What is the main difference between a globe and a map?

2. What is one advantage of using a globe instead of a map?

Global Gores

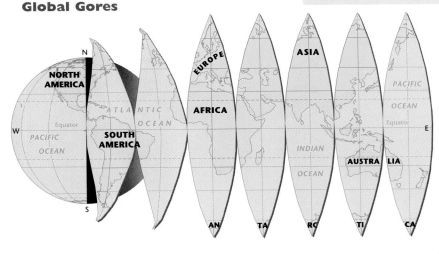

◀ **Location**
When mapmakers flatten the surface of the Earth, curves become straight lines. As a result, size, shape, and distance are distorted.

Teaching Resources

📁 **Comparing Globes and Maps,** in the Social Studies and Geography Skills booklet, p. 12, helps students understand and apply the skill of understanding differences between maps and globes.

Lesson Objective

Compare maps and globes as representations of the Earth.

Lesson Plan

1 Engage
Warm-Up Activity

Ask students what it might be like to see the Earth from space.

Activating Prior Knowledge

Ask students whether they would use a map or a globe to plan a vacation. Discuss how they might use both.

2 Explore

Have students read the page and study the illustrations. Discuss with them similarities and differences between maps and globes.

3 Teach

Roughly sketch the continents on a large grapefruit with a ballpoint pen. Explain that the grapefruit is like the Earth. Carefully peel the grapefruit and then challenge students to reassemble the continents into a flat map.

4 Assess

Assess students' understanding by asking them to complete the Practice Your World Explorer Skills.

Answers to ...

PRACTICE YOUR WORLD EXPLORER SKILLS

1. A globe is a scale model of the Earth; a map is a drawing of the Earth or a region of it.
2. Students should be able to support their choices of either accurate shape, true direction, or accurate distance.

1 Define the hemispheres of the Earth.

2 Locate places on a map using the coordinates of latitude and longitude.

Lesson Plan

1 Engage

Warm-Up Activity

Present this challenge to the class. Tell students that they are sailing alone around the world. They have been in a huge storm and have run out of food. They have not seen land for weeks, but when they radio for extra supplies, they can give their exact location. How? (They know their latitude and longitude.)

Activating Prior Knowledge

Draw an unlabeled grid on the chalkboard. Place a large dot somewhere on the grid. Ask students how they could use the grid to describe where the dot is.

Locating Places on a Map or a Globe

The Hemispheres

Another name for a round ball like a globe is a sphere. The Equator, an imaginary line halfway between the North and South Poles, divides the globe into two hemispheres. (The prefix *hemi* means "half.") Land and water south of the Equator are in the Southern Hemisphere. Land and water north of the Equator are in the Northern Hemisphere.

Mapmakers sometimes divide the globe along an imaginary line that runs from North Pole to South Pole. This line, called the Prime Meridian, divides the globe into the Eastern and Western Hemispheres.

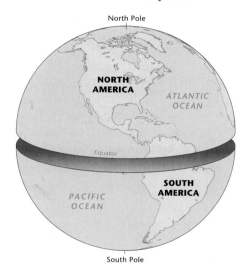

▲ The Equator divides the Northern Hemisphere from the Southern Hemisphere.

▲ The Prime Meridian divides the Eastern Hemisphere from the Western Hemisphere.

Resource Directory

Teaching Resources

 Understanding Hemispheres, in the Social Studies and Geography Skills booklet, p. 7, helps students understand and apply the skill of identifying hemispheres.

Media and Technology

Color Transparency 98

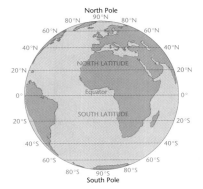

Parallels of Latitude

The Equator, at 0° latitude, is the starting place for measuring latitude or distances north and south. Most globes do not show every parallel of latitude. They may show every 10, 20, or even 30 degrees.

The Global Grid

Two sets of lines cover most globes. One set of lines runs parallel to the Equator. These lines, including the Equator, are called *parallels of latitude*. They are measured in degrees (°). One degree of latitude represents a distance of about 70 miles (112 km). The Equator has a location of 0°. The other parallels of latitude tell the direction and distance from the Equator to another location.

The second set of lines runs north and south. These lines are called *meridians of longitude*. Meridians show the degrees of longitude east or west of the Prime Meridian, which is located at 0°. A meridian of longitude tells the direction and distance from the Prime Meridian to another location. Unlike parallels, meridians are not the same distance apart everywhere on the globe.

Together the pattern of parallels of latitude and meridians of longitude is called the global grid. Using the lines of latitude and longitude, you can locate any place on Earth. For example, the location of 30° north latitude and 90° west longitude is usually written as 30°N, 90°W. Only one place on Earth has these coordinates—the city of New Orleans, in the state of Louisiana.

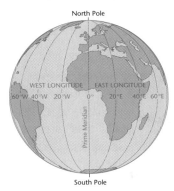

Meridians of Longitude

The Prime Meridian, at 0° longitude, runs from pole to pole through Greenwich, England. It is the starting place for measuring longitude or distances east and west. Each meridian of longitude meets its opposite longitude at the North and South Poles.

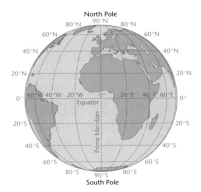

The Global Grid

By using lines of latitude and longitude, you can give the absolute location of any place on the Earth.

PRACTICE YOUR WORLD EXPLORER SKILLS

1. Which continents lie completely in the Northern Hemisphere? The Western Hemisphere?

2. Is there land or water at 20°S latitude and the Prime Meridian? At the Equator and 60°W longitude?

2 Explore

Read through these two pages with students. Using a large map, have students begin at the Prime Meridian and put their fingers on each of the meridians of longitude as they move east and then west. Do the same with the parallels of latitude, moving from the Equator to the North Pole and then to the South Pole. Some students may need help in understanding the definition of *parallel*. (Parallel lines are lines that never meet.)

3 Teach

Ask a volunteer to work with a large map or globe. Have other students name cities around the world. The volunteer must locate them and state their coordinates.

4 Assess

To assess students' understanding, give students coordinates that you have found in an atlas and ask them to locate the city. Have students discuss the process. Use students' discussion to assess their understanding of how to locate places on maps and globes.

Teaching Resources

 Understanding Latitude and Longitude and Using Latitude and Longitude, in the Social Studies and Geography Skills booklet, pp. 10–11, helps students understand and apply the skill of reading latitude and longitude lines.

Media and Technology

Color Transparency 99

Answers to . . .

PRACTICE YOUR WORLD EXPLORER SKILLS

1. Asia, North America, Europe; North America, South America
2. water; land

I magine trying to flatten out a complete orange peel. The peel would split. The shape would change. You would have to cut the peel to get it to lie flat. In much the same way, maps cannot show the correct size and shape of every landmass or body of water on the Earth's curved surface. Maps shrink some places and stretch others. This shrinking and stretching is called distortion—*a change made to a shape.*

To make up for this disadvantage, mapmakers use different map projections. Each map projection is a way of showing the round Earth on flat paper. Each type of projection has some distortion. No one projection can accurately show the correct area, shape, distance, and direction for the Earth's surface. Mapmakers use the projection that has the least distortion for the information they are studying.

Same-Shape Maps

Some map projections can accurately show the shapes of landmasses. However, these projections often greatly distort the size of landmasses as well as the distance between them.

One of the most common same-shape maps is a Mercator projection, named for the mapmaker who invented it. The Mercator projection accurately shows shape and direction, but it distorts distance and size. In this projection, the northern and southern areas of the globe appear stretched more than areas near the Equator. Because the projection shows true directions, ships' navigators use it to chart a straight line course between two ports.

Mercator Projection

Equal-Area Maps

Some map projections can show the correct size of landmasses. Maps that use these projections are called equal-area maps. In order to show the correct size of landmasses, these maps usually distort shapes. The distortion is usually greater at the edges of the map and less at the center.

Robinson Maps

Many of the maps in this book use the Robinson projection. This is a compromise between the Mercator and equal-area projections. It gives a useful overall picture of the world. The Robinson projection keeps the size and shape relationships of most continents and oceans but does distort size of the polar regions.

Azimuthal Maps

Another kind of projection shows true compass direction. Maps that use this projection are called azimuthal maps. Such maps are easy to recognize—they are usually circular. Azimuthal maps are often used to show the areas of the North and South Poles. However, azimuthal maps distort scale, area, and shape.

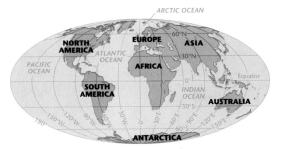

Equal-Area Projection

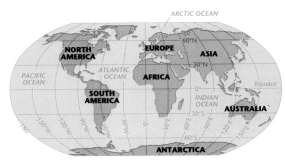

Robinson Projection

Azimuthal Projection

PRACTICE YOUR WORLD EXPLORER SKILLS

1. What feature is distorted on an equal-area map?

2. Would you use a Mercator projection to find the exact distance between two locations? Tell why or why not.

3. Which would be a better choice for studying the Antarctic—an azimuthal projection or a Robinson projection? Explain.

2 Explore

After students have read the two pages, have them look up the word *distortion* in a dictionary. Ask them why we use maps that we know are distorted. (All maps are somewhat distorted.)

3 Teach

Students can practice the skill by comparing the maps to a globe. Ask them to note especially the sizes and positions of Greenland and Antarctica.

To apply their understanding of the skill, students can suggest reasons why many maps use the Robinson projection. (It shows the sizes and shapes of the continents with the least amount of distortion.)

4 Assess

Assess students' understanding by the accuracy of their answers.

Media and Technology

 Color Transparency 100

Answers to...

PRACTICE YOUR WORLD EXPLORER SKILLS

1. shapes
2. No; the Mercator projection distorts distances.
3. An azimuthal projection centered on the South Pole would show all of Antarctica, a Robinson projection would not.

Mapmakers provide several clues to help you understand the information on a map. As an explorer, it is your job to read and interpret these clues.

Compass
Many maps show north at the top of the map. One way to show direction on a map is to use an arrow that points north. There may be an N shown with the arrow. Many maps give more information about direction by displaying a compass showing the directions, north, east, south, and west. The letters N, E, S, and W are placed to indicate these directions.

Title
The title of a map is the most basic clue. It signals what kinds of information you are likely to find on the map. A map titled *West Africa: Population Density* will be most useful for locating information about where people live in West Africa.

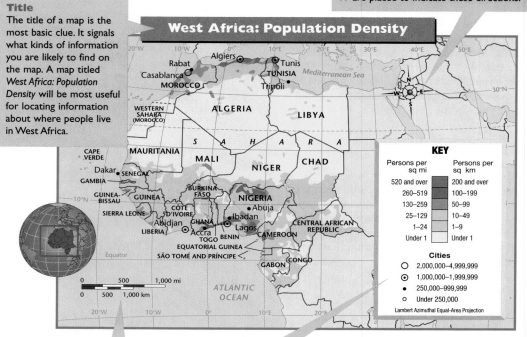

West Africa: Population Density

Scale
A map scale helps you find the actual distances between points shown on the map. You can measure the distance between any two points on the map, compare them to the scale, and find out the actual distance between the points. Most map scales show distances in both miles and kilometers.

Key
Often a map has a key, or legend, that shows the symbols used on the map and what each one means. On some maps, color is used as a symbol. On those maps, the key also tells the meaning of each color.

PRACTICE YOUR WORLD EXPLORER SKILLS

1. What part of a map tells you what the map is about?

2. Where on the map should you look to find out the meaning of this symbol? •

3. What part of the map can you use to find the distance between two cities?

234   MAP AND GLOBE HANDBOOK

Comparing Maps of Different Scale

ere are three maps drawn to three different scales. The first map shows Moscow's location in the northeastern portion of Russia. This map shows the greatest area—a large section of northern Europe. It has the smallest scale (1 inch = about 900 miles) and shows the fewest details. This map can tell you what direction to travel to reach Moscow from Finland.

Find the red box on Map 1. It shows the whole area covered by Map 2. Study Map 2. It gives a closer look at the city of Moscow. It shows the fea-

tures around the city, the city's boundary, and the general shape of the city. This map can help you find your way from the airport to the center of town.

Now find the red box on Map 2. This box shows the area shown on Map 3. This map moves you closer into the city. Like the zoom on a computer or camera, Map 3 shows the smallest area but has the greatest detail. This map has the largest scale (1 inch = about 0.8 miles). This is the map to use to explore downtown Moscow.

Map 1

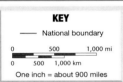

KEY

— National boundary

0   500   1,000 mi

0   500   1,000 km

One inch = about 900 miles

Map 2

KEY

▢ Built-up area

— Road or street

0   5   10 mi

0   5   10 km

One inch = about 12.5 miles

Map 3

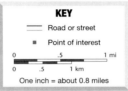

KEY

⋯ Road or street

■ Point of interest

0   .5   1 mi

0   .5   1 km

One inch = about 0.8 miles

PRACTICE YOUR WORLD EXPLORER SKILLS

1 Which map would be best for finding the location of Red Square? Why?

2 Which map best shows Moscow's location relative to Poland? Explain.

3 Which map best shows the area immediately surrounding the city?

MAP AND GLOBE HANDBOOK   **235**

Teaching Resources

📁 **Comparing Maps of Different Scale,** in the Social Studies and Geography Skills booklet, p. 6, helps students understand and use maps of different scale.

Lesson Objective

Use political maps.

Lesson Plan

1 Engage

Warm-Up Activity

To introduce the skill, tell students that American writer Mark Twain once wrote about people in a hot-air balloon who were confused because the ground below them was not colored like maps.

Activating Prior Knowledge

Point out that the word *political* comes from a Greek word meaning "citizen." A political map is one that emphasizes the boundaries of an area established by its citizens.

2 Explore

Read through the page with students. Make sure they realize that a political map mainly shows how people have divided and named the land.

3 Teach

Ask students to practice using a political map by locating a boundary between countries, the capital of Russia, and a river that is also a boundary.

4 Assess

Have students complete the Practice Your World Explorer Skills. Assess their understanding by the accuracy of their answers.

Answers to ...

PRACTICE YOUR WORLD EXPLORER SKILLS

1. red line 2. star in a circle; solid circle 3. none

Political Maps

apmakers create maps to show all kinds of information. The kind of information presented affects the way a map looks. One type of map is called a political map. Its main purpose is to show continents, countries, and divisions within countries such as states or provinces. Usually different colors are used to show different countries or divisions within a country. The colors do not have any special meaning. They are used only to make the map easier to read.

Political maps also show where people have built towns and cities. Symbols can help you tell capital cities from other cities and towns. Even though political maps do not give information that shows what the land looks like, they often include some physical features such as oceans, lakes, and rivers.

Political maps usually have many labels. They give country names, and the names of capital and major cities. Bodies of water such as lakes, rivers, oceans, seas, gulfs, and bays are also labeled.

PRACTICE YOUR WORLD EXPLORER SKILLS

1. What symbol shows the continental boundary?

2. What symbol is used to indicate a capital city? A major city?

3. What kinds of landforms are shown on this map?

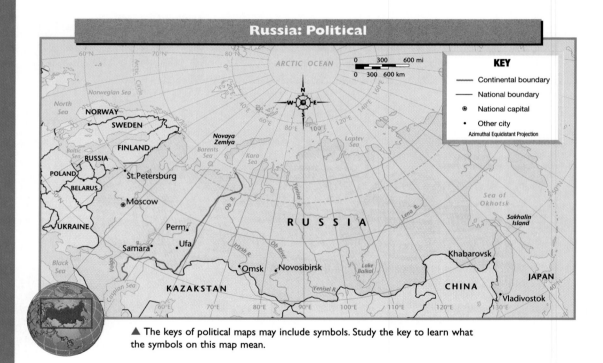

▲ The keys of political maps may include symbols. Study the key to learn what the symbols on this map mean.

Resource Directory

Teaching Resources

Reading a Political Map, in the Social Studies and Geography Skills booklet, p. 19, helps students practice using political maps.

Physical Maps

Like political maps, physical maps show country labels and labels for capital cities. However, physical maps also show what the land of a region looks like by showing the major physical features such as plains, hills, plateaus, or mountains. Labels give the names of features such as mountain peaks, mountains, plateaus, and river basins.

In order to tell one landform from another, physical maps often show elevation and relief.

Elevation is the height of the land above sea level. Physical maps in this book use color to show elevation. Browns and oranges show higher lands while blues and greens show lands that are at or below sea level.

Relief shows how quickly the land rises or falls. Hills, mountains, and plateaus are shown on relief maps using shades of gray. Level or nearly level land is shown without shading. Darkly shaded areas indicate steeper lands.

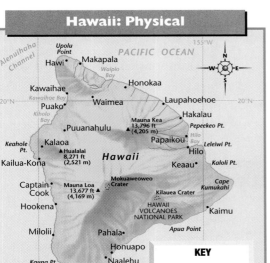

Hawaii: Physical

PRACTICE YOUR WORLD EXPLORER SKILLS

1. How is relief shown on the map to the left?

2. How can you use relief to decide which areas will be the most difficult to climb?

3. What information is given with the name of a mountain peak?

▲ On a physical map, shading is sometimes used to show relief. Use the shading to locate the mountains in Hawaii.

▼ Mauna Kea, an extinct volcano, is the highest peak in the state of Hawaii. Find Mauna Kea on the map.

237

Teaching Resources

📁 **Elevation on a Map,** in the Social Studies and Geography Skills booklet, p. 20, helps students understand and read physical maps that show elevation of land.

Lesson Objective

Use physical maps.

Lesson Plan

1 Engage
Warm-Up Activity

To introduce the skill, tell students that they are going for a hike in the mountains. Encourage them to consider that a map showing the heights of the mountains might be useful.

Activating Prior Knowledge

Remind students that political maps do not necessarily show features of the landscape.

2 Explore

Have students read the page. Point out that a physical map makes the physical features of a place clearer than a political map does.

3 Teach

Students can practice using a physical map by checking this one for the highest mountain it shows. Have students apply the skill by pointing out other physical features on the map.

4 Assess

Have students complete the Practice Your World Explorer Skills. Assess their understanding by the accuracy of their answers.

Answers to . . .

PRACTICE YOUR WORLD EXPLORER SKILLS

1. shading
2. Darkly shaded areas are steep and more difficult to climb.
3. its elevation

As you explore the world, you will encounter many different kinds of special purpose maps. For example, a road map is a special purpose map. The title of each special purpose map tells the purpose and content of the map. Usually a special purpose map highlights only one kind of information. Examples of special purpose maps include land use, population distribution, recreation, transportation, natural resources, or weather.

The key on a special purpose map is very important. Even though a special purpose map shows only one kind of information, it may present many different pieces of data. This data can be shown in symbols, colors, or arrows. In this way, the key acts like a dictionary for the map.

Reading a special purpose map is a skill in itself. Look at the map below. First, try to get an overall sense of what it shows. Then, study the map to identify its main ideas. For example, one main idea of this map is that much of the petroleum production in the region takes place around the Persian Gulf.

1. What part of a special purpose map tells what information is contained on the map?

2. What part of a special purpose map acts like a dictionary for the map?

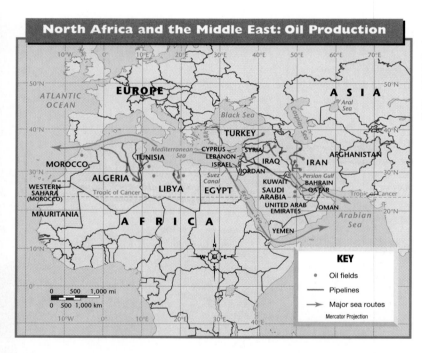

North Africa and the Middle East: Oil Production

KEY
- • Oil fields
- — Pipelines
- → Major sea routes

Mercator Projection

◄ The title on a special purpose map indicates what information can be found on the map. The symbols used on the map are explained in the map's key.

Landforms, Climate Regions, and Natural Vegetation Regions

Maps that show landforms, climate, and vegetation regions are special purpose maps. Unlike the boundary lines on a political map, the boundary lines on these maps do not separate the land into exact divisions. A tropical wet climate gradually changes to a tropical wet and dry climate. A tundra gradually changes to an ice cap. Even though the boundaries between regions may not be exact, the information on these maps can help you understand the region and the lives of people in it.

Landforms

Understanding how people use the land requires an understanding of the shape of the land itself. The four most important landforms are mountains, hills, plateaus, and plains. Human activity in every region in the world is influenced by these landforms.

- **Mountains** are high and steep. Most are wide at the bottom and rise to a narrow peak or ridge. Most geographers classify a mountain as land that rises at least 2,000 feet (610 m) above sea level. A series of mountains is called a mountain range.

- **Hills** rise above surrounding land and have rounded tops. Hills are lower and usually less steep than mountains. The elevation of surrounding land determines whether a landform is called a mountain or a hill.
- A **plateau** is a large, mostly flat area of land that rises above the surrounding land. At least one side of a plateau has a steep slope.
- **Plains** are large areas of flat or gently rolling land. Plains have few changes in elevation. Many plains areas are located along coasts. Others are located in the interior regions of some continents.

▶ A satellite view of the Earth showing North and South America. What landforms are visible in the photograph?

239

Teaching Resources

📁 **Four Types of Landforms,** in the Social Studies and Geography Skills booklet, p. 21, helps students understand and read maps that show mountains, hills, plateaus, and plains.

2 Explore

Write the terms *landforms, climate regions,* and *natural vegetation regions* on the chalkboard. As students read the material on this page and the following page, have them find examples for each term.

3 Teach

Divide the class into small groups. Ask each group to draw a picture of one of the following landforms: a mountain, a hill, a plateau, a plain. Then ask each group to find the landform on a map in this book or in an atlas.

Direct each student to choose one of the 12 climate types. Ask them to use the maps in this book or in an atlas to find a place in the world with that climate. Then have students use one of the natural vegetation maps in the textbook to figure out which of the 12 natural vegetation regions covers that climate location.

Climate Regions

Another important influence in the ways people live their lives is the climate of their region. Climate is the weather of a given location over a long period of time. Use the descriptions in the table below to help you visualize the climate regions shown on maps.

Climate	Temperatures	Precipitation
Tropical		
Tropical wet	Hot all year round	Heavy all year round
Tropical wet and dry	Hot all year round	Heavy when sun is overhead, dry other times
Dry		
Semiarid	Hot summers, mild to cold winters	Light
Arid	Hot days, cold nights	Very light
Mild		
Mediterranean	Hot summers, cool winters	Dry summers, wet winters
Humid subtropical	Hot summers, cool winters	Year round, heavier in summer than in winter
Marine west coast	Warm summers, cool winters	Year round, heavier in winter than in summer
Continental		
Humid continental	Hot summers, cold winters	Year round, heavier in summer than in winter
Subarctic	Cool summers, cold winters	Light
Polar		
Tundra	Cool summers, very cold winters	Light
Ice Cap	Cold all year round	Light
Highlands	Varies, depending on altitude and direction of prevailing winds	Varies, depending on altitude and direction of prevailing winds

Resource Directory

Teaching Resources

Reading a Climate Map, in the Social Studies and Geography Skills booklet, p. 26, helps students understand and read maps that show different climate regions.

Natural Vegetation Regions

Natural vegetation is the plant life that grows wild without the help of humans. A world vegetation map tells what the vegetation in a place would be if people had not cut down forests or cleared grasslands. The table below provides descriptions of natural vegetation regions shown on maps. Comparing climate and vegetation regions can help you see the close relationship between climate and vegetation.

Vegetation	Description
Tropical rain forest	Tall, close-growing trees forming a canopy over smaller trees, dense growth in general
Deciduous forest	Trees and plants that regularly lose their leaves after each growing season
Mixed forest	Both leaf-losing and cone-bearing trees, no type of tree dominant
Coniferous forest	Cone-bearing trees, evergreen trees and plants
Mediterranean vegetation	Evergreen shrubs and small plants
Tropical savanna	Tall grasses with occasional trees and shrubs
Temperate grassland	Tall grasses with occasional stands of trees
Desert scrub	Low shrubs and bushes, hardy plants
Desert	Little or no vegetation
Tundra	Low shrubs, mosses, lichens; no trees
Ice Cap	No vegetation
Highlands	Varies, depending on altitude and direction of prevailing winds

PRACTICE YOUR WORLD EXPLORER SKILLS

1. How are mountains and hills similar? How are they different?

2. What is the difference between a plateau and a plain?

Teaching Resources

📁 **Reading a Natural Vegetation Map,** in the Social Studies and Geography Skills booklet, p. 25, helps students understand and read maps that show natural vegetation regions.

4 Assess

Ask students to complete the Practice Your World Explorer Skills. Assess their understanding of landforms by the accuracy of their answers.

Assess students' understanding of the effect of climate on vegetation by asking them to share the results of their work in finding places with their assigned landform, climate, and vegetation. Have students check one another's work and match appropriate climate and vegetation regions.

Answers to ...

PRACTICE YOUR WORLD EXPLORER SKILLS

1. Mountains and hills rise above the surrounding land. Hills are usually lower and less steep than mountains.
2. Both plains and plateaus are mostly flat areas. A plateau rises above the surrounding land, and one side may have a steep slope.

Atlas

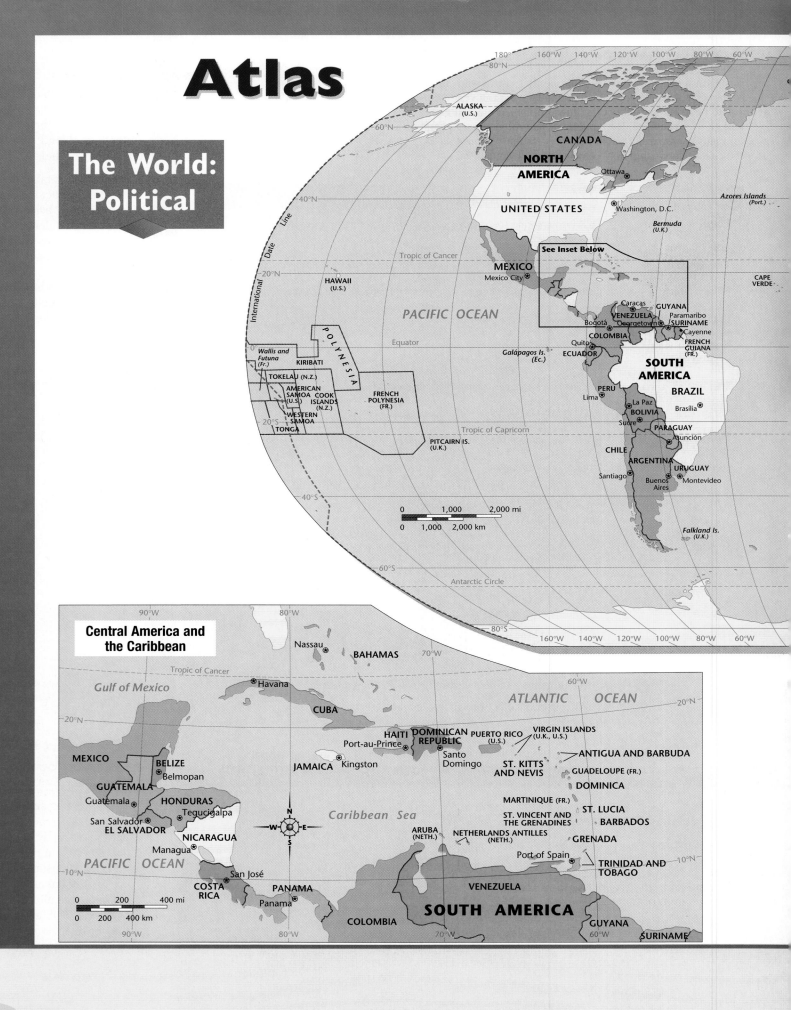

ALASKA (U.S.)

CANADA

NORTH AMERICA

Ottawa ⊛

Azores Islands (Port.)

UNITED STATES

Washington, D.C. ⊛

Bermuda (U.K.)

Tropic of Cancer

See Inset Below

MEXICO

Mexico City ⊛

CAPE VERDE

HAWAII (U.S.)

PACIFIC OCEAN

Caracas ⊛
VENEZUELA
Georgetown ⊛
GUYANA
Paramaribo ⊛
SURINAME

Bogotá ⊛
COLOMBIA
Quito ⊛
ECUADOR

Cayenne
FRENCH GUIANA (FR.)

Equator

Galápagos Is. (Ec.)

SOUTH AMERICA

International Date Line

Wallis and Futuna (Fr.)
KIRIBATI

POLYNESIA

TOKELAU (N.Z.)

AMERICAN SAMOA (U.S.)
COOK ISLANDS (N.Z.)

FRENCH POLYNESIA (FR.)

WESTERN SAMOA
TONGA

PERU
Lima ⊛

La Paz ⊛
BOLIVIA
Sucre ⊛

BRAZIL

Brasília ⊛

PARAGUAY
Asunción ⊛

Tropic of Capricorn

PITCAIRN IS. (U.K.)

CHILE

ARGENTINA

URUGUAY

Santiago ⊛

Buenos Aires ⊛
Montevideo ⊛

0   1,000   2,000 mi
0   1,000   2,000 km

Falkland Is. (U.K.)

Antarctic Circle

Central America and the Caribbean

90°W   80°W

Nassau ⊛
BAHAMAS
70°W

Tropic of Cancer

Gulf of Mexico

⊛ Havana

CUBA

ATLANTIC OCEAN

60°W

20°N

MEXICO

BELIZE
⊛ Belmopan

HAITI
Port-au-Prince ⊛
JAMAICA
Kingston ⊛

DOMINICAN REPUBLIC
Santo Domingo

PUERTO RICO (U.S.)

VIRGIN ISLANDS (U.K., U.S.)

ANTIGUA AND BARBUDA

ST. KITTS AND NEVIS

GUADELOUPE (FR.)

DOMINICA

GUATEMALA
Guatemala ⊛

HONDURAS
Tegucigalpa ⊛

MARTINIQUE (FR.)

ST. VINCENT AND THE GRENADINES

ST. LUCIA

BARBADOS

San Salvador ⊛
EL SALVADOR

NICARAGUA
Managua ⊛

Caribbean Sea

ARUBA (NETH.)

NETHERLANDS ANTILLES (NETH.)

GRENADA

PACIFIC OCEAN

COSTA RICA
San José ⊛

PANAMA
Panama ⊛

VENEZUELA

Port of Spain ⊛

TRINIDAD AND TOBAGO

10°N

0   200   400 mi
0   200   400 km

COLOMBIA

SOUTH AMERICA

GUYANA

SURINAME

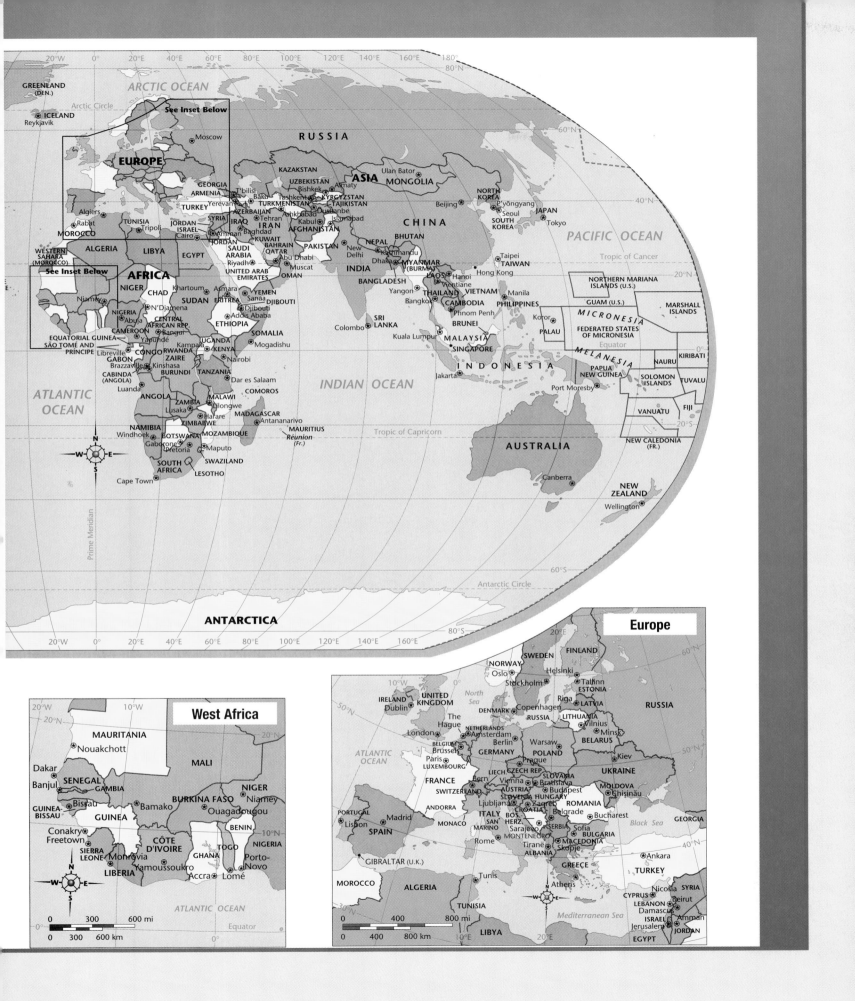

ATLAS 243

The World: Physical

ARCTIC OCEAN

GREENLAND (DEN.)

Beaufort Sea

Yukon R.

Mackenzie R.

Bering Sea

Aleutian Islands

ROCKY MOUNTAINS

GREAT PLAINS

NORTH AMERICA

CANADIAN SHIELD

Hudson Bay

Missouri R.

Great Lakes

St. Lawrence R.

Colorado R.

Rio Grande

SIERRA MADRE ORIENTAL

SIERRA MADRE OCCIDENTAL

Mississippi R.

APPALACHIAN MTS.

ATLANTIC OCEAN

Tropic of Cancer

Gulf of Mexico

West Indies

Caribbean Sea

Hawaiian Islands

P O L Y N E S I A

PACIFIC OCEAN

Equator

Orinoco R.

GUIANA HIGHLANDS

AMAZON BASIN

Amazon R.

SOUTH AMERICA

BRAZILIAN HIGHLANDS

ANDES MOUNTAINS

Tropic of Capricorn

PAMPAS

Rio de la Plata

PATAGONIA

Cape Horn

Drake Passage

Antarctic Circle

ANTARCTIC PENINSULA

180° 160°W 140°W 120°W 100°W 80°W 60°W

80°N
60°N
40°N
20°N
0°
20°S
40°S
60°S
80°S

160°W 140°W 120°W 100°W 80°W 60°W

KEY

Elevation

Feet		Meters
Over 13,000		Over 3,960
6,500–13,000		1,980–3,960
1,600–6,500		480–1,980
650–1,600		200–480
0–650		0–200
Below sea level		Below sea level

Ice cap

Ice shelf

Robinson Projection

South Pole

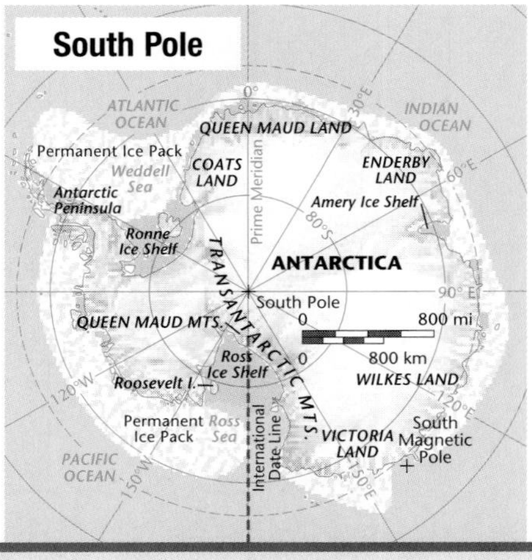

ATLANTIC OCEAN

QUEEN MAUD LAND

INDIAN OCEAN

Permanent Ice Pack

Weddell Sea

COATS LAND

ENDERBY LAND

Antarctic Peninsula

Amery Ice Shelf

Ronne Ice Shelf

Prime Meridian

ANTARCTICA

South Pole

0   800 mi

0   800 km

QUEEN MAUD MTS.

TRANSANTARCTIC MTS.

Ross Ice Shelf

WILKES LAND

Roosevelt I.

Permanent Ice Pack

Ross Sea

VICTORIA LAND

South Magnetic Pole

PACIFIC OCEAN

International Date Line

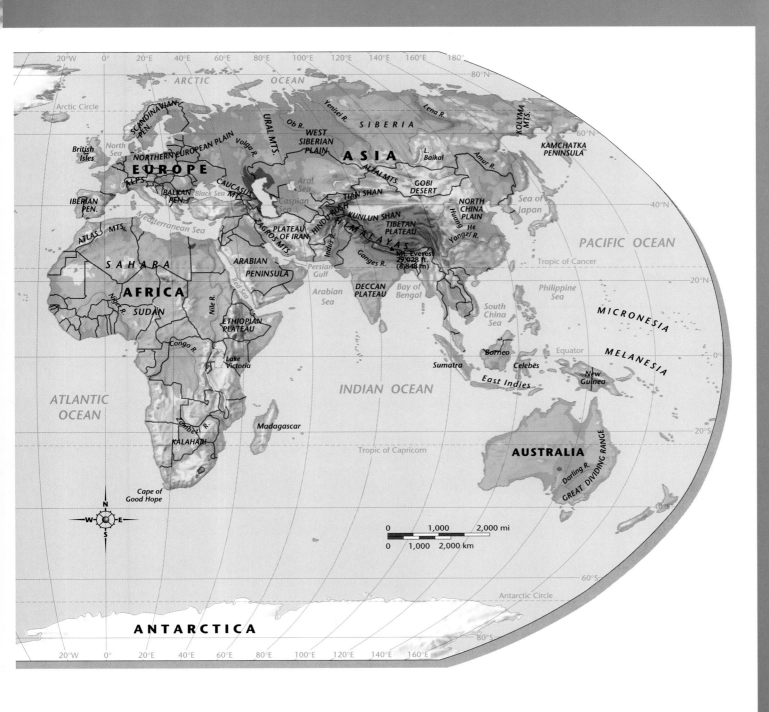

ARCTIC OCEAN

80°N

60°N

Arctic Circle

SCANDINAVIAN PEN.

British Isles

North Sea

Yenisei R. SIBERIA Lena R.

Ob R. WEST SIBERIAN PLAIN

KOLYMA MTS.

NORTHERN EUROPEAN PLAIN Volga R. URAL MTS.

ASIA

KAMCHATKA PENINSULA

EUROPE

L. Baikal

ALPS

CAUCASUS MTS. Aral Sea ALTAI MTS. GOBI DESERT

40°N

IBERIAN PEN.

BALKAN PEN. Black Sea

Caspian Sea TIAN SHAN

Amur R. Sea of Japan

ATLAS MTS. Mediterranean Sea

ZAGROS MTS. PLATEAU OF IRAN HINDU KUSH KUNLUN SHAN

NORTH CHINA PLAIN

PACIFIC OCEAN

SAHARA

ARABIAN PENINSULA

Persian Gulf

TIBETAN PLATEAU

Huang He Yangzi R.

Tropic of Cancer

AFRICA

Red Sea

Arabian Sea

Indus R. HIMALAYAS Mt. Everest 29,028 ft. (8,848 m)

20°N

Niger R. SUDAN Nile R.

Ganges R.

DECCAN PLATEAU

Bay of Bengal

South China Sea

MICRONESIA

ETHIOPIAN PLATEAU

Philippine Sea

0°

Congo R.

Lake Victoria

INDIAN OCEAN

Sumatra

Borneo

Celebes

Equator

New Guinea

MELANESIA

East Indies

ATLANTIC OCEAN

Zambezi R.

Madagascar

KALAHARI

20°S

Cape of Good Hope

Tropic of Capricorn

AUSTRALIA

Darling R. GREAT DIVIDING RANGE

N
W E
S

0   1,000   2,000 mi
0   1,000 2,000 km

60°S

Antarctic Circle

80°S

ANTARCTICA

20°W   0°   20°E   40°E   60°E   80°E   100°E   120°E   140°E   160°E

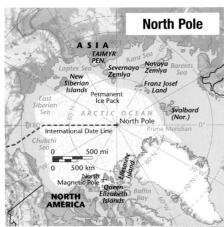

North Pole

ASIA

TAIMYR PEN.

Laptev Sea

Kara Sea

Severnaya Zemlya

Novaya Zemlya

Barents Sea

New Siberian Islands

Permanent Ice Pack

Franz Josef Land

East Siberian Sea

ARCTIC OCEAN North Pole

Svalbard (Nor.)

Chukchi Sea

International Date Line

Prime Meridian

0   500 mi
0   500 km

North Magnetic Pole

Ellesmere Island

Baffin Bay

NORTH AMERICA

Queen Elizabeth Islands

United States: Political

ARCTIC OCEAN

RUSSIA

ALASKA

CANADA

Arctic Circle

70°N

70°N

60°N

Bering Strait

Yukon River

Anchorage

Juneau

Bering Sea

Gulf of Alaska

60°N

| 0 | 250 | 500 mi |
| 0 | 250 | 500 km |

160°W

140°W

50°N

120°W

110°W

WASHINGTON

Olympia

Seattle

Spokane

River

Minot

Columbia

MONTANA

Bismarck

Portland

Salem

Helena

Billings

OREGON

IDAHO

Boise

Sheridan

Missouri River

Klamath Falls

Snake River

Jackson

WYOMING

Pierre

Rapid City

Eureka

40°N

Twin Falls

Winnemucca

Great Salt Lake

NEBRASKA

Sacramento

Carson City

Salt Lake City

Cheyenne

San Francisco

NEVADA

UTAH

Denver

Colorado River

Grand Junction

COLORADO

Cedar City

Pueblo

Arkansas

CALIFORNIA

Las Vegas

PACIFIC

Los Angeles

Santa Fe

OCEAN

Albuquerque

San Diego

ARIZONA

NEW MEXICO

Phoenix

Roswell

Tucson

Rio Grande

El Paso

MEXICO

160°W

155°W

Honolulu

N

PACIFIC OCEAN

HAWAII

20°N

20°N

Hilo

155°W

| 0 | 50 | 100 mi |
| 0 | 50 | 100 km |

Tropic of Cancer

120°W

110°W

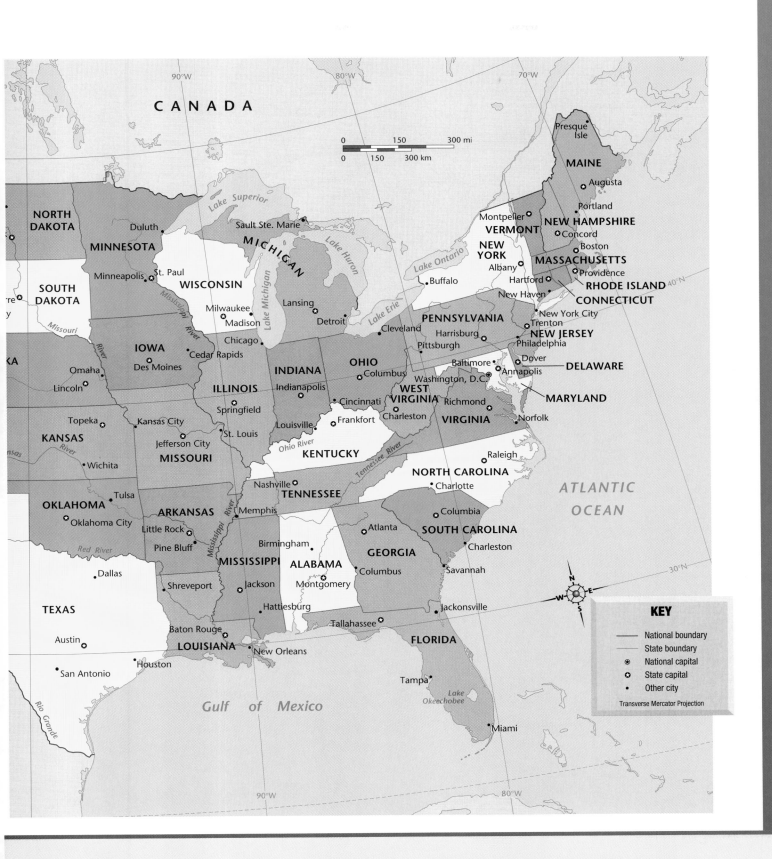

CANADA

NORTH DAKOTA
SOUTH DAKOTA

Duluth

MINNESOTA

Minneapolis · ·St. Paul

Sault Ste. Marie

MICHIGAN

Lake Superior

Lake Michigan

Lake Huron

WISCONSIN

Milwaukee ·
· Madison

Lansing
·

Detroit ·

Lake Erie

Lake Ontario

MAINE

Presque
Isle

· Augusta

· Portland

Montpelier ⊕ **NEW HAMPSHIRE**

VERMONT ⊕ Concord

· Boston

NEW YORK

Albany ⊕

MASSACHUSETTS
⊕Providence

RHODE ISLAND

Hartford ⊕

New Haven

CONNECTICUT

· Buffalo

Mississippi River

IOWA
Des Moines ⊕

· Cedar Rapids

Chicago ·

Cleveland ·

PENNSYLVANIA

Harrisburg ⊕
Pittsburgh ·

New York City ·

Trenton ⊕
NEW JERSEY

Philadelphia
⊕ Dover

· Omaha

ILLINOIS

Indianapolis ⊕

INDIANA

OHIO

Columbus ⊕

Baltimore ·
· ⊕Annapolis

DELAWARE

Lincoln ⊕

Springfield ⊕

Cincinnati ·

Washington, D.C.⊛

WEST VIRGINIA

MARYLAND

Topeka ⊕

Kansas City ·

Louisville ·
· Frankfort

Charleston ⊕

Richmond ⊕

Norfolk ·

VIRGINIA

KANSAS

Jefferson City ⊕
St. Louis ·

Ohio River

KENTUCKY

Tennessee River

Raleigh ·

· Wichita

MISSOURI

NORTH CAROLINA

Kansas River

Nashville ⊕

· Charlotte

OKLAHOMA

Tulsa ·

ARKANSAS

Memphis ·

TENNESSEE

Columbia ⊕

SOUTH CAROLINA

Oklahoma City ⊕

Little Rock ⊕

Mississippi River

· Atlanta

Charleston ·

Pine Bluff ·

Birmingham ·

MISSISSIPPI

ALABAMA

Columbus ·

GEORGIA

Savannah ·

Red River

· Dallas

Shreveport ·

· Jackson ⊕

Montgomery ⊕

TEXAS

Hattiesburg ·

Jackonsville ·

Baton Rouge ⊕

Tallahassee ⊕

FLORIDA

Austin ⊕

LOUISIANA · New Orleans

· San Antonio

· Houston

Rio Grande

Gulf of Mexico

Tampa ·

Lake
Okeechobee

· Miami

*ATLANTIC
OCEAN*

90°W   80°W   70°W

40°N

30°N

90°W   80°W

0   150   300 mi

0   150   300 km

N
W   E
S

KEY

—— National boundary

—— State boundary

⊛ National capital

⊕ State capital

· Other city

Transverse Mercator Projection

ATLAS   247

North and South America: Political

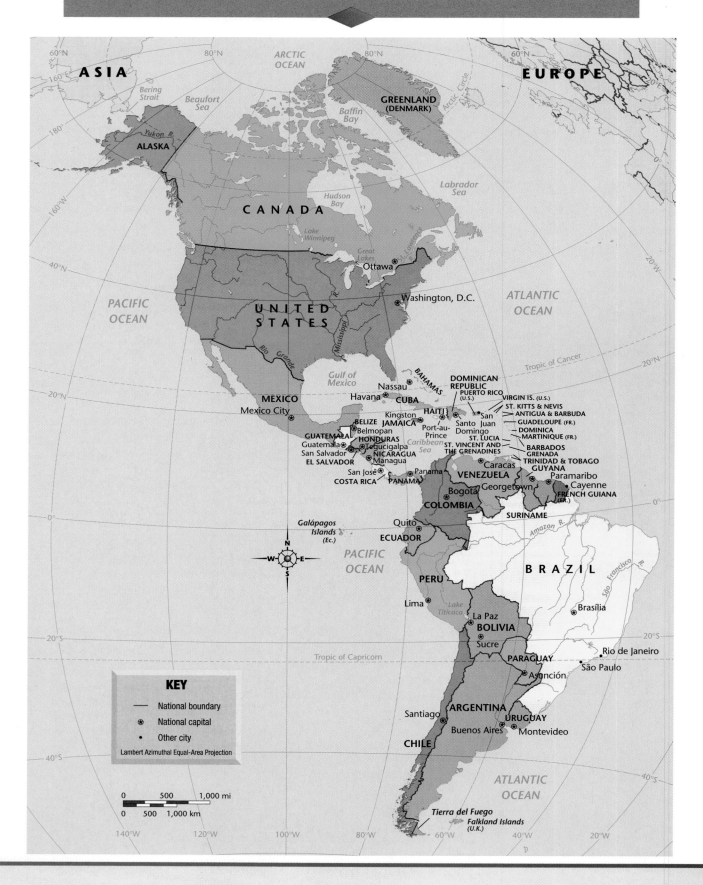

ASIA

ARCTIC OCEAN

EUROPE

Bering Strait

Beaufort Sea

GREENLAND (DENMARK)

Baffin Bay

ALASKA

Yukon R.

Labrador Sea

Hudson Bay

CANADA

Lake Winnipeg

Great Lakes

Ottawa

PACIFIC OCEAN

ATLANTIC OCEAN

UNITED STATES

Washington, D.C.

Rio Grande

Mississippi

Tropic of Cancer

Gulf of Mexico

Nassau

BAHAMAS

DOMINICAN REPUBLIC

PUERTO RICO (U.S.)

VIRGIN IS. (U.S.)

MEXICO

Havana

CUBA

ST. KITTS & NEVIS

ANTIGUA & BARBUDA

Mexico City

Kingston

HAITI

Santo

San Juan

GUADELOUPE (FR.)

BELIZE

JAMAICA

Port-au-Prince

Domingo

DOMINICA

Belmopan

MARTINIQUE (FR.)

GUATEMALA

HONDURAS

ST. LUCIA

Guatemala

Tegucigalpa

Caribbean Sea

ST. VINCENT AND THE GRENADINES

BARBADOS

San Salvador

NICARAGUA

GRENADA

EL SALVADOR

Managua

TRINIDAD & TOBAGO

GUYANA

San José

Panama

Caracas

COSTA RICA

PANAMA

VENEZUELA

Paramaribo

Cayenne

Bogotá

Georgetown

FRENCH GUIANA (FR.)

COLOMBIA

SURINAME

Galápagos Islands (Ec.)

Quito

ECUADOR

Amazon R.

0°

BRAZIL

São Francisco R.

PACIFIC OCEAN

PERU

Lima

Lake Titicaca

Brasília

La Paz

BOLIVIA

Sucre

Rio de Janeiro

Tropic of Capricorn

PARAGUAY

São Paulo

Asunción

KEY

—— National boundary

⊛ National capital

• Other city

Lambert Azimuthal Equal-Area Projection

Santiago

ARGENTINA

URUGUAY

Buenos Aires

Montevideo

CHILE

ATLANTIC OCEAN

0   500   1,000 mi

0   500 1,000 km

Tierra del Fuego

Falkland Islands (U.K.)

North and South America: Physical

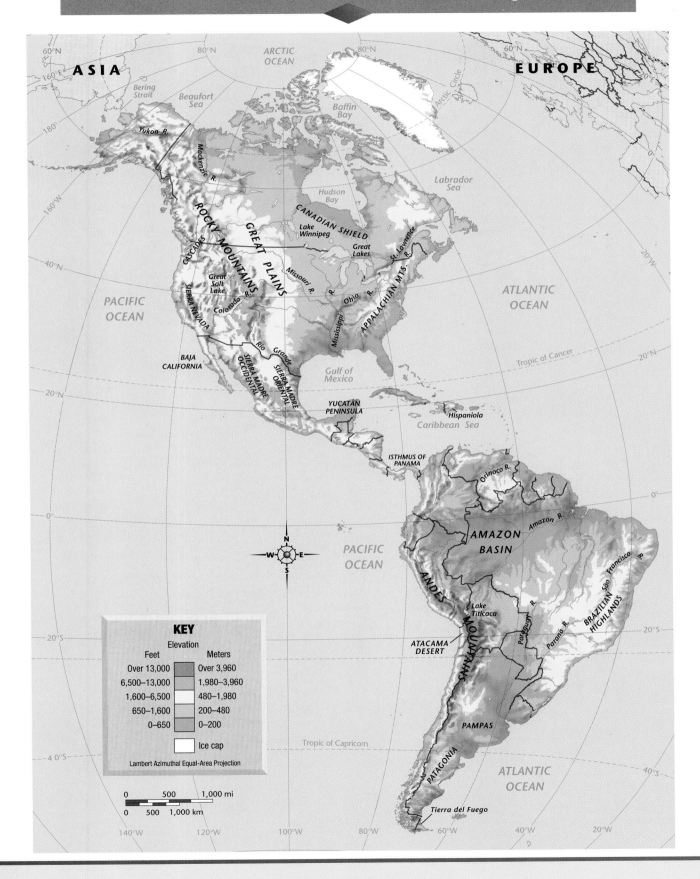

KEY

Elevation

Feet	Meters
Over 13,000	Over 3,960
6,500–13,000	1,980–3,960
1,600–6,500	480–1,980
650–1,600	200–480
0–650	0–200
Ice cap	

Lambert Azimuthal Equal-Area Projection

0   500   1,000 mi

0   500   1,000 km

Europe: Political

KEY

— National boundary
⊛ National capital
• Other city

Lambert Azimuthal Equal-Area Projection

ARCTIC OCEAN

ATLANTIC OCEAN

Arctic Circle

Reykjavik • **ICELAND**

Faeroe Is. (Den.)

Shetland Is. (U.K.)

Prime Meridian

NORWAY
Lillehammer •
Oslo ⊛

SWEDEN
Stockholm ⊛
• Göteborg

Gulf of Bothnia

FINLAND
Turku • • Helsinki
Tallinn ⊛ • St. Petersburg

ESTONIA

RUSSIA
Moscow ⊛

Riga ⊛ **LATVIA**

Baltic Sea

LITHUANIA
Vilnius ⊛

BELARUS
Minsk •

North Sea

DENMARK
Copenhagen ⊛

RUSSIA

Gdańsk •

POLAND
Warsaw ⊛
Łódź •

Kiev ⊛

IRELAND
Dublin ⊛

UNITED KINGDOM
• Manchester

London ⊛

NETHERLANDS
Amsterdam ⊛
The Hague ⊛

Brussels ⊛
BELGIUM

LUXEMBOURG
Luxembourg ⊛

Berlin ⊛

GERMANY
• Cologne
• Bonn
• Frankfurt

Katowice • • Kraków

Prague ⊛ **CZECH REPUBLIC**
Brno •

SLOVAKIA
Bratislava ⊛

UKRAINE

MOLDOVA
Chişinău ⊛

Paris ⊛

LIECHTENSTEIN
Bern ⊛
SWITZERLAND

Munich •

Danube R.

Vienna •
AUSTRIA

• Budapest
HUNGARY

• Cluj
ROMANIA
Bucharest ⊛

Bay of Biscay

FRANCE

Milan •

Ljubljana ⊛
SLOVENIA
Zagreb ⊛
CROATIA

BOSNIA & HERZEGOVINA
Sarajevo ⊛

Belgrade ⊛
SERBIA

Black Sea

PORTUGAL

ANDORRA

Marseille •

MONACO

SAN MARINO

ITALY

Podgorica ⊛
MONTENEGRO

BULGARIA
Sophia ⊛

Skopje ⊛
MACEDONIA

Adriatic Sea

Corsica

VATICAN CITY
Rome ⊛

ALBANIA
Tiranë ⊛

Madrid ⊛
• Barcelona

SPAIN

Lisbon ⊛

Sardinia

Naples •

Aegean Sea

Tyrrhenian Sea

GREECE
• Athens

Balearic Is.

Strait of Gibraltar

GIBRALTAR (U.K.)

Mediterranean Sea

Sicily

Ionian Sea

MALTA

Crete

AFRICA

0   250   500 mi
0   250   500 km

N
W   E
S

Europe: Physical

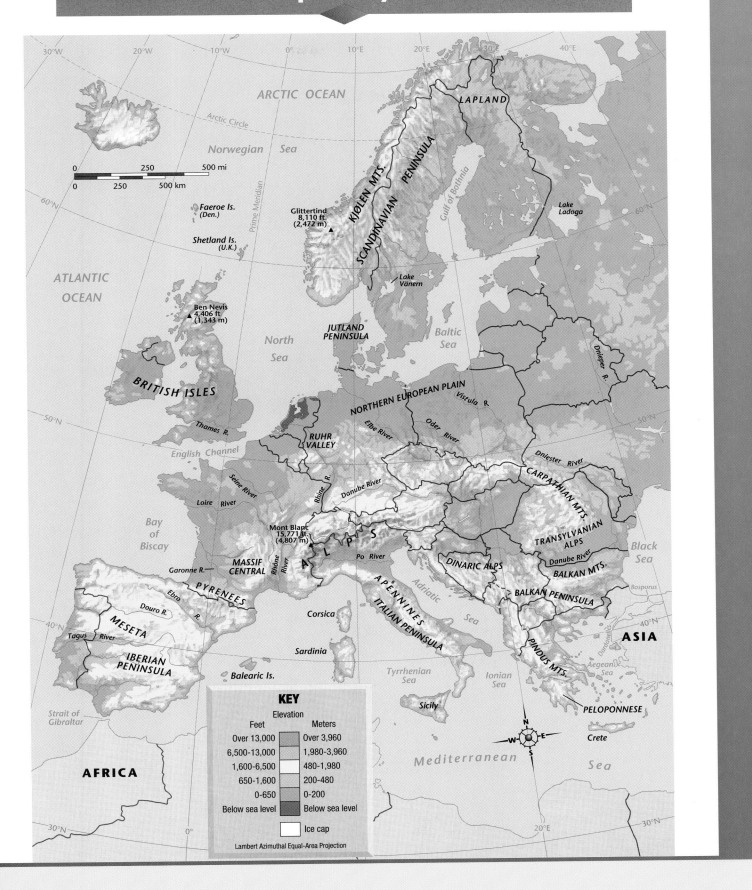

ARCTIC OCEAN

LAPLAND

Norwegian Sea

Arctic Circle

Prime Meridian

Faeroe Is. (Den.)

Glittertind 8,110 ft. (2,472 m)

KJØLEN MTS.

SCANDINAVIAN PENINSULA

Gulf of Bothnia

Lake Ladoga

Shetland Is. (U.K.)

ATLANTIC OCEAN

Ben Nevis 4,406 ft. (1,343 m)

Lake Vänern

JUTLAND PENINSULA

Baltic Sea

North Sea

Dnieper R.

BRITISH ISLES

NORTHERN EUROPEAN PLAIN

Vistula R.

Thames R.

Elbe River

Oder River

RUHR VALLEY

English Channel

Rhine R.

Danube River

Dniester River

CARPATHIAN MTS.

Seine River

Loire River

Bay of Biscay

Mont Blanc 15,771 ft. (4,807 m)

A L P S

Po River

TRANSYLVANIAN ALPS

Danube River

Black Sea

MASSIF CENTRAL

Rhône River

DINARIC ALPS

BALKAN MTS.

Garonne R.

PYRENEES

A P E N N I N E S

Adriatic Sea

BALKAN PENINSULA

Bosporus

Ebro R.

Douro R.

MESETA

Corsica

ITALIAN PENINSULA

PINDUS MTS.

Dardanelles

ASIA

Tagus River

IBERIAN PENINSULA

Sardinia

Aegean Sea

Balearic Is.

Tyrrhenian Sea

Ionian Sea

PELOPONNESE

AFRICA

Sicily

Crete

Strait of Gibraltar

KEY

Elevation

Feet		Meters
Over 13,000		Over 3,960
6,500–13,000		1,980–3,960
1,600–6,500		480–1,980
650–1,600		200–480
0–650		0–200
Below sea level		Below sea level
	Ice cap	

Lambert Azimuthal Equal-Area Projection

Mediterranean Sea

Africa: Political

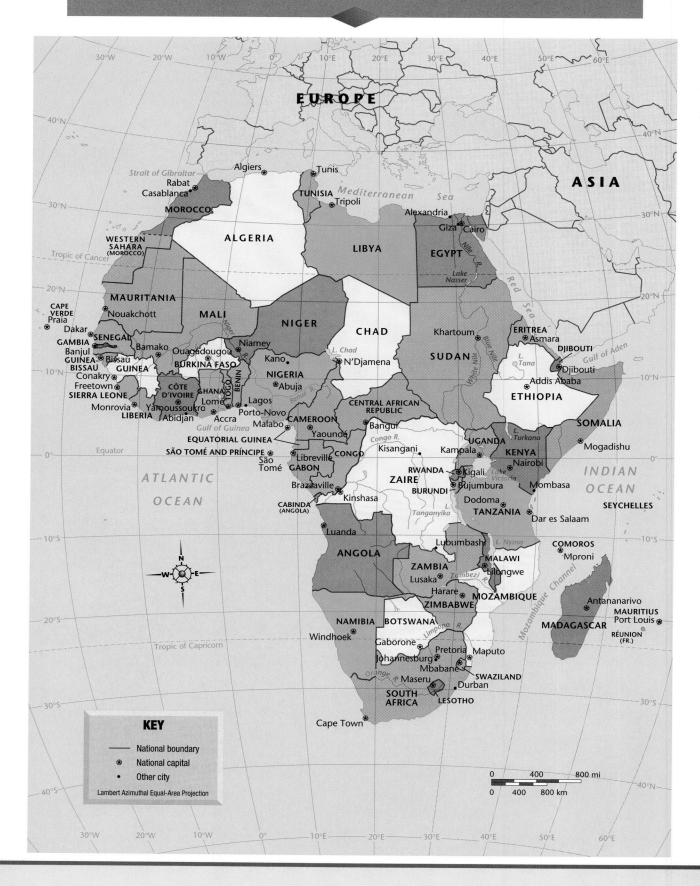

EUROPE

ASIA

Mediterranean Sea

Strait of Gibraltar

Algiers · Tunis
Rabat TUNISIA · Tripoli
Casablanca
MOROCCO
Alexandria
Giza · Cairo

WESTERN SAHARA (MOROCCO)
ALGERIA
LIBYA
EGYPT

Tropic of Cancer

Nile R.

Lake Nasser

Red Sea

MAURITANIA

CAPE VERDE
Praia
Nouakchott
MALI
NIGER
CHAD
Khartoum
ERITREA
Asmara
DJIBOUTI

Gulf of Aden

Dakar
SENEGAL
Bamako
Niamey
L. Chad
SUDAN
L. Tana
Djibouti

GAMBIA
Banjul
GUINEA BISSAU
Bissau
BURKINA FASO
Kano
N'Djamena
Addis Ababa

Conakry
GUINEA
NIGERIA
Abuja
Blue Nile

Freetown
SIERRA LEONE
CÔTE D'IVOIRE
GHANA
TOGO BENIN
Lagos
CENTRAL AFRICAN REPUBLIC
White Nile
ETHIOPIA

Monrovia
Yamoussoukro
Lomé
Porto-Novo
SOMALIA

LIBERIA
Abidjan
Accra
Malabo
CAMEROON
Bangui
L. Turkana

Gulf of Guinea
EQUATORIAL GUINEA
Yaoundé
Congo R.
UGANDA
Mogadishu

SÃO TOMÉ AND PRÍNCIPE
São Tomé
Libreville
GABON
CONGO
Kisangani
Kampala
KENYA

Equator
Brazzaville
ZAIRE
RWANDA
Kigali
Lake Victoria
Nairobi

CABINDA (ANGOLA)
Kinshasa
BURUNDI
Bujumbura
Dodoma
Mombasa

Luanda
Tanganyika
TANZANIA
Dar es Salaam
SEYCHELLES

ATLANTIC OCEAN

INDIAN OCEAN

ANGOLA
Lubumbashi
L. Nyasa
COMOROS
Moroni

ZAMBIA
MALAWI
Lilongwe

Lusaka
Zambezi R.

NAMIBIA
BOTSWANA
Harare
ZIMBABWE
MOZAMBIQUE
Mozambique Channel

MADAGASCAR
Antananarivo
MAURITIUS
Port Louis

Windhoek
Gaborone
Limpopo R.

RÉUNION (FR.)

Tropic of Capricorn

Pretoria
Maputo
Johannesburg
SWAZILAND
Mbabane

Orange R.
Maseru
Durban

SOUTH AFRICA
LESOTHO

Cape Town

KEY

—— National boundary

⊛ National capital

• Other city

Lambert Azimuthal Equal-Area Projection

0   400   800 mi

0   400   800 km

Africa: Physical

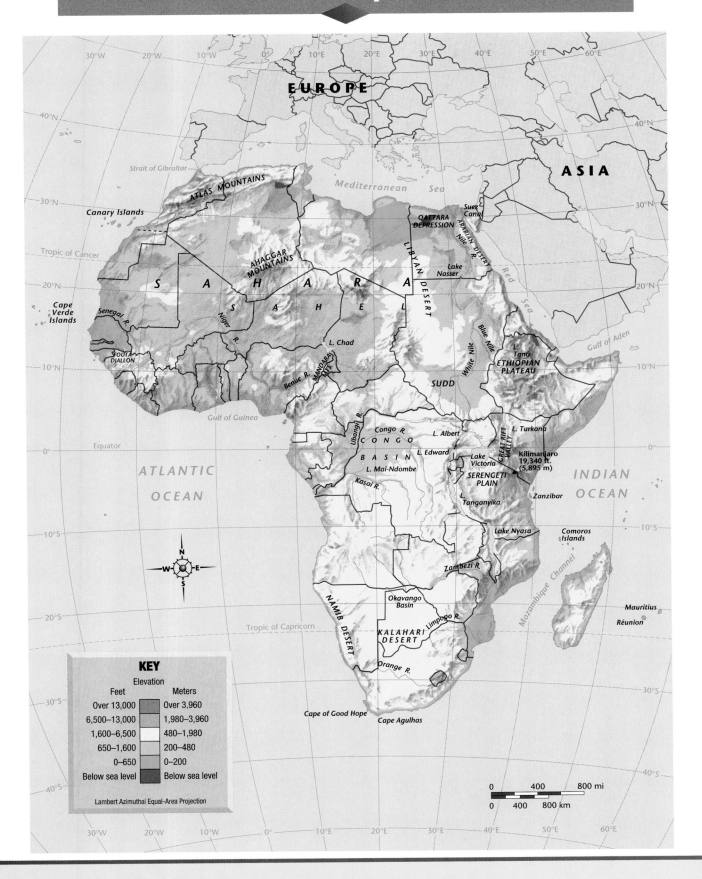

EUROPE

ASIA

Strait of Gibraltar

Mediterranean Sea

ATLAS MOUNTAINS

Canary Islands

Tropic of Cancer

QATTARA DEPRESSION

Suez Canal

ARABIAN DESERT

Nile R.

AHAGGAR MOUNTAINS

Lake Nasser

S A H A R A

LIBYAN DESERT

Red Sea

Cape Verde Islands

Senegal R.

Niger R.

S A H E L

Gulf of Aden

FOUTA DJALLON

L. Chad

MANDARA MTS.

White Nile

Blue Nile

L. Tana

ETHIOPIAN PLATEAU

Benue R.

SUDD

Gulf of Guinea

Ubangi R.

Congo R.

CONGO BASIN

L. Albert

GREAT RIFT VALLEY

L. Turkana

Equator

L. Edward

Lake Victoria

Kilimanjaro 19,340 ft. (5,895 m)

ATLANTIC OCEAN

L. Mai-Ndombe

Kasai R.

SERENGETI PLAIN

INDIAN OCEAN

L. Tanganyika

Zanzibar

Lake Nyasa

Comoros Islands

Mauritius

Réunion

Zambezi R.

Mozambique Channel

NAMIB DESERT

Okavango Basin

Limpopo R.

Tropic of Capricorn

KALAHARI DESERT

Orange R.

Cape of Good Hope

Cape Agulhas

KEY

Elevation

Feet	Meters
Over 13,000	Over 3,960
6,500–13,000	1,980–3,960
1,600–6,500	480–1,980
650–1,600	200–480
0–650	0–200
Below sea level	Below sea level

Lambert Azimuthal Equal-Area Projection

0   400   800 mi

0   400   800 km

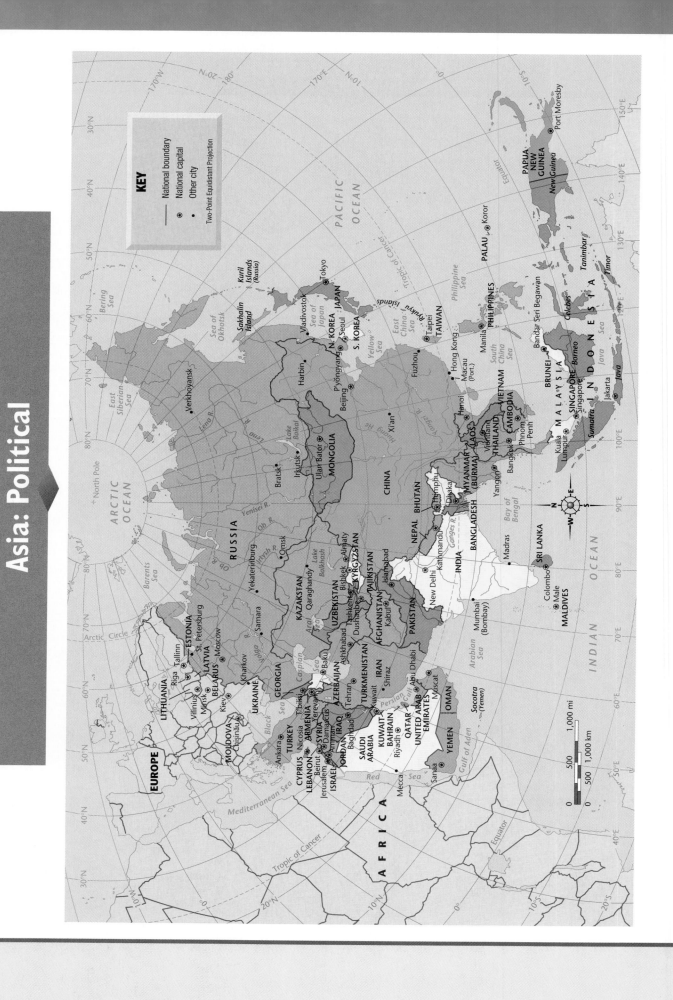

Asia: Political

KEY

— National boundary
⊛ National capital
• Other city

Two-Point Equidistant Projection

ARCTIC OCEAN

North Pole

Barents Sea

East Siberian Sea

Bering Sea

Sea of Okhotsk

Verkhoyansk

Sakhalin Island

Kuril Islands (Russia)

RUSSIA

Vladivostok

Tokyo

JAPAN

Sea of Japan

N. KOREA

Pyŏngyang

Seoul

S. KOREA

Yellow Sea

Harbin

Beijing

PACIFIC OCEAN

Lena R.

Lake Baikal

Bratsk

Irkutsk

Ulan Bator

MONGOLIA

CHINA

Xi'an

Huang He

Fuzhou

East China Sea

Ryukyu Islands

Taipei

TAIWAN

Hong Kong

Macau (Port.)

South China Sea

Philippine Sea

PHILIPPINES

Manila

PALAU

Koror

Yenisei R.

Ob R.

Omsk

Yekaterinburg

Irtysh R.

Lake Balkhash

KAZAKHSTAN

Qaraghandy

Almaty

KYRGYZSTAN

Bishkek

TAJIKISTAN

Dushanbe

Tashkent

UZBEKISTAN

Ashkhabad

Aral Sea

BHUTAN

Thimphu

NEPAL

Kathmandu

Ganges R.

BANGLADESH

Dhaka

MYANMAR (BURMA)

Yangon

LAOS

Vientiane

THAILAND

Bangkok

VIETNAM

Hanoi

CAMBODIA

Phnom Penh

Bay of Bengal

INDIA

New Delhi

Madras

Mumbai (Bombay)

SRI LANKA

Colombo

Male

MALDIVES

INDIAN OCEAN

Arabian Sea

PAKISTAN

Islamabad

AFGHANISTAN

Kabul

TURKMENISTAN

IRAN

Tehran

Shiraz

MALAYSIA

Kuala Lumpur

SINGAPORE

Singapore

BRUNEI

Bandar Seri Begawan

Sumatra

Borneo

Celebes

Java Sea

Jakarta

Java

INDONESIA

Timor

Tanimbar

PAPUA NEW GUINEA

New Guinea

Port Moresby

Volga

Samara

Caspian Sea

Baku

AZERBAIJAN

GEORGIA

Tbilisi

ARMENIA

Yerevan

St. Petersburg

Moscow

Kharkov

Kiev

UKRAINE

BELARUS

Minsk

LITHUANIA

Vilnius

LATVIA

Riga

ESTONIA

Tallinn

MOLDOVA

Chişinău

EUROPE

Black Sea

TURKEY

Ankara

CYPRUS

Nicosia

LEBANON

Beirut

SYRIA

Damascus

ISRAEL

Jerusalem

JORDAN

Amman

IRAQ

Baghdad

Kuwait

KUWAIT

BAHRAIN

QATAR

Riyadh

SAUDI ARABIA

Abu Dhabi

UNITED ARAB EMIRATES

OMAN

Muscat

Gulf of Oman

Persian Gulf

YEMEN

Sanaa

Socotra (Yemen)

Gulf of Aden

Mecca

Red Sea

AFRICA

Mediterranean Sea

Arctic Circle

Tropic of Cancer

Equator

Tropic of Cancer

N

E

W

S

0   500   1,000 mi

0   500   1,000 km

Asia: Physical

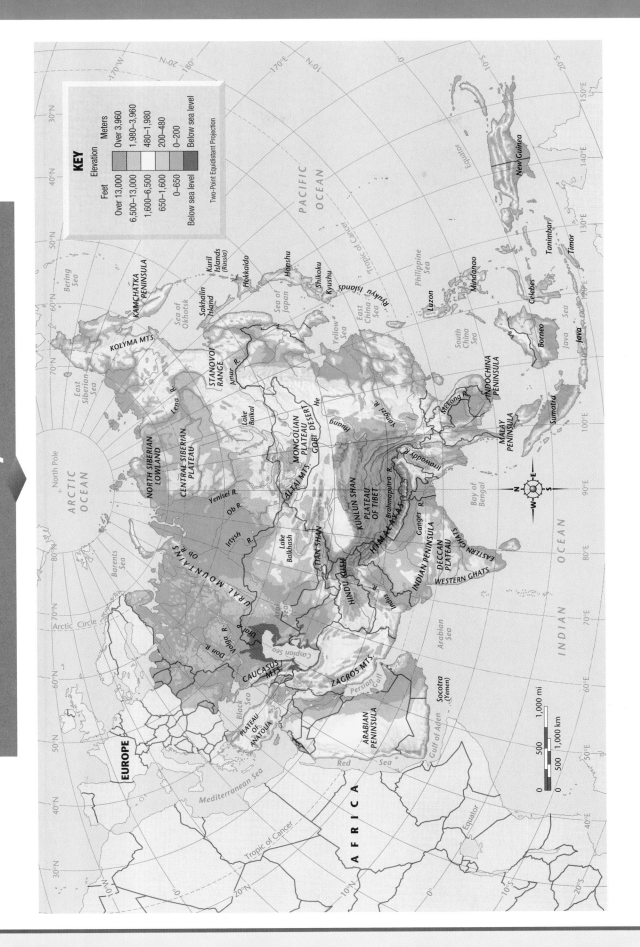

KEY

Elevation

Feet	Meters
Over 13,000	Over 3,960
6,500–13,000	1,980–3,960
1,600–6,500	480–1,980
650–1,600	200–480
0–650	0–200
Below sea level	Below sea level

Two-Point Equidistant Projection

Australia, New Zealand, and the Pacific Islands: Physical–Political

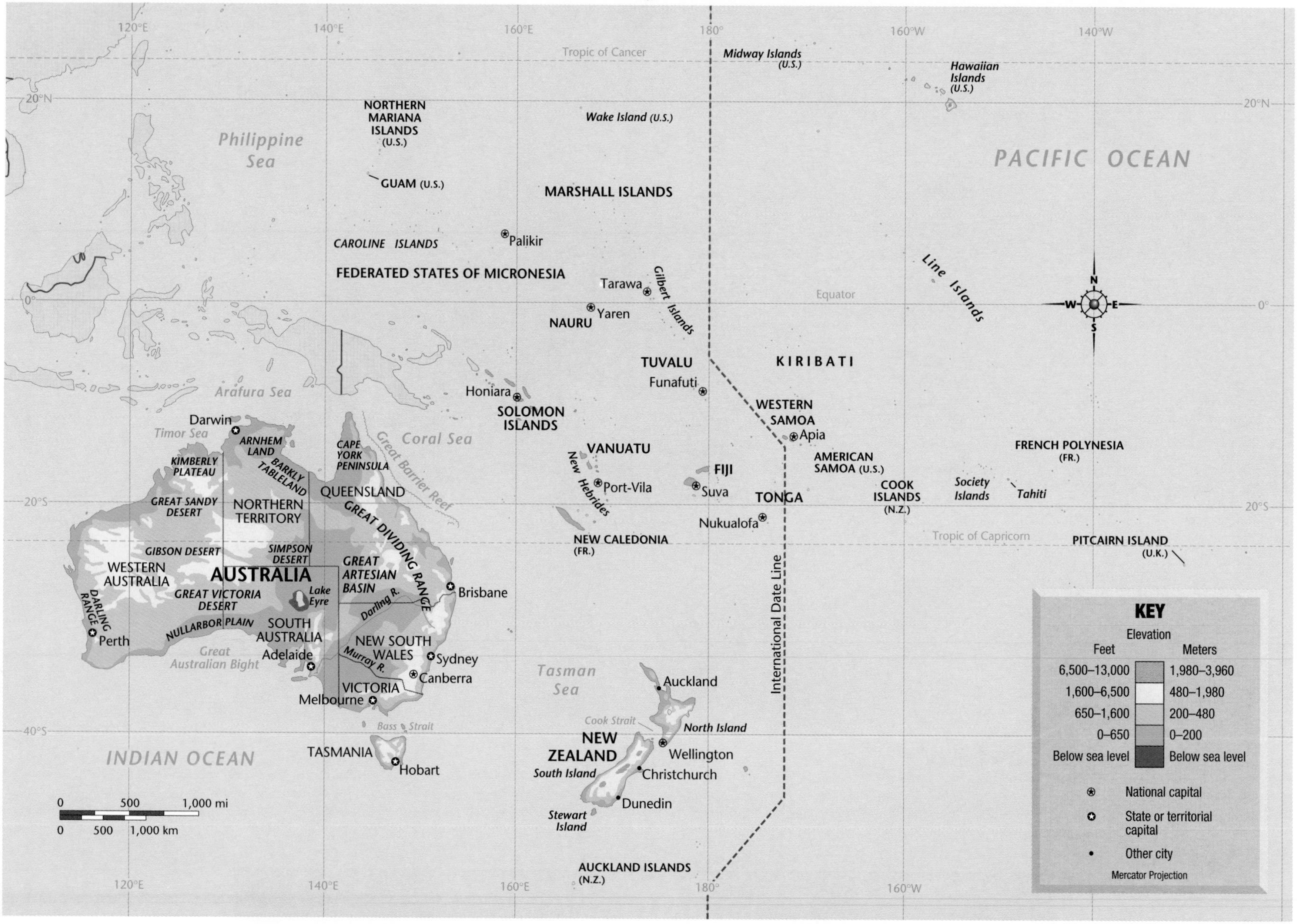

PACIFIC OCEAN

Philippine Sea

NORTHERN MARIANA ISLANDS (U.S.)

GUAM (U.S.)

CAROLINE ISLANDS

FEDERATED STATES OF MICRONESIA

*Palikir

MARSHALL ISLANDS

Wake Island (U.S.)

Midway Islands (U.S.)

Hawaiian Islands (U.S.)

Line Islands

KIRIBATI

Tarawa
Gilbert Islands

NAURU
*Yaren

TUVALU
*Funafuti

WESTERN SAMOA
*Apia

AMERICAN SAMOA (U.S.)

COOK ISLANDS (N.Z.)

FRENCH POLYNESIA (FR.)

Society Islands
Tahiti

PITCAIRN ISLAND (U.K.)

Tropic of Capricorn

Equator

Tropic of Cancer

SOLOMON ISLANDS
Honiara

VANUATU
*Port-Vila
New Hebrides

FIJI
*Suva

TONGA
Nukualofa

NEW CALEDONIA (FR.)

International Date Line

Tasman Sea

Auckland
North Island

Wellington
Christchurch
Dunedin

NEW ZEALAND
South Island

Stewart Island

AUCKLAND ISLANDS (N.Z.)

Cook Strait

Coral Sea

Great Barrier Reef

CAPE YORK PENINSULA

QUEENSLAND

GREAT DIVIDING RANGE

Brisbane

Sydney
*Canberra

NEW SOUTH WALES

GREAT ARTESIAN BASIN

Darling R.

Murray R.

VICTORIA
Melbourne

Bass Strait

Hobart

TASMANIA

ARNHEM LAND

Darwin

NORTHERN TERRITORY

BARKLY TABLELAND

SIMPSON DESERT

Lake Eyre

SOUTH AUSTRALIA

Adelaide

AUSTRALIA

KIMBERLY PLATEAU

GREAT SANDY DESERT

GIBSON DESERT

GREAT VICTORIA DESERT

NULLARBOR PLAIN

Great Australian Bight

WESTERN AUSTRALIA

DARLING RANGE
*Perth

Timor Sea

Arafura Sea

INDIAN OCEAN

KEY

Elevation

Feet	Meters
6,500–13,000	1,980–3,960
1,600–6,500	480–1,980
650–1,600	200–480
0–650	0–200
Below sea level	Below sea level

⊛ National capital

✪ State or territorial capital

• Other city

Mercator Projection

1,000 mi

500   1,000 km

0   500

The Arctic

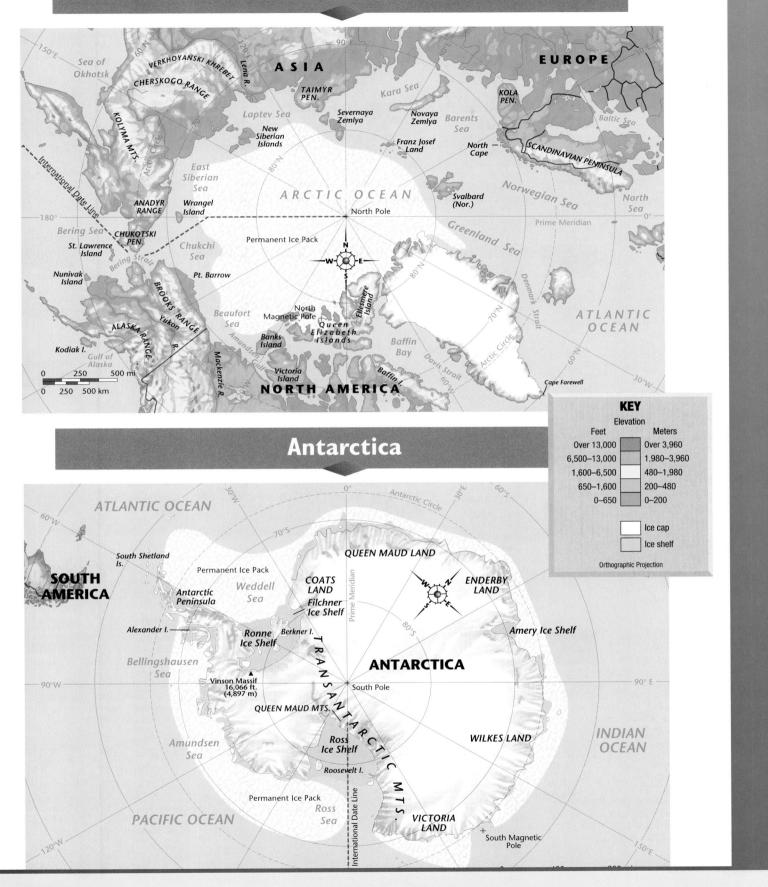

Sea of Okhotsk
150°E
60°N
VERKHOYANSKI KHREBET
CHERSKOGO RANGE
Lena R.
120°E
90°E
ASIA
EUROPE
KOLYMA MTS.
TAIMYR PEN.
Kara Sea
Severnaya Zemlya
KOLA PEN.
Laptev Sea
New Siberian Islands
Novaya Zemlya
Barents Sea
Baltic Sea
Franz Josef Land
SCANDINAVIAN PENINSULA
Arctic Circle
80°N
North Cape
East Siberian Sea
ARCTIC OCEAN
Svalbard (Nor.)
Norwegian Sea
ANADYR RANGE
Wrangel Island
North Pole
Greenland Sea
Prime Meridian
North Sea
0°
180°
International Date Line
Bering Sea
CHUKOTSKI PEN.
St. Lawrence Island
Chukchi Sea
Permanent Ice Pack
80°N
Denmark Strait
ATLANTIC OCEAN
Nunivak Island
BROOKS RANGE
Pt. Barrow
Beaufort Sea
North Magnetic Pole
Ellesmere Island
70°N
Kodiak I.
ALASKA RANGE
Yukon R.
Banks Island
Queen Elizabeth Islands
Baffin Bay
Arctic Circle
60°N
Gulf of Alaska
Amundsen Gulf
Mackenzie R.
Victoria Island
Baffin I.
Davis Strait
30°W
0   250   500 mi
NORTH AMERICA
Cape Farewell
0   250   500 km

Antarctica

KEY

Elevation

Feet		Meters
Over 13,000		Over 3,960
6,500–13,000		1,980–3,960
1,600–6,500		480–1,980
650–1,600		200–480
0–650		0–200

Ice cap

Ice shelf

Orthographic Projection

ATLANTIC OCEAN
60°W
30°W
0°
Antarctic Circle
30°E
60°S
60°E
SOUTH AMERICA
South Shetland Is.
Permanent Ice Pack
70°S
QUEEN MAUD LAND
ENDERBY LAND
Antarctic Peninsula
Weddell Sea
COATS LAND
Prime Meridian
Amery Ice Shelf
Alexander I.
Filchner Ice Shelf
Ronne Ice Shelf
Berkner I.
80°S
Bellingshausen Sea
TRANSANTARCTIC MTS.
ANTARCTICA
90°W
Vinson Massif 16,066 ft. (4,897 m)
South Pole
90°E
QUEEN MAUD MTS.
WILKES LAND
INDIAN OCEAN
Amundsen Sea
Ross Ice Shelf
Roosevelt I.
Permanent Ice Pack
International Date Line
Ross Sea
VICTORIA LAND
PACIFIC OCEAN
120°W
South Magnetic Pole
150°E

World View

Afghanistan

CAPITAL: Kabul
POPULATION: 21,251,821
MAJOR LANGUAGES: Pashtu, Afghan Persian, Turkic, and 30 various languages
AREA: 250,010 sq mi; 647,500 sq km
LEADING EXPORTS: fruits and nuts, handwoven carpets, and wool
CONTINENT: Asia

Albania

CAPITAL: Tiranë
POPULATION: 3,413,904
MAJOR LANGUAGES: Albanian, Tosk dialect, and Greek
AREA: 11,101 sq mi; 28,750 sq km
LEADING EXPORTS: asphalt, metals and metallic ores, and electricity
CONTINENT: Europe

Algeria
CAPITAL: Algiers
POPULATION: 28,539,321
MAJOR LANGUAGES: Arabic (official), French, and Berber dialects
AREA: 919,626 sq mi; 2,381,740 sq km
LEADING EXPORTS: petroleum and natural gas
CONTINENT: Africa

Andorra
CAPITAL: Andorra La Vella
POPULATION: 65,780
MAJOR LANGUAGES: Catalan (official), French, and Castilian
AREA: 174 sq mi; 450 sq km
LEADING EXPORTS: electricity, tobacco products, and furniture
CONTINENT: Europe

Angola
CAPITAL: Luanda
POPULATION: 10,069,501
MAJOR LANGUAGES: Portuguese (official), Bantu, and various languages
AREA: 481,370 sq mi; 1,246,700 sq km
LEADING EXPORTS: oil, diamonds, and refined petroleum products
CONTINENT: Africa

Anguilla
CAPITAL: The Valley
POPULATION: 7,099
MAJOR LANGUAGE: English (official)
AREA: 35 sq mi; 91 sq km
LEADING EXPORTS: lobster and salt
LOCATION: Caribbean Sea

Antigua and Barbuda
CAPITAL: Saint John's
POPULATION: 65,176
MAJOR LANGUAGES: English (official) and various dialects
AREA: 170 sq mi; 440 sq km
LEADING EXPORTS: petroleum products and manufactures
LOCATION: Caribbean Sea

Argentina
CAPITAL: Buenos Aires
POPULATION: 34,292,742
MAJOR LANGUAGES: Spanish (official), English, Italian, German, and French
AREA: 1,068,339 sq mi; 2,766,890 sq km
LEADING EXPORTS: meat, wheat, corn, oilseed, and manufactures
CONTINENT: South America

Armenia
CAPITAL: Yerevan
POPULATION: 3,557,284
MAJOR LANGUAGES: Armenian and Russian
AREA: 11,506 sq mi; 29,800 sq km
LEADING EXPORTS: gold and jewelry, and aluminum
CONTINENT: Asia

Australia
CAPITAL: Canberra
POPULATION: 18,322,231
MAJOR LANGUAGES: English and various languages
AREA: 2,968,010 sq mi; 7,686,850 sq km
LEADING EXPORTS: coal, gold, meat, wool, and alumina
CONTINENT: Australia

Austria
CAPITAL: Vienna
POPULATION: 7,986,664
MAJOR LANGUAGE: German
AREA: 32,376 sq mi; 83,850 sq km
LEADING EXPORTS: machinery and equipment, and iron and steel
CONTINENT: Europe

Azerbaijan

CAPITAL: Baku
POPULATION: 7,789,886
MAJOR LANGUAGES: Azeri, Russian, Armenian, and various languages
AREA: 33,438 sq mi; 86,600 sq km
LEADING EXPORTS: oil and gas, chemicals, and oil field equipment
CONTINENT: Europe and Asia

Bahamas
CAPITAL: Nassau
POPULATION: 256,616
MAJOR LANGUAGES: English and Creole
AREA: 5,382 sq mi; 13,940 sq km
LEADING EXPORTS: pharmaceuticals, cement, rum, and crawfish
LOCATION: Caribbean Sea

Bahrain

CAPITAL: Manama
POPULATION: 575,925
MAJOR LANGUAGES: Arabic, English, Farsi, and Urdu
AREA: 239 sq mi; 620 sq km
LEADING EXPORTS: petroleum and petroleum products
CONTINENT: Asia

Bangladesh

CAPITAL: Dhaka
POPULATION: 128,094,948
MAJOR LANGUAGES: Bangla and English
AREA: 55,600 sq mi; 144,000 sq km
LEADING EXPORTS: garments, jute and jute goods, and leather
CONTINENT: Asia

Barbados
CAPITAL: Bridgetown
POPULATION: 256,395
MAJOR LANGUAGE: English
AREA: 166 sq mi; 430 sq km
LEADING EXPORTS: sugar and molasses, and rum
LOCATION: Caribbean Sea

Belarus
CAPITAL: Minsk
POPULATION: 10,437,418
MAJOR LANGUAGES: Byelorussian and Russian
AREA: 79,926 sq mi; 207,600 sq km
LEADING EXPORTS: machinery and transportation equipment
CONTINENT: Europe

Belgium
CAPITAL: Brussels
POPULATION: 10,081,880
MAJOR LANGUAGES: Dutch, French, and German
AREA: 11,780 sq mi; 30,510 sq km
LEADING EXPORTS: iron and steel, and transportation equipment
CONTINENT: Europe

Belize

CAPITAL: Belmopan
POPULATION: 214,061
MAJOR LANGUAGES: English (official), Spanish, Maya, and Garifuna
AREA: 8,865 sq mi; 22,960 sq km
LEADING EXPORTS: sugar, citrus fruits, bananas, and clothing
LOCATION: Caribbean Sea

Benin
CAPITAL: Porto-Novo
POPULATION: 5,522,677
MAJOR LANGUAGES: Fon, Yoruba, and at least 6 various languages
AREA: 43,484 sq mi; 112,620 sq km
LEADING EXPORTS: cotton, crude oil, palm products, and cocoa
CONTINENT: Africa

Bermuda

CAPITAL: Hamilton
POPULATION: 61,629
MAJOR LANGUAGE: English
AREA: 19.3 sq mi; 50 sq km
LEADING EXPORTS: semitropical produce and light manufactures
CONTINENT: North America

Bhutan
CAPITAL: Thimphu
POPULATION: 1,780,638
MAJOR LANGUAGES: Dzongkha (official), Tibetan dialects, and Nepalese dialects
AREA: 18,147 sq mi; 47,000 sq km
LEADING EXPORTS: cardamon, gypsum, timber, and handicrafts
CONTINENT: Asia

Bolivia
CAPITAL: La Paz
POPULATION: 7,896,254
MAJOR LANGUAGES: Spanish, Quechua, and Aymara
AREA: 424,179 sq mi; 1,098,580 sq km
LEADING EXPORTS: metals, natural gas, soybeans, jewelry, and wood
CONTINENT: South America

Bosnia and Herzegovina

CAPITAL: Sarajevo
POPULATION: 3,201,823
MAJOR LANGUAGE: Serbo-Croatian
AREA: 19,782 sq mi; 51,233 sq km
LEADING EXPORTS: none
CONTINENT: Europe

Botswana

CAPITAL: Gaborone
POPULATION: 1,392,414
MAJOR LANGUAGES: English and Setswana
AREA: 231,812 sq mi; 600,370 sq km
LEADING EXPORTS: diamonds, copper and nickel, and meat
CONTINENT: Africa

Brazil

CAPITAL: Brasília
POPULATION: 160,737,489
MAJOR LANGUAGES: Portuguese, Spanish, English, and French
AREA: 3,286,600 sq mi; 8,511,965 sq km
LEADING EXPORTS: iron ore, soybean, bran, and orange juice
CONTINENT: South America

British Virgin Islands

CAPITAL: Road Town
POPULATION: 13,027
MAJOR LANGUAGE: English
AREA: 58 sq mi; 150 sq km
LEADING EXPORTS: rum, fresh fish, gravel, sand, and fruits
LOCATION: Caribbean Sea

Brunei

CAPITAL: Bandar Seri Begawan
POPULATION: 292,266
MAJOR LANGUAGES: Malay, English, and Chinese
AREA: 2,228 sq mi; 5,770 sq km
LEADING EXPORTS: crude oil and liquefied natural gas
CONTINENT: Asia

Bulgaria

CAPITAL: Sofia
POPULATION: 8,775,198
MAJOR LANGUAGE: Bulgarian
AREA: 42,824 sq mi; 110,910 sq km
LEADING EXPORTS: machinery and agricultural products
CONTINENT: Europe

Burkina Faso

CAPITAL: Ouagadougou
POPULATION: 10,422,828
MAJOR LANGUAGES: French (official) and Sudanic languages
AREA: 105,873 sq mi; 274,200 sq km
LEADING EXPORTS: cotton, gold, and animal products
CONTINENT: Africa

Burundi

CAPITAL: Bujumbura
POPULATION: 6,262,429
MAJOR LANGUAGES: Kirundi, French, and Swahili
AREA: 10,746 sq mi; 27,830 sq km
LEADING EXPORTS: coffee, tea, cotton, and hides and skins
CONTINENT: Africa

Cambodia

CAPITAL: Phnom Penh
POPULATION: 10,561,373
MAJOR LANGUAGES: Khmer and French
AREA: 69,902 sq mi; 181,040 sq km
LEADING EXPORTS: timber, rubber, soybeans, and sesame
CONTINENT: Asia

Cameroon

CAPITAL: Yaounde
POPULATION: 13,521,000
MAJOR LANGUAGES: 24 various languages, English, and French
AREA: 183,574 sq mi; 475,440 sq km
LEADING EXPORTS: petroleum products and lumber
CONTINENT: Africa

Canada

CAPITAL: Ottawa
POPULATION: 28,434,545
MAJOR LANGUAGES: English and French
AREA: 3,851,940 sq mi; 9,976,140 sq km
LEADING EXPORTS: newsprint, wood pulp, timber, and crude petroleum
CONTINENT: North America

Cape Verde

CAPITAL: Praia
POPULATION: 435,983
MAJOR LANGUAGES: Portuguese and Crioulo
AREA: 1,556 sq mi; 4,030 sq km
LEADING EXPORTS: fish, bananas, and hides and skins
CONTINENT: Africa

Cayman Islands

CAPITAL: George Town
POPULATION: 33,192
MAJOR LANGUAGE: English
AREA: 100 sq mi; 260 sq km
LEADING EXPORTS: turtle products and manufactured goods
LOCATION: Caribbean Sea

Central African Republic

CAPITAL: Bangui
POPULATION: 3,209,759
MAJOR LANGUAGES: French, Sangho, Arabic, Hunsa, and Swahili
AREA: 240,542 sq mi; 622,980 sq km
LEADING EXPORTS: diamonds, timber, cotton, coffee, and tobacco
CONTINENT: Africa

Chad

CAPITAL: N'Djamena
POPULATION: 5,586,505
MAJOR LANGUAGES: French, Arabic, Sara, Songo, and over 100 various languages and dialects
AREA: 495,772 sq mi; 1,284,000 sq km
LEADING EXPORTS: cotton, cattle, textiles, and fish
CONTINENT: Africa

Chile

CAPITAL: Santiago
POPULATION: 14,161,216
MAJOR LANGUAGE: Spanish
AREA: 292,269 sq mi; 756,950 sq km
LEADING EXPORTS: copper and other metals and minerals
CONTINENT: South America

China

CAPITAL: Beijing
POPULATION: 1,203,097,268
MAJOR LANGUAGES: Mandarin, Putonghua, Yue, Wu, Minbei, Minnan, Xiang, and Gan and Hakka dialects
AREA: 3,705,533 sq mi; 9,596,960 sq km
LEADING EXPORTS: textiles, garments, footwear, and toys
CONTINENT: Asia

Colombia

CAPITAL: Bogota
POPULATION: 36,200,251
MAJOR LANGUAGE: Spanish
AREA: 439,751 sq mi; 1,138,910 sq km
LEADING EXPORTS: petroleum, coffee, coal, and bananas
CONTINENT: South America

Comoros

CAPITAL: Moroni
POPULATION: 549,338
MAJOR LANGUAGES: Arabic, French, and Comoran
AREA: 838 sq mi; 2,170 sq km
LEADING EXPORTS: vanilla, ylang-ylang, cloves, and perfume oil
LOCATION: Indian Ocean

Congo

CAPITAL: Brazzaville
POPULATION: 2,504,996
MAJOR LANGUAGES: French, Lingala, Kikongo, and other languages
AREA: 132,051 sq mi; 342,000 sq km
LEADING EXPORTS: crude oil, lumber, plywood, sugar, and cocoa
CONTINENT: Africa

Cook Islands

CAPITAL: Avarua
POPULATION: 19,343
MAJOR LANGUAGES: English and Maori
AREA: 95 sq mi; 240 sq km
LEADING EXPORTS: copra, fresh and canned fruit, and clothing
LOCATION: Pacific Ocean

Costa Rica

CAPITAL: San José
POPULATION: 3,419,114
MAJOR LANGUAGES: Spanish and English
AREA: 19,730 sq mi; 51,100 sq km
LEADING EXPORTS: coffee, bananas, textiles, and sugar
CONTINENT: Central America

Côte d'Ivoire

CAPITAL: Yamoussoukro
POPULATION: 14,791,257
MAJOR LANGUAGES: French, Dioula, and 59 other dialects
AREA: 124,507 sq mi; 322,460 sq km
LEADING EXPORTS: cocoa, coffee, tropical woods, and petroleum
CONTINENT: Africa

Croatia

CAPITAL: Zagreb
POPULATION: 4,665,821
MAJOR LANGUAGE: Serbo-Croatian
AREA: 21,830 sq mi; 56,538 sq km
LEADING EXPORTS: machinery and transportation equipment
CONTINENT: Europe

Cuba

CAPITAL: Havana
POPULATION: 10,937,635
MAJOR LANGUAGE: Spanish
AREA: 42,805 sq mi; 110,860 sq km
LEADING EXPORTS: sugar, nickel, shellfish, and tobacco
LOCATION: Caribbean Sea

Cyprus

CAPITAL: Nicosia
POPULATION: 736,636
MAJOR LANGUAGES: Greek, Turkish, and English
AREA: 3,572 sq mi; 9,250 sq km
LEADING EXPORTS: citrus, potatoes, grapes, wines, and cement
LOCATION: Mediterranean Sea

Czech Republic

CAPITAL: Prague
POPULATION: 10,432,774
MAJOR LANGUAGES: Czech and Slovak
AREA: 30,388 sq mi; 78,703 sq km
LEADING EXPORTS: manufactured goods
CONTINENT: Europe

Denmark

CAPITAL: Copenhagen
POPULATION: 5,199,437
MAJOR LANGUAGES: Danish, Faroese, Greenlandic, and German
AREA: 16,630 sq mi; 43,070 sq km
LEADING EXPORTS: meat and meat products, and dairy products
CONTINENT: Europe

Djibouti

CAPITAL: Djibouti
POPULATION: 421,320
MAJOR LANGUAGES: French, Arabic, Somali, and Afar
AREA: 8,495 sq mi; 22,000 sq km
LEADING EXPORTS: hides and skins, and coffee (in transit)
CONTINENT: Africa

Dominica

CAPITAL: Roseau
POPULATION: 82,608
MAJOR LANGUAGES: English and French patois
AREA: 290 sq mi; 750 sq km
LEADING EXPORTS: bananas, soap, bay oil, and vegetables
LOCATION: Caribbean Sea

Dominican Republic

CAPITAL: Santo Domingo
POPULATION: 7,511,263
MAJOR LANGUAGES: Spanish
AREA: 18,815 sq mi; 48,730 sq km
LEADING EXPORTS: ferronickel, sugar, gold, coffee, and cocoa
LOCATION: Caribbean Sea

Ecuador

CAPITAL: Quito
POPULATION: 10,890,950
MAJOR LANGUAGES: Spanish, Quechua, and various languages
AREA: 109,487 sq mi; 283,560 sq km
LEADING EXPORTS: petroleum, bananas, shrimp, and cocoa
CONTINENT: South America

Egypt

CAPITAL: Cairo
POPULATION: 62,359,623
MAJOR LANGUAGES: Arabic, English, and French
AREA: 386,675 sq mi; 1,001,450 sq km
LEADING EXPORTS: crude oil and petroleum products
CONTINENT: Africa

El Salvador

CAPITAL: San Salvador
POPULATION: 5,870,481
MAJOR LANGUAGES: Spanish and Nahua
AREA: 8,124 sq mi; 21,040 sq km
LEADING EXPORTS: coffee, sugar cane, and shrimp
CONTINENT: Central America

Equatorial Guinea

CAPITAL: Malabo
POPULATION: 420,293
MAJOR LANGUAGES: Spanish, Pidgin English, Fang, Bubi, and Ibo
AREA: 10,831 sq mi; 28,050 sq km
LEADING EXPORTS: coffee, timber, and cocoa beans
CONTINENT: Africa

Eritrea

CAPITAL: Asmara
POPULATION: 3,578,709
MAJOR LANGUAGES: Tigre, Kunama, Cushitic dialects, Nora Bana, and Arabic
AREA: 46,844 sq mi; 121,320 sq km
LEADING EXPORTS: salt, hides, cement, and gum arabic
CONTINENT: Africa

Estonia

CAPITAL: Tallinn
POPULATION: 1,625,399
MAJOR LANGUAGES: Estonian, Latvian, Lithuanian, and Russian
AREA: 17,414 sq mi; 45,100 sq km
LEADING EXPORTS: textiles, food products, vehicles, and metals
CONTINENT: Europe

Ethiopia

CAPITAL: Addis Ababa
POPULATION: 55,979,018
MAJOR LANGUAGES: Amharic, Tigrinya, Orominga, Guaraginga, Somali, Arabic, English, and various languages
AREA: 435,201 sq mi; 1,127,127 sq km
LEADING EXPORTS: coffee, leather products, and gold
CONTINENT: Africa

Fiji

CAPITAL: Suva
POPULATION: 772,891
MAJOR LANGUAGES: English, Fijian, and Hindustani
AREA: 7,054 sq mi; 18,270 sq km
LEADING EXPORTS: sugar, clothing, gold, processed fish, and lumber
LOCATION: Pacific Ocean

Finland

CAPITAL: Helsinki
POPULATION: 5,085,206
MAJOR LANGUAGES: Finnish, Swedish, Lapp, and Russian
AREA: 130,132 sq mi; 337,030 sq km
LEADING EXPORTS: paper and pulp, machinery, and chemicals
CONTINENT: Europe

France

CAPITAL: Paris
POPULATION: 58,109,160
MAJOR LANGUAGES: French and regional dialects and languages
AREA: 211,217 sq mi; 547,030 sq km
LEADING EXPORTS: machinery and transportation equipment
CONTINENT: Europe

Gabon

CAPITAL: Libreville
POPULATION: 1,185,749
MAJOR LANGUAGES: French, Fang, Myene, Bateke, Bapounou/Eschira, and Bandjabi
AREA: 103,351 sq mi; 267,670 sq km
LEADING EXPORTS: crude oil, timber, manganese, and uranium
CONTINENT: Africa

The Gambia

CAPITAL: Banjul
POPULATION: 989,273
MAJOR LANGUAGES: English, Mandinka, Wolof, Fula, and various languages
AREA: 4,363 sq mi; 11,300 sq km
LEADING EXPORTS: peanuts and peanut products, and fish
CONTINENT: Africa

Georgia

CAPITAL: T'bilisi
POPULATION: 5,725,972
MAJOR LANGUAGES: Armenian, Azeri, Georgian, Russian, and various languages
AREA: 26,912 sq mi; 69,700 sq km
LEADING EXPORTS: citrus fruits, tea, and wine
CONTINENT: Asia

Germany

CAPITAL: Berlin
POPULATION: 81,337,541
MAJOR LANGUAGE: German
AREA: 137,808 sq mi; 356,910 sq km
LEADING EXPORTS: machines and machine tools, and chemicals
CONTINENT: Europe

Ghana

CAPITAL: Accra
POPULATION: 17,763,138
MAJOR LANGUAGES: English, Akan, Moshi-Dagomba, Ewe, Ga, and various languages
AREA: 92,104 sq mi; 238,540 sq km
LEADING EXPORTS: cocoa, gold, timber, tuna, and bauxite
CONTINENT: Africa

Greece

CAPITAL: Athens
POPULATION: 10,647,511
MAJOR LANGUAGES: Greek, English, and French
AREA: 50,944 sq mi; 131,940 sq km
LEADING EXPORTS: manufactured goods, foodstuffs, and fuels
CONTINENT: Europe

Grenada

CAPITAL: Saint George's
POPULATION: 94,486
MAJOR LANGUAGES: English and French patois
AREA: 131 sq mi; 340 sq km
LEADING EXPORTS: bananas, cocoa, nutmeg, and fruits and vegetables
LOCATION: Caribbean Sea

Guatemala

CAPITAL: Guatemala
POPULATION: 10,998,602
MAJOR LANGUAGES: Spanish, Quiche, Cakchiquel, Kekchi, and various languages and dialects
AREA: 42,044 sq mi; 108,890 sq km
LEADING EXPORTS: coffee, sugar, bananas, cardamom, and beef
CONTINENT: Central America

Guinea

CAPITAL: Conakry
POPULATION: 6,549,336
MAJOR LANGUAGES: French and various languages
AREA: 94,930 sq mi; 245,860 sq km
LEADING EXPORTS: bauxite, alumina, diamonds, gold, and coffee
CONTINENT: Africa

Guinea Bissau

CAPITAL: Bissau
POPULATION: 1,124,537
MAJOR LANGUAGES: Portuguese, Criolo, and various languages
AREA: 13,946 sq mi; 36,210 sq km
LEADING EXPORTS: cashews, fish, peanuts, and palm kernels
CONTINENT: Africa

Guyana

CAPITAL: Georgetown
POPULATION: 723,774
MAJOR LANGUAGES: English and various dialects
AREA: 83,003 sq mi; 214,970 sq km
LEADING EXPORTS: sugar, bauxite/alumina, rice, and shrimp
CONTINENT: South America

Haiti

CAPITAL: Port-au-Prince
POPULATION: 6,539,983
MAJOR LANGUAGES: French and Creole
AREA: 8,784 sq mi; 22,750 sq km
LEADING EXPORTS: light manufactures and coffee
LOCATION: Caribbean Sea

Holy See (Vatican City)

CAPITAL: Vatican City
POPULATION: 830
MAJOR LANGUAGES: Italian, Latin, and various languages
AREA: 17 sq mi; 44 sq km
LEADING EXPORTS: none
CONTINENT: Europe

Honduras

CAPITAL: Tegucigalpa
POPULATION: 5,549,743
MAJOR LANGUAGES: Spanish and various dialects
AREA: 43,280 sq mi; 112,090 sq km
LEADING EXPORTS: bananas, coffee, shrimp, lobsters, and minerals
CONTINENT: Central America

Hungary

CAPITAL: Budapest
POPULATION: 10,318,838
MAJOR LANGUAGES: Hungarian and various languages
AREA: 35,920 sq mi; 93,030 sq km
LEADING EXPORTS: raw materials and semi-finished goods
CONTINENT: Europe

Iceland

CAPITAL: Reykjavik
POPULATION: 265,998
MAJOR LANGUAGE: Icelandic
AREA: 39,770 sq mi; 103,000 sq km
LEADING EXPORTS: fish and fish products, and animal products
CONTINENT: Europe

India

CAPITAL: New Delhi
POPULATION: 936,545,814
MAJOR LANGUAGES: English, Hindi, Bengali, Telugu, Marathi, Tamil, Urdu, Gujarati, Malayam, Kannada, Oriya, Punjabi, Assamese, Kashmiri, Sindhi, Sanskrit, and Hindustani (all official)
AREA: 1,269,389 sq mi; 3,287,590 sq km
LEADING EXPORTS: clothing, and gems and jewelry
CONTINENT: Asia

Indonesia

CAPITAL: Jakarta
POPULATION: 203,583,886
MAJOR LANGUAGES: Bahasa Indonesia, English, Dutch, Javanese, and various dialects
AREA: 741,052 sq mi; 1,919,251 sq km
LEADING EXPORTS: manufactures, fuels, and foodstuffs
CONTINENT: Asia

Iran

CAPITAL: Tehran
POPULATION: 64,625,455
MAJOR LANGUAGES: Farsi (official) and Turkic languages
AREA: 634,562 sq mi; 1,643,452 sq km
LEADING EXPORTS: petroleum, carpets, fruit, nuts, and hides
CONTINENT: Asia

Iraq

CAPITAL: Baghdad
POPULATION: 20,643,769
MAJOR LANGUAGES: Arabic, Kurdish, Assyrian, and Armenian
AREA: 168,760 sq mi; 437,072 sq km
LEADING EXPORTS: crude oil and refined products, and fertilizers
CONTINENT: Asia

Ireland

CAPITAL: Dublin
POPULATION: 3,550,448
MAJOR LANGUAGES: Irish Gaelic and English
AREA: 27,136 sq mi; 70,280 sq km
LEADING EXPORTS: chemicals and data processing equipment
CONTINENT: Europe

Israel

CAPITAL: Jerusalem
POPULATION: 7,566,447
MAJOR LANGUAGES: Hebrew, Arabic, and English
AREA: 10,421 sq mi; 26,990 sq km
LEADING EXPORTS: machinery and equipment, and cut diamonds
CONTINENT: Asia

Italy

CAPITAL: Rome
POPULATION: 58,261,971
MAJOR LANGUAGES: Italian, German, French, and Slovene
AREA: 116,310 sq mi; 301,230 sq km
LEADING EXPORTS: metals, and textiles and clothing
CONTINENT: Europe

Jamaica

CAPITAL: Kingston
POPULATION: 2,574,291
MAJOR LANGUAGES: English and Creole
AREA: 4,243 sq mi; 10,990 sq km
LEADING EXPORTS: alumina, bauxite, sugar, bananas, and rum
LOCATION: Caribbean Sea

Japan

CAPITAL: Tokyo
POPULATION: 125,506,492
MAJOR LANGUAGE: Japanese
AREA: 145,888 sq mi; 377,835 sq km
LEADING EXPORTS: machinery, motor vehicles, and electronics
CONTINENT: Asia

Jordan

CAPITAL: Amman
POPULATION: 4,100,709
MAJOR LANGUAGES: Arabic and English
AREA: 34,447 sq mi; 89,213 sq km
LEADING EXPORTS: phosphates, fertilizers, and potash
CONTINENT: Asia

Kazakhstan

CAPITAL: Almaty
POPULATION: 17,376,615
MAJOR LANGUAGES: Kazakh and Russian
AREA: 1,049,191 sq mi; 2,717,300 sq km
LEADING EXPORTS: oil, and ferrous and nonferrous metals
CONTINENT: Asia

Kenya

CAPITAL: Nairobi
POPULATION: 28,817,227
MAJOR LANGUAGES: English, Swahili, and various languages
AREA: 224,970 sq mi; 582,650 sq km
LEADING EXPORTS: tea, coffee, and petroleum products
CONTINENT: Africa

Kiribati

CAPITAL: Tarawa
POPULATION: 79,386
MAJOR LANGUAGES: English and Gilbertese
AREA: 277 sq mi; 717 sq km
LEADING EXPORTS: copra, seaweed, and fish
LOCATION: Pacific Ocean

Korea, North

CAPITAL: P'yongyang
POPULATION: 23,486,550
MAJOR LANGUAGE: Korean
AREA: 46,542 sq mi; 120,540 sq km
LEADING EXPORTS: minerals and metallurgical products
CONTINENT: Asia

Korea, South

CAPITAL: Seoul
POPULATION: 45,553,882
MAJOR LANGUAGES: Korean and English
AREA: 38,025 sq mi; 98,480 sq km
LEADING EXPORTS: electronic and electrical equipment
CONTINENT: Asia

Kuwait

CAPITAL: Kuwait
POPULATION: 1,817,397
MAJOR LANGUAGES: Arabic and English
AREA: 6,881 sq mi; 17,820 sq km
LEADING EXPORT: oil
CONTINENT: Asia

Kyrgyzstan

CAPITAL: Bishkek
POPULATION: 4,769,877
MAJOR LANGUAGES: Kyrgyz and Russian
AREA: 76,644 sq mi; 198,500 sq km
LEADING EXPORTS: wool, chemicals, cotton, metals, and shoes
CONTINENT: Asia

Laos

CAPITAL: Vientiane
POPULATION: 4,837,237
MAJOR LANGUAGES: Lao, French, English, and various languages
AREA: 91,432 sq mi; 236,800 sq km
LEADING EXPORTS: electricity, wood products, coffee, and tin
CONTINENT: Asia

Latvia

CAPITAL: Riga
POPULATION: 2,762,899
MAJOR LANGUAGES: Lettish, Lithuanian, Russian, and various languages
AREA: 24,750 sq mi; 64,100 sq km
LEADING EXPORTS: oil products, timber, and ferrous metals
CONTINENT: Europe

Lebanon

CAPITAL: Beirut
POPULATION: 3,695,921
MAJOR LANGUAGES: Arabic, French, Armenian, and English
AREA: 4,016 sq mi; 10,400 sq km
LEADING EXPORTS: agricultural products, chemicals, and textiles
CONTINENT: Asia

Lesotho

CAPITAL: Maseru
POPULATION: 1,992,960
MAJOR LANGUAGES: Sesotho, English, Zulu, and Xhosa
AREA: 11,719 sq mi; 30,350 sq km
LEADING EXPORTS: wool, mohair, wheat, cattle, and peas
CONTINENT: Africa

Liberia

CAPITAL: Monrovia
POPULATION: 3,073,245
MAJOR LANGUAGES: English and Niger-Congo
AREA: 43,002 sq mi; 111,370 sq km
LEADING EXPORTS: iron ore, rubber, timber, and coffee
CONTINENT: Africa

Libya
CAPITAL: Tripoli
POPULATION: 5,248,401
MAJOR LANGUAGES: Arabic, Italian, and English
AREA: 679,385 sq mi; 1,759,540 sq km
LEADING EXPORTS: crude oil and refined petroleum products
CONTINENT: Africa

Liechtenstein
CAPITAL: Vaduz
POPULATION: 30,654
MAJOR LANGUAGES: German and Alemannic
AREA: 62 sq mi; 160 sq km
LEADING EXPORTS: small specialty machinery and dental products
CONTINENT: Europe

Lithuania
CAPITAL: Vilnius
POPULATION: 3,876,396
MAJOR LANGUAGES: Lithuanian, Polish, and Russian
AREA: 25,175 sq mi; 65,200 sq km
LEADING EXPORTS: electronics, petroleum products, and food
CONTINENT: Europe

Luxembourg
CAPITAL: Luxembourg
POPULATION: 404,660
MAJOR LANGUAGES: Luxembourgisch, German, French, and English
AREA: 998 sq mi; 2,586 sq km
LEADING EXPORTS: finished steel products and chemicals
CONTINENT: Europe

Macedonia
CAPITAL: Skopje
POPULATION: 2,159,503
MAJOR LANGUAGES: Macedonian, Albanian, Turkish, Serb, Gypsy, and various languages
AREA: 9,781 sq mi; 25,333 sq km
LEADING EXPORTS: manufactured goods and machinery
CONTINENT: Europe

Madagascar
CAPITAL: Antananarivo
POPULATION: 13,862,325
MAJOR LANGUAGES: French and Malagasy
AREA: 226,665 sq mi; 587,040 sq km
LEADING EXPORTS: coffee, vanilla, cloves, shellfish, and sugar
CONTINENT: Africa

Malawi
CAPITAL: Lilongwe
POPULATION: 9,808,384
MAJOR LANGUAGES: English, Chichewa, and various languages
AREA: 45,747 sq mi; 118,480 sq km
LEADING EXPORTS: tobacco, tea, sugar, coffee, and peanuts
CONTINENT: Africa

Malaysia
CAPITAL: Kuala Lumpur
POPULATION: 19,723,587
MAJOR LANGUAGES: Malay, English, Mandarin, Tamil, Chinese dialects, and various languages and dialects
AREA: 127,322 sq mi; 329,750 sq km
LEADING EXPORTS: electronic equipment
CONTINENT: Asia

Maldives
CAPITAL: Male
POPULATION: 261,310
MAJOR LANGUAGES: Divehi dialect and English
AREA: 116 sq mi; 300 sq km
LEADING EXPORTS: fish and clothing
CONTINENT: Asia

Mali
CAPITAL: Bamako
POPULATION: 9,375,132
MAJOR LANGUAGES: French, Bambara, and various languages
AREA: 478,783 sq mi; 1,240,000 sq km
LEADING EXPORTS: cotton, livestock, and gold
CONTINENT: Africa

Malta
CAPITAL: Valletta
POPULATION: 369,609
MAJOR LANGUAGES: Maltese and English
AREA: 124 sq mi; 320 sq km
LEADING EXPORTS: machinery and transportation equipment
CONTINENT: Europe

Marshall Islands
CAPITAL: Majuro
POPULATION: 56,157
MAJOR LANGUAGES: English, Marshallese dialects, and Japanese
AREA: 70 sq mi; 181.3 sq km
LEADING EXPORTS: coconut oil, fish, live animals, and trichus shells
LOCATION: Pacific Ocean

Mauritania
CAPITAL: Nouakchott
POPULATION: 2,263,202
MAJOR LANGUAGES: Hasaniya Arabic, Wolof, Pular, and Soninke
AREA: 397,969 sq mi; 1,030,700 sq km
LEADING EXPORTS: iron ore, and fish and fish products
CONTINENT: Africa

Mauritius
CAPITAL: Port Louis
POPULATION: 1,127,068
MAJOR LANGUAGES: English (official), Creole, French, Hindi, Urdu, Hakka, and Bojpoori
AREA: 718 sq mi; 1,860 sq km
LEADING EXPORTS: textiles, sugar, and light manufactures
LOCATION: Indian Ocean

Mayotte
CAPITAL: Mamoutzou
POPULATION: 97,088
MAJOR LANGUAGES: Mahorian and French
AREA: 145 sq mi; 375 sq km
LEADING EXPORTS: ylang-ylang and vanilla
CONTINENT: Africa

Mexico
CAPITAL: Mexico City
POPULATION: 93,985,848
MAJOR LANGUAGES: Spanish and Mayan dialects
AREA: 761,632 sq mi; 1,972,550 sq km
LEADING EXPORTS: crude oil, oil products, coffee, and silver
CONTINENT: North America

Micronesia
CAPITAL: Federated states of Kolonia (on the Island of Pohnpei)
*a new capital is being built about 10 km southwest in the Palikir Valley
POPULATION: 122,950
MAJOR LANGUAGES: English, Turkese, Pohnpeian, Yapese, and Kosrean
AREA: 271 sq mi; 702 sq km
LEADING EXPORTS: fish, copra, bananas, and black pepper
LOCATION: Pacific Ocean

Moldova
CAPITAL: Chisinau
POPULATION: 4,489,657
MAJOR LANGUAGES: Moldovan (official), Russian, and Gagauz dialect
AREA: 13,012 sq mi; 33,700 sq km
LEADING EXPORTS: foodstuffs, wine, and tobacco
CONTINENT: Europe

Monaco
CAPITAL: Monaco
POPULATION: 31,515
MAJOR LANGUAGES: French (official), English, Italian, and Monegasque
AREA: .73 sq mi; 1.9 sq km
LEADING EXPORTS: exports through France
CONTINENT: Europe

Mongolia
CAPITAL: Ulaanbaatar
POPULATION: 2,493,615
MAJOR LANGUAGES: Khalkha Mongol, Turkic, Russian, and Chinese
AREA: 604,270 sq mi; 1,565,000 sq km
LEADING EXPORTS: copper, livestock, animal products, and cashmere
CONTINENT: Asia

Morocco
CAPITAL: Rabat
POPULATION: 29,168,848
MAJOR LANGUAGES: Arabic (official), Berber dialects, and French
AREA: 172,420 sq mi; 446,550 sq km
LEADING EXPORTS: food and beverages
CONTINENT: Africa

Mozambique
CAPITAL: Maputo
POPULATION: 18,115,250
MAJOR LANGUAGES: Portuguese and various dialects
AREA: 309,506 sq mi; 801,590 sq km
LEADING EXPORTS: shrimp, cashews, cotton, sugar, copra, and citrus
CONTINENT: Africa

Myanmar (Burma)
CAPITAL: Rangoon
POPULATION: 45,103,809
MAJOR LANGUAGE: Burmese
AREA: 261,979 sq mi; 678,500 sq km
LEADING EXPORTS: pulses and beans, teak, rice, and hardwood
CONTINENT: Asia

Namibia
CAPITAL: Windhoek
POPULATION: 1,651,545
MAJOR LANGUAGES: English (official), Afrikaans, German, Oshivambo, Herero, Nama, and various languages
AREA: 318,707 sq mi; 825,418 sq km
LEADING EXPORTS: diamonds, copper, gold, zinc, and lead
CONTINENT: Africa

Nauru

CAPITAL: Government offices in Yaren District
POPULATION: 10,149
MAJOR LANGUAGES: Nauruan and English
AREA: 8 sq mi; 21 sq km
LEADING EXPORTS: phosphates
LOCATION: Pacific Ocean

Nepal

CAPITAL: Kathmandu
POPULATION: 21,560,869
MAJOR LANGUAGES: Nepali (official) and 20 various languages divided into numerous dialects
AREA: 54,365 sq mi; 140,800 sq km
LEADING EXPORTS: carpets, clothing, and leather goods
CONTINENT: Asia

Netherlands

CAPITAL: Amsterdam
POPULATION: 15,452,903
MAJOR LANGUAGE: Dutch
AREA: 14,414 sq mi; 37,330 sq km
LEADING EXPORTS: metal products and chemicals
CONTINENT: Europe

New Caledonia

CAPITAL: Noumea
POPULATION: 184,552
MAJOR LANGUAGES: French and 28 Melanesian-Polynesian dialects
AREA: 7,359 sq mi; 19,060 sq km
LEADING EXPORTS: nickel metal and nickel ore
LOCATION: Pacific Ocean

New Zealand

CAPITAL: Wellington
POPULATION: 3,407,277
MAJOR LANGUAGES: English and Maori
AREA: 103,741 sq mi; 268,680 sq km
LEADING EXPORTS: wool, lamb, mutton, beef, fish, and cheese
LOCATION: Pacific Ocean

Nicaragua

CAPITAL: Managua
POPULATION: 4,206,353
MAJOR LANGUAGES: Spanish (official), English, and various languages
AREA: 50,000 sq mi; 129,494 sq km
LEADING EXPORTS: meat, coffee, cotton, sugar, seafood, and gold
LOCATION: Caribbean Sea

Niger

CAPITAL: Niamey
POPULATION: 9,280,208
MAJOR LANGUAGES: French (official), Hausa, and Djerma
AREA: 489,208 sq mi; 1,267,000 sq km
LEADING EXPORTS: uranium ore and livestock products
CONTINENT: Africa

Nigeria

CAPITAL: Abuja
POPULATION: 101,232,251
MAJOR LANGUAGES: English (official), Hausa, Yoruba, Ibo, and Fulani
AREA: 356,682 sq mi; 923,770 sq km
LEADING EXPORTS: oil, cocoa, and rubber
CONTINENT: Africa

Niue

CAPITAL: (Free association with New Zealand)
POPULATION: 1,837
MAJOR LANGUAGES: Polynesian and English
AREA: 100 sq mi; 260 sq km
LEADING EXPORTS: canned coconut cream, copra, and honey
LOCATION: Pacific Ocean

Norway

CAPITAL: Oslo
POPULATION: 4,330,951
MAJOR LANGUAGES: Norwegian (official), Lapp, and Finnish
AREA: 125,186 sq mi; 324,220 sq km
LEADING EXPORTS: petroleum and petroleum products
CONTINENT: Europe

Oman

CAPITAL: Muscat
POPULATION: 2,125,089
MAJOR LANGUAGES: Arabic (official), English, Baluchi, Urdu, and Indian dialects
AREA: 82,034 sq mi; 212,460 sq km
LEADING EXPORTS: petroleum, re-exports, and fish
CONTINENT: Asia

Pakistan

CAPITAL: Islamabad
POPULATION: 131,541,920
MAJOR LANGUAGES: Urdu (official), English (official), Punjabi, Sindhi, Pashtu, Urdu, Balochi, and other languages
AREA: 310,414 sq mi; 803,940 sq km
LEADING EXPORTS: cotton, textiles, clothing, rice, and leather
CONTINENT: Asia

Palau

CAPITAL: Koror
POPULATION: 16,661
MAJOR LANGUAGES: English (official), Sonsorolese, Angaur, Japanese, Tobi, and Palauan
AREA: 177 sq mi; 458 sq km
LEADING EXPORTS: trochus, tuna, copra, and handicrafts
LOCATION: Pacific Ocean

Panama

CAPITAL: Panama
POPULATION: 2,680,903
MAJOR LANGUAGES: Spanish (official) and English
AREA: 30,194 sq mi; 78,200 sq km
LEADING EXPORTS: bananas, shrimp, sugar, clothing, and coffee
CONTINENT: Central America

Papua New Guinea

CAPITAL: Port Moresby
POPULATION: 4,294,750
MAJOR LANGUAGES: English, pidgin English, and Motu
AREA: 178,266 sq mi; 461,690 sq km
LEADING EXPORTS: gold, copper ore, oil, logs, and palm oil
LOCATION: Pacific Ocean

Paraguay

CAPITAL: Asuncion
POPULATION: 5,358,198
MAJOR LANGUAGES: Spanish (official) and Guarani
AREA: 157,052 sq mi; 406,750 sq km
LEADING EXPORTS: cotton, soybeans, timber, and vegetable oils
CONTINENT: South America

Peru

CAPITAL: Lima
POPULATION: 24,087,372
MAJOR LANGUAGES: Spanish (official), Quechua (official), and Aymara
AREA: 496,243 sq mi; 1,285,220 sq km
LEADING EXPORTS: copper, zinc, and fish meal
CONTINENT: South America

Philippines

CAPITAL: Manila
POPULATION: 73,265,584
MAJOR LANGUAGES: Pilipino and English (official)
AREA: 115,834 sq mi; 300,000 sq km
LEADING EXPORTS: electronics, textiles, and coconut products
CONTINENT: Asia

Poland

CAPITAL: Warsaw
POPULATION: 38,792,442
MAJOR LANGUAGE: Polish
AREA: 120,731 sq mi; 312,680 sq km
LEADING EXPORTS: intermediate goods
CONTINENT: Europe

Portugal

CAPITAL: Lisbon
POPULATION: 10,562,388
MAJOR LANGUAGE: Portuguese
AREA: 35,553 sq mi; 92,080 sq km
LEADING EXPORTS: clothing and footwear, and machinery
CONTINENT: Europe

Qatar

CAPITAL: Doha
POPULATION: 533,916
MAJOR LANGUAGES: Arabic (official) and English
AREA: 4,247 sq mi; 11,000 sq km
LEADING EXPORTS: petroleum products, steel, and fertilizers
CONTINENT: Asia

Romania

CAPITAL: Bucharest
POPULATION: 23,198,330
MAJOR LANGUAGES: Romanian, Hungarian, and German
AREA: 91,702 sq mi; 237,500 sq km
LEADING EXPORTS: metals and metal products, and mineral products
CONTINENT: Europe

Russia

CAPITAL: Moscow
POPULATION: 149,909,089
MAJOR LANGUAGES: Russian and various languages
AREA: 6,952,996 sq mi; 17,075,200 sq km
LEADING EXPORTS: petroleum and petroleum products
CONTINENT: Europe and Asia

Rwanda

CAPITAL: Kigali
POPULATION: 8,605,307
MAJOR LANGUAGES: Kinyarwanda (official), French (official), and Kiswahili
AREA: 10,170 sq mi; 26,340 sq km
LEADING EXPORTS: coffee, tea, cassiterite, and wolframite
CONTINENT: Africa

Saint Kitts and Nevis

CAPITAL: Basseterre
POPULATION: 40,992
MAJOR LANGUAGE: English
AREA: 104 sq mi; 269 sq km
LEADING EXPORTS: machinery, food, and electronics
LOCATION: Caribbean Sea

Saint Lucia

CAPITAL: Castries
POPULATION: 156,050
MAJOR LANGUAGES: English and French patois
AREA: 239 sq mi; 620 sq km
LEADING EXPORTS: bananas, clothing, cocoa, and vegetables
LOCATION: Caribbean Sea

Saint Vincent and the Grenadines

CAPITAL: Kingstown
POPULATION: 117,344
MAJOR LANGUAGES: English and French patois
AREA: 131 sq mi; 340 sq km
LEADING EXPORTS: bananas, and eddoes and dasheen (taro)
LOCATION: Caribbean Sea

San Marino

CAPITAL: San Marino
POPULATION: 24,313
MAJOR LANGUAGE: Italian
AREA: 23 sq mi; 60 sq km
LEADING EXPORTS: building stone, lime, wood, and chestnuts
CONTINENT: Europe

Sao Tome and Principe

CAPITAL: Sao Tome
POPULATION: 140,423
MAJOR LANGUAGE: Portuguese (official)
AREA: 371 sq mi; 960 sq km
LEADING EXPORTS: cocoa, copra, coffee, and palm oil
CONTINENT: Africa

Saudi Arabia

CAPITAL: Riyadh
POPULATION: 18,729,576
MAJOR LANGUAGE: Arabic
AREA: 757,011 sq mi; 1,960,582 sq km
LEADING EXPORTS: petroleum and petroleum products
CONTINENT: Asia

Senegal

CAPITAL: Dakar
POPULATION: 9,007,080
MAJOR LANGUAGES: French (official), Wolof, Pulaar, Diola, and Mandingo
AREA: 75,752 sq mi; 196,190 sq km
LEADING EXPORTS: fish, ground nuts, and petroleum products
CONTINENT: Africa

Serbia and Montenegro

CAPITAL: Belgrade
POPULATION: 11,101,833
MAJOR LANGUAGES: Serbo-Croatian and Albanian
AREA: 39,436 sq mi; 102,350 sq km
LEADING EXPORTS: none
CONTINENT: Europe

Seychelles

CAPITAL: Victoria
POPULATION: 72,709
MAJOR LANGUAGES: English (official), French (official), and Creole
AREA: 176 sq mi; 455 sq km
LEADING EXPORTS: fish, cinnamon bark, and copra
CONTINENT: Africa

Sierra Leone

CAPITAL: Freetown
POPULATION: 4,753,120
MAJOR LANGUAGES: English (official), Mende, Temne, and Krio
AREA: 27,700 sq mi; 71,740 sq km
LEADING EXPORTS: rutile, bauxite, diamonds, coffee, and cocoa
CONTINENT: Africa

Singapore

CAPITAL: Singapore
POPULATION: 2,890,468
MAJOR LANGUAGES: Chinese, Malay, Tamil, and English
AREA: 244 sq mi; 633 sq km
LEADING EXPORTS: computer equipment
CONTINENT: Asia

Slovakia

CAPITAL: Bratislava
POPULATION: 5,432,383
MAJOR LANGUAGES: Slovak and Hungarian
AREA: 18,860 sq mi; 48,845 sq km
LEADING EXPORTS: machinery and transportation equipment
CONTINENT: Europe

Slovenia

CAPITAL: Ljubljana
POPULATION: 2,051,522
MAJOR LANGUAGES: Slovenian, Serbo-Croatian, and various languages
AREA: 7,837 sq mi; 20,296 sq km
LEADING EXPORTS: machinery and transportation equipment
CONTINENT: Europe

Solomon Islands

CAPITAL: Honiara
POPULATION: 399,206
MAJOR LANGUAGES: Melanesian pidgin and English
AREA: 10,985 sq mi; 28,450 sq km
LEADING EXPORTS: fish, timber, palm oil, cocoa, and copra
LOCATION: Pacific Ocean

Somalia

CAPITAL: Mogadishu
POPULATION: 7,347,554
MAJOR LANGUAGES: Somali (official), Arabic, Italian, and English
AREA: 246,210 sq mi; 637,660 sq km
LEADING EXPORTS: bananas, live animals, fish, and hides
CONTINENT: Africa

South Africa

CAPITAL: Pretoria (administrative), Cape Town (legislative), Bloemfontein (judicial)
POPULATION: 45,095,459
MAJOR LANGUAGES: Afrikaans, English, Ndebele, Pedi, Sotho, Swazi, Tsonga, Tswana, Venda, Xhosa, and Zulu (all official)
AREA: 471,027 sq mi; 1,219,912 sq km
LEADING EXPORTS: gold, other minerals and metals, and food
CONTINENT: Africa

Spain

CAPITAL: Madrid
POPULATION: 39,404,348
MAJOR LANGUAGES: Spanish, Catalan, Galician, and Basque
AREA: 194,892 sq mi; 504,750 sq km
LEADING EXPORTS: cars and trucks, and semifinished goods
CONTINENT: Europe

Sri Lanka

CAPITAL: Colombo
POPULATION: 18,342,660
MAJOR LANGUAGES: Sinhala (official) and Tamil
AREA: 25,333 sq mi; 65,610 sq km
LEADING EXPORTS: garments and textiles, teas, and diamonds
CONTINENT: Asia

Sudan

CAPITAL: Khartoum
POPULATION: 30,120,420
MAJOR LANGUAGES: Arabic (official), Nubian, Ta Bedawie, Nilotic, Nilo-Hamitic, and Sudanic dialects
AREA: 967,532 sq mi; 2,505,810 sq km
LEADING EXPORTS: gum arabic, livestock/meat, and cotton
CONTINENT: Africa

Suriname

CAPITAL: Paramaribo
POPULATION: 429,544
MAJOR LANGUAGES: Dutch (official), English, Sranang, Tongo, Hindustani, and Japanese
AREA: 63,041 sq mi; 163,270 sq km
LEADING EXPORTS: alumina, aluminum, and shrimp and fish
CONTINENT: South America

Swaziland

CAPITAL: Mbabane
POPULATION: 966,977
MAJOR LANGUAGES: English (official) and SiSwati (official)
AREA: 6,641 sq mi; 17,360 sq km
LEADING EXPORTS: sugar, edible concentrates, and wood pulp
CONTINENT: Africa

Sweden

CAPITAL: Stockholm
POPULATION: 8,821,759
MAJOR LANGUAGES: Swedish, Lapp, and Finnish
AREA: 173,738 sq mi; 449,964 sq km
LEADING EXPORTS: machinery, motor vehicles, and paper products
CONTINENT: Europe

Switzerland

CAPITAL: Bern
POPULATION: 7,084,984
MAJOR LANGUAGES: German, French, Italian, Romansch, and various languages
AREA: 15,943 sq mi; 41,290 sq km
LEADING EXPORTS: machinery and equipment
CONTINENT: Europe

Syria

CAPITAL: Damascus
POPULATION: 15,451,917
MAJOR LANGUAGES: Arabic (official), Kurdish, Armenian, Aramaic, Circassian, and French
AREA: 71,501 sq mi; 185,180 sq km
LEADING EXPORTS: petroleum, textiles, cotton, and fruits
CONTINENT: Asia

Taiwan

CAPITAL: Taipei
POPULATION: 21,500,583
MAJOR LANGUAGES: Mandarin Chinese (official), Taiwanese, and Hakka dialects
AREA: 13,892 sq mi; 35,980 sq km
LEADING EXPORTS: electrical machinery and electronics
CONTINENT: Asia

Tajikistan

CAPITAL: Dushanbe
POPULATION: 6,155,474
MAJOR LANGUAGES: Tajik (official) and Russian
AREA: 55,253 sq mi; 143,100 sq km
LEADING EXPORTS: cotton, aluminum, fruits, and vegetable oil
CONTINENT: Asia

Tanzania
CAPITAL: Dar Es Salaam
POPULATION: 28,701,077
MAJOR LANGUAGES: Swahili, English, and various languages
AREA: 364,914 sq mi; 945,090 sq km
LEADING EXPORTS: coffee, cotton, tobacco, tea, and cashew nuts
CONTINENT: Africa

Thailand
CAPITAL: Bangkok
POPULATION: 60,271,300
MAJOR LANGUAGES: Thai and English
AREA: 198,463 sq mi; 511,770 sq km
LEADING EXPORTS: machinery and manufactures
CONTINENT: Asia

Togo
CAPITAL: Lome
POPULATION: 4,410,370
MAJOR LANGUAGES: French, Ewe and Mina, Dagomba, and Kabye
AREA: 21,927 sq mi; 56,790 sq km
LEADING EXPORTS: phosphates, cotton, cocoa, and coffee
CONTINENT: Africa

Tonga
CAPITAL: Nukualofa
POPULATION: 105,600
MAJOR LANGUAGES: Tongan and English
AREA: 289 sq mi; 748 sq km
LEADING EXPORTS: squash, vanilla, fish, root crops, and coconut oil
LOCATION: Pacific Ocean

Trinidad and Tobago
CAPITAL: Port-of-Spain
POPULATION: 1,271,159
MAJOR LANGUAGES: English, Hindu, French, and Spanish
AREA: 1,981 sq mi; 5,130 sq km
LEADING EXPORTS: petroleum and petroleum products
LOCATION: Caribbean Sea

Tunisia

CAPITAL: Tunis
POPULATION: 8,879,845
MAJOR LANGUAGES: Arabic and French
AREA: 63,172 sq mi; 163,610 sq km
LEADING EXPORTS: hydrocarbons and agricultural products
CONTINENT: Africa

Turkey

CAPITAL: Ankara
POPULATION: 63,405,526
MAJOR LANGUAGES: Turkish, Kurdish, and Arabic
AREA: 301,394 sq mi; 780,580 sq km
LEADING EXPORTS: manufactured products, and foodstuffs
CONTINENT: Europe and Asia

Turkmenistan
CAPITAL: Ashgabat
POPULATION: 4,075,316
MAJOR LANGUAGES: Turkmen, Russian, Uzbek, and various languages
AREA: 188,463 sq mi; 488,100 sq km
LEADING EXPORTS: natural gas, cotton, and petroleum products
CONTINENT: Asia

Tuvalu
CAPITAL: Fongafale, on Funafuti atoll
POPULATION: 9,991
MAJOR LANGUAGES: Tuvaluan and English
AREA: 10 sq mi; 26 sq km
LEADING EXPORT: copra
LOCATION: Pacific Ocean

Uganda
CAPITAL: Kampala
POPULATION: 19,573,262
MAJOR LANGUAGES: English, Luganda, Swahili, Bantu languages, and Nilotic languages
AREA: 91,139 sq mi; 236,040 sq km
LEADING EXPORTS: coffee, cotton, and tea
CONTINENT: Africa

Ukraine
CAPITAL: Kiev
POPULATION: 51,867,828
MAJOR LANGUAGES: Ukranian, Russian, Romanian, Polish, and Hungarian
AREA: 233,098 sq mi; 603,700 sq km
LEADING EXPORTS: coal, electric power, and metals
CONTINENT: Europe

United Arab Emirates

CAPITAL: Abu Dhabi
POPULATION: 2,924,594
MAJOR LANGUAGES: Arabic, Persian, English, Hindi, and Urdu
AREA: 29,183 sq mi; 75,581 sq km
LEADING EXPORTS: crude oil, natural gas, re-exports, and dried fish
CONTINENT: Asia

United Kingdom

CAPITAL: London
POPULATION: 58,295,119
MAJOR LANGUAGES: English, Welsh, and Scottish Gaelic
AREA: 94,529 sq mi; 244,820 sq km
LEADING EXPORTS: manufactured goods, machinery, and fuels
CONTINENT: Europe

United States

CAPITAL: Washington, D.C.
POPULATION: 263,814,032
MAJOR LANGUAGES: English and Spanish
AREA: 3,618,908 sq mi; 9,372,610 sq km
LEADING EXPORTS: capital goods and automobiles
CONTINENT: North America

Uruguay
CAPITAL: Montevideo
POPULATION: 3,222,716
MAJOR LANGUAGES: Spanish and Brazilero
AREA: 68,041 sq mi; 176,220 sq km
LEADING EXPORTS: wool and textile manufactures
CONTINENT: South America

Uzbekistan

CAPITAL: Tashkent
POPULATION: 23,089,261
MAJOR LANGUAGES: Uzbek, Russian, Tajik, various languages
AREA: 172,748 sq mi; 447,400 sq km
LEADING EXPORTS: cotton, gold, natural gas, and minerals
CONTINENT: Asia

Vanuatu
CAPITAL: Port-Vila
POPULATION: 173,648
MAJOR LANGUAGES: English, French, pidgin, and Bislama
AREA: 5,699 sq mi; 14,760 sq km
LEADING EXPORTS: copra, beef, cocoa, timber, and coffee
LOCATION: Pacific Ocean

Venezuela
CAPITAL: Caracas
POPULATION: 21,004,773
MAJOR LANGUAGES: Spanish and various languages
AREA: 352,156 sq mi; 912,050 sq km
LEADING EXPORTS: petroleum, bauxite and aluminum, and steel
CONTINENT: South America

Vietnam

CAPITAL: Hanoi
POPULATION: 74,393,324
MAJOR LANGUAGES: Vietnamese, French, Chinese, English, Khmer, and various languages
AREA: 127,248 sq mi; 329,560 sq km
LEADING EXPORTS: petroleum, rice, and agricultural products
CONTINENT: Asia

Western Samoa
CAPITAL: Apia
POPULATION: 209,360
MAJOR LANGUAGES: Samoan and English
AREA: 1,104 sq mi; 2,860 sq km
LEADING EXPORTS: coconut oil and cream, taro, copra, and cocoa
LOCATION: Pacific Ocean

Yemen
CAPITAL: Sanaa
POPULATION: 14,728,474
MAJOR LANGUAGE: Arabic
AREA: 203,857 sq mi; 527,970 sq km
LEADING EXPORTS: crude oil, cotton, coffee, hides, and vegetables
CONTINENT: Asia

Zaire

CAPITAL: Kinshasa
POPULATION: 44,060,636
MAJOR LANGUAGES: French, Lingala, Swahili, Kingwana, Kikongo, and Tshiluba
AREA: 905,599 sq mi; 2,345,410 sq km
LEADING EXPORTS: copper, coffee, diamonds, cobalt, and crude oil
CONTINENT: Africa

Zambia
CAPITAL: Lusaka
POPULATION: 9,445,723
MAJOR LANGUAGES: English (official) and about 70 various languages
AREA: 290,594 sq mi; 752,610 sq km
LEADING EXPORTS: copper, zinc, cobalt, lead, and tobacco
CONTINENT: Africa

Zimbabwe
CAPITAL: Harare
POPULATION: 11,139,961
MAJOR LANGUAGES: English, Shona, and Sindebele
area: 150,809 sq mi; 390,580 sq km
LEADING EXPORTS: agricultural products and manufactures
CONTINENT: Africa

Glossary of Geographic Terms

basin
a depression in the surface of the land; some basins are filled with water

bay
a part of a sea or lake that extends into the land

butte
a small raised area of land with steep sides

▲ butte

canyon
a deep, narrow valley with steep sides; often has a stream flowing through it

cataract
a large waterfall; any strong flood or rush of water

delta
a triangular-shaped plain at the mouth of a river, formed when sediment is deposited by flowing water

flood plain
a broad plain on either side of a river, formed when sediment settles on the riverbanks

glacier
a huge, slow-moving mass of snow and ice

hill
an area that rises above surrounding land and has a rounded top; lower and usually less steep than a mountain

island
an area of land completely surrounded by water

isthmus
a narrow strip of land that connects two larger areas of land

mesa
a high, flat-topped landform with cliff-like sides; larger than a butte

mountain
an area that rises steeply at least 2,000 feet (300 m) above surrounding land; usually wide at the bottom and rising to a narrow peak or ridge

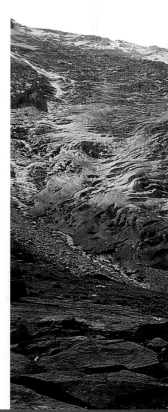

▶ glacier

◀ cataract

◀ delta

mountain pass
a gap between mountains

peninsula
an area of land almost completely surrounded by water and connected to the mainland by an isthmus

plain
a large area of flat or gently rolling land

plateau
a large, flat area that rises above the surrounding land; at least one side has a steep slope

river mouth
the point where a river enters a lake or sea

strait
a narrow stretch of water that connects two larger bodies of water

tributary
a river or stream that flows into a larger river

volcano
an opening in the Earth's surface through which molten rock, ashes, and gasses from the Earth's interior escape

▶ volcano

Gazetteer

A

Alexandria (31.12°N, 29.58°E) ancient Hellenistic city in Egypt, p. 178

Assyria a historical kingdom of northern Mesopotamia around present-day Iraq and Turkey, p. 38

Athens (38°N, 23.38°E) the capital city of Greece, p. 165

B

Babylonia (32.15°N, 45.23°E) an ancient region around southeastern Mesopotamia and between the Tigris and Euphrates rivers; now present-day Iraq, p. 36

C

Canaan a historical and Biblical area around Palestine, p. 48

Carthage (37.04°N, 10.18°E) an ancient city on the northern coast of Africa; now a suburb of the city of Tunis, p. 195

Chang Jiang (30.3°N, 117.25°E) the longest river in China and Asia and third-longest river in the world, p. 125

Colosseum (41.54°N, 12.29°E) a large amphitheatre built in Rome around A.D. 70; site of contests and combats between people and animals, p. 200

Constantinople (41.02°N, 29°E) the ancient capital of Byzantium; now Istanbul, Turkey, p. 217

E

East Africa an eastern region of the continent of Africa that is made up of the countries of Burundi, Kenya, Rwanda, Tanzania, Uganda, and Somalia, p. 14

Euphrates River (36°N, 40°E) a river flowing south from Turkey through Syria and Iraq, p. 30

F

Fertile Crescent a region in Southwest Asia; site of the world's first civilizations, p. 30

G

Ganges River (24°N, 89.3°E) a river in northern India and Bangladesh, flowing from the Himalaya Mountains to the Bay of Bengal, p. 96

Gaul (46.39°N, 0.47°E) a region inhabited by the ancient Gauls; now present-day France and parts of Belgium, Germany, and Italy, p. 196

Giza (30.01°N, 31.12°E) an ancient city capital of Upper Egypt; site of the Great Pyramids, p. 77

Greece (39°N, 21.3°E) a country in Mediterranean Europe; site of a great ancient civilization, p. 153

H

Himalaya Mountains (29.3°N, 85.02°E) a mountain system of south central Asia, extending along the border between India and Tibet and through Pakistan, Nepal, and Bhutan, p. 95

Huang He (35.06°N, 113.39°E) the second-longest river in China, p. 125

I

Indus River Valley (26.43°N, 67.41°E) a valley and early civilization along the Indus River, one of the longest rivers in the world, p. 96

Israel (32.4°N, 34°E) a country in Southwest Asia, p. 50

Italy (43.58°N, 11.14°E) a boot-shaped country in southern Europe, including the islands of Sicily and Sardinia, p. 192

J

Jerusalem (31.46°N, 35.14°E) the capital city of Israel; holy to Jews, Christians, and Muslims, p. 49

Judah the name of the southern half of the Kingdom of the Israelites (the northern half retained the name Israel); Jerusalem was its capital; also spelled *Judea*, p. 50

Judea see above

K

Kerma a market town in present-day Sudan; an ancient Nubian city, p. 86

L

Lower Egypt an area in ancient Egypt, in the northern Nile River region, p. 62

Lower Nubia an ancient region in northern Africa extending from the Nile Valley in Egypt to present-day Sudan, specifically, between the first and second Nile cataracts, p. 62

M

Macedonia ancient kingdom north of Greece, p. 175

Marathon a city in the Attic Peninsula where the Greeks defeated the Persians in 490 B.C., p. 172

Meroë a city of ancient Nubia in present-day Sudan, p. 86

Mesopotamia (34°N, 44°E) an ancient region between the Tigris and Euphrates rivers in Southwest Asia, p. 29

Mohenjo-Daro (27.2°N, 68.1°E) an ancient city on the banks of the Indus River in southern Pakistan, p. 96

N

Napata one of the three most powerful Nubian kingdoms; located between the third and fourth cataracts of the Nile River in Upper Nubia, p. 86

New Babylonian Empire a revival of the old Babylonian Empire stretching from the Persian Gulf to the Mediterranean Sea, p. 39

North China Plain a large plain in East Asia, built up by soil deposits of the Huang He, p. 124

P

Parthenon the chief temple of the Greek goddess Athena on the hill of the Acropolis in Athens, Greece, p. 161

Persia the historical name for the region in and around present-day Iran, p. 172

Phoenicia an ancient region in present-day Lebanon, p. 46

R

Rome (41.52°N, 12.37°E) the capital city of Italy; capital of the ancient Roman Empire, p. 191

S

Silk Road an ancient trade route between China and Europe, p. 140

Sparta an ancient city-state in Greece, p. 170

Sumer the site of the earliest known civilization; located in Mesopotamia, in present-day southern Iraq; later became Babylonia, p. 29

T

Tiber River a major river in Italy; Rome is built on its banks, p. 191

Tigris River a river in Iraq and Turkey, p. 30

Troy (39.59°N, 26.14°E) an ancient city in north-western Anatolia, the Asiatic part of Turkey, p. 154

U

Upper Egypt an area in ancient Egypt in the Nile Valley, south of the river's delta and the 30th northern parallel, p. 62

Upper Nubia an ancient region in northeastern Africa that extended from the Nile Valley in Egypt to present-day Sudan, specifically, between the second and sixth cataracts, p. 62

Biographical Dictionary

A

Abraham first leader of the Israelites; according to the Bible, he led his family to a new land, Canaan, where he became the founder of a new nation, p. 51

Alexander the Great king of Macedonia (356 B.C.–323 B.C.); conquered Persia and Egypt and invaded India; spread Hellenism, p. 176

Archimedes (ar kuh MEE deez) (born 290 B.C.) Greek inventor and mathematician; invented the formulas for the surface area and volume of a sphere, p. 179

Asoka (uh SOH kuh) (died c. 238 B.C.) Chandragupta's grandson and last major emperor of India's Maurya empire; credited with having built the greatest empire in India's history; helped spread Buddhism, p. 113

Augustus (63 B.C.–A.D. 14) first Roman emperor; ruled after Julius Caesar's death in 44 B.C. until his own death, p. 197

C

Champollion, Jean François (zhahn frahn SWAH shahm poh LYOHN) (A.D. 1790–1832) French scholar; first to decode Egyptian hieroglyphics, p. 83

Chandragupta (chuhn druh GUP tuh) (died 297 B.C.) founded India's Maurya empire in 321 B.C.; unified most of India under one ruler, p. 111

Confucius (kuhn FYOO shuhs) (551 B.C.–479 B.C.) Chinese philosopher and teacher; his beliefs, known as Confucianism, greatly influenced Chinese life, p. 129

Constantine (KAHN stuhn teen) (c. A.D. 278–337) emperor of Rome from A.D. 312 to 337; encouraged the spread of Christianity, p. 213

D

Deborah (c. 1100s B.C.) judge and prophet of the Old Testament; started a war against the Canaanites, p. 53

D

Diocletian (dy uh KLEE shuhn) (A.D. 245–316) emperor of Rome from A.D. 284 to 305; reorganized the Roman government, p. 216

E

Etruscans ancient people who lived in Etruria in Italy from at least 650 B.C. to about 500 B.C.; lived before the Romans and influenced their culture, p. 193

Euclid (YOO klid) (c. 300 B.C.) Greco-Roman mathematician; known for the *Elements,* a book on geometry, p. 178

G

Gautama, Siddhartha (sihd DAHR tuh goh TUH muh) (lived sometime between 500 B.C. and 350 B.C.) founder of Buddhism; born a prince, he left his family and wealth to find the cause of human suffering; called the Buddha, p. 106

H

Hadrian (HAY dree uhn) (A.D. 76–138) emperor of Rome from A.D. 117 to 138; one of Rome's greatest emperors; worked to unify the empire, p. 199

Hammurabi (hahm uh RAH bee) (died 1750 B.C.) king of Babylon from about 1792 B.C. to 1750 B.C.; creator of the Babylonian empire; established one of the oldest codes of law, p. 36

Hatshepsut (haht SHEHP soot) (died c. 1482 B.C.) stepmother of Thutmose III; ruled Egypt as regent and then as pharaoh (c. 1482 B.C.); achieved economic success, especially in trade, p. 67

Herodotus (huh RAHD uh tuhs) (c. 484 B.C.–420 B.C.) Greek author who traveled throughout the known world; wrote about the wars between Greece and Persia in the *History,* the first major historical work of ancient times, p. 61

Homer (c. 800 B.C.) Greek poet; credited with composing the epics the *Iliad* and the *Odyssey,* p. 155

I

Iceman of the Alps one of the oldest and best-preserved bodies ever found; discovered on the border between Austria and Italy in 1991; is believed to be from Europe's Copper Age (4000 B.C.–2200 B.C.), p. 9

J

Jesus (c. 4 B.C.–A.D. 30) founder of Christianity; believed by Christians to be the Messiah; executed by the Roman government; followers said he spoke to them after his death and rose bodily to heaven, p. 208

Julius Caesar (c. 100 B.C.–44 B.C.) Roman political and military leader; became dictator for life in 44 B.C.; greatly improved the Roman government; was murdered by Roman senators because of his great power, p. 195

L

Liu Bang (LEE oo bahng) founder of the Han dynasty of China in 202 B.C.; born a peasant; stabilized the government and promoted education, p. 138

M

Martial (MAR shuhl) Roman poet (c. A.D. 38–103); wrote poems about the early Roman Empire, p. 203

Menes (MEE neez) (lived c. 2925 B.C.) founder of the first Egyptian dynasty; unified Upper and Lower Egypt; founded the capital of Memphis, p. 68

Moses (c. 1200s B.C.) Israelite leader; led the Israelites from Egypt to Canaan; according to the Bible, he received the Ten Commandments from God, p. 48

N

Nebuchadnezzar II (nehb uh kuhd NEHZ uhr) (c. 630 B.C.–561 B.C.) king of the New Babylonian empire from about 605 B.C. to 561 B.C., p. 39

Nero (c. A.D. 37–68) Roman emperor from A.D. 54 to 68; known for his mistreatment of the Christians, p. 198

O

Octavian (63 B.C.–A.D. 14) Rome's first emperor; wise and strong leader whose rule led to peace and wealth; also known as Augustus, p. 196

P

Paul (c. A.D. 10–62) disciple of Jesus; spent his later life spreading Jesus' teachings, p. 210

Pericles (PEHR ih kleez) (c. 495 B.C.–429 B.C.) Athenian leader; played a major role in the development of democracy and the Athenian empire, p. 159

Philip (382 B.C.–336 B.C.) king of Macedonia; seized power in 359 B.C.; conquered the Greek city-states; father of Alexander the Great, p. 175

R

Romulus and Remus twin brothers; according to legend, founded Rome in 753 B.C., p. 191

S

Seneca (c. 4 B.C.–A.D. 65) writer, philosopher, and statesman of ancient Rome, p. 206

Shi Huangdi (shee hoo ahng DEE) (c. 259 B.C.–210 B.C.) emperor of the Qin dynasty (c. 221 B.C.–210 B.C.); was the first to unify the Chinese empire, p. 134

Sima Qian (soo MAH chen) (c. 495 B.C.–429 B.C.) Chinese scholar, astronomer, and historian; wrote the most important history of ancient China, *Historical Records*, p. 144

Socrates (SOK ruh teez) (c. 470 B.C.–399 B.C.) Athenian philosopher of late 400s B.C.; taught through questioning; helped form many values of Western culture; was put to death for challenging Athenian values, p. 162

Solon (c. 630 B.C.–560 B.C.) Athenian statesman; made Athens more democratic, p. 158

T

Taharka prince of Nubia; became king of Nubia and Egypt in 690 B.C., p. 85

Thutmose III (thoot MOH suh) (died 1426 B.C.) stepson of Hatshepsut; considered the greatest pharaoh of the New Kingdom of Egypt; reigned from 1479 B.C. to 1426 B.C.; expanded empire to include Syria and Nubia, p. 70

W

Wudi (woo dee) (c. 156 B.C.–86 B.C.) Chinese emperor from 140 B.C. to 86 B.C.; brought the Han dynasty to its peak; expanded the Chinese empire; made Confucianism the state religion, p. 139

Glossary

A

absolute power complete control over someone or something, p. 112

acropolis a high, rocky hill on or near which early people built cities, p. 156

afterlife the next life, in which the dead are believed to live again, p. 73

agora [AG uh ruh] a public market and meeting place in an ancient Greek city, p.166

ahimsa [uh HIM sah] in Hinduism, the idea of being nonviolent, p. 105

alphabet a set of symbols that represent the sounds of a language, p. 47

aqueduct a structure that carries water over long distances, p. 202

archaeologist a scientist who examines bones, tools, structures, and other objects to learn about past peoples and cultures, p. 11

aristocrat a member of a rich and powerful family, p. 157

artisan a worker who is especially skilled in making something, such as baskets, leather goods, tools, jewelry, pottery, or clothes, p. 87

assassinate to murder for political reasons, p.176

astronomer a scientist who studies the stars and other objects in the sky, p. 83

B

barbarian a person considered to be wild and uncivilized, p. 175

bazaar a market selling different kinds of goods, p. 37

blockade the cutting off of an area by enemy forces that closes it to travel and trade, p. 174

C

caravan a group of traders traveling together, p. 37

caste a social class of people, p. 100

cataract a rock-filled rapid in a river, p. 62

circus an arena in ancient Rome; also the show held there, p. 205

citadel a fortress in a city, p. 97

city-state a city with its own traditions and its own government and laws; both a city and a separate independent state, pp. 32, 156

civilization a society with cities, a central government run by official leaders, and workers who specialize in certain jobs, leading to social classes. Writing, art, and architecture also characterize a civilization, p. 21

civil service the group of people whose job is to carry out the work of government, p. 132

code an organized list of laws or rules, p. 40

consul one of two officials who led the ancient Roman Republic, p. 194

convert to change one's beliefs, p. 113

covenant a binding agreement, p. 52

cuneiform [kyoo NEE uh form] a form of writing that uses groups of wedges and lines; used to write several languages of the Fertile Crescent, p. 44

currency the kind of money used by a group or a nation, p. 138

D

delta the place at the mouth of a river where it splits into several streams to form an area shaped like a triangle, p. 63

democracy a form of government in which citizens govern themselves, p. 157

dharma [DAHR muh] in Hinduism, the religious and moral duties of each person, p. 104

diaspora [dy AS puhr uh] the scattering of people who have a common background or beliefs, p. 54

dictator a person in the ancient Roman Republic appointed to rule for six months in times of emergency, with all the powers of a king, p. 194

dike a protective wall that controls or holds back water, p. 126

disciple a follower of a person or belief, p. 209

domesticate to tame animals and raise them to be used by humans, p. 17

dynasty a family of rulers, p. 68

E

empire many territories and people who are controlled by one government, p. 36

epic a long poem that tells a story, p. 155

epistle [ee PIS uhl] a letter; in the Christian Bible, letters written by disciples like Paul to Christian groups, p. 211

exile to force someone to live in another country, p. 50

extended family closely related people of several generations, such as brothers and sisters, parents, uncles and aunts, grandparents, and great-grandparents, p. 127

F

famine a time when there is so little food that many people starve, p. 48

fertile land or soil that contains substances plants need in order to grow well, p. 17

G

Gospel in the Christian Bible, the books of Matthew, Mark, Luke, and John, which are the first four books of the New Testament, p. 209

H

Hellenistic describing Greek culture after the death of Alexander the Great, including the three main kingdoms formed by the breakup of Alexander's empire, p. 177

hieroglyphs [HY ur oh glifs] a kind of picture writing in which some pictures stand for ideas or things and others stand for sounds, p. 82

history the written and other recorded events of people, p. 10

I

immortal someone or something that lives forever, p. 162

inflation an economic situation in which there is more money of less value, p. 216

irrigation supplying land with water through a network of canals, p. 19

L

loess [les] yellow-brown soil, p. 125

M

martyr a person who chooses to die for a cause he or she believes in, p. 212

meditate to think deeply about sacred things, p. 107

mercenary a foreign soldier who serves in an army only for pay, p. 215

messiah a savior in Judaism and Christianity, p. 209

migrate to relocate; to move from one place to settle in another area, p. 99

missionary a person who spreads his or her religious beliefs to others, p. 108

monotheism the belief in one god, p. 48

monsoon a strong wind that blows across a region at certain times of the year, p. 96

mummy a dead body preserved in lifelike condition, p. 75

myth a traditional story; in some cultures, a legend that explains people's beliefs, p. 33

N

nirvana the lasting peace that Buddhists seek by giving up selfish desires, p. 108

nomad a person who has no single, settled home, p. 16

O

oral tradition stories passed down through generations by word of mouth, p. 12

P

papyrus [puh PY ruhs] an early form of paper made from a reedlike plant found in the marshy areas of the Nile delta, p. 82

patrician member of a wealthy, upper-class family in the ancient Roman Republic, p. 194

peninsula an area of land nearly surrounded by water, p. 153

pharaoh [FAIR oh] the title of the kings of ancient Egypt, p. 67

philosopher someone who uses reason to understand the world. In Greece, the earliest philosophers used reason to explain natural events, p. 162

philosophy system of beliefs and values, p. 131

plague a widespread disease, p. 174

plebeian an ordinary citizen in the ancient Roman Republic, p. 194

polytheism the belief in many gods, p. 33

prehistory before history; the events in the period of time before writing was invented, p. 10

prophet a religious leader who told the Israelites what God wanted them to do, p. 54

province a unit of an empire; the provinces of the Roman Empire each had a governor supported by an army, p. 198

pyramid a huge building with four sloping outside walls shaped like triangles. In Egypt, pyramids were built as royal tombs, p. 77

R

regent someone who rules for a child until the child is old enough to rule, p. 70

reincarnation rebirth of a soul in the body of another living thing, p. 104

republic a type of government in which citizens who have the right to vote select their leaders; the leaders rule in the name of the people, p. 194

S

scribe a professional writer, p. 29

silk a valuable cloth originally made only in China from threads spun by caterpillars called silkworms, p. 142

silt rich, fertile soil deposited by the flooding of a river, p. 63

social class a group, or class, that is made up of people with similar backgrounds, wealth, and ways of living, p. 23

subcontinent a large landmass that juts out from a continent; India is considered a subcontinent, p. 95

surplus more of a thing or product than is needed, p. 20

T

tragedy a type of serious drama that ends in disaster for the main character, p. 163

tribute a payment made by a less powerful state or nation to a more powerful one, p. 160

tyrant a ruler who takes power with the support of the middle and working classes; not necessarily cruel and violent, p. 157

V

veto the Latin word for "forbid"; the rejection of a bill by the President or of any planned action or rule by a person in power, p. 194

W

warlord a leader of an armed group, p. 139

Index

The *italicized* page numbers refer to illustrations. The *m, c, p,* or *t* preceding the number refers to maps *(m)*, charts *(c)*, pictures *(p)*, or tables *(t)*.

Acknowledgments

Program Development, Design, Illustration, and Production

Proof Positive/Farrowlyne Associates, Inc.

Cover Design

Olena Serbyn and Bruce Bond

Cover Photo

Jon Chomitz

Maps

GeoSystems Global Corp.

Text

16, map from *World Civilizations: The Global Experience,* Volume A by Peter N. Stearns, Michael Adas, and Stuart B. Schwartz. Copyright 1993 by HarperCollins College Publishers. Reprinted by permission of Addison Wesley Educational Publishers Inc. 33, from Mary Anne Frese Witt et al, *The Humanities: Cultural Roots and Continuities, Volume 1, Three Cultural Roots,* Fourth Edition. Copyright 1993 by D.C. Heath and Company. 40, from *Everyday Life in Babylonia and Assyria,* by H.W.F. Saggs. Copyright 1965 by H. W. F. Saggs. Used by permission of B.T. Batsford Ltd. 51, from *The Torah: A Modern Commentary.* Copyright 1981 by The Union of American Hebrew Congregations. Reprinted by permission of The Union of American Hebrew Congregations. 101, from the Rig-Veda, 1.154, verses 1–3 adapted from *Hinduism* by V.P. (Hermant) Kanitkar, Stanley Thornes (Publishers) Ltd, 1989. 120, from *The Fables of India* by Joseph Gaer. Copyright 1955 by Joseph Gaer; © renewed 1983 by Fay Gaer. By permission of Little, Brown and Company. 131, from *Book of Songs,* translated by Arthur Waley. Copyright 1937 by Arthur Waley. Used by permission of Grove/Atlantic, Inc. 159, from *The Peloponnesian War,* by Thucydides. Copyright 1951 by Random House, Inc. 186, from THE ADVENTURES OF ULYSSES by Bernard Evslin. Copyright 1969 by Scholastic Inc. Reprinted by permission of Scholastic Inc.

Photo Research

Feldman & Associates, Inc.

Photos

1 TL, © D.J. Dianellis/Photri, 1 TR, © Charles Walker Collection/Stock Montage, 1 B, © D.E. Cox/Tony Stone Images, 4 TL, TR, © SuperStock International, 4 BL, © Doug Armand/Tony Stone Images, 4 BR, © Christopher Arensen/Tony Stone Images, 4 inset, © Mark Thayer, Boston, 5, © The Granger Collection, 6–7, © Erich Lessing/PhotoEdit, 8, © Douglas Mazonowicz/Art Resource, 9, © SyGMA, 10 L, R, © Kenneth Garrett/National Geographic Society Image Collection, 11 TL, BL, R, © Lee Boltin/Boltin Picture Library, 12, © Jason Laure'/Laure' Communications, 13, © Yann Layma/Tony Stone Images, 14, © Lee Boltin/Boltin Picture Library, 17, © Robert S. Peabody Museum of Archaeology, Phillips Academy, Andover, Massachusetts All Rights Reserved/Robert S. Peabody Museum of Archaeology, 18, © Ed Simpson/Tony Stone Images, 19, 21, © SuperStock International, 23 L, R, © Erich Lessing/Art Resource, 24, © Michael Newman/PhotoEdit, 29, © Lee Boltin/Boltin Picture Library, 31, © SuperStock International, 32, © British Museum, 33, © The Granger Collection, 34, © Courtesy University of Chicago/Oriental Institute, 35, © Erich Lessing/Art Resource, 37, © The Granger Collection, 38, © Erich Lessing/Art Resource, 39, © British Museum, 40, © Giraudon/Art Resource, 41 L, © The Granger Collection, 41 R, © Erich Lessing/Art Resource, 42, © Giraudon/Art Resource, 43 L, R, © The Granger Collection, 45, © Art Resource, 47, © The Granger Collection, 49, © SuperStock International, 50, © Corbis-Bettmann, 51, © Jewish Museum/Art Resource, 53 T, B, © The Granger Collection, 54, © Erich Lessing/Art Resource, 56, © Lucas Films/Kobal Collection, 61, © Werner Forman/Art Resource, 62, © The Bettmann Archive/Corbis-Bettmann, 63, © Eliot Elisofon/National Geographic Society Image Collection, 64, 65, © SuperStock International, 66, © Lee Boltin/Boltin Picture Library, 67, © SuperStock International, 68, © Werner Forman Archive/Art Resource, 71, © SuperStock International, 72 L, © The Granger Collection, 72 R, © SuperStock International, 73, © Erich Lessing/Art Resource, 74, © Scala/Art Resource, 75 L, © The Granger Collection, 75 R, Egyptian National Museum, Cairo/SuperStock International, 77, © Hugh Sitton/Tony Stone Images, 78, © Richard T. Nowitz/Photri, 79, © Chip & Rosa María de la Cueva Peterson, 80, © Erich Lessing/Art Resource, 81 T, © Robert Frerck/Odyssey Productions, 81 B, 82, © The Granger Collection, 83 TR, © Bridgeman/Art Resource, 83 BL, © The Granger Collection, 84 L, R, © Lee Boltin/Boltin Picture Library, 85, © The Granger Collection, 87 T, © Director's Contingent Fund (40.469) Courtesy of/Museum of Fine Arts Boston, 87 B, © The Granger Collection, 88, © Museum Expedition, Nubian Gallery (20.333) Courtesy of/Museum of Fine Arts Boston, 89, © Museum Expedition, Nubian Gallery (20.1059) Courtesy of/Museum of Fine Arts Boston, 90–91, © The Granger Collection, 95, © Nicholas DeVore/Tony Stone Images, 97, © Trip/Trip Photographic, 98 T, BL, BR, © Jehangir Gazdar/Woodfin Camp & Associates, 99, © Kevin Downey Photography, 101, © Robert & Linda Mitchell Photography, 102, Krishna, by Dhruv Khanna, age 12, India. Courtesy of the International Children's Art Museum, 103, © GUPTA/Dinodia Picture Agency, 104, © Robert & Linda Mitchell/Robert & Linda Mitchell Photography, 105, © Anil A. Dave/Dinodia Picture Agency, 106, © Lee Boltin/Boltin Picture Library, 107, © Robert & Linda Mitchell Photography, 108, © D.E. Cox/Tony Stone Images, 109, © Robert & Linda Mitchell Photography, 111, 112, © Corbis-Bettmann, 113, © Dinodia/Dinodia Picture Agency, 114, © Chris Haigh/Tony Stone Images, 115, © Kevin Miller/Tony Stone Images, 116 T, © David W. Hamilton, 116 B, © Michael Newman/PhotoEdit, 123, © Charles Walker Collection/Stock Montage, 124, © Kevin Downey Photography, 125, © Wolfgang Kaehler Photography, 126, © H. Rogers/Trip Photographic, 127, © The Granger Collection, 128, © Photri, 129, © The Granger Collection, 130, © Giraudon/Bridgeman Art Library, 131, © UPI/Corbis-Bettmann, 132, © The Great Bronze Age of China/Metropolitan Museum, 134, 135, TL, B, © O. Louis Mazzatenta/National Geographic Society Image Collection, 135 TR, © K. Cardwell/Trip Photographic, 136, © Keren Su/Tony Stone Images, 139, © The Granger Collection, 140, © Masaharu Uemura/Tony Stone Images, 142 L, R, © The Granger Collection, 142 inset, © Robert & Linda Mitchell/Robert & Linda Mitchell Photography, 143 L, © J. Stanley/Trip Photographic, 143 R, © Photri, 144 T, BL, © The Granger Collection, 144 BR, © Photri, 147, © Michael Newman/PhotoEdit, 151, © Ric Ergenbright/Ric Ergenbright Photography, 153, © Werner Forman/Art Resource, 154, © George Grigoriou/Tony Stone Images, 155, Trojan Horse, by Sissy Pachiadaki, age 12, Greece. Courtesy of the International Children's Art Museum, 156, © Robert Frerck/Odyssey Productions, 157, © George Grigoriou/Tony Stone Images, 158 L, © Corbis-Bettmann, 158 R, © Gjon Mili, Life Magazine © Time Inc./Time Picture Syndication, 159, 160, 161, © Robert Frerck/Odyssey Productions, 162, © The Granger Collection, 163, © Paul Merideth/Tony Stone Images, 164, © Jean Pragen/Tony Stone Images, 165, © Scala/Art Resource, 166, © D.J. Dianellis/Photri, 167, © Robert Frerck/Odyssey Productions, 168, © Nimatallah/Art Resource, 169, © The Metropolitan Museum of Art Fletcher Fund 1931 (31.11.10) Photograph by Schecter Lee/Metropolitan Museum of Art, 170, © Lee Boltin/Boltin Picture Library, 171, © SuperStock International, 172, © Erich Lessing/Art Resource, 174, © Scala/Art Resource, 175 TL, © The Granger Collection, 175 BR, © Lee Boltin/Boltin Picture Library, 178, © Stock Montage, 184, © Michael Newman/PhotoEdit, 187, © AISA/Photri, 188, © A. Giampiccolo/FPG International, 191, © Scala/Art Resource, 192, © Joe Cornish/Tony Stone Images, 193, © The Granger Collection, 195, © Capena. Italia/Photri, 196, © Hulton Getty Picture Collection, 197, © Stephen Studd/Tony Stone Images, 198, © Stock Montage, 199, © Nimatallah/Art Resource, 200, © Robert Frerck/Odyssey Productions, 203, © Scala/Art Resource, 205, © Hulton Getty Picture Collection, 206 TR, © Robert Frerck/Odyssey Productions, 206 BL, © Giraudon/Art Resource, 208, © Erich Lessing/Art Resource, 209, 211 L, R, 212, © Scala/Art Resource, 213, © INDEX/Photri, 214 T, © The Granger Collection, 214 BL, © Lee Boltin/Boltin Picture Library, 214 BR, © The Granger Collection, 216, © Corbis-Bettmann, 217, © The Granger Collection, 222, 225, © Mark Thayer, Boston, 226 I, © Steve Leonard/Tony Stone Images, 226 B, © Robert Frerck/Odyssey Productions, 227 T, © Wolfgang Kaehler/Wolfgang Kaehler Photography, 227 BL, © John Elk/Tony Stone Images, 227 BR, © Will & Deni McIntyre/Tony Stone Images, 237, © G. Brad Lewis/Tony Stone Images, 239, © Nigel Press/Tony Stone Images, 266 T, © A & L Sinibaldi/Tony Stone Images, 266 B, © John Beatty/Tony Stone Images, 267 T, © Hans Strand/Tony Stone Images, 267 BL, © Spencer Swanger/Tom Stack & Associates, 267 BR, © Paul Chesley/Tony Stone Images.

Teacher's Notes

Teacher's Notes

Teacher's Notes

Teacher's Notes

Teacher's Notes

Teacher's Notes

Teacher's Notes

Teacher's Notes

Teacher's Notes

Teacher's Notes